YUGA:

An
Anatomy
of
our Fate

MARTY GLASS

YUGA

AN
ANATOMY
OF
OUR FATE

Sophia Perennis
Ghent NY

First published in the USA
by Sophia Perennis, Ghent, NY 2001
Series editor: James R. Wetmore
© copyright 2001

For information, address:
Sophia Perennis, 343 Rte 21C
Ghent NY 12075
Printed in the United States of America

✠

By the same author:

The Sandstone Papers
Eastern Light in Western Eyes

Library of Congress Cataloging-in-Publication Data

Glass, Marty, 1938–
Yuga: an anatomy of our fate / Marty Glass

p. cm.
Includes index
ISBN 0 900588 29 2 (pbk.: alk. paper)
ISBN 0 900588 36 5 (cloth.: alk. paper)
1. Spiritual life. 2. Civilization, Modern. I. Title
BL624.G58 2001
291.2—dc21   2001000393

I would like to dedicate this book
to the memory of my Mother,
Esther.
1906–1998
This world insulted her, as it insults you,
but it could not defeat her, as I hope it will not defeat you.
The virtue that assured her glorious victory
over this world
and the suffering it inflicted,
and shone as imperishable beauty of soul,
and informed her indomitable courage,
was the purity of heart
of which she was unaware,
but which was surely noted in heaven,
and inspires her son.

Truth is the austerity of the Kali Age.

~ Sri Ramakrishna

I must dare to speak the truth, when truth is my theme.

~ Plato (*Phaedrus*, 247D)

None of the Emperor's clothes had ever met with such a success.
'But he hasn't got any clothes on!' gasped out a little child.
'Good heavens! Hark at the little innocent!' said the father,
and the people whispered to one another what the child had said.

~ Hans Christian Andersen

In reality, the *philosophia perennis*, actualized in the West,
though on different levels, by Plato, Aristotle, Plotinus,
the Fathers and the Scholastics,
constitutes a 'definitive' intellectual heritage,
and the great problem of our times
is not to replace them with something better
— for this something could not exist
according to the point of view in question here —
but to return to the sources, both around us and within us,
and to examine all the data of contemporary life
in the light of the one, timeless truth.

~ Frithjof Schuon

Adoration unto the supreme Being, pure, eternal and all-pervading,
the changeless Reality, the one Being, meditating upon whom
sages attain liberation, eternal and undifferentiated,
the One out of whom the visible world, the scene of diversity,
comes into existence, in whom it rests, and to whom it returns in the end
when the world-cycles come to a close.

~ Brahmapurana

It was a dry wind
And it swept across the desert
And it curled into the circle of birth
And the dead sand
Falling on the children
The mothers and the fathers
And the automatic earth
It's a turn-around jump shot
It's everybody jump start
Its every generation throws a hero up the pop charts
Medicine is magical and magical is art
The Boy in the Bubble
And the baby with the baboon heart
And I believe
These are the days of lasers in the jungle
Lasers in the jungle somewhere
Staccato signals of constant information
A loose affiliation of millionaires
And billionaires and baby
These are the days of miracle and wonder
This is the long distance call
The way the camera follows us in slo-mo
The way we look to us all
The way we look to a distant constellation
That's dying in a corner of the sky
These are the days of miracle and wonder
And don't cry baby, don't cry, don't cry

from the Graceland Concert
words by Paul Simon
Music by Paul Simon and Forere Motloheloa
Accordion: Forere Motloheloa
Bass: Baghiti Klumalo
Drums: Vusi Khumalo
Percussion: Makhaya Mahlangu
Synthesizer guitar: Adrian Belew
Acoustic guitar: Paul Simon
Synthesizer: Rob Mounsey
Recorded at The Hit Factory
New York, U.S.A.

Table of Contents

THIS is a funny Table of Contents. Unconventional. It's consistent with how this book is disorganized. It doesn't proceed logically, building up an analysis or point of view or intellectual structure step by step, although each 'chapter' definitely assumes assimilation of what has gone before. Terms are defined when they are introduced, but all 'definitions' are progressively and necessarily deepened and expanded in the course of the text, as are our own insights in the course of the deepening and expanding of our experience. The book doesn't really have 'chapters' unified around a single theme, but rather sections or essays, excursions voyaging through irresistible afterthoughts, serendipitous digressions or related parts of the picture, varying widely in length and scope, a sequence of 'hits', mutually reinforcing and hopefully illuminating elements of a single exposition, or demonstration, or provocation.

But the foregoing implies that this is a book about something 'out there' — and in part, of course, it is — whereas it's actually more like a journey, as I pointed out in the Introduction. It's really a journey through a world that is simultaneously inner and outer, 'the world' as it really is, in other words. Through yourself, hopefully opening the door to liberating decisions. And through the providential 'situation' it is your stupendous fate to inhabit, your choice to escape.

I. Invitation [1]

A polite euphemism; actually, it's a summons, because the quest for Truth is strictly enjoined, the directive imperious, originating as they do in your very humanity...

II. Surveillance [2]

We gather information about ourselves, every last speck and dribble, never quite sure what it means, worried a bit, anxious, but reassured that at least we have the data...

III. History & Way [3]

What is History? How did it begin? The vanished Way and the Fall into Time: two *immense* categories of comprehension, absolutely indispensable—and 'surveillance is fruitless'…

IV. Progress & Tradition [4]

Picking up from Chapter III: our two ways of seeing ourselves, our two ways of living, and this is *one of the very big ideas in the book*, first introduced now — and with inexpressible gratitude to Mircea Eliade, who wrote *Cosmos and History*…

V. Self-Inflicted yet Autonomous, Unreal yet Fatal [6]

Many basic terms of the discussion, characteristics of the *yuga*, first introduced in this very pithy chapter: television and elders, Capitalism, Information Technology (I.T.), Artificial Intelligence (A.I.), Entertainment vs. Reality, Genetic Engineering, the 'Post-Human Era', the disappearance of Nature…

VI. Humanity, Posterity, Eternity [9]

Impossible to epitomize this chapter, give it a name. 'Historical Humanity and Eternal Humanity' comes closest, I suppose, but there's talk about the Heart of Light, Power and Terror, the Four Illimitable Sublime Truths, and the indigenous Darkness…

   ✳ The things we hope for are hope's dreams; the things we fear, fear's nightmares.

VII. Clockwatch [12]

Clock-time! And a warning from Lao Tzu, repeated, given *twice*, as if to make sure we'll have no excuse…

VIII. Time & Temples [14]

The building of churches, closer scrutiny of 'the contrast between past and present', and no mountains and rivers are seen from jet planes...

✻ It's impossible to make a pilgrimage on a freeway...
✻ The grave decision we face in eternity and evade in time...

IX. The Information Coronation [17]

The Computer. Newsgroup, chat room, clip art, webpage, homepage, hyperlink, netiquette, netizen, screen saver, search engine, and spam. When you grasp the significance of the Computer, you've seen the Whole Picture, and vice versa; *but*: it's either *both* or *neither*! What can I say? It's cards on the table with this one. Roszak's book, *The Cult of Information*, is best, Sherry Turkle's *The Second Self* is also fine — enormous bibliography here, of course...

✻ Whatever displaces Life can only be Death.
✻ Which alleges . . . that human minds are simply 'computers made of meat'.

X. Import in Depth [29]

Definitely a polemic. Extremist? One-sided? Exaggerated? Bilious? Bombastic? Or a protest, a cry from the heart, an indictment of infamy, a passionate broadside, a testimony by someone who 'doesn't count' (get the double meaning?), who's been driven (like so many of us, in so very many trying situations) to an insistence that sounds 'tasteless' or 'strident' only to those who fear (or know) that he speaks the truth. The fact is, anything that sounds 'reasonable', 'responsible', 'judicious', sounds like the discourse you always hear, is a defense and actual creation of the world in which that discourse originates and is valid, like the TV news, *and can never make that world, that Lie, visible to you*: think of Chuang Tse and Hui Neng, Rumi and Kabir, Villon and Rimbaud, Meister Eckhart, Kierkegaard, William Blake... but above all, how can *any* language be disproportionate to the leering dishonour we inhabit, or even be equal to it, how can anyone 'over-react' to what is, after all, not that silly old 'Moloch' and 'Mammon' stuff, but the *Kali-Yuga* itself?

✳ We discover that the great Drama, from beginning to end, is one eternal Moment within us...

✳ Man ... has lost the secret of how to make himself human.

⁓LEWIS MUMFORD, 1956.

✳ We are equally ignorant of what has possessed us and what it has usurped. Of what we have made of ourselves, in Time, in History, and of what we are eternally, in Heaven.

XI. Up to Speed [36]

Speed, attention spans, Telemanity, hunters and gatherers, John Muir, haiku, the end of the Age of Typography...

✳ Time has speeded up, just as the sages assured us it would in the *Kali-Yuga*.

XII. Invisible Absences [39]

Briefly, our present condition summarized; at greater length, what we've lost: our losses, the 'invisible fatal absences', and our 'baffled restlessness' without the presences that make us happy, human. *But*: lost only to the collective, accessible forever to individuals.

✳ This quiet, furtively tended little candle of shame...

✳ Our cardiac intelligence, the Heart-Intellect, in which Love and Knowledge, compassion and gnosis, are One.

XIII. Awakening [42]

Misinterpretation of the Cosmic Dream, mistaken solidarity with a desacralized Cosmos, wisdom of Mircea Eliade. Distinguishing the Real from the unreal. The first small seed here of a major theme...

✳ We can liberate ourselves from the groundless hopes and fears that bind us to the Dream...

XIV. The Name of the Age [44]

The loss of reality, French origin of a particular usage of the word 'terror.' This chapter simply states bluntly something everyone already knows but

✳ What is at stake here? What is really at stake here? At the end of the day, it's not salvation, or honorable withdrawal, or metaphysical rectitude, or even living in the Truth. At stake is the preservation of our capacity to love humanity. Lose this, and we've lost everything.

XVII. Taking Care of Business [62]

The longest 'chapter' so far: an analysis of 'collective enterprise in the *Kali-Yuga*.' How did I put it together? I took an article from the *Guardian of London and Manchester* (7/27/90), describing a perfect representative 'enterprise', and used it as the thread upon which the themes of the analysis are strung, and it leads to a fundamental 'lesson' I had in mind from the beginning. In this chapter you will meet a very great French Master, Jacques Ellul; a profoundly insightful, apparently overlooked American philosopher, George Morgan; and, for the second time, one of the finest minds of our century, Ananda Coomaraswamy, author of the classic 'On Being in One's Right Mind', from which we will learn something about metanoia... Bon Voyage!

✳ A protective ignorance, rooted in confirmed despair, insured by an insuperable shallowness and dissembled by a relaxed arrogance...

✳ Progress can admit problems: but nothing more serious.

✳ The conquest of power, the *choice* of power, is already self-destructive...

✳ We ride the back of an autonomously unfolding technological history *which is ourselves*...

✳ Today, *technique has taken over the whole of civilization.*

∼ELLUL

✳ This sort of transformation — or, I should say, humanity's metamorphosis in the *Kali-Yuga* — is quintessentially invisible.

✳ Human purpose is defined by Spirit. Spirit is our End, as it is our Origin and Truth ... that cosmic interdependence or 'interbeing' of the Avatamsaka Sutra.

✳ The world *in divinis* is qualitative.

✳ And the front page of every newspaper on earth is filled with numbers.

✳ 'Planet Hollywood', which is as perfect a name for the hyper-real world of the *Kali-Yuga* as could be conceived.

✳ Frozen in the icy unyielding objectivity of the present technological moment...

✳ The name of the vacuum...

✳ Metanoia is, then, a transformation of one's whole being.

∼COOMARASWAMY

XVIII. Remember What the Dormouse Said! Feed your Head! Feed your Head! [97]

'I would like to gather together at this point some brief reflections and commentaries on aspects of our lives in the *Kali-Yuga* which, given the ground we have covered, should not require elaboration.' That's how this 'chapter' begins. It's a series of separate pieces, which could have just as well, some of them, been 'chapters' themselves, although there are links here and there. I can't recall why I chose to do it this way.

✳ Only the transient, only the perishable and ambivalent, define us.

✳ Now write their letters to Santa Claus on computers . . . Santa Claus, the closest thing to Christ we could come up with in these trying times...

✳ The ferocious emphasis on action . . . the dispraise and effacement of thoughtfulness.

✳ The whole key in life is to make your body look great, whether by exercise or fashion.

⁓ ELLE MAGAZINE

✳ The Tibetan 'peasants' didn't know they were being exploited by their 'landlords', and didn't hate them, until...

✳ The question young people must face, 'What will I be when I grow up?'

✳ And the wedding is organized and choreographed for the video.

✳ The world came to an end by becoming unreal.

✳ Reality in the 90s is a computer-generated cartoon where you can kill people.

⁓ SAN FRANCISCO CHRONICLE

✳ THE BRAVE NEW WORLD OF COMPUTER SEX

⁓ELLE MAGAZINE

✳ The gradual disappearance of 'the recollected countenance'...

✳ 'Knowing' the stars to be 'nothing but' balls of flaming gases...

✳ Gained Power, lost the world.

✳ Today's British village is not a place but a set of communications systems...

⁓GUARDIAN OF LONDON AND MANCHESTER

✳ A manipulative artificiality as our latest and final mode of existence.

✳ Real crime! Real slime! These shows all exploit their subjects' ordeals. What is it that so fascinates us?

⁓ NEWSWEEK

✳ We learn a new word here: 'soundbite.'

✳ Television is a destruction human beings *grow into*...

✳ Time speeds up in the *Kali-Yuga*, the cosmic substance flows ever faster.

✳ The real world, the world in our hearts, is not redeemed, for it was never separated from Grace, from the Origin, from God.

✳ Indeed, he is the showers, the ocean, the stars, the foliage.

～ D. T. SUZUKI

✳ This world that we are is the real one. Find it.

XIX. One Way [126]

Message and implications of Chapter 18 of the *Tao Te Ching*. And Chapter 38, known as the Te Classic. The essential insight into cyclic unfolding from the Taoist perspective. *Very* shrewd, *very* unanswerable. (And there are a few quotes from Toshihiko Izutsu's great book, *Sufism and Taoism*; also Lin Yutang.)

✳ When life for many people no longer seems worth living... the 'suicide hot lines' appear...

✳ A threshold has been crossed in these instances...

✳ He who loses the Way feels lost.

～ TAO TE CHING

✳ Ellul's brilliant insight is here metaphysically situated, consummated, in Taoist teleology.

✳ Metaphysical intelligence knows that the *Kali-Yuga* must display *li* in its terminal form.

✳ In forgetfulness, here we are: in remembrance, nothing has happened at all.

✳ It's all like an iron ball rolling down a flight of steps.

✳ But neither the sun nor the cloud know anything about each other...

XX. Zen & The Art of Cosmic Cycle Discountenance [144]

The 'Zen Buddhist angle on our original state and its loss.' Here we drink at the immortal Buddhist fountain of wisdom, the pitchers poured for us by one of the very great Masters, a *guy everybody loves*, D. T. Suzuki: 'sweetness and light.'

✳ If you want to understand Zen, understand it right away.

～ SUZUKI

✳ The forest sages, holy hermits and anchorites, monastics in their mountain fastnesses…

✳ *Wabi, sabi, fuga,* and *kaminagara no michi*…

✳ All four of the Japanese terms cited by Suzuki refer, with varying emphases, to turning one's back on History or Civilization or Society.

✳ The *sabi* of this bamboo vase consists in the very fact of this leakage.

⸺Lord Fumai

✳ At this time, 'a lone traveller grows pensive over the destiny of human life.

✳ I live in another realm here, beyond the world of men.

⸺Li T'ai-po

✳ We know we have strayed from something, something of our beautiful truth, our core of joy.

✳ There is in every one of us a desire to return to a simpler form of living…

⸺Suzuki

✳ We shall not, as historical humanity, re-enter the Garden…

✳ This is the time, as Zen would declare, when Chiyo really sees the flower and the flower in turn sees the poetess.

⸺Suzuki

✳ The Eddie Bauer turtleneck, spandex in the collar….elastic-reinforced shoulder seams…Women's $15.

⸺Atlantic Monthly

XXI. Three [160]

The 'three bodies of testimony' upon which this study is based. 'I just realized it this morning, just put it together in my mind.' Seems like this should have been included in the Introduction, doesn't it?

XXII. Four [162]

XXIII. What a Long Strange Trip It's Been [168]

Now this is one incredible 'chapter.' It holds itself together, but not all that tightly; room to move. The central theme: children growing up in this world. Our children. (I have five.) But it's also the chapter where we get into Baudrillard ('hyper-reality'), whose writings, in the words of Douglas Kellner, 'constitute perhaps the first radical high-tech, new wave social theory.'

Cutting edge pomo stuff. And all this, so we don't lose touch with Reality, set on the Vedantic foundation of *Atma* (Spirit), *Jagat* (the world), and *Jiva* (the human person). Also Marx (the *real* Marx), René Guénon, Eliade again, Black Elk, and Don Quixote. (This was a challenging book to write; the way it came out is the way it came out.) And many others. The flow of thought is leisurely here, so feel comfortable going slowly; and just getting 'the feel', the thrust, of Marx and Guénon is enough. Same goes for Baudrillard, who's really simply trying to invent a vocabulary to describe, and situate, what you already know intuitively: something already implicit in your mature cynicism.

✳ We don't know what will become of our children, we who live in the *Kali-Yuga*.
✳ And we suffer, suffer because we love...
✳ The road into the *Kali-Yuga*, the road called Progress.
✳ Let's begin on a Foundation.
✳ Hyper-reality . . . the 'reality' in which our children 'discover themselves' in the *Kali-Yuga*.
✳ 'Man-made': it begins as a thin film, transparent, its future unforeseeable, over Nature...
✳ Baudrillard's work follows upon Marx's.
✳ Not the 'brilliant but shallow' *Communist Manifesto* crap of his youth...
✳ Three inner and outer landscapes... production, consumption, hyper-reality.
✳ A fundamental mutation in the ecology of the human species.
～ BAUDRILLARD
✳ It's amusing to imagine an encounter between him and Marx: 'Are we actually seeing the same thing here? That creep, and me?'
✳ Our children, 'hanging out' where selves are purchased, are called 'mall rats'.
✳ All living forms must be brought into harmony with the mechanical world picture...
～ MUMFORD
✳ This direction has been designated as that of the 'solidification' of the world.
～ GUÉNON
✳ All three of these guys are seeing and saying the same thing, in different ways.
✳ Actually a perception of the *Kali-Yuga*...
✳ People saw all this coming, back in the thirties, this bizarre invisible transformation of human beings and human life into numbers and objects...
✳ In fact, of course, this 'productive' worker cares as much about the crappy shit he has to make as does the capitalist himself who employs him.
～ MARX (*Grundrisse*, p273)

✳ For quantification is the disappearance of reality. . . . The created world is the ecstasy of its qualities...

✳ In rejecting or losing celestial values, man became the victim of time... time is the decadence which carries us away from the origin.

〜 FRITHJOF SCHUON

✳ Expressed initially in his concept of sign value and sign fetishism.

✳ THEY SEE THEIR PRO KIDS AS MEAL TICKETS.

✳ The complex, to be called 'The Mall of America', is projected to attract more visitors than Mecca or the Vatican, he said.

〜 SAN FRANCISCO EXAMINER

✳ Apollonius of Tyana to the King of Babylon:

✳ Picking up the thread again. (We go with the flow here. It was either digressions or footnotes: I chose digressions.)

✳ All of this seemingly groping and tormented vocabulary is a deadly serious and determined attempt to describe something mind-boggling... 'Strawberry Fields Forever...'

✳ The very experience and ground of the 'real' disappears.

〜 KELLNER

✳ The 'hyperreality of simulations' in the media are more real than real, and come to produce and define a new reality.

✳ The *buddhi, intelligentia spiritualis,* the *takhayyul mutlaq* or Theophanic Imagination of Sufism.

✳ Sex and hype, violence and freeways and credit cards and fuel injection... what Baudrillard calls 'cyberblitz.'

✳ In the same invisible intangible way that *we are Capital,* that *we are Technique...* that *we are the Megamachine...*

✳ In this same invisible way *we are Hyper-reality.*

✳ Then comes the best part. I turn on the VCR and get caught up in my soaps. At about midnight I fall asleep.

〜 UNNAMED STUDENT

✳ The magical fax, porno-perfecto, your own PC, the gleaming credit card and the instant replay of the turn-around jump shot.

✳ What is involved if the human race is not to lose its grip on reality entirely is something like a profound and ultimately planet-wide re-orientation of modern culture...

〜 MUMFORD

✳ Plato's famous *anamnesis* . . . which unveils the fabulous pleromatic *illud tempus* which man has to remember if he is to know the *truth* and participate in *Being.*

〜 ELIADE

✳ It is not merely that on the television screen entertainment is the metaphor for all discourse. It is that off the screen the same metaphor prevails.

〜 NEIL POSTMAN

❋ Disneyland is presented as imaginary in order to make us believe that the rest is real, when in fact…

~ BAUDRILLARD

❋ The New Global Popular Culture: Is it American? Is it Good for America? Is it Good for the World? Conference organizer and AEI Senior Fellow Ben J.Wattenberg's answers to those questions were Yes, Yes, and Yes…

~ WILSON QUARTERLY

❋ Hyper-reality, predictably, presents a serious challenge to novelists.
❋ And now Don Quixote having satisfy'd his Appetite, he took a Handful of Acorns, and looking earnestly upon 'em…

~ MIGUEL DE CERVANTES SAAVEDRA

❋ According to Coontz, when most Americans mention 'family values', they are thinking of 1950s and 1960s TV shows such as 'Leave it to Beaver' and 'The Adventures of Ozzie and Harriet.'
❋ Time now to begin circling in on the landing field: on our children's inheritance of a hyper-real world as an event in our hearts, in the heart of humanity.
❋ Something else here, something elusive…
❋ Once upon a time, when I looked at my son or daughter…
❋ Now, when I look at my son or daughter…
❋ For archaic man, reality is a function of the imitation of a celestial archetype…

~ ELIADE

❋ We are reminded of Zen's *kaminagara no michi.*
❋ Profane man is the result of a desacralization of human existence.

~ ELIADE

❋ Once upon a time… when I looked at my father or mother…
❋ Now when I look at my mother or father…
❋ The whole thing centers around *innocence*…
❋ But the themes and scope of the preceding commentary on 'reality'… call for a commensurate finale… We must always return. That is the motion of the Tao.
❋ We should understand well that all things are the works of the Great Spirit.

~ BLACK ELK

❋ Civilized, crying how to be human again: this will tell you how.

~ ROBINSON JEFFERS

❋ Every form you see has its archetype in the divine world, beyond space…

~ JALAL AL-DIN RUMI

❋ Lead me from the unreal to the Real.

~ INVOCATION, *Brihadaranyaka Upanishad*

XXIV. Christ and the *Kali-Yuga* [242]

Adequacy to the demand, on all levels, of the subject being treated here is dependent upon forgiveness and Grace. And from our side, the conviction of obedience. There's nothing 'heavier' than the question addressed in this chapter.

XXV. Last Chapter, End of the Book [306]

Au revoir, mes amis! And a blessing from the Irish:
May the road rise up to meet you
May the wind be always at your back
May the sun shine warm upon your face
The rains fall soft upon your fields
And until we meet again
May God hold you in the palm of His hand.
    That about covers it.

Appendix [327]

Index [345]

Apologia Pro Opus Suum

As I edited this text for publication I kept asking myself,
Is it really that bad,
that hopeless?
Did I go too far?
What's the verdict here?
Well, at the end of the day, as they say in England,
it's your life to live.
Your call.
I merely unveil the question.
Forgive me.

Introduction

At a certain point solemnity collapses under its own weight. Why is this so? I'll tell you. It's because the heart of the universe is Joy, Ananda, and it invariably reasserts Itself. 'From Bliss all these beings arise.' So solemnity, along with sobriety, gloom, grief, contrition and the rest of the clan, has a shelf life, as it were. The Reality, that Joy, inevitably reasserts Itself, because It is always there anyway: behind the shifting scenes, utterly untouched by and independent of our fleeting moods and states — as the doctrines unanimously and ecstatically proclaim. It is always the Truth, and that means our Truth: Absolute and Eternal, while everything else, not only our moods and states but the entire cycle of birth-and death, the samsara, is relative and transient. Heart of the universe, Heart of my heart.

So no matter how grim the situation or episode, sooner or later someone shrugs his or her shoulders and winks, someone chuckles and comes up with an old saying, someone catches somebody's eye and smiles, someone rises to his or her feet and walks out to carry on with life because that's the way of things, the way we learn to live in this world: the dispensation, the Law. We're not in charge here. The indestructible affirmation reasserts itself without fail, and whether we know it or not, that affirmation, the life that we are, the life that carries on, is Joy.

Now why do I say this?

Because a shift in sensibility something like the paradigm I just described took place in the course of writing this book, and a dialogue between the two dimensions, the eternal and the transient, is at the heart of the book's message. We have a grim situation to explore here, or at least it looks that way on the surface, and we have an eternal Truth behind it. We have history, we have Heaven: a grim scenario, and the changeless Reality: we appear to be imprisoned in and inescapably conditioned by the former, but we are actually eternally free in the latter. We are the Reality which is Joy Everlasting, and the grim scenario this book seeks to explore, the *Kali-Yuga*, is actually the glorious Mahamaya, the Great Illusion, the divine Lila or Play of God, the Shakti of Shiva Mahadeva: as Oberon put it, speaking to Puck, 'the fierce vexation of a dream.' Not real. 'The whole of existence is imagination within imagination, while true Being is God alone.' (Ibn 'Arabi) This is the Teaching, *scientia sacra*, the *sanatana dharma* or Eternal Truth.

The shift in sensibility expressed itself through a change in the tone of the writing, a gradual metamorphosis of voice. I only discovered it after the fact; it wasn't intentional. The solemnity, gravit,y and self-conscious seriousness, the urgent concern, of the opening sections is punctured with increasing frequency and gradually entirely replaced, although not without intermittent flashbacks, by a sort of reckless disdain, a cheerful indifference to the gruesome subject matter and an almost contemptuous detachment from its dire implications. A sort of reverse *contemptus mundi* attitude emerges, something like Milarepa must have felt when he said, 'I made a pillow of my mother's bones and remained in an undistracted state of tranquillity.' After all, this is a deadly serious book about *maya*, the Great Illusion, written by someone who *knows* that: how are you supposed to write such a book? *Why* would it be written? (You will see.) If you know all this is *maya*, as I do and we are taught, you can't take it very seriously (you 'wear the world as a loose garment', as the Sufis say): and if you do take it seriously, as I have for a purpose, you have to forget it's *maya*. You see the dilemma. It presents itself as a problem of tone and style, voice and attitude. Subtleties of English prose, how to say it and keep the balance. The exposition itself is remorselessly consistent and continuous; the tone is an unfolding drama in which serious challenges to motivation, sincerity and personal *sadhana* have to be met.

This brings us to the book's message. Living in the *Kali-Yuga*, the closing phase of the cosmic cycle, is a solemn matter indeed, and those among us who think about things very seriously, and try to make serious decisions about how they'll live their lives, are doing so, whether they know it or not, precisely because they live in this terminal period, where we are all cast into the crisis. And yet at the same time the *Kali-Yuga*, the cosmic cycles, this world and everything in it, are not the Reality. They are, as gnosis teaches us, *maya*, the 'world-appearance' or Cosmic Dream. If we can wake up from it— and that's one of the really big if's—we become Enlightened: a drop-out. One with the infinite Bliss. That's why this book, in an earlier draft, was subtitled 'A Head Trip to Reality.' It's a journey from and through the unreal to the Real. (*Asatoma sadgamaya*... lead me from the unreal to the Real...) Nothing has truly happened here, nothing has *ever* happened, 'appearances' to the contrary notwithstanding. It's a Dream, glorious to be sure, an appearance in consciousness, the *pure* consciousness, the 'Infinite Consciousness' celebrated in Yoga Vasishtha, in the Atman or Self or Supreme Spirit realized by the sages in their meditation, having no more substance than the play of light on the water. But we want to know all about it anyway: all about the Dream, everything that happened in it, the Story of Humanity, and we want to know all about it because we sense that we need to make serious decisions based upon what happened in that Dream and we don't want to make them in the dark. Knowledge, we feel, liberates; and we are right about that. 'To be human is to know.'

So this is a book about what happened to us, where we are and how we got here — about the Dream, in other words — written in the hope of contributing to a decision-making process none of us can evade, but reminding us all along that nothing has happened and we are always in heaven and there is no one anywhere to 'make decisions' and God alone is Real. *Brahman satyam, jagan mithya*: Brahman is Real, the world is not. *Ayam Atma Brahma*: This Self is Brahman. Shankara's summation.

Now I'm going to start this Introduction all over again and talk about the book in terms of Enlightenment. Same problematic, another angle.

This book is a passionately concerned analysis of a situation which the Enlightened regard with tranquil detachment and only the unenlightened regard with passionate concern. It is also a cheerful acquiescence to a situation which the unenlightened regard with desperate urgency and only the Enlightened can view with cheerful acquiescence. The Enlightened, witnesses to Wisdom, are detached; the unenlightened, spokespersons for Ignorance, are passionate. Without claims or apologies, this book is both. It is at once a relentless indictment of an ignominy (literally 'deprivation of one's good name') the Enlightened regard with detached compassion, and a disdainfully indifferent survey of a situation the unenlightened regard with bitter self-reproach or blank despair. The unenlightened, as everyone knows, are unanimous in their conviction that the world which *appears* real *is* real — a conviction which is the very definition of Ignorance — and this is an impassioned, belligerently partisan and deadly serious book about that world written by someone who knows full well that Wisdom sees the Truth. He just loves that world too much to be wise.

But there's good reason for this two-fold approach.

The fact is, enlightened people — pilgrims merely passing through, exiles returning home, 'renunciates' who know they've renounced Nothing — don't spend much time developing an in-depth analysis of what's going on in a world they know isn't real anyway. (There's no way, as far as I can see, to go into this without sounding misleadingly facetious or whimsical from time to time, a bit light-headed or -hearted; there's just something incorrigibly funny, as Zen people well know, about the eye-to-eye between Enlightenment and 'the world.') The motivation just isn't there. And they are in command of an extremely powerful, indeed invincible, shorthand which reduces such an analysis to the identification of a very few basic Errors, sometimes called 'defilements', sometimes rebellion or disobedience, which provide a sufficient explanation for the baffling wretchedness experienced by unenlightened people. An explanation indeed sufficient to illuminate the entire crisis of the planet. Ignorance, Craving, Pride and unwholesome thoughts, concupiscence, the 'wound of malice', willfulness, delusion, the identification of the Self with the non-Self, mistaking the rope for a snake (*Atma* for *maya*), egoism in its innumerable guises — these are often offered for our sober appraisal.

This approach seems reductive, even simplistic, to the unenlightened, and laughably so to Western intelligence which has proven itself brilliantly capable of understanding the West in all its filthy satanic reality from every imaginable angle and with enthusiastically exhaustive thoroughness, even relish. But it's not; not reductive, not simplistic. Wisdom, being timeless, is addressed to the individual human person, whose decisive attributes and appropriate modes of comportment in its earthly career are also timeless. Timelessness in the form of Wisdom addresses timelessness in the form of the human soul, or *jiva*, having their common root in the *imago dei*. Wisdom, in other words, is indifferent with perfect justification to the vicissitudes of historical circumstance, to the *particular* morbidities of the West, which are, after all, and if you want to take the time, traceable to what the Abrahamic monotheisms call Sin and the Eastern revelations call Ignorance. In other words, the gigantic middle ground, as it were, between Wisdom and individuals, the institutional forms in which these transgressions manifest themselves as collective history, are irrelevant, actually invisible, to gnosis. Stated differently, Eastern sages (you have perhaps noticed this yourself) haven't the faintest clue about what is happening in the West, and not only because the middle ground is invisible to them but because from their point of view, which is absolutely correct, nothing is happening at all. (Pointing a finger at 'materialism' is about the deepest they ever get.) They speak to individuals, to theomorphic humanity *sub specie aeternitatis*, 'the *forma humanitatis* who is independent of all orders of time and has neither beginning nor end', as Coomaraswamy stated it with his usual eloquent precision, and all they can offer is Enlightenment.

But we, we of the West, want more, or less, than Enlightenment. We really, indeed desperately, want to understand what's happening to us, and in the language we speak; we want to know the meaning of History. Above all, we want to understand the collective destiny: what's going down now. It is, to say the very least and for reasons I surely need not list, uppermost on all our minds.

Now that need has been met, brilliantly and thoroughly as I've said, by the collective enterprise of serious Western writers, and it is their work that composes the bibliography which, I hope, informs this book: for the West understands itself, intimately and with a vengeance. And strangely enough, certain astute commentators on the collective destiny, Westerners, borrow a term from the East to describe it. And you guessed it: that term is *Kali-Yuga*, the final stage of the cosmic cycle. *Kali-Yuga*, then, is the name given in Eastern cosmologies to the grim situation perceived, in varying states and degrees of horror, alarm and cynical or bemused resignation, by almost everyone. Wisdom, of course, knows that the *Kali-Yuga* is a phantasm of *maya*, and the Self alone is Real. The unenlightened well-intentioned, on the other hand, facing a kaleidoscopic galaxy of harrowing and continually erupting 'problems', are in desperate pursuit of effective strategies and an agenda to avert an apparently inexorable gradual catastrophe which is actually both inevitable and illusory. Inevitable, illusory, and providential! Strange stuff. We discover yet another interpretation of the Buddha's invariable enigmatic half-smile.

Many Western observers, however, and among them some of the keenest minds of all, don't use the Eastern term. These observers, giants among the Ignorant, regard the world as real — they think the rope is a snake; they've heard of ropes but don't believe they exist — and may be identified as 'unconscious prophets of the *Kali-Yuga*.' Innocent of the eastern sage's tendency to oversimplification, and unaware of the unreality of their subject matter, these giants explore the intricacies of historical humanity's career with truly savage insight and thoroughness, in discourses of challenging complexity. A German, Karl Marx, two Frenchmen, Jacques Ellul and Jean Baudrillard, and an American, Lewis Mumford, are perhaps the brightest lights in this group. In a second rank we'd discover Theodore Roszak (*The Cult of Information*), Neil Postman (*Amusing Ourselves to Death*), Jeremy Rifkin (*Algeny*), Jerry Mander (*In the Absence of the Sacred*), and Bill McKibben (*The End of Nature*). The lesser figures are legion. Virtually every commentator on modern life, from ad writers to movie directors to the editor of your local newspaper to the teenager next door, and you yourself, is an 'unconscious prophet of the *Kali-Yuga*.' It's an open secret. Everyone knows.

So the paradox. The unconscious prophets, always Westerners, are far and away the sharpest, really the only people worth listening to, but they

XXXII ❋ YUGA: AN ANATOMY OF OUR FATE

don't understand that actually they are talking about nothing (words are merely arising and subsiding in their minds, as these are in your now for you and in my now for me), *legerdemain* of the illusory subject-object dichotomy, castles in the air ('ether', infinite space, locus of the manifestation, Sanskrit *acasa*) in their generous hearts, the 'world-appearance', and need not be distressed in the slightest; and those, always Easterners lost in Bliss, who do know that nothing has ever happened have, in consequence, nothing to offer us but divine Wisdom. I draw heavily upon both, Western Masters and the *sophia perennis* or Wisdom tradition: religion, as it is usually named: Revelation. The contribution of the few who are at home in both universes of discourse, in both archives, such as Frithjof Schuon, Ananda Coomaraswamy, René Guénon, Seyyed Hossein Nasr, Marco Pallis, Mircea Eliade, Martin Lings, and Huston Smith, is priceless, and they are my principal Masters.

Which brings me to the following. The analysis proposed in this book, given its incredible scope, is inherently collective. Many voices speak here; no one could have presumed to take this on alone. The names I've mentioned, and many more, sit at a round table in my brain. They make suggestions, fit things together and essentially write the book; I simply set it down as best I can. We all have to help out here. Behind this discourse is the love of our species, of this particular being: that's the inspiration. We're talking about the fate of Humanity. The finale of that symphony, the last tune in the set, the music we love, the music in our hearts. Johnny Hartman singing 'Unforgettable.' Bill Evans playing 'Here's That Rainy Day'.

About the text. If I had a reputation to build or defend (a ridiculous thought), I might have chosen to paraphrase my Masters' insights, to express them in my own words, giving a false impression of individual enterprise. I don't do that. Instead I have chosen, especially toward the second half of the book, to quote their own words, often at length. Three reasons: first, the work, as I said, is inherently collective and should be presented as such, as a self-awareness of humanity at large; second, they are generally eloquent, they are the real Masters, and you deserve to hear them first-hand; and third, no one would be moved to take all this seriously if it appeared to originate in a single mind. It would seem private. It's not; and I want to make dead sure no one draws that wrong conclusion. I am a bibliography. And I am the common life.

I think this text needs to be introduced one last time. I don't feel I've been blunt enough.

This is a book about our times, and it offers no hope for the Protagonist, historical humanity. (Hope, the 'great falsifier of truth' — Gracian, 'the worst of all evils, because it prolongs the torments of man'—Nietzsche; 'Hope is the cause of the greatest misery; abandonment of hope is the highest bliss'— the Avadhuta who had twenty-four teachers, *Srimad Bhagavatam*.) For individuals yes; for the collective no. For individuals yes, in the form of that spiritual Realization or Enlightenment or Love of God which is the only hope they have ever had anyway, time out of mind. But for the collective, no. There is no 'ray of hope' here, no automatic mandatory 'last chapter message' of the kind we invariably find in the proliferation of books containing urgent warnings about where we are heading and what will happen if we don't 'come to our senses' soon. Perhaps I'm wrong; but I doubt it.

And I feel that I am writing not for 'kindred spirits' but for almost any-one, for more people today than yesterday, because we all live in the same world and it's all going in one direction and we all got our hunch, our suspi-cion, from the same sources: from everything, really, the whole society, the whole contemporary human scene, from scraps of conversation, cumulative life experience, overwhelmingly from the sense of technological transforma-tions, from the television 'community' and the media, from honest books, from our own stories and the stories of our friends, from historical and institutional trends, from quiet introspection and insistent intuition, from the convergence of all these.

We may be summoned, or driven, to consider the adoption of a life in Spirit by an inability to identify any longer with historical humanity in its entirety, and with these times specifically, as well as by the eternal magne-tism of heaven. This dying world, or dying humanity, is sufficient incentive to seek an alternative to our fate within its definition and orbit, to our neces-sarily tormented identification with its suicidal disorientations and fever-ishly marketed 'hope.' Suicidal, ecocidal. The world itself, seen for what it really is, in sober witness to the truth on all levels, drives us to seek a way out of it, and by His Grace offers one: that is to say, a contemplative disen-gagement which does not contradict or exclude a responsible life here. This is, of course, as always; but now more than ever. A Way, a Path, a Deliver-ance. 'From the moment you came into the world of being, a ladder was placed before you that you might escape' — *Divani Shamsi Tabriz*.

What follows is an anatomy of the *Kali-Yuga*. It's about this concrete world, you and me and our kids and the lives we live. The Reign of Quan-tity, the Fall into Time, the Mutation into Machinery, the End of Nature, the Prison of Unreality — or of the 'hyper-reality' identified by Jean Baudril-lard et. al. Those are the five hallmarks. The end of the cosmic cycle, and of a humanity sufficiently recognizable as such to warrant our commitment to its future. Not a proof, for proof, in this context, is not possible nor is its pursuit morally justifiable. Rather a provocation. The rejection or reorientation of our allegiance to posterity takes place in a region of the soul beyond the reach of argument or exposition. The region of eternal allegiance to eternal Truth, to the Reality, which, because we are divine, made in His image, is allegiance to Humanity as well. Eternal Humanity. Such is the grace of the *Kali-Yuga*.

In the outer world there's always a horizon, beyond which we cannot see. But in the inner world we see the infinite.

Suggestions to the Reader

First of all, it's not really a 'book'. Not that particular social artifact which surfaces in bookstores and libraries and is called a 'book.' Looks like one, but isn't. It's another kind of artifact, whose nearest relative is the subversive pamphlet or protest song or a muttered ironic remark about pyramid-building or mass human sacrifice or the necessity of an inquisition, and it makes its way through the world, from mind to mind, soul to soul, on another kind of path, and it isn't read the way a book is read.

This is because of what it says and the way it says it and their relationship to the culture in which the text appears. (See the 'Table of Contents' entry for Chapter X.) It can never be received into the world it examines, exposes, meaning never become a 'book', because there's no way to transform it into a commodity: no way it can be purveyed, marketed, advertised, critiqued, no way to 'promote' it in that world, no way to *sell it, and no way even to talk about it in public dialogue.* It is the quintessentially unmentionable. It falls outside the circle of legitimate discourse, and for many reasons. (Other adjectives I could have used: conventional, consensual, official, familiar, established, comprehensible, validated, digestible, acceptable, customary, intelligible… and so on.) Its 'argument' can never be respectable. What I've said here is anathema: that which is loathed and detested, denounced with utter abhorrence by authority.

And that being clarified, now on to the reading of it.

You don't have to read the whole thing. By no means. What you want to do is 'get it': get the idea, get the sense of it, the point, the drift, the mind and soul of the voice, and that could happen anywhere and anytime because the same voice, beneath shifting moods, is there on every page, and it might take only one page for you to hear it. Once you've 'got' what this text seeks to communicate, once you've grasped it with your mind and heart, your Cardiac Intellect, and assessed its accuracy and import, it's yours and you can continue 'reading' it, if you wish, by the way you live your life, the way you interpret things, respond to experience and make decisions. You can put the book down then. Or continue reading it to acquire reinforcement, or encouragement, or simply to satisfy curiosity.

The text is best described—and I do so in the Introduction and elsewhere—as a provocation. Something to stimulate your spirit, your intelligence, your latent defiance, your aliveness and resolve, something to confirm and fortify your secret suspicion. (Everyone has a secret suspicion now.) Skip around in it if that's your style, till a word or phrase, a passage or an idea, a citation, hits you, and then stop reading and dwell upon it: talk about it with the people you talk about things with. Embellish it with material drawn from your own experience, or confront it with that material and see where that leads, or examine your own experience in its light. If you're a disciplined type, read it straight through, patiently, forgiving the flaws inevitable in so demanding an enterprise undertaken by a father of five who goes to work every day and gets as worn out as you do.

Read the whole 'Table of Contents' first. It's a reliable anticipation of the text, consisting, as it does, of quotations from the text. And, if you're 'ready'—'the readiness is all' in this affair (Hamlet)—it may be all you need to read.

Read my Masters, the textual citations. This was a bibliography project. The citations were gleaned from many thousands of pages. They're powerful and profound, very often eloquent, and always unmistakably true. The style of my Masters—and yours, they're yours too, they loved us and told it like it is for us because we're made for the truth—is emphatic and compressed; their writing is informed by an unwavering integrity that demands and achieves exhaustive precision. Absorb their words, if not mine. These are our best minds, collectively the Mind of humanity. They are our own will, our own right, to understand ourselves, our maximum intelligence, both moral, because the universe is a moral drama, as all human cultures attest, and relentless, because where truth is concerned the stakes are infinite. And if anything they say is just too hard to grasp, pass over it and move right along. It's all right. Ellul, Baudrillard, Eliade, Marx, Guénon, Schuon, Mumford, Coomaraswamy, Nasr, and others, Ellen Chen's commentary on the *Tao Te Ching*, Toshihiko Izutsu on Sufism, really are difficult, for the simple reason that the subject they deal with, humanity, is 'difficult' (double meaning intended!): complex, elusive, subtle, profound: many-faceted, inexhaustible, inherently deceptive. But the reward of grasping, even glimpsing, what they are getting at is priceless.

In Chapter XXIV, the next-to-the-last, the water is considerably, really infinitely, over our heads: no one, no mere human, is 'on top of' this subject, not even Schuon. This chapter was the hardest to write, and probably the hardest to read. Do what you can with it. Meditate on it, or just forget about it. It was a matter of thoroughness. This chapter had to be written.

And by the way: if you can't accept the assumption of a Divine Reality—can't accept 'religion' on its own claim, transcendence, a celestial Center and Origin, Divine Wisdom, Divine Truth, Beatitude, the Perennial Philosophy, an Absolute, a Supreme which is both Personal and Impersonal, God and Nirvana, and so on—if your position here is irreversible because you're just so sure, put this book down now: it's fallen into the wrong hands. Return it or pass it along, it's not for you.

The opening sentences of Chapter IX become more all-embracing, more devastatingly true, every day, in myriad ways no one would have anticipated six years ago when I wrote them. If I were still writing I'd add a lot more to Chapter IX; but if you catch the drift of the text, and have been blessed with a thoughtful appraisal of the Age of Information, you'll be able to do that quite easily yourself. (But maybe not so easily: you might benefit from Chapter III of Jerry Mander's excellent and insightful *In the Absence of the Sacred*, where he discusses the ingredients of 'the pro-technology paradigm.' And there's a 'Technology Update' appendix in this text.) Remember, always remember: the Emperor has no clothes. Many names, many masks, many technological incarnations, many dialects, but no clothes. The Great Claim is a Lie. Think of it this way: you are *always* being lied to—manipulated, programmed, indoctrinated, exploited, degraded, insulted, misled, dishonored—by the culture you inhabit. (And nearly all the time innocently! By people just doing their job! Isn't that maddening? And thought-provoking? What *is* a 'job'?) As you perhaps suspect.

Love informed the writing of this book, and love is what ought to motivate your reading of it. 'Love is all there is, it makes the world go round!' (Bobby Dylan) And 'Thou art the Love that became the universe.'

Read the last chapter. It's easy stuff, sort of a summary, and I think it's where the inner motivating impulse here, the heart of the text, the soul of the motivating purpose, comes closest to attaining purity of expression.

Hearing or reading *Ramayana* you will get
from Rama what you wish for,
so be aware! Don't ask too little. Guard yourself
—everything counts, and so be kind.
Good fortune to you all.
This is the world's first best poem.
In the first age of the world
men crossed the ocean of existence
by their spirit alone.
In the second age sacrifice and ritual began,
and then Rama lived,
and by giving their every act to him
men lived well their ways.
Now in our age what is there to do
but worship Rama's feet?
But my friend, the last age
of this world shall be the best.
For then no act has any worth, all is useless...
except only to say *Rama*.
The future will read this. Therefore I tell them,
when all is in ruin around you, just say *Rama*.
We have gone from the spiritual to the passionate.
Next will come Ignorance. Universal war.
Say *Rama* and win! Your time cannot touch you!

~RAMAYANA

Holy Father,
keep through thine own name
those whom thou hast given me,
that they may be one, as we are...
They are not of the world,
even as I am not of the world.

~John 17: 11, 16

You find yourself in this transient, joyless world.
Turn from it, and take your delight in me.
Fill your heart and mind with me, adore me,
make all your acts an offering to me,
bow down to me in self-surrender.
If you set your heart upon me thus,
and take me for your ideal above all others,
you will come into my Being.

~Bhagavad Gita, IX

I

Invitation

I think it has become appropriate for men and women of good will to give some thought to the future of humanity in the light of present conditions and trends. We may find that we are able, on the basis of provisional assessments of that future, to answer certain fundamental questions about how we should live our lives now.

We ought to proceed with perfect serenity of spirit. We are capable of that. We ought to be completely honest. Reassurances do not alter reality; hope does not guide us to the truth. Our sympathies should be with the protagonist, but we can't allow ourselves to be swayed by them; all the more so because the actual identity of the protagonist, and therefore our own as individuals, is not something we can take for granted, but is rather one of the questions we will be trying to answer. We are summoned to the heart of matters, to the roots and depths of things; to our own hearts, our own roots and depths.

II

Surveillance

THE controversy about the fate of humanity is central and inherent in our cultural life. An apprehensive watchfulness hangs in the air. This is a sign of the times. There is no end to the facts and statistics cited as evidence in support of the opinions about where we are heading. Optimism and pessimism, enthusiasm and alarm, all shades, all degrees. There are penetrating insights, and illuminating interpretations of institutions, behavior and events. Persuasive arguments and diagnoses, an abundant bibliography, and a sleepless irony that misses nothing. We watch ourselves closely.

Every endangered species, every river, every forest. Every shift in the patterns of domestic and communal life. Every technological and pedagogical innovation. Every emerging pathology, every new strategy, every new character on the stage. Symptoms, indicators, figures of speech. Styles: of music, child-rearing, therapy and life. Which way people jump from the Golden Gate Bridge, how they cope, how they relax, how they unwind. Every image, every nuance. We take note of it all. We try to distinguish what is dangerous from what is simply novel, always aware that wrong turns, leading possibly to disaster, are a permanent peril. Surveillance.

III

History & Way

BUT nothing is ever proven one way or another in the debate about where we are heading. Nothing demonstrated, nothing conclusively established. The surveillance is fruitless, both as a source of understanding and as the preliminary to intervention. We watch it all happening before our eyes. We speculate, extrapolate and argue. But the debate is itself only another stone in the avalanche.

The history we monitor unfolds like something elemental, and at an ever-increasing speed. Something we call 'the pace of life' continuously accelerates. No one seems to be in control. We feel as if an utterly indifferent, inscrutable, unreachable and remorseless agency is directing the performance, down to the most minute detail and in every moment, of a Master Plan so unintelligible to us that we can't tell whether it's hostile, insane or simply capricious.

This is the very nature of history. Once things began happening, they took on a life of their own. What is history? It is the departure from an ancestral Way in which we were one with cyclical Nature, and in which nothing new ever happened. There was only an eternal repetition of the archetypal patterns and exemplary models of responsible human life. I was as my father or mother; I lived the same life, sang the same songs, and knew the same sorrows, joys, seasons, landmarks and truths: and my sons and daughters would be like me. This Way has vanished forever, and we have never recovered from the loss, and never will. Its death-knell was sounded, and the new mode of being inaugurated, in the narratives of the Old Testament, where for the first time in human experience a unique significance, as part of an unfolding one-way divine intention, was accorded to events. We are still reeling, still stunned, even now. It can't be assimilated. We can never feel comfortable with it. History has been called the Fall into Time. It brought a new kind of terror into the world.

IV
Progress
& Tradition

BROADLY speaking, there are two perspectives, which may be called the secular and the traditional. They are irreconcilable, and they appear, in innumerable guises, whenever a serious dialogue about humanity and its fate is pursued to ultimate implications, and whenever we think deeply about the meaning, direction and purpose of our lives.

In the secular perspective, reality is History, knowledge is given to us by Science and happiness by technology, everything is relative, and the criterion of rectitude is practicality. In the traditional perspective, there's an eternal Norm or Law or Way—a *dharma*—from which we have departed, a Truth or Wisdom or Simplicity which we have forgotten, and an Absolute, which may or may not be a personal God, which is alone real, whose existence we now deny. What is seen from the former as Progress and the multiplication of human potentials is seen from the latter as dehumanization and impoverishment. These opposing perspectives, occasionally explicit but most often implicit, confront each other with growing frequency as the sense of crisis deepens. Their manners of expression are ramified indefinitely, and into bewildering complexity.

The first perspective, however, is also the world. It is enthroned Power. When we talk about History, Science and Progress, we are talking about this world, our common experience and the forces that shape it. The second perspective is a dedication and a Witness; on its own terms, a Witness of Error, Ignorance and Death. It is powerless, and does not seek power. The first, as active, as history and the force behind it, is predominantly 'outer', and proudly visible. It is also the modern mind; it informs secular philosophies and nearly everyone's fundamental, but increasingly threatened, assumptions about the past and the future. The second perspective, as contemplative, is predominantly 'inner' and intangible. It views outer things, the ever-changing world and the ever-flowing river of events, as insubstantial because ephemeral; the divine archetypes alone are real. In its full realization, however, in meditative or ecstatic insight, it perceives a perfect identity of inner and outer, of Self and world, in an eternal present.

Each perspective regards the other, with respect to these last grand alternatives and wherever their encounter takes place, as mistaken about the nature of reality. Our decision about how we shall live our lives will depend upon what we regard or experience as real.

V

Self-Inflicted
yet Autonomous,
Unreal yet Fatal

THERE are people among us old enough to remember what life was like before television. If they're in their seventies they can even remember young adulthood without television. But of course their numbers steadily decrease. And if they've been 'watching' television for the past forty years, they have been metamorphosed anyway; they will have been dispossessed of their own experience, and cannot bear personal witness, as they alone could have, to our present death and former life. They are truly tragic figures. We stare at their faces with bitter love, for they are our mothers and fathers, and try to blink away the sorrow, the strange disorienting sense of absence. They were supposed to become wise, we were supposed to look to them for wisdom; but they were struck down in their prime. Where once a light shone in their eyes, and where now there should glow the joy and depth of wisdom, there is distracted vacancy. They will never become what they were meant to be. I coin a word, a word for our time: spiricide. Television is spiricide. And we who know this are the last humans.

This seems an exaggerated accounting. And perhaps it is. But only in the sense that more responsibility is attributed to television than it actually incurs. Other causes contribute to the destruction of wisdom in elders. The perpetual innovation, for example, that characterizes historical societies and the capitalist mode of production in particular. If your world has been dismantled, of what use to your descendants is your experience? Of what use what you learned? And where is there room for wisdom anyway, when knowledge and truth, and even ideas, have been replaced by 'information', by 'data', and thought itself presumed to be merely a Turing machine, a sequence of algorithms? (Defined by a renowned expert in 'the physics of consciousness' as 'simply a calculational procedure of some kind.') The world of 'A.I', Artificial Intelligence, in which the Computer Age was born, is also spiricide. Our parents escaped it, but our children will not.

Television, computers, manic discontinuity defined as Progress. Edutainment, infomercial, dramedy, channel surfing, couch potato, ear candy. Television humanity, Computer humanity. Reality becomes Entertainment, and vice versa. Minds become Machines, and vice versa. Only those who resist can survive. Only those who recall, who recollect, who look within. And their survival is not in this world.

Money is the objective community, our relationship to one another. Capital, as Marx demonstrated, is not a thing, it is a social relationship. Television is the subjective community, the common mind: the news, the sports spectaculars, the commercials, the videos: the shared world on all levels. The Computer, the Internet, is the spectacular supremely versatile fruit of their union, consummation of the screen community in commodity culture, wunderkind, the genial supervision, facilitator and confirmation of both dimensions, objective and subjective at once in its ubiquitous administration. These three define realism and reality. They determine what we can do, define what we are and report what we have done. We are created in their images.

It could be argued, and has been, that we are the descendants of human beings, and that this is the Post-Human Era. Consider, for example, that there's no longer any such thing as Nature. That genetic engineering has already undertaken a 'new creation', sometimes referred to as 'Genesis II', which will include the improvement of the human species as well as the manufacture of living 'marketable products'. Science and commerce are working together, billions already invested. Information Technology, 'I.T', is at the heart of it all. The marriage of genetic engineering and computer science is the New Age, the Brave New World we have already entered. It was celebrated while we were watching television, and we'll be informed about it by television. We ourselves, along with the whole world of life, are now finally understood to be 'systems of information', recorded in the genetic code. We, and all of Nature, can and will be programmed.

Nature as such, as an immutable background, an autonomous, inviolate and eternal setting, a Creation, is already vanished from human experience, and in reality as well: our footprints are everywhere, in the rains and the seasons, the oceans and the air. There is no Nature anymore. It is gone forever. Its physical remains will be 'programmed' and 'engineered' to suit the purposes of beings who no longer remember what human purposes are, who no longer remember what it was like to be human, and who will program and engineer themselves, in the electronic darkness they now inhabit, out of existence, We, too, will be gone forever.

Until now, no matter what insult and damage we inflicted upon ourselves through social inventions, at least we were all born human, born intact. In the midst of the inescapable uncertainties, and hazards, at least human birth, 'so precious to get' according to the Teachings, the Supreme Grace, the great promise perpetually renewed, was guaranteed. Until now.

VI

Humanity, Posterity, Eternity

ALLEGIANCE to posterity. The conviction of inescapable involvement with a future of the human race and of the Earth, as if one's own destiny were at stake. Solidarity with the humanity of time and space, a
collective temporal and physical being, with its past, its crisis and its fate.
This is the identity of men and women of good will.

It is specific to historical existence as that existence climaxes in the global
self-awareness made possible by modern technology. What originated in
Biblical messianic expectations of collective righteousness or a restoration of
felicity culminates in apprehension of the apocalypse, of ecocide, holocaust,
universal mechanization, racial extinction, or any of the ingenious dystopias
of science fiction. *Twelve Monkeys*, *Escape from L.A.*, *Road Warrior*, *Blade
Runner*. Hope and fear: the experience of History, of the Fall into Time.

Now at last there is no one but us. No Creator, no Creation. Nothing to
worship. Nothing beyond us, nothing containing us, nothing within us but
tissues, organs and bones, nothing we must flow with or submit to or accept
with patient serenity as our appointed dispensation. We create ourselves
now. We are our History, and History is what we make. Our own, and the
Earth's as well. We determine where and whether the rivers will flow, the
composition of the oceans and the atmosphere, the length of the seasons,
the population of all creatures, their survival or extinction. The temperature
of the planet. The wavelengths of sunlight. We are Power. Our final state of
being is Power. Power and Terror.

It is time, I believe, to become aware of and carefully examine our identification with historical humanity and its temporal situations. That identification is an error. Humanity is not really a physical being confined within a

linear numerical continuum called Time, crawling on the surface of a whirl-ing ball of stone in a measureless universe made of matter. It has no history, and it is not a material being. It is eternal. It is a Consciousness, a Heart of Light. Nothing can ever happen to it. It was and will be what it always is, for it exists outside of time and space. And that is true of the world as well. The world, the Earth, every petal, bird-call, and morning, every moment in Nature, is now and was then what it always was and always will be, forever. Everything is eternal, and indestructible. Eternal in your heart, which is the Heart of the universe. The Fall into Time, the world unfolding in Time, the world devoured by Time, and Time itself—all are imaginary. Reality is else-where; there is nothing to hope for, and nothing to fear. The things we hope for are hope's dreams; the things we fear, fear's nightmares. Everything is accomplished, and everything is immortal, Now.

In the traditional wisdom, what is transient is unreal. Human beings are bound to this transience, and its inevitable sorrow, by the pursuit of their personal goals. By concupiscence, by desire, by the illusion of the ego. They want things for themselves, and they think that when they get them they will be happy. They pursue pleasure and success. This is universal Igno-rance, the indigenous Darkness in which the uncomprehended Light shines forever. There is no happiness in the finite.

Men and women of good will are bound to transience by their solidarity with historical humanity. They identify with the hopes and fears of the human race, with the historical drama and the contemporary situation of the protagonist. This is a nobler bondage; but for that very reason, because there's a genuine element of noble self-sacrifice about it, a virtue and righ-teousness, we are reluctant to point out its ultimate futility, its unavoidable entrapment in the transience and relativity of all earthly affairs. It justifiably contrasts itself favorably with the first bondage, selfish and short-sighted. We acknowledge and respect its acceptance of responsibility, its ability to feel and be guided by compassion, its recognition of oneness. Partisans of historical humanity make revolutions in the name of freedom, justice and equality, they enter the political arena, they campaign for and contribute to just causes; they organize resistance to oppression, they champion the dis-possessed and disenfranchised. Their knowledge is of the past, their reality is the present stage of the struggle, their devotion is to the future. Their thought is ideological and strategic, and they are guided by visions of a bet-ter or ideal world, in which people and nations live in peaceful harmony with each other. They are the heroes and heroines of the historical drama, to those who share their views, and they have earned their good names. But they disappear, the inspiring leaders and the loyal foot-soldiers, gradually, inevitably, into the dust of compromise and relativity, ground into unforeseeable new shapes and roles by the attrition of subsequent events, and the simple accumulation of years, and finally no one can say with certainty what they really did or meant or amounted to, or what, if anything, they left behind.

Historical Humanity, eternal Humanity. The second contains the first within it, but as it really is, a dream. Allegiance to historical Humanity, to posterity, and allegiance to eternal Humanity, to the Light. The second contains the first within it: but as it really is, as witness to the Intention, fidelity to the Truth, obedience to the Law. An end in itself, achieving nothing durable because there is nothing durable in this world. The Buddha taught compassion, loving-kindness, sympathy and impartiality, the Four Illimitable Sublime Moods, knowing full well that there is no one to bestow them on, and no one to bestow them. The realities are in heaven. In this world, their shadows.

VII

Clockwatch

What made the machine truly novel was the device that prevented the free fall of the weights and interrupted their drop into regular intervals… It was called an escapement, since it was a way of regulating the 'escape' of the motive power into the clock, and it held revolutionary import for human experience… These interrupted movements eventually measured off the minutes and, later, the seconds. When, in due course, clocks became common, people would think of time no longer as a flowing stream but as the accumulation of discrete measured moments. The sovereign time that governed daily lives would no longer be the sunlight's smooth-flowing elastic cycles. Mechanized time would no longer flow. The tick-tock of the clock's escapement would become the voice of time… There are few greater revolutions in human experience than this movement from the seasonal or 'temporary' hour to the equal hour. Here was man's declaration of independence from the sun, new proof of his mastery over himself and his surroundings. Only later would it be revealed that he had accomplished this mastery by putting himself under the domination of a machine with imperious demands all its own.
~Daniel J. Boorstin, *The Discoverers*

Clocks do not measure time: they produce it. There is no independent world 'out there' composed of measurable intervals and sequences. The world of minutes and seconds is produced by machines called clocks. It did not exist before their invention, it does not exist in Nature, and it only exists now in our enslavement to its false claim. With the invention of the clock, the progenitor and supreme archetype of all mechanisms, human time, which could only have been a fluid living sense of duration woven out of events in human experience, capable of flowing swiftly or slowly in both directions, and even standing still, was replaced by something new in the world: clock-time. Arithmetic rigor and precision. Accuracy. Earth time, human time, was replaced by mechanical time. Quality by quantity, sentience by machinery, natural by artificial, life by death. As always. These displacements are the signposts of Progress.

We are now securely bolted to that momentous innovation. An invisible clock ticks ceaselessly in the air, in our days and nights, even in our minds. Silent integers flash into the liquid crystal, positioning our memories, intentions and possibilities. Through the infinity of numbers, it nails everything that ever happened and ever will happen to its exact location on a calibrated one-way track. It decrees tension, desperation, panic and their release. Wages could not be determined without it; communication would become impossible, we could not even think. The world would fall apart. This was an irreversible transformation, like so many others that define our lives today. The old time, for it is human time and we remain human, can still be experienced. But only when we forget the world from which it was expelled.

> Caught, pinioned, blinded, sealed and cased in Time,
> Summoned, elected, armed and crowned by Time,
> Tried and condemned, stripped and disowned by Time…
> Buried alive and buried dead by Time:
> If there's no crack or chink, no escape from Time…
> If there's no power can burst the rock of Time…
> Nothing in earth or heaven to set us free:
> Imprisonment's forever; we're the mock of Time,
> While lost and empty lies eternity
> ~Edwin Muir (1887–1959)

The clock, like television and the invasion of Artificial Intelligence, the Computer, is spiricide. Its appearance should not be seen as a calamity, however. Like the other spiricides, it is simply inevitable death, inevitable unfolding. The Manifestation is breathed forth from the Principle, and grows increasingly distant from It. Thus there is privation, Evil. At the same time, they are always One. Atman and *Maya*, Nirvana and Samsara, always One. Authentic Humanity, which is Paradise, is recoverable by those who seek it with earnest sincerity and whole-souled devotion. Seek it where it always was, within. *Intra te quaere deum*. Its destruction is purely external, and therefore purely apparent. Within us it is immortal. And when we find it there, the distinction between inner and outer disappears. Nothing can ever happen to the changeless Reality that we are. And furthermore: 'Whatever is contrary to Tao will not last long.' The warning is repeated. 'That which goes against the Tao comes to an early end.

VIII
Time
& Temples

IT isn't age that hallows the centuries-old houses of worship. Their aura of sanctity, their humble or majestic certitude about what they are and why they exist, reside in our awareness of the piety with which they were built and attended. They are hallowed because believers worshipped in them, because they were built in the age of belief. They are authentic. The builders and believers were authentic, at one with their lives as we are not, and seem to stare out at us across an abyss that can never be bridged. This was another world.

Because piety is gone, it is no longer possible to build a house of worship. The structures we build will never be experienced as hallowed, and even now are experienced as modern versions, replicas or imitations, of the originals. Instead, they'll become historic. Like old railway stations, public buildings and city squares. The last temples, the last houses of worship of the human race, have all been built.

Structures built with power machinery are necessarily profane. A church with automatic glass doors is profane, any structure whatsoever built in the era of power machinery and automatic glass doors is profane. And this for two reasons. First, for the obvious reason that the era of power machinery is the secular era, and its creations bear the stamp of its cultural values. And second, because construction machinery, heavy equipment — its roar, its smell, its arrogance of violent power, its brutal irresistibility, its operators' natural assumption, the natural assumption of their whole society, that speed and power are good in themselves — are inconsistent with Spirit. The churches and cathedrals were built by artisans, whose minds were in their hands, working at a human pace and within the range of human mental and physical prowess; this unity of mind and hand is visible in their work, and must be visible in all work dedicated to Spirit. It is the presence of this unity that elicits our contemplative appreciation of any human work. We only truly exist in our wholeness. In the operation of heavy equipment there is no such unity. The temple must be built by people: not machines. Its paraphernalia and adornment hand-crafted; not machine-made. And the same holds true of the automatic glass doors. Ease, convenience, casual efficiency, a silent electrical triumph over the effort necessary to open a door, all are inconsistent with Spirit. We have to be willing to push the door open. It's impossible to make a pilgrimage on a freeway, what we see through the window of a jet plane are not mountains and rivers, and if we want to enter a House of God and worship there, we have to push the door open. It's that simple. And yet, because 'Mercy is more real than the whole world' (SCHUON), because there's a Reality beyond our assertions, beyond our dreamworld and immune to its discourse and deviations, a contrite heart will never be denied. Anywhere.

The old houses of worship are hallowed by the human hands that erected them, carrying the stones, wielding the wooden tools, and tending to details that, in the artless immediacy of their imperfections and irregularities, announce the human presence—its seriousness and concentration, its affirmation of the symmetry and geometry whose indifference to mathematical accuracy characterizes living beauty—rather than technological precision. Hallowed, finally, by the builders and attendants unquestioning acceptance of the reason this thing was done, and their unquestioning belief in the sacred Truth that inspired the work. *This is a House of God: He will be worshipped here.*

Now this seems to be a comparison between past and present at the expense of the latter. It isn't. The contrast between past and present—and many more will be drawn here—is always a metaphor. It stands for the timeless distinction between our spiritual truth, our appropriate Way, our successful identification of and with our true humanity, on the one hand, and on the other, our departure from the Way, the Truth and the Life (John 14:6), our transgression of the Norm, our ignorance, error and failure. These two alternatives are always present; but only for individuals, because it is only to individuals that the Message, the Truth and the Law, the promise of Grace, are addressed. Collective humanity cannot escape the one-way descent into darkness, which is the very nature of the Fall into historical time. Cannot halt or reverse the descending trajectory, the stupendous and inexorable unfolding of the cosmic cycles referred to in the East as *Yugas*. This distinction between the individual dispensation and the collective fate must be deeply pondered, for it is central to our understanding of the grave decision we face in eternity and evade in time. It doesn't counsel a rejection of responsibility and compassion—this has never been the Teaching—but a detachment from their earthly goals.

The metaphor, the 'contrast between past and present', is imposed upon us by the illusory Fall into Time. It's an unavoidable, and actually quite useful, even indispensable, 'manner of speaking'. It should be understood, however, that within the metaphor there are always plausible and deadlocked 'arguments on both sides'. In the traditionalist perspective, traditional societies are characterized by accidental evil and essential good, the modern world by essential evil and accidental good. In the secular perspective, History is Progress, and everything is relative, including such terms as 'good' and 'evil'. Both perspectives are within the metaphor, taking the 'contrast between past and present' literally, and neither resolution nor reconciliation are possible because there isn't any real encounter, what is real to one being unreal to the other. In my own usage, the 'contrast between past and present' is always a figure of speech.

We don't want to become entangled in fruitless debate here. The argument in which a romantic and uncritical idealization of the past provokes a defensive and uncritical celebration of the present, and vice versa, is a pitfall. A diversion, in both senses of the word. The world cannot be understood, cannot 'make sense' to human minds, and we cannot know how to live our lives, in the absence of a timeless Truth outside of historical relativism. As it has been said, we are 'made for the Absolute'. Timeless Truth does exist. It is within us, and It can be known directly, in inexhaustible variety of expression. But not by what some Buddhists call 'little mind' or the ego. It is known by 'big mind', or the Self, which is one with It, and which we are.

IX

The Information Coronation

'Why doesn't God get a computer so he can figure all this out?' Ashley asked the doctor.
〜 *Life Magazine*, 'The American Family', Part Five

WINDOWS LIVES IN THE MACHINE BUT ITS POWER & ITS PERSONALITY COME FROM YOU.

A Digital-Nervous-System relies on connected PCs and integrated software to make information flow more rich, rapid and accurate... Everyone on the same page. Everyone hungry. Things just work.
〜 Microsoft

To sleep perchance to dream perchance to mess with reality fantasy is just another word for fearless there will always be a place in the world for rebels the key to creativity is yanking convention inside out DO YOU DREAM IN SONY?

'I surf [the Net], therefore I am.'

'YOU'VE GOT THE WHOLE WORLD IN YOUR HAND BECAUSE I'VE GOT OUR WHOLE NETWORK ON OUR DESKTOP.'

SPEAKING IN BYTE-SIZE SENTENCES In Silicon Valley, the geeks and the go-getters have their own way of talking about life Take that offline... Watch out. He's sucking his own exhaust.... What's your space?... Let's do some dumpster diving. ... Isn't she a serial entrepreneur? ... Yeah, he's vesting in peace... And your exit strategy?... Wow, she's hard-wired!... Don't bother him. He's pre-IPO... Her birthday's close to mine-Q2!

In our times it is the machine which tends to become the measure of man, and thereby it becomes something like the measure of God, though of course in a diabolically illusory manner; for the more 'advanced minds' it is in fact the machine, techniques, experimental science, which will henceforth dictate to man his nature, and it is these which create the truth- as is shamelessly asserted- or rather what usurps its place in consciousness. It is difficult for man to fall lower, to realize a greater mental perversion, a more complete abandonment of himself, a more perfect betrayal of his intelligent and free personality: in the name of 'science' and of 'human genius' man consents to become the creature of what he has created and to forget what he is to the point of expecting to get the answer about this from machines and from the blind forces of nature; he has waited till he is no longer anything and now claims to be his own creator. Swept away by a torrent, he glories in his incapacity to resist it.

⁓FRITHJOF SCHUON, *Stations of Wisdom*

Modern civilization, by its divorce from any principle, can be likened to a headless corpse of which the last motions are convulsive and insignificant.

⁓ANANDA COOMARASWAMY

The Computer, the Net, and the Web! What can I say?

The present planetary undertaking, usurping, drowning out or simply transforming into itself, with a zeal that bankrupts hyperbole, every aspect of personal and communal life, is actually our feverish funeral preparations, an ecstasy of Ignorance, or the funeral itself, the choice of metaphor depending upon our degree of sentimentality or sense of theatre. Its scope and sheer delirious frenzy is unprecedented in historical experience, a cavalcade of self-celebration putting to shame even the ferocious global expansion of the market economy. And given the supreme stature of the Protagonist, *imago dei*, the One Comprehensor, 'wearing a crown of uncreated light', this is altogether fitting and proper, the only way it could and should go. We exit in style. Triumphantly on-line, flourishing our mice, feeling absolutely terrific.

Those who concur with this interpretation should be very careful, however, very selective, about suggesting it to people. Think twice and then again about trying to demonstrate or prove it, and to whom and when. And to understand why I say that is itself evidence that our true situation has been recognized, its depth and solemnity, its irreversibility, its inexpressible gravity. Our situation cannot be grasped by worldly discourse and cognition; it floats above them, incomprehensible to those whose very lives it defines, in serene unreachability and independence, as the summer clouds float above the shrill cries and laughter of children playing on the ground below them. The famous simile of the Buddha, 'like children asleep in a burning house', comes to mind. This world will not understand itself through reliance on its own methods of interpretation. And it is disrespectful to try to make people aware of how they have been damaged by faiths and beliefs they haven't the power to disavow. Let it lie. Leave them to heaven.

✳

The myriad forms of our death-agony, our dehumanization, are everywhere about us, an uninterrupted cacophony, They become visible as such not by being pointed out, but by contrast with the humanity whose legitimate estate and jurisdiction they have usurped, as sickness is visible only by contrast with health. They cannot be seen in themselves, because they are socially defined, within the fictitious universe projected around and within us by the modern mass media, as normal. If not normal, they are troublesome anomalies, traceable to oversight or neglect that have emerged in the sea of customary normality like temporary islands uplifted by underwater volcanoes. They are simply 'problems', demanding for their solution only determination and the appropriate strategies and techniques. It is pointless to try to prove anything that contradicts the axioms of this administered self-contained world.

We come to understand why the Computer is evil, and absolutely so, only by knowing, and loving, what we actually are. And what our world is. This requires the external reference I have referred to as Wisdom, or the traditional perspective, or timeless Truth. But Wisdom, tradition and Truth have by now, in the metaphor of past and present, almost vanished completely, and soon will be retained only as commodities and oratorical devices. They were destroyed and replaced by the concept of Progress, and by Science itself. By the scientific world-view, in which all reality is physical, and everything from consciousness to the origin of the universe is apprehended by instruments and explained by equations, the twin tools of the physicist. In which complex numbers, Hamiltonian mechanics, quantum mechanics, computability, Gödel undecidability, phase space, Hilbert space, photon spin, the Lorentz equation, Schrödinger's equation, Dirac's equation, entropy, black holes, white holes, the Big Bang, Hawking radiation, quasicrystals and the Mandelbrot set are the important realities, and the men who think about them the legislators of our experience, while the Teaching of Jesus, the Buddha and the Tao, and the messages of Nature and the heart, and such 'concepts' as holiness, beatitude, enlightenment, salvation and grace, are simply pastimes and curiosities of the mind in reverie.

The scientific work-flow will prevail. Excellent studies exposing the emptiness and fatality of the Computer, such as Theodore Roszak's thorough and insightful *The Cult of Information*, are helpless against it. And so are all the other studies: Neil Postman's irrefutable exposure of the degradation of humanity by television, *Amusing Ourselves to Death*; Jeremy Rifkin's deeply considered and relentlessly insightful unmasking of the ideology and practice of genetic engineering, *Algeny*; Bill McKibben's *The End of Nature*; and the eloquent legacy of so wise, genial, faithful and prolific a champion of humanity as Lewis Mumford, who began warning us even in 1956, with *The Transformations of Man*, that humanity was being displaced by machinery, the organic by the mechanical, and the natural by the artificial, in all dimensions of our being, a tragedy that could only culminate in the totalitarian technocracy he labelled the Megamachine. These voices as well: helpless against the scientific world-view. Speaking through the mouths of our friends, it will argue that the benefits of computer science greatly outweigh the 'negative side effects' and the exaggerated 'dangers of misuse'. This argument, invincible within the uncontested value system of our society, is readily identified as the invariable rhetoric of Progress. We should not be tricked into engaging it, and those who innocently mouth it merit our compassion.

In the Computer's displacement of Truth by information, of knowledge by data, of quality by quantity, of human encounter by interactive software, of thought, understanding, insight and intentionality by sequences of algorithms, of the inexhaustible richness and subtlety in human discourse by serial yes-or-no statements, the self-consciousness of humanity, of society and of our world, becomes insentient. Consciousness itself becomes inorganic, which is to say dead. The self-awareness of the Earth, whose immemorial flora and fauna will soon be supplemented, replacing those lost through 'genetic erosion', by the genetically engineered mutations in whose profitability billions of dollars have already been invested, will become a computerized global grid of 'information' functioning to insure the health and growth of 'the economy'. That self-awareness used to be a Life: a living interaction and inter-sensitivity, a spontaneous perfection, an absolute Beauty. Creation, in other words. We never really had a precise word for the inner living Mind of the Earth that the Computer is now replacing, other than the personifications, the great Goddesses and Mothers, now regarded as 'myth'. But one thing is certain: it wasn't insentient, it wasn't calculating, it wasn't supervision or administration or management, it wasn't a watchdog overseer who kept things 'under control' and 'running smoothly'. It was not domination. It was Life. It was Joy, ineffable Harmony, and the Tao of Heaven. Whatever displaces Life can only be Death.

✳

It is assumed by the ideology of Information Technology that insufficient data is and has been the principal source of difficulty in solving social problems, the principal (and invisible) deprivation we have suffered, delaying the fulfillment of our individual and communal potential and deferring our accession to true happiness. The roots and depths of things, the inner dimensions, the moral and ethical imperatives whose violation cannot fail to carry consequences, the verified conviction that true understanding only is attained when a human mind focuses on one thing and goes deeper and deeper into it until the point of commitment is reached, the intangibles that exist only in the human experience of them, will all be absent from the societal consciousness informed by this assumption and activated, irreversibly institutionalized, by the computer technology of the Internet Age. Reality will be, and is now being, defined and addressed in terms that can be made intelligible to a Turing machine, the prototype of the modern algorithmic theory upon which binary computer 'thinking' is based. It is not an actual machine, but a mathematical abstraction conceived in 1935 by an English mathematician and code-breaker named Alan Turing in response to German mathematician David Hilbert's *Entscheidungsproblem*, his 'tenth problem', presented in 1900 at the Paris International Congress of Mathematicians and again, in more completed form, at the 1928 Bologna International Congress. Hilbert had asked if there was 'some general mechanical procedure which could *in principle* solve all the problems of mathematics', a 'general algorithmic procedure for resolving mathematical questions.' (Roger Penrose, *The Emperor's New Mind*) This mechanical procedure is the *algorithm*, the basic unit of all computer 'thinking'. In the computer, in other words, human reality, the entire life of the Earth, is approached as if it were a zone of mathematical entities; it is perceived and interpreted, defined and 'understood', in those terms. 'Thinking' becomes a procedure for processing quantifiable information. 'Procedural thinking', sequences of algorithms, means step-by-step logic, what we do with our minds when, for example, we work out the route for a trip by close study of a road map, or figure out what might have gone wrong with an engine that refuses to start, or calculate the next move in a chess game. It is, quintessentially, the way Sherlock Holmes thought, the series of logical deductions with which he acquired information about his visitors and solved his cases. That sort of thinking. 'Elementary'. This is what computers do. If A, then B. If not A, then not B. And so on. But Holmes can speak for himself. *Elementary Basic*, by Henry Ledgard and Andrew Singer (Fontana/Collins, 1982), is a textbook that teaches computer programming in the format of a discourse by Sherlock Holmes on the use of a device he invented, called an 'Analytical Engine'.

'Well, my friend', I said, after examining the list, 'these may be very good clues, but a glance at them does not tell me who the murderer was. Precisely why the police neglected them, and that is where the Analytical Engine comes into use. These clues are worthless unless we can determine the particular relationship of one to another and see how they fit into a larger scheme. To do so we need to devise an *algorithm* that both we and the Engine can follow.'
'This all sounds very mathematical, Holmes', I suggested.
'It is, Watson,' he replied. 'But the mathematics themselves are childishly simple. Our algorithm may be compared to a recipe—a set of instructions to be carried out in a specific order. Our ingredients and how they are to be used, however, must be stated rigorously if the Engine is to follow them correctly. There are a few items of importance concerning algorithms that I must relate to you. First and foremost, only one instruction is performed at a time; and secondly, after each instruction, the next step must be made absolutely clear, Finally, there must be a clearly defined stopping place, indicating that the problem has been solved and that the execution of the algorithm ends.'
'But Holmes,' I asked, 'since the clues themselves are steps by which one logically arrives at the solution, why do they not constitute an algorithm?'
'This is the key, Watson. The clues are data, not instructions. They have no orderly arrangement that shows their inter-relationship. It is just such an orderly arrangement that the algorithm confers. Now, Watson, if you wish to follow my future investigations, you would do well to learn the technique of creating algorithms yourself, for there is really no other way to understand the Analytical Engine's operations."

The authors go on to say, 'Of all the topics we will discuss in this book, the most fundamental is the concept of an *algorithm*. The rigor demanded by a computer algorithm is the essence of programming, no matter which special language you are working in.' They summarize:

> Generally, an algorithm is a sequence of instructions given to solve some problem. Any algorithm must have the following characteristics:
> It must be organized properly...
> It must go step by step...
> It must be precise...
> It must make the data explicit...
> It must contain no irrelevant information...
> It must be correct.

What is left out here is what will be left out of the world. Give it its name. Its many names. Or maybe it has no name at all. Maybe it's something so fundamental, so inherent, that we could only become aware of it when it started to disappear. When we sensed the loss. The absence.

Eventually, Turing's ingenious design model for the modern computer algorithm, the early adding machines and addressographs, the flood of research and development provoked by Norbert Wiener's *Cybernetics* and Claud Shannon's 'ground-breaking' and highly technical paper, 'A Mathematical Theory of Communication', both appearing in 1948, the elevation of the concept of 'feedback' into the very secret of life and mind, and the introduction of the primitive keypunch machines seized upon by the banking, insurance and government bureaucracies, were refined into a new field of study called Artificial Intelligence. Now listed in college catalogues as a new 'major' called Cognitive Science, two of whose founding theorists have declared that 'the programmed computer and human problem solver are both species belonging to the genus "Information Processing System".' The consciousness in which such statements originate, which alleges, if I may quote another major theorist, that human minds are simply 'computers made of meat', this consciousness and sensibility that characterize the 'strong A.I.' community, is not simply an imbecile obscenity and moral stupidity originating in a mutilated and impoverished experience of life. Its origins lie much deeper. It is informed, I suggest, by an impulse to humiliate humanity. By a complacent contempt for humanity and by jealousy of those whose humanity is a stranger to self-loathing. Informed most basically, I think, by an embittered sense that humanity, like a God that failed, had betrayed those who believed in it. (Such people there are. And 'He is the most Merciful of those who show mercy.' ∼ Koran 12:64) Information Technology arises from the bloodstained radioactive rubble and choking moans of Western Civilization's two great World Wars. Its genocides. Verdun, the Meuse-Argonne, the Somme, Auschwitz, Omaha Beach, Hiroshima, Nuremburg. Its crimes against itself, and other peoples, and the Earth. The ubiquitous complicities, the gradual establishment of a universal cynicism. Its true face was unveiled in this century. Those who have seen it cannot escape the need to re-examine the assumptions that govern their lives. The West is the fate of humanity, the glittering irresistible trash of Europe the fate of the world.

So our surrender to the Computer, to the Web and the Net, and our celebration of that surrender, came about. Determined not by the particular circumstances which, given the nature of things, might always have been otherwise, but by a profound collapse of self-confidence, a profound despair, within the heart of historical humanity. We could no longer understand ourselves, and realized that we never had, and so we abdicated to machine 'intelligence', to the omniscient Central Computer of science fiction. We succumbed to what Lewis Mumford called the Myth of the Machine. Millions of television viewers were first dazzled by the mystique of the computer screen, and the unchallengeable prestige of anyone seated before it, in the 1969 coverage of the Apollo 11 expedition, with its images of imperturbable technicians co-ordinating incomprehensible computer data at the Houston Mission Control Center. Screens within screens. No one now is ever very far away from the screen, the keyboard and the disk drive, and no classroom, very soon, will be without them. Even where the Computer is not physically present, its assumptions are everywhere, in all realms of life; significance is reduced to information and quantities. The annual Number One Bestseller is *The Guinness Book of World Records*; our most popular adult game is 'Trivial Pursuit'. Children speculate about the mysteries of life and consciousness now by comparing themselves not to other living creatures, but to the computer; they try to decide whether the machines are alive, and whether they are machines. Some of the chapter titles in Sherry Turkle's *The Second Self* are sufficiently eloquent: 'Adolescence and Identity: Finding Yourself in the Machine'; 'The New Computer Cultures: The Mechanization of the Mind'; 'Hackers: Loving the Machine for Itself'; 'The New Philosophers of Artificial Intelligence: A Culture with Global Aspirations'; 'Thinking of Yourself as a Machine'; and 'The Human Spirit in a Computer Culture'. Nothing will stop it. The teacher says, 'If you don't get into your seat your computer privileges will be taken away.' Adults too, of course. 'The Internet has spawned a new phenomenon—the notion of the disembodied self as the true self, a lone wanderer in cyberspace... Online we cultivate new versions of ourselves, suspended in the ether.' (*Atlantic Monthly*, February 2000). O brave new world, that hath such creatures in it!

✳

Love of truth, love of depth, love of life, love of nature, love of humanity. Awareness of the living intangible infinite richness, the secret, the mystery, beneath the surface of every human moment and encounter, and the knowledge that this richness is the substance of our humanity, the substance of our lives, the essence of joy. Love of the mind, of living consciousness, of intelligence and language. Of the human qualities and attributes: virtue, respect, insight, devotion, self-mastery, forgiveness, forbearance, empathy, kindness, sacrifice, concern, nobility, integrity of motive. All of them. Love, in other words, of the specifically human, knowledge of what is authentically human, conscious joy in being human, and radiant certitude that human existence is miraculous, of infinite significance, that we truly are made in the image of Divinity, and are truly the Center of a universe that is divine.

All this, *being human*, is necessary in order to see that the Computer is spiricide, our terminal metamorphosis. That it defames, assaults and usurps the core of our humanity. That what it gives—99% of which is only an intensification of the institutionalized deceit, exploitation, dislocations, disorientations and self-destructions from which we already suffer, an intensification of the culture's misinformed assumptions and conclusions, of merchandising, irrelevance, trivialization, sensationalism, superficiality, 'information glut', speed as value, and above all *slick shit*, and the release, the unleashing of latent morbidities awaiting the appropriate technological vehicle—is out of all proportion, all measure, with the immensity of what it takes from us: which was, as a matter of fact, already taken, already absent, and perhaps still vaguely, occasionally, mourned, before the coronation of cyberworld simultaneously drowned out and drove deeper the misgivings that prove we are not yet dead. We were groomed for it. By Capital, by Science, by Power. Well groomed.

A few final comments: 'sweeping generalizations', or '*die reine wahrheit*'? 'Inquire within', as it says on the *Funny Times* T-shirt showing a picture of the *Tathagata*.

✳

An 'information age' is a terminal chaos, producing humans whose inner
state, to the degree that they live 'on-line', is itself a chaos: restless, eagerly
pursuing, perpetually changing, incoherent, 'excited', a bubbling crackling
all-absorbing discontinuity leading only back into itself, looking for more.
What else can I find here? Hungry forever for more of the same, more
pulses of distraction. (Past participle of *distrahere*, to draw asunder; to agi-
tate by conflicting passions or by a variety of motives or cares; to confuse, to
craze, to madden; perplexity, disorder, mental derangement.) On the one
hand, traditional society or humanity, where knowledge was mutually refer-
ential, producing human integrity and the whole person; on the other, an
information society, producing the uniform blankness composed of inexhaustible data. It's the difference between a landscape and a dump. I am
reminded of Neil Postman's discussion of 'context-free information' in
Amusing Ourselves to Death:

> The idea of context-free information; that is, the idea that the value of infor-
> mation need not be tied to any function it might serve in social and political
> decision-making and action, but may attach merely to its novelty, interest,
> and curiosity... As Thoreau implied, telegraphy made relevance irrelevant.
> The abundant flow of information had very little or nothing to do with those
> to whom it was addressed... For the first time in human history, people were
> faced with the problem of information glut, which means that simulta-
> neously they were faced with the problem of a diminished social and political
> potency... the contribution of the telegraph to public discourse was to dig-
> nify irrelevance and amplify impotence.

We've come a long way since the introduction of the telegraph. The key
words in the above citation from Postman's excellent book are 'relevance' and
'irrelevance'. You know: Who am I? What is all this? What can I know for
sure? What must I do? That sort of thing.

And there's this angle as well. The P.C., Internet, Worldwide Web, the
bullshit soundbite 'global village', being 'on-line', bring now into our homes
what was formerly elsewhere, the entire 'public sphere' of capitalist bureau-
cratic exploitative commercial propagandistic 'alienated' society, the prior
absence of which left our homes and personal lives intact, untouched, places
of face-to-face human encounter, inviolate: whatever they may have been, at
least our own. This transformation was the work of radio and television
first, of course, but the dot-com culture is the final closing of the circle, fill-
ing in the gaps, as it were, because the chaos of garbage that was formerly

received, 'watched', is now 'chosen', and vigorously pursued. And it's not an 'invasion': it's the answer to an invitation, because, as always, we are both victim and executioner—nobody here but us. Did electronic infotainment/infomercial drive out what was there or fill a vacuum? The answer, of course, is both. It's a simultaneous event, *occurring in the unfolding of individual lives.* What was formerly historical is now biographical: technological change is so rapid now that we are transformed in the course of our life-spans by the remorselessly erupting innovations, the 'breakthroughs' in a world where '*everything* is new'. Time speeds up in the *Kali-Yuga.*

The Internet stands as the final perversion, inversion, of God, of the Sacred. It is now the invisible all-pervading *Presence*—we can all feel it in the air!—which 'knows' everything, offers us triumph and fulfillment, the answers we need, looming miraculous and incomprehensible, 'beyond' any individual but not beyond 'access'. Heaven is Cyberspace, the Creator is the Scientist, the Altar is the Screen, the theology is computer technology, the monks are the nerds and hackers, Holy Writ is the Program, the Priests are the Consultants, Salvation is Being On-Line, and Paradise is The Information Age.

The cyborg isn't some kind of half-human, half-robot, not the android of Blade Runner. It's our collective being, Dot-Com Culture. Money, machinery, and people: One at last.

Now Everyone Gets to Hog the Internet.

Surf

The AnyPoint Home Network connects all
your PCs to the Internet simultaneously

So your family can surf at the same time.
And you don't need a new Internet account. Or a
new phone line. You simply plug into existing
phone jacks. You can also share any printer, drive
or file from an PC in the house. The Intel
AnyPoint Home Network. Now instead of
waiting in line, your family can be online.

Find out more at www.intel.com/anypoint

✳

In the late sixteenth century, Huanchu Daoren, retired into Taoist apprenticeship after a lifelong career in public service, wrote:

> On a winter night when the land is covered with snow and the moon is in the sky, your state of mind is clarified simply and spontaneously. When you feel the gentle energy of the spring breeze, your psychological realm is also naturally harmonized. Creation and the human mind merge intimately without separation.

Again and always, we are not contrasting the past with the present, but the timeless Truth or Way with our departure from it. The Truth is not left behind; it is suppressed, or ignored, or forgotten, or concealed beneath a layer of lies. But it is always present. It never abandons us.

Identification with the truly human, with eternal Humanity immersed in the holiness of eternal Life, enables us to perceive historical humanity in its death-agony. A sensibility to which everything is relative, and the sacred a fiction, is deaf and blind to this perspective. It denies the eternal Truth that can always be discerned, by those who seek it, beneath the impassive merciful paradox of the revealed Word; denies the wisdom of the heart as well. Religious witness, witness to 'your Original Face before you were born', to the reality of the Unseen, to the immortal Dharma that sustains the universe, is patronized and exploited. To the scientific mind, the mind that conceived and assimilates itself to the Computer, these references can only be unintelligible. Their assertion in the twentieth century only amusing.

> To know God, the Real in itself, the supremely Intelligible, and then to know things in the light of this knowledge, and in consequence also to know ourselves: these are the dimensions of intrinsic and integral intelligence, the only one worthy of the name, strictly speaking, since it alone is properly human.
> ⁓FRITHJOF SCHUON

Our witness is visible only to ourselves, and to God. This is sufficient, and its own reward. One with Love, one with the Light. What more could we ask?

'When the fool hears about the Tao, he only laughs at it; it would not be the Tao if he did not laugh at it.'

More on the Computer throughout this text, and in the Appendix 'Technology Update.'

X

Import
in Depth

THE facts are there. The simple indisputable facts of the matter. What we have done and are doing to ourselves and the Earth, what is actually happening here. And the explanations also. How it all came about, continues to come about, and continually eludes our efforts to intervene.

But we never get to the next step. The facts and explanations that ought to form the basis for a deepening self –understanding, followed by an experience of repentance and moral conversion, are instead reduced to impotent platitudes, and the trite cynicism of those whose concern went deep enough to become a disposition. Common knowledge, standing helpless before an inscrutable brick wall of priorities extrinsic to human concern, is reduced by the system's infallible mechanisms of self-preservation to the catchwords and slogans with which we bemoan our galaxy of ills. To television specials, and the incessant publication of statistics, and debates on 'the budget'. Even the 'efforts to intervene' do not actually exist, in any genuine sense, but are merely smokescreens erected or permitted in order to satisfy a societal need to believe that something is being done, that crises, or aspects of them, are being addressed. We all know this. Some pretend otherwise; but that is simply their fate.

The horrors we observe around us are not aberrations but in fact cliches. They are redefined, by the official voices of our damnation, into 'Problems' whose mere public mention is sufficient evidence that they are being dealt with and can be safely driven from our perpetually relieved minds by the next item on the 'news'. Insights are everywhere, but never their import. The hopelessness of our situation, its unravellable complexity, the slow incomprehensible suicide of Progress, and our despair itself, have all become tedious truisms. Not worth mentioning. To speak of them with urgency, without the appropriate irony, is a mark of immaturity, A lack of realism.

But these platitudes and tedious truisms are the vital truth. They are precisely what can and must determine the life decisions of serious people. What we have to do is just the opposite of what is done by our society. We have to explore their significance, on every level and to their ultimate implications, until we get to the very heart of the matter. Until their message is deciphered.

✳

For example, we all know that Western Civilization did things to the world. 'Mastered' it to suit its own purposes, developed the omnipotent technology with which we now equate our success as a species. This is a truism. What followed? Power became an end in itself, the supreme 'good', a disastrous and terminal perversion which Lewis Mumford warns us about on nearly every page of his eloquent masterpiece, *The Pentagon of Power*. And this meant that a new mode appeared, a new posture of humanity, in which it is impossible to see in the world the image of a sacred Grandeur from which it necessarily and clearly originates. A calculating appraisal of potential use, an acquisitive rapacity, replaced awe, adoration and humility, and the simple grateful sense of residence in a miracle, the miracle of Existence, The Gift. This was a stage of the Fall from Grace. 'Our contemporary Western outlook', wrote Huston Smith in *Forgotten Truth*, 'differs in its very soul from what might otherwise be called "the human unanimity".' When the world is perceived as Creation, as a Presence, it teaches us an essential truth about ourselves and reality. We experience infinite joy, for we know that we are intended, that we are what we are, and the world is what it is, by a divine Intention. To dwell in that Intention, to worship and adore it, is contemplative life, the truly human life, the Way and the Goal. When, on the other hand, the world is perceived as something to be conquered and exploited, with no claims of its own or essential relationship to our own essential being, we shrivel inwardly and sink into spiritual darkness, our facial expressions become murderous to human eyes; we become monstrosities in the universe. That happened. 'Monstrosities' is the right word. Finally, when this mode became fully mechanized, physically and socially, it was fulfilled. It was done, and our fate was sealed.

All this is metaphor, or a dream. Nothing was done, no fate was sealed. Nothing whatsoever has happened. The substance of all apparent events and episodes is the changeless Self, which is what we are: *Tat tvam asi*, That art Thou. When we focus our meditation upon the Drama, when we 'know' the Drama from within, perceive it with and in the Light with which we have realized our eternal identity, it is transfigured, as we ourselves are, and we enter the one divine Moment, which is all of Reality, in a particular manner, one among countless, and in a particular depth and wealth, whose specific virtue, in this specific emphasis, is the awakening of the realization that we are one with Humanity. We discover that the great Drama, from beginning to end, is one eternal Moment within us, the whole 'history of the world' one eternal indestructible Moment, suspended in the Eternal Now of God, the one 'I am' which is our very Self. All Love, all Bliss, Eternal Life. Everyone is saved because birth and death were illusions all along. Brahman alone is real. We only fall into the Story, into time and space and the Great Mortality, the transmigratory travail, when He is no longer beheld in the mirror of the Heart.

The truth about Capitalism, like the truth about the West, has also become an irrelevant infamy of vital import. The deliberate and unashamed production of measureless volumes of trash is a chief characteristic of the society, or social relationship, Marx called Capital, *Das Kapital*. Trash to adorn the body, to furnish and decorate the house, to save labour and time, to evidence success, to divert the mind. Therefore the frenzied inflammation of an appetite to consume, to own, to experience, to disport oneself in every conceivable manner. The incensement of an insatiable acquisitiveness as the basic rationale of society, whose alternating episodes of fleeting satisfaction and vigorous renewed pursuit are defined as the twin modes of human fulfilment. Therefore universal deception, exploitation and manipulation, with trained experts who specialize in the techniques of appeal appropriate to children, teen-age girls, teen-age boys, parents, widows, manual labourers, the aged: to every imaginable social category, including the experts themselves, and to categories literally imagined in order to create new markets. And all of this socially sanctioned, encouraged, celebrated, flaunted before the envious fervor of 'developing nations'. All this is normal. We bask in the sycophantic irony of the entrapped and defeated. Capital is something like a tyrant from another planet whose opaque remorseless predilections, sadistic rapacity, glacial indifference, strange tolerances and calculated concessions are 'explained' by 'economists' and 'political scientists', flattered and lampooned in satirical cartoons, and embodied by 'lawyers', 'politicians' and 'executives', our societal life, in this bizarre dispensation, being a perpetual desperate negotiation with an alien arrangement of things with which we have, necessarily, identified ourselves and our success, unaware of the ineluctable accommodation that was our demise. (Or, in the hackneyed simile, it's a mechanism in which we are all interchangeable parts: 'cogs in the machine'.) Capitalism is spiricide. A herald of the End.

✳

The End. This is the term we must penetrate, the pivotal term. We sense it 'out there', in global presentiments, but always as a hackneyed hyperbole. It can be interpreted in several ways, but never as 'the end of the world.'

In Marxian terms, now no longer burdened by the theory, embarrassed by the practice or inspired by the hope of communism, it is Capital itself, the social relationship of the commodity form, that is the End. Capital, in its transformation of all things, everything on Earth including human beings, even sunlight and moonlight, into their exchange value, into *money*, is the final stage of the 'Reign of Quantity' that characterizes the end of a cosmic cycle.

Quantification can go no further. All talk about our public lives, and nearly all 'serious' talk about our private lives, is talk about 'money'. Quantities of money. And 'money' is merely a figure of speech. The universal quantification with which we are now identical required a word for units of itself. These quantities that define our entire social reality, our own identities and all the relationships among us, are now stored in the 'memory banks' of the Computer, the technological consummation reflecting and confirming the historical consummation of Capital. As Capital, for there is no one here but us, we are both the tyrant from another planet and the race that has been vanquished through transformation into his image, and invisible to ourselves in both roles. Marx would have relished this metaphor, in his own peculiar 'scientific' way; he was the only man in the world, the shabbily-dressed German immigrant striding through the streets of mid-nineteenth-century London, who saw the incredible thing that Capital actually was, and we can read in the scintillating magisterial congeries of the *Grundrisse* the desperation of his determination to warn us.

More fundamentally, in terms of our decision, the End refers to the end of a humanity sufficiently recognizable as such to warrant a commitment to its future. Allegiance to posterity means allegiance to historical humanity, and it is precisely the humanness of historical humanity's future that is placed in question. What is our proper relationship to the fate of what may no longer be the self-evident object of that boundless love which humanity has always inspired in us? As Lewis Mumford wrote, in 1956:

> Never before was man so free from natures restrictions; but never before was he more the victim of his own failure to develop, in any fullness, his own specifically human traits: in some degree, as I have already suggested, he has lost the secret of how to make himself human.

And finally, the End refers to the end of humanity capable of identifying with, or even recalling, it's divine paradigm, its Truth. Incapable of believing that the words 'divine' or 'truth' could have any meaning, that they are anything other than archaisms, that anything exists other than the unfolding of events on a linear continuum in a material world. In other words, historical humanity itself, as such, is the End. The End is the Fall into Time, but it is not an event. It happens eternally, whenever we turn away from Him.

History, Progress, the Triumph of the West. All this drama, this passion, this irresistible summons to adore and celebrate ourselves. The Story of Humanity, the glorious and vainglorious Prometheanism, the timeless rectitude it drove back to heaven. This is the dream we love: with all our hearts. Even when we awaken from it, the love remains—but now as the eternal Love that is God, and appears as His world.

✳

What could we honestly expect from this being? A being that poisons its own home, polluting its air, its water, its soil, its food, its own bodies, invents 'acceptable levels', and then lies to itself about the results of its measurements of those 'levels'? What stage has it reached? What is revealed by a nearly universal daily experience described as 'going through the motions'? The common experience that what we are supposed to be doing is a fiction, and that we are really doing something else or nothing at all? Why do we put artificial smiles on our faces? Exactly what are we doing when we are 'talking small talk'? Our lives, captured by meaningless mechanism, exhaust our will to experience them, and we say, with mechanical cheerfulness, 'T.G.I.F.' How can we propose escape, when this mechanization is the very direction of History, the definition of Progress? What does it mean that millions of people alter their state of consciousness with addictive and self-destructive chemicals in order to make their lives bearable, and are then diagnosed as 'addictive personalities', or victims of a scrupulously quantified social fate called 'unemployment', whose deviation from 'acceptable levels' is monitored, 'adjusted' and announced with triumph or alarm practically every hour, and which is actually essential and indispensable to the functioning of the system it presumably indicts? What does it mean that it is only by 'putting things from our minds' that we are able to carry on without collapsing into a grief-stricken somnambulism, and that the technology that generates the horrors we must put from our minds, through countless direct applications and indirect consequences of the social priorities it determines, is the same technology that 'enables' us to know about them, and as 'entertainment'? What does it mean that we are waging a continuous and widely publicized war against the violence whose lurid portrayal is one of our principal sources of diversion, and at continually escalating levels of brutality? Who imposes anxiety, depression and 'stress' upon us but we ourselves, and why do 'we' do it? Who decreed the Computer and its worship? Who decreed our entire way of life?

It was not wisdom, and it was not democracy. It was, and remains with increasing vengeance, the interlocking impersonal dynamisms of Capital, Science and Technology, and the rudderless 'creativity' we call Progress. The stupendous fateful *karma* whose inexorable unfolding and ever accumulating weight we call Freedom. We are equally ignorant of what has possessed us and what it has usurped. Of what we have made of ourselves, in Time, in History, and of what we are eternally, in Heaven. We are not even capable of comprehending this kind of language anymore. That degraded. Hence darkness. Hence mechanism. Hence death.

See it clearly. The capitulation to mechanism is what we extol as Progress. It filled the terrifying vacuum left behind when we lost the capacity to believe there was anything sacred in the universe or anything essential and changeless, inviolate, within ourselves, by which we could guide our lives and govern our conduct. There was only matter, and history. We became hollow. The world became dead. We salvaged our self-respect by calling the new order Progress—but with ever-increasing irony. This is the West, the undisputed exemplary civilization, the human destiny.

People drinking coffee in corner cafes in the morning, the meaningless 'information' of the daily newspapers passing across their blank minds and then immediately forgotten, people listening to the radio weather and traffic reports in freeway gridlocks, people staring dispiritedly at the ranks of numbers and splinters of instruction and information glowing provocatively and imperiously on the computer screens, are all in something like a state of brain-death, casualties of the normal spiricide. How many other normal everyday words are there, like 'advertising', and normal everyday settings, like 'shopping malls', and normal everyday institutions, like 'insurance companies', that ought to provoke the same revulsion and disbelief we would feel at, for example, the spectacles presented in the Circus Maximus, the same sense of outrage, desolation and dishonor, but don't? You know, simply to have rendered one species extinct is already a certain herald of the End, to those who have eyes that can see. Any of a million moments on television, in the classroom, in the factories, any of a million pages in the newsweeklies and teenage magazines, any of a million public experiences, is a certain herald of the End, to those who have eyes that can see, and who want to know the truth. Evidence of the End is actually an unrestricted plenitude coextensive with the entire contemporary reality. Everything is testimony.

✳

Speculations and assertions like these, always open to charges of exaggeration and one-sidedness—how could it be otherwise?—cannot fail, however, to cross or strike a chord in the minds of thoughtful people, by whom their inescapable import must be pondered. To provoke, at least, a reverie of bemused mixed feelings, or a faint smile, sardonic or melancholy, in recognition of the enormities beneath the facade. The truisms, the commonplace ironies, the everyday normalities are telling us something, or at least suggesting it. We have to listen to them, we have to interpret them, examine their implications. We are beings of unsurpassable dignity, we are made for the Truth. Our ability to identify the tragedies and travesties we see around us implies, confirms the very Light they deny. The inner Eternity, the divine Humanity, *forma humanitatis*, the Nirvana that they deny. *Lex Aeterna* and *Spiritus Sanctus*. Our truth is outside of time, and eternal within us. The joy of seeking and knowing the truth, the truth about what we have made of ourselves in Ignorance, the indestructible Truth that we are despite it, is unequalled. This is the Teaching. We have no choice.

XI

Up to Speed

'Our customers are moving at Internet speed, so they need us to
respond at Internet speed'
∼'Fast Company', Spring 1999

TIME has speeded up, just as the sages assured us it would in the
Kali-Yuga. We experience it as the accelerated 'pace of life'. The 'pace of life' is
not external to us, however. It is we ourselves, since we are our time, who
now speed through our ever-shortening days, and shorten them by that very
speeding, and celebrate each 'time-saving' innovation with the same automatic enthusiasm. Everywhere we equate speed with skill, victory and
Progress.

We 'drive' through Nature, through Creation, on strips of concrete called
'freeways' and 'highways', in 'cars'. I place these quintessentially familiar
words in quotation marks because they refer to customs and artifacts so
central to our culture's unexamined definitions of success that we are not
conscious of how they determine, and deform, our experience. The whole
culture of the modern world is comprised of such deformations, invisible to
those dehumanized by them, due to the saturating power of technology.
Formerly we walked. John Muir, in April of 1868, walked from San Francisco to Yosemite Valley in the Sierras. People took walking tours of Europe
even into the nineteenth century. We could, and did, stop when there was
something to receive or adore, to contemplate, worship or ponder. Nothing
short of Enlightenment itself awaited us, as the Japanese *haiku* testify. It
takes time to do these things, and we had time. We cannot have human
experience in a mechanized setting, and this should be axiomatic. No
human experience inside machines, within earshot of machines, or in environments built for machines, where the determining values are power and
speed. On highways, in other words, in cars. That's the image of freedom
and fulfillment, you know: a car on a highway. The thrill of glamour also:
the instilling of envy, of hunger.

And between 'commutes', many over an hour each way, we 'work'. In 'factories' and 'office buildings'. Bolted to clock-time, to 'production goals', to machines, and supervised always by the soundless deafening roar of Money, the Demon Master of the *Kali-Yuga*. 'Wage-slaves' of 'the Almighty Dollar'. Rewarded on 'pay-day' with the Master's measure of our worth to him: a quantity of himself, calculated to the smallest unit, and always begrudged. We patronize our primitive forebears, because Progress cannot be denied without a fatal collapse of morale. But 'reports on hunters and gatherers… suggest a mean of three to five hours per adult worker per day in food production.' According to a seventeenth-century explorer, 'Savage days are nothing but a pastime.' (Marshall Sahlins, quoted by Huston Smith in *Forgotten Truth*.) And this labour in the silence or music of Nature. In that immemorial Beauty, that Life. We have 'gained' speed… but we've lost the world. And it's not there anymore anyway, the world, Nature; it's all 'known', criss-crossed with electricity and jet trails, populated literally or technologically. Wilderness not is, but was 'the preservation of the world'. We 'enjoy the scenery' now, and study the meticulously accurate topo maps made possible by aerial photography. Each hillock, each dell a hachure line, a number. As I have been suggesting, there are life decisions to be made on the basis of observations such as these: intuitions to be re-examined, strengths to be tested. The stakes are infinite. It's not a matter of casual nostalgia or absent-minded resignation.

Our minds also speed. The attention span of television humanity, which perhaps merits another neologism, 'telemanity', can be measured in seconds. A human mind, if it is actually thinking and learning, grasping reality, must be free to stop and reflect, make connections and draw inferences, return to reconsider, leap or linger, all at its own pace. As in reading, or reverie. But the Age of Typography has given way to the Age of Television. This transition, it has been argued, is the most momentous of the twentieth century.

Now… this is commonly used on radio and television newscasts to indicate that what one has just heard or seen has no relevance to what one is about to hear or see, or possibly to anything one is ever likely to hear or see. The newscaster means that you have thought long enough on the previous matter (approximately forty-five seconds), that you must not be morbidly preoccupied with it (let us say, for ninety seconds), and that you must now give your attention to another fragment of news or a commercial… For on television, nearly every half hour is a discrete event, separated in content, context, and emotional texture from what precedes and follows it. In part because television sells its time in seconds and minutes, in part because television must use images rather than words, in part because its audience can move freely to and

from the television set, programs are structured so that almost each eight-
minute segment may stand as a complete event in itself. Viewers are rarely
required to carry over any thought or feeling from one parcel of time to
another.

~NEIL POSTMAN, *Amusing Ourselves to Death*

There is no end to what could be pointed out about television's transforming impact on our humanity. Postman's insights are devastating on
every page. Where are the disastrous consequences, one might ask, if television has been so destructive of our humanity? The question is entirely reasonable. But even the people who have chosen not to own television sets will
be unable to answer it. We are all weakened. 'Telemanity' is the ubiquitous
social presence, the presence of the world we all inhabit: it is, like Capital, a
social relationship. The destruction of an authentic public reality, and therefore of an authentic human community, and therefore of authentic human
experience, and therefore of authentic human beings, is not visible to those
who identify—with enthusiasm or misgivings, *bon gre mal gre*—with their
replacements. Television humanity, the electronic collective, is a tragically
disfigured humanity: a metamorphosis, a degradation. It is no longer the
being to whom divine Wisdom, which alone makes us human, is or can be
addressed. Again, that End. 'Make one fast choice now and no second!
Come, clear your heart and quickly walk with me into Brahma, while there
is time!'

~RAMAYANA.

XII

Invisible
Absences

On the one hand, the descriptive and defining terms with which we are now familiar. The conditions, the signs and symptoms, the diseases. The Fall into Time, History and historical humanity. Progress; the cult of Power; universal quantification, universal mechanization, the reign of Science and Technology; relativism, materialism, secularism; television and mass media, Information Technology and the Computer; genetic engineering; Capital. Urban-industrial-vehicular-commercial-technological-pharmaceutical-electronic-information-spectator society and the synthetic environment. The West. 'Europe's disintegrated soul, the hell of modern existence.' (Coomaraswamy) Ecocide, dehumanization, destruction and devastation of the planet's integrity and life, the sense and presence of a mind-boggling suicidal craziness, a terminal crisis, an End. ('Dehumanization', incidentally, is one of the more trenchant 'terms of indictment' that have become platitudes: 'bogus', 'plastic', 'celluloid', 'endangered', 'genocide', 'stress-related', 'polluted', etc.) The *Kali-Yuga*—where, in merciful recognition of our extremity, our spiritual enfeeblement and dilapidation, nothing more is asked, or needed, than devotional repetition of a Holy Name. 'Water suffices to put out fire, the sunrise to disperse the darkness: in the *Kali-Yuga* the repetition of the Name of Hari suffices to destroy all errors' (Vishnu Purana).

And then innumerable subheadings. The whole human story is summarized at the End, just as, we are told, the whole life of a dying person flashes across his mind in the final moment—a person who may realize then, to complete the analogy, in the joy of a blinding illumination, that that instant of passing is all there ever is of life, and that all along 'he' or 'she' was the immortal Absence: the Self, which is alone real. Every human theme and every human moment is present at the end of the drama, elements of a cosmic

Review, a summing up, suspended in the Pure Consciousness that we are, each demanding its measure of acknowledgement, each claiming its right to eulogy. Our dignity requires that we understand what we did to ourselves, how it happened, that we know what our story was from the beginning to the end. That we make our death, if such it is, our own.

On the one hand, then, our condition, our present state, what we have become as historical beings. And on the other hand, the casualties. The casualties of the *Kali-Yuga*. Not what we have become, the shape and features of our death, not what happened, how we got here, but what we have lost. What enabled us, in belief or access, to be human. What are they?

We've lost God: the Holy, the Sacred, the Divine in all its senses. Lost Truth. We have no Wisdom. We do not believe these exist. Nature, both as a dimension of our experience, in the absence of which we are no longer human, and as a setting: also lost. Oneness and Wholeness. The Way, in all its sublime reflections here below. We've lost Reality, in other words. Lost Joy: 'for from Bliss all things arise.' There's really nothing left at all. Just a shapeless and fruitless commotion. An elemental inertia. A noise. Which is as it had to be. The end is prefigured in the beginning, as death is prefigured in birth.

But let there be clarity here; so much can be misunderstood. They are lost to our collective experience, vanished from cultural assumption and intention, but in themselves they are eternal and indestructible. Lost irreversibly to historical humanity, and hence its present death agony, but accessible eternally, with the guidance provided by a revealed Tradition and the 'proof' provided by initiatory experience, to individuals. 'That Reality which pervades the universe is indestructible. No one has the power to change the Changeless.' The Light shineth in the darkness. Worship of God, knowledge of Truth, conformity to Wisdom, harmony with Nature, and love of all four: these make us human. They are Dharma. They guarantee our contact, indeed our identity, with Reality.

Nor can these disappearances from our lives be comprehended in isolation from one another, still less from the language, the perspective, that is Light itself. God, Truth, Wisdom and Nature, the Reality they summarize and with which, in our authentic humanity, our theomorphism—the 'Original Face', the 'uncarved block', the primordial or Edenic state, our eternal as opposed to temporal nativity, the Atman, the Buddha-nature—we are ultimately One: these words are interpreted and their referents equivalent in many ways. They overlap and converge, they are fluid; they are the words that enable us to talk about and comprehend what has happened to us, the words that point to and acknowledge what can only be realized in silence. 'His secret Name is Truth of the Truth', 'Brahman alone is Real', 'I regard the wise as my very Self', 'All this is Brahman', 'Arjuna, I am the Cosmos revealed, and its germ that lies hidden', 'I am the Way and the Truth and the Life', 'Whatever happens, in any form or at any time or place, is but a variation of the one self existent Reality', 'Therefore the sage keeps to One and becomes the standard for the world.' Nature is Creation: the Way of Heaven and Earth, the Valley Spirit that never fails: His Manifestation, conceived in Love and sustained in Wisdom. *Hagia Sophia*: Divine Wisdom. And though the losses occur on this profound and decisive level, the level where our very humanity is at stake and the question of our final ends is addressed, they reverberate throughout the texture of our daily experience, and can be illustrated there. We can and should distinguish Truth, Wisdom and Reality from truth, wisdom and reality, the former referring to the divine and eternal, the Origin and Ground, the latter to their prolongations into the context of our earthly affairs, the relative plane characterized by contingency and finitude, the Manifestation. But since denial of the former necessarily carries with it loss or corruption of their derivatives and reflections, it can be said that we are murdered or mutilated right here, right now, without interruption, in every room in the world. Devastated from within by invisible fatal absences. Nothing that labor can produce or money can buy can fill that void. The glittering wonders of science and technology, the megatons of entertainment, and all the fun and excitement in the world, cannot fill a single cubic centimeter of that void. Not even our tears.

This death is what must be seen. This failure, this baffled restlessness and unfulfillment, this mystified desperation: this quiet, furtively tended little candle of shame. This grief. And seen with 'the eye of the heart': our cardiac intelligence, the Heart-Intellect, in which Love and Knowledge, compassion and gnosis, are One. Success, in other words, yours and mine, does not depend upon a convincing and thorough articulation, an exhaustive exposition, a proof. It's a matter of resolute honesty, candor, self-respect. It begins with a feeling about things, a disquietingly insistent suspicion. It knows indignation, alarm, desperate anguish and bereavement. It culminates in a surrender. As I have already said, there is no 'argument' here. Rather a provocation, a discourse that might provide the occasion for a life-determining recognition. A single intuition, a single flash of insight would suffice, a single admission. One of those lucid reveries we later describe as 'putting it all together'. The whole is contained in each part, each piece implies the whole pattern. It's all so obvious.

XIII
Awakening

Maya, the world-appearance. The Dream we find so enchanting, so irresistible. 'And when I go hence, may my last words be that what I have seen was unsurpassable' (TAGORE). And, in a manner of speaking, it was. Unsurpassable.

We can awaken from it, this incredible Dream, and we can, with detached compassion, reenter it at will, as witnesses to the oneness of all beings and things in God, the Dreamer.

But it shouldn't be misinterpreted. There is the danger. Misinterpretation of the Dream originates in worldliness, in attachment, in worldly hopes and desires, in mistaken solidarity with a desacralized universe. There is our bondage.

> *This* world is rejected, *this* life depreciated, because it is known that *something else* exists, beyond becoming, beyond temporality, beyond suffering…
> Again and again Indian texts repeat this thesis—that the cause of the soul's 'enslavement' and, consequently, the source of its endless sufferings lie in *man's solidarity with the cosmos*, in his participation, active and passive, direct or indirect, in nature. Let us translate: solidarity with a *desacralized* world, participation in a *profane* nature. *Neti! Neti!* cries the sage of the Upanishads: 'No, no! thou art not *this*; nor art thou *that!*' In other words: you do not belong to the fallen cosmos, *as you see it now*; you are not necessarily engulfed in *this* creation; necessarily—that is to say, by virtue of the law of your own being.
> ~ELIADE, *Yoga: Immortality and Freedom*

Solidarity with the Dream is always an error, because it is solidarity with transience, impermanence, with what becomes, changes and vanishes, with what comes and goes, with *history*, in other words, with what is *not real*, whereas we are and are made for the Eternal, which alone is Real. Enlightenment is, among other things, the ability to distinguish the unreal from the real.

If solidarity with the cosmos is the consequence of a progressive desacralization of human existence, and hence a fall into ignorance and suffering, the
road toward freedom necessarily leads to a desolidarization from the cosmos
and profane life.

⁓ELIADE, ibid.

Therefore the danger of optimistic misinterpretations of the Dream—the
belief in Progress, in other words, or in the 'limitless resourcefulness' of terrestrial humanity: they encourage a mistaken and fatal solidarity with an
imaginary protagonist whose abandonment of its celestial archetype is a certain guarantee of its equally imaginary doom. We can liberate ourselves
from the groundless hopes and fears that bind us to the Dream by facing
squarely the testimony of our present condition, understanding what is
actually happening here, what we have made and are feverishly making of
ourselves, and accepting the conclusions of a dispassionate assessment. It is
an end in itself, for Truth is Joy, and the knowers of Truth become what they
know.

XIV

The Name
of the Age

Go, Soul, the body's quest,
Upon a thankless arrant;
Fear not to touch the best;
The truth shall be thy warrant.
Go, since I needs must die,
And give the world the lie.

~ 'The Lie', WALTER RALEIGH (1552–1618)

REALITY with a lower-case 'r'. We've lost even that. There is only perpetual novelty, perpetual meaningless innovation, a series of technicolor spectacles exploding at microsecond intervals in the media delirium which has become our reality. Nothing endures, there are no mountains, no landmarks, no verities. Nothing 'familiar' but the latest fad or image or buzzword or soundbite or click. Nothing is genuine here. Which is why our most common disqualifying term, applied to situations, statements, events and people every minute of the day, is *bullshit*. The *Kali-Yuga* is the *Age of Universal Bullshit*. This is why people who have an intuition of their true stature as human beings speak ironically or contemptuously about the arena of public affairs and the characters and motivations of those who are vociferous there: the language of irony corresponds to the Age of Bullshit. The word is appropriate, actually perfect, because it simultaneously exposes the ubiquitous Lie, the ubiquitous unreality, and expresses our attitude of contempt. 'The dogs bark, the caravan passes.' Everything in public life is bullshit just as water is always wet, and our personal lives are perpetually menaced by the same verdict to the degree that we identify with the imbecilic garbage projected by this culture as the images of fulfillment and success to which we should aspire with hope and zeal, galvanized by fear and envy. (Glamour: the evocation of envy.) We speak with justified contempt of the nauseating 'reality' we have made for ourselves, the universal phoney Hollywood-Disneyland-Internet-Superbowl-Shopping-Mall-TV-Credit Card 'reality', and this contempt, like its object, is a graphic sign of the times. We know, we all know, at the deepest levels of our consciousness, and with a certain wary apprehension, that our world is a fake and a sham.

And therefore inherently, structurally inimical, hostile, malevolent, a masquerade of the Adversary. *Not hollow.* This we also know. Not hollow at all. We've all glimpsed, at least, the inferno raging behind the global television screen. Behind the Sickness, the universal pretense, the mannequin charade: the great Commercial we are offered as reality. There are dangers here, new dangers, never seen or dreamed of before, impossible to anticipate. And a vague chilling all-pervading Danger, a Master Danger, sentient and implacable, the terror of History itself. Terror: as in the French usage which originated in what came to be called the Reign of Terror, meaning the pervasive subterranean fear experienced by those living in a period characterized by a murderous violence both systematic and unpredictable, varying in degree with the accidents of geographical location and social station, but haunting everyone in its myriad guises. We are all aware that in our times, 'evil proves to be no longer only an individual decision but, increasingly, a transpersonal structure of the historical World' (ELIADE, *The Myth of the Eternal Return*, 1954). Sharp articulation! We have turned our backs on the Eternal, turned our backs on heaven. You can't do that without opening your eyes immediately in hell. Separated from God, Truth, Wisdom and Nature, and given that *corruptio optimi pessima*, what else could we expect?

Keep a straight mind
In the evil time
In the mad-dog time.
Why may not an old man run mad?
History falls like rocks in the dark,
All will be worse confounded soon.

Count that girl's beauty, count the coast-range
The steep rock that stops the Pacific,
Count the surf on its precipice, The hawk in its air,
For all will be worse confounded soon...

Count its eagles and wild boars,
Count the great blue-black winter storms,
Heavy rain and the hurricane,

Get them by heart,
For all will be worse confounded soon...

History passes like falling
Rocks in the dark,
And all will be worse confounded soon.

⁓ROBINSON JEFFERS, probably around 1940

XV

The Degradation
of Discourse

OVER a year ago, when I was living in Wales, a friend of mine from San Francisco, attending a conference in Liverpool, came by to visit. By chance, no one was at home but me, the rest of my family away on vacation in Italy, and no one else 'dropped in', and the phone never rang. He was not 'running late', nor 'swinging by' on his way to somewhere else. Andrew looks people steadily in the eye, smiles rarely and appropriately, and calmly and soberly speaks the truth as he understands it. The type of man who values and respects his life and the world in which it unfolds, and had made serious decisions, consequent upon that evaluation, about how he should conduct himself in social intercourse. A human norm, in other words.

He listened attentively, maintaining eye contact. No 'games' were played, and there was no 'small talk'. No subject was introduced in order to 'keep the conversation going'. He remembered what had been said, and was conscious of the quality of his experience. His attention span began to flicker, like mine, only with physical exhaustion, at which point the dialogue was steered to a conclusion with respect for whatever priorities had been established, and with courtesy. He understood verbal decorum and knew that the art of conversation was a technique of the sacred and a form of communion. An access to a reality worthy and demanding of our assertion, significant in our lives, and immediately present. We had spoken frankly and thoughtfully about important things, or the important implications in mundane things, and had often laughed with delight. The whole thing was a joy. I had one other evening like this one about a month later, with a younger man whose purity of heart, genuine Christian intelligence and eager intuition of depth and truth were sufficient to the demands of such encounters. Since then I haven't had such a conversation again. Snatches, approximations, for I know many fine people; but always 'squeezed in', or circumspect, or abruptly shattered by an interruption, or fading out at the reaching of an inner limit of endurance.

Now this may reflect a certain impoverishment in my life. And on an abstract level of course it does. But that interpretation would be valid, and my experience really nothing more than a private dilemma or aberration devoid of social significance, only if the sort of encounter whose quality I have attempted to evoke is common in our culture, and in fact it isn't. Quite the contrary. It's very rare, and certainly increasingly so.

✳

The physical, social and psychological settings in which the truth may be respectfully petitioned, gravely uttered and humbly acknowledged are disappearing. The corresponding mental and verbal prerequisites are also disappearing. A human type is disappearing. This is happening primarily because the belief that there *is* such a thing as truth is disappearing, which causes those who still believe in it to seem presumptuous, tasteless or naive. And also threatening. Threatening, because they force upon others an embarrassing suspicion, which is also an authentic perception, of inner emptiness or triviality of character. The scene becomes very rapidly awkward or tense, sensibilities have been tactlessly offended; the superficial mechanical equilibrium of social convention has been disturbed and must be restored, either by 'poking fun' or 'changing the subject' or any of countless conversational stratagems and maneuvers. Although chances are that nothing will need to be done consciously, or even unconsciously, because the situation will take care of itself. The phone will ring, someone will enter or leave the room, someone will turn on the television set or a tape or a blender, some food or drink will now be ready or require replenishing, something or other will need to be attended to: there will be an interruption or distraction. And anyway, with attention spans dwindling literally to matters of seconds, and as the settings in which the exercise of longer attention spans is encouraged are vanishing, the serious communal contemplation of anything whatsoever for more than the briefest interlude is automatically stifled. Our thinking and talking are no longer able to persevere long enough to be equal to the understanding of what we are thinking and talking about. We can't 'hold on' to anything long enough to comprehend it: 'Get to the point!' That depth at which truth may be experienced, not as a 'fact' but as a state of fulfilment or equivalence, in which we recall, with gratitude and humility, our true stature as human, is never even approached. Even simple sincerity can only be tolerated for a brief time before it must be neutralized by joviality, or a return to those practical considerations which alone are deemed serious. The speed-up of time in the *Kali-Yuga* provides a partial explanation here. But fear of depth and authenticity, fear of anything that might threaten the facade of 'normal' interpretation and 'normal' response, and thereby expose our servitude, which cannot really be helpless, to the social conventions that 'shield' us from the truth, also plays a role.

✳

I have been speaking here of the disappearance of what might be called 'the truth-speaking voice', the voice that speaks with dignity about genuinely serious matters and is heard with respect, as well as the social and psychological settings in which that voice is invoked, from our personal lives, where it would have had its best chance to survive. That such a voice or sensibility does not and cannot exist in public life scarcely needs to be argued. The *Kali-Yuga*, as I have suggested, is the Age of Universal Bullshit. More specifically, since technology is the hallmark of this Yuga, the Age of Television. The relationship between television and truth is illustrated in Postman's 'Media as Epistemology' chapter.

> As a culture moves from orality to writing to printing to televising, its ideas of truth move with it... Truth, like time itself, is a product of a conversation man has with himself about and through the techniques of communication he has invented... A major new medium changes the structure of discourse; it does so by encouraging certain uses of the intellect, by favoring certain definitions of intelligence and wisdom, and by demanding a certain kind of content—in a phrase, by creating new forms of truth-telling. I will say once again that I am no relativist in this matter, and that I believe the epistemology created by television not only is inferior to a print-based epistemology but is dangerous and absurdist... We have reached, I believe, a critical mass in that electronic media have decisively and irreversibly changed the character of our symbolic environment. We are now a culture whose information, ideas and epistemology are given form by television, not by the printed word... They delude themselves who believe that television and print coexist, for coexistence implies parity. There is no parity here. Print is now merely a residual epistemology, and it will remain so.
> ⁓ POSTMAN, *Amusing Ourselves to Death*

And if television degrades truth through expropriation by a medium which, as epistemology, is inherently debasing and manipulative, inherently poisonous to our humanity through its power to degrade the content of collective consciousness, its values, aspirations and sense of reality, into a reflection of the ridiculous moronic trash-world it beams into countless millions of living rooms, kitchens, bedrooms, dens and 'TV rooms', Information Technology joins its assault on truth by leveling:

> In much the same way, in its new technical sense, *information* has come to denote whatever can be coded for transmission through a channel that connects a source with a receiver, regardless of semantic content. For Shannon's purposes, all the following are 'information':
>
> E = mc²
> Jesus saves.
> Thou shalt not kill.
> I think, therefore I am
> Phillies 8, Dodgers 5.
> 'Twas brillig and the slithy toves did gyre and gimble in the wabe.'
>
> And indeed, these are no more or less meaningful than any string of haphazard bits (x:44jGH?566MRK) I might be willing to pay to have telexed across the continent… All are 'information'. The word comes to have a vast generality, but at a price; the *meaning* of things communicated comes to be leveled, and so too the value.
> ～ROSZAK, *The Cult of Information*

Leveling, then; as if the algorithmic reductionism we have already discussed were not fully adequate to achieve the elimination of anything humanly meaningful from computer 'discourse', from *our* discourse, *our* communication 'network'.

✳

But it's more than television and Information Technology that do it, more than the subtle erosion and sabotage of the internal and external settings conducive to the expression of the truth-speaking voice. The modern world's conviction that all values are relative, conditioned by social and historical circumstance, or are simply matters of expedience, or, with complete indifference to consistency, that *any* position must be deemed principled by definition, effectively invalidates the idea of truth, the appeal to significance, meaningfulness: to what matters and, ultimately, what alone matters. Scientific facts, verifiable by repeating the experiment, alone are 'truth', and the rest is a matter of subjectivity or 'different strokes for different folks'.

As I have suggested, there are Truth and truth, upper-case and lowercase, metaphysical or principial and 'this-worldly' or derivative. In a human culture, the latter are woven into the texture of daily life and discourse, and as they become increasingly profound gradually 'shade off' into the former. Their function is to lead us toward the Light, toward our essential and authentic humanity; ultimately, toward Illumination and Salvation, and Peace. Lowercase truths refer primarily to the determination of values. Questions of right and wrong, wise and foolish, worthwhile and worthless, meaningful and meaningless, even smart and stupid. How we should guide and govern our lives: our conduct, public and private. The right thing to do or think or say. How to avoid the mistakes that make us and others miserable. How to be happy—at one with ourselves and each other and the world. What we learn from our myths and moral epics, our exemplary figures, fictional or historical, the paradigmatic episodes, the maxims, adages and didactive illustrative tales of the world. From the world's great literature and visual art, in their moral message and their illumination of our experience; even from music, for 'Beauty is the splendor of the Real'. Finally, we emerge into the Truth: the *Dhammapada*, the *Gita*, the *Tao Te Ching*, the *Koran*. *Proverbs* and *Ecclesiastes* and the Psalms of David and the Parables of Jesus. Revelation. This is the human journey. In a truly human commonweal there is a realm, a forum of responsibility, internal and external, where truth and wisdom reside. Its atmosphere is characterized by reverence and humility. Its origin is heaven, the primordial and eternal Mercy, it is a gift of Grace and a proof of our holiness, and its presence preserves us from error here below and directs us on the Path that leads back to that Origin. The realm, in our blasted shattered lives, in this blindingly self-betrayed 'commonwoe', of weariness and cynicism, confusion and dissension, and longing. Even mourning.

> Dasaratha said, 'You may take him. You are Sumantra the best charioteer, the best driver ever born in all this world, this world where there is but one right road, where the directions and the *ways are hard to see, hard to find, hard to remember.'*
> ◠RAMAYANA

XVI

Not Impartial: Dispassionate

Every morning is the same morning.
Freshness. Nothing exists but the present. This is always true, that nothing exists but
the present; but it seems clearest, most evident, in the morning. The freshness becomes
us, enhances the quality of consciousness, brings out our intrinsic nativity here, and the
world's nativity within us. Puts things in place. We are the freshness of the morning.
The earth clothed in the freshness of the morning, the beauty. It's a good time to medi-
tate, some say the best. Good to be the freshness of the morning, bliss to discover that
truth in meditation. Clarity, emptiness, peace. Silence, and the Presence. What Taoists
call 'the world of dust', and others call Maya and karma and desire, and others dual-
ity, and others the transmigratory travail, has not yet summoned us from the timeless
Oneness into the great hallucination. As it will.

LIFE in the *Kali-Yuga* is without foundation. There is no foundation here.
So its victims, its inmates, are necessarily plagued by uncertainty, irresolu-
tion, fear. This is a sign of mortal damage, it's a mortal wound, for certitude
is inherent in intelligence, the *raison d'être* presupposed by it. 'Should I be
here, now, doing this? Is this right for me, my place, do I belong here?
Should I be married to this man, this woman, or unmarried, or among these
people? Is this my proper life? Is this a human life? Am I happy? What do I
want for my children? Should I look for another job, train for a different
career? Am I a loser?' Absence of foundation, perpetual innovation and universal relativism, historical society: all refer to the same condition, the same
omen. Our experience of the foundation on nothingness is uncertainty, anxiety, searching. Forced enthusiasms, energetic performances of the current
stereotypes, the currently advertised life style; helpless consciousness of

pretense, phoniness, entrapment. An embittered or ironic, and finally accustomed, even cheerful, resignation. Diminished expectations, diminished awareness, diminished humanity. The nagging suspicion of a wasted life, of time running out. The form, which must be respected, but not the substance, of dignity. I have lost the source of this citation, but I read somewhere, in a book probably written by someone who had delved into Hellenic esoterisms, that a world without God, without the light of Knowledge, is a world condemned to *scotos*, or darkness, *aporia*, or bewilderment, (literally 'roadlessness', not knowing where to go), *ecplexis* or shock, *stenochoria*, or anguish, *zophos* or gloom and *phobos*, or terror. I think we find this catalogue confirmed in our adult assessments; rarely on the surface, of course, but always intuitable beneath the facade. In the lives of the friends we love. All but the first are subjective states, experienced at different times and in varying degrees. The first, Darkness, is *Maya* itself, in its aspect of resistance to *Atma*, 'comprehending it not', whether through willfulness or fatality. Or simply metaphysical Ignorance. The Darkness is Ignorance, the ego, which is separation from Reality. 'But there is a taint worse than all taints — Ignorance is the greatest taint. O mendicants! Throw off that taint and become taintless' (DHAMMAPADA 243).

The experience of collective destiny in historical society is a complement to the personal anxiety of life without foundation. For those who 'care', who are unaware (equally with those who *don't* 'care') that the 'reality' they take seriously, accept at face value, is actually a media spectacular — Jean Baudrillard's 'hyper-reality' of simulations without originals; signs and codes, 'cybernetic noise': television, in other words, *entertainment*, the 'Post-Modern Carnival' — the experience is one of feeling continually 'disturbed' or 'disgusted' by 'the way things are going', i.e. by History. ('History falls on your head like rocks...' JEFFERS) Worried, anxiously, they watch through the windshield their children skipping off to school, they read the newspapers and innumerable informative magazine articles, the 'reports', watch the TV 'news' and 'specials', shaking their heads, sensing the impending catastrophe at the end of the apparently irreversible breakdown. And eventually, exhaustion. It's impossible to go on caring, impossible to continually respond to a permanently and hopelessly escalating aggravation of our plight. Or, which amounts to the same thing, impossible to go on taking it all seriously. Just as it becomes impossible to respond with enthusiastic interest or appetite to the continuous innovations in technology, life style and distraction that characterize capitalist society, the production-consumption machine invented by Western 'civilization' whose definition of 'wellbeing' has been 'bought' by the entire world. Both are insults to our dignity. What words have emerged emptier than 'Freedom' and 'Progress', more meaningless than 'standard of living', more treacherous than 'creativity'?

✻

We live from video to video, pseudo-event to pseudo-event, commodity to commodity. (Pseudo-event: an event specifically staged to be reported. In a profound sense, this includes *everything* ever 'shown' on television, 'live' or taped, for that moment has itself been staged: preconceived, fitted together and 'served up.' In a more restricted sense, the term would refer to 'events' like press conferences, public statements and appearances, 'press releases', election time activities, etc. 'Celebrities' — movie stars, sports idols, entertainers — are human pseudo-events. National Geographic Society expeditions? The war in the Persian Gulf? Who can say? Who can say what is real in the *Kali-Yuga*? The word loses its meaning.) We mark time by their appearances, by the changing *prices* of *things* The categories and strategies with which we explain our lives have no foundation in durable meanings, no durable reference points; there is nothing constant, known to us, in whose light the transient details can be interpreted and integrated. Which is why the tone and style of discourse is always discontinuous, now urgent now light-hearted, now acrimonious now matter-of-fact, and punctuated by innocently evasive reassuring smiles. Incoherence of personality emerges from the universal incoherence of relativism and ephemerality, fragmentation of discourse from fragmentation of life, for 'fallen or post-edenic man is a kind of fragmentary being...' (SCHUON) We cannot infer from one opinion what someone's other opinions might be; relationships and consequences in modern society make no human sense, and their senselessness is simply our mature assumption, 'taken for granted'. We laugh at the madness and absurdity of our own lives, and are 'entertained' (I always feel the need to put quotation marks around this word, its stupendous significance in our lives is so profoundly different from its dictionary definition) by people, called 'comedians', who specialize in ferreting out the laughable aspects we hadn't noticed. We sense the titanic malevolent power of chaotic forces swirling and lashing beneath the surface of our lives, in the primordial and terminal amorphousness symbolized in tradition by water, the Waters: 'the primal substance from which all forms come and to which they will return either by their own regression or in a cataclysm.' (ELIADE, *Patterns in Comparative Religion*) Our human, hence divine, contours are hammered into deformity by

the technological rationality of urban-industrial society, the reign of Science,
the Accumulation of Capital. By an insanity both willful and unwilling,
despised and embraced.

MONDO 2000 DIG IT, BOYS AND GIRLS, IS *NOT YOUR FATHER'S
MAGAZINE.* Unless, of course, Daddykins happens to be a stone cyberpunk digital freak hooked on 'Virtual Reality', life extension, artificial IQ
enhancement, pleasure-pulse implants, nanotechnology, the post-industrial
leisure avant-garde, hip-hop culture, hacker-pranking, space skateboarding
and the zooming, booming electronic landscape of the 21st century. Talk
about your quantum generation gap. If you're not accelerating you're out of
the race. Mondo 2000, currently the hottest rumor in the computer industry
and huge in England and Japan, is the ultra-contemporary 'performance'
magazine that says the computer/video kids are at the controls. That sweet,
slow, dopey ol' mom 'n' pop are simply incapable of processing the MTV-style
microblips fast enough to keep pace. That all the old passe paradigms are
crumbling at warp speed. That the 'cybernet' is in place and 'total possibilities'
are thinkable. That 'radical assaults on the limits of biology, gravity and time'
are just around the cybernetic corner. Got it? Care to jump aboard for a
zippy little ride into the fun-filled (and fearsome) future?
⸺San Francisco Examiner, October, 1990

And so on. This 'article' is not a grotesque aberration. It's merely one of
the countless dialects in which the Voice of the Computer, the Information
Age, speaks to us. Language, context, emphasis and sensibility vary widely.
But the content, the message, the 'vision' are not marginal in our culture.
They are central. (And as I sit here, August 27, 1998, staring at this passage
and at the bay tree outside wondering if I should gather more samples, more
evidence, I decide not to bother. I'm sure you know why.)

So our lives, in this dawning nitwit technocratic hell, become a kaleidoscope of bewildered fantasies, floating in emptiness, vulnerable to every gust
of emotion, prey to serial crises of identity; haunted by uncertainty, by a
nagging unidentifiable presentiment of hollowness, error or failure. We drag
ourselves from weekend to weekend, for we invented work and a society
characterized by the commodity nature of labor power, and banter 'small
talk' or mutter recriminations until, tense and exhausted, we slump into
after-dinner stupefaction and metamorphose into 'prime time'. Heaven,
Nature and the Law, with the truths, values and norms they generate, are
still operative in our lives, for they are eternal and their authority is
forever—but answering now not with Mercy to our acquiescence, but to our

defiance, our ignorant, innocent, completely unintentional defiance, with Rigor.

✳

Everyone senses these things. The drama, the loss of our souls, the defeat at our own hands. The subterranean derangement. A sizeable chunk of public discourse is a strange sort of double-talk, simultaneously celebrating and deploring, valiantly confronting and slyly caricaturing, the current 'trends'. Negotiating with them, as it were, without losing face. But to protest against what is happening to us seems almost inane. To propose alternatives, even to try to conceive them, an impious presumption. Obviously it all unfolded as it did with a logic both inexorable and transparent, as if ordained, almost comforting in its seamless inevitability. We have no right to complain.

Nor need to lament. What we call 'the world' is but an image of the true world, the 'original' world or Origin which is the world *in divinis*, or the immortal Self. *Al-haqq*, the absolute Reality, realm of the eternal Archetypes of which everything here below is a manifestation and a symbol. The image decays, as it must, corroded by time; but the Reality, the world *in divinis*, is eternal in the Eternal Now. It is 'the world in our hearts'. We sever our allegiance to posterity, to historical humanity and its 'future', and instead establish our solidarity with Humanity as divine, the deiform being whose eternal oneness with God is the indestructible eternity of its world as well. This world, this Earth. This Paradise. Sever our allegiance to a desacralized cosmos, which can only mean to nothing, and adore the Reality which casts forth these myriad forms, in all their ineffable intoxicating, irresistible beauty, whose transience we have no need to mourn, knowing, in direct transcendental experience, their eternity in Heaven, in our Love. Knowing Humanity's eternity in Heaven, in our Love. We love the human essence, which is God: humanity *in divinis*, which is everlasting, and the womb of an infinity of universes. We identify and bear witness to That, and disengage ourselves from misconceived allegiance to the magic spell It weaves, the Lila, the Creation, the Dream. This is our salvation, in itself, and from hope or despair. The salvation of the world as well. 'Nothing is born, nothing is destroyed. Away with your dualism, your likes and dislikes. Every single thing is just the One Mind. When you have perceived this, you will have mounted the Chariot of the Buddhas.' Nothing has happened. Nothing at all.

Realizing this truth, then, perceiving it directly in our meditation, we become the Primary Man, the Primary Woman:

When *prajna-intuition* takes place it annihilates space and time relationships, and all existence is reduced to a point-instant. It is like the action of a great fire at the end of a *kalpa* (era) which razes everything to the ground and prepares a new world to evolve. In this new *prajna*-world there is no three-dimensional space, no time divisible into the past, present, and future. At the tip of my finger Mount Sumeru rises; before I utter a word and you hear it, the whole history of the universe is enacted. This is no play of poetic imagination, but the Primary Man manifesting himself... The Primary Man is Prince Nata, and, in fact, every one of us, when the flesh is returned to the mother, and the bones to the father... By the Primary Man is meant ultimate reality or *prajna*, as the case may be.
⟋D.T. Suzuki

The end of a cycle of terrestrial humanity, the *Kali-Yuga*, is an incentive to Self-Realization—Supreme Identity, *Summum Bonum,* 'the Station of No-what-ness'—to a turning toward Spirit, and in this sense it is a grace, just as, conversely, self-realization is, and always 'was', annihilation of the world.' *Brahman satyam, jagat mithya*: Brahman is real, the world is unreal, *Ayam Atma Brahman*: This Self is Brahman. I can't imagine a greater clarity and eloquence than we find in Coomaraswamy's essay, 'The Flood in Hindu Tradition':

'Floods' are a normal and recurrent feature of the cosmic cycle... [they] are essentially resolutions of manifested existences into their undetermined potentiality, the Waters; and each renewed cycle of manifestation is a bringing forth on the next 'day' of forms latent as potentiality in the floods of reservoir of being. In each case the seeds, ideas, or images of the future manifestation persist during the interval or inter-Time of resolution on a higher plane of existence, unaffected by the destruction of manifested forms. As to this, it will be understood, of course, that the chronological symbolism, inevitable from the empirical point of view, cannot be thought of as really characterizing the timeless actuality of all the possibilities of existence in the indivisible present of the Absolute, for Whom all multiplicity is mirrored in a single image. As, then, there can be no destruction of things as they are in the Self, but only of things as they are in themselves, the eternity, or rather timelessness, of ideas is a metaphysical necessity. Hence, indeed, the conception of another transformation, an *atyantika pralaya*, ultimate or absolute resolution, to be accomplished by the individual when or wherever he may

be, as Realization: when, in fact, by self-naughting a man effects for himself
the transformation of things as they are in themselves, and knows them only
as they are in the Self, he becomes immortal.absolutely, as independent of
time and of every other contingency.

Two fates. The fate of 'the world' in the *Kali-Yuga*, the end of the cosmic
cycle, and the fate of 'the world' wherever Self-Realization occurs, where *prajna*-intuition takes place; where an aspirant perceives and becomes one with
the Truth. In both cases, time and space are annihilated, and discourse is
terminated, for we have reached the limit of the expressible. Perhaps, in our
position on the cosmic trajectory, there is an added element of consolation
unknown to the saints and sages with whose memory and example we are
blessed—although there isn't really anyone to be consoled. There never was
a 'world', as we interpret that word spontaneously, nor were there ever individuals, and the two fates are actually identical: the end of an illusion. Neither the *Kali-Yuga* nor Self-Realization occur in chronological time or
empirical space, for time and space are the constituent dimensions of the
illusion they dissipate. Within the Dream, we call it real. Awakened, we call
it a Dream. From within the Dream, the *Kali-Yuga* and Self-Realization are
incomprehensible. Awakened, nothing has happened at all. Nothing ended,
and no one awoke.

As Coomaraswamy himself put it, in one of his incredible renowned
footnotes ('*Akimcanna*: Self-Naughting'), 'The Traveler is bound for a
world's End that is within himself.' That's about as succinct an epitome of
the theme and thrust of the present text as one could expect to discover.

❊

What is at stake here? What is really at stake here? At the end of the day, as
they say in England, it's not salvation, or honorable withdrawal, or metaphysical rectitude, or even living in the Truth. At stake is the preservation of
our capacity to love humanity. Lose this, and we've lost everything. It's the
place where the point of the sword seeks to enter: kill that love and we're
truly dead. When all is said and done this is the fundamental thing, because
of its all-pervading reverberations in our earthly lives. This love is essential,
and must inform any serious choice we make, any commitment, any witness. It is the real target of the *Kali-Yuga's* assault on our humanity, and the
only threat we need take seriously. As historical humanity becomes steadily
less human, we must rediscover, meaning *recollect*—'we': a minority, as

always, a few; those who can hear the Summons and have the strength to respond; those who have taken the true measure of our situation and who know, through their faith, that there has to be an answer that preserves and affirms our wholeness—the eternal divine paradigm from which it is departing now, at the close of the cycle, in the reign of quantity and mechanization and the twilight of Nature, and love *that*. It alone is real. And this love of the paradigm, the Archetype, the Consciousness, is love of God as well. Love of God, or *bhakti*, and *jñana*: oneness with the indestructible Reality, our very Self, in which the drama unfolds and the illusory calamity presents its very real challenge. This is the *Kali-Yuga*. Time to go home.

✳

I haven't spoken here of worldly hope, the hope or conviction that things will or must get better, except as the incorrigible but thoroughly understandable fiction that has consoled people ever since the Fall into Time, from its initial appearance in the form of messianic expectation in the Biblical era to its final crystallization in the ideology of Progress. But if there were any hope for historical humanity, for a prolongation of the Dream in which quantification, mechanization, cyberworld and the Power Complex—the Reign of Science, in other words—were repudiated instead of increasingly affirmed, it could only be through identification of and with our authentic Humanity, and with its guidance. That is, a rediscovery of the truth of Primordial Tradition, *Sophia Perennis et Universalis*. This will not happen. This will not happen, and those who proclaim it as the only hope really succeed only in confirming, on the highest level, the pointlessness of hope—driving the last nail in the coffin, as it were—so clearly inevitable is the triumph of a dark future, and so absurdly unreal the prospects of the Light, in the apocalyptic alternative they quite correctly identify. Anagarika Govinda, for example, puts it this way:

> Because humanity stands at the cross-roads of great decisions: before it lies the Path of Power, through control of the forces of nature—a path leading to enslavement and self-destruction—and the Path of Enlightenment, through control of the forces within us—leading to liberation and self-realization. To show this path (the *Bodhisattva-marga*) and to transform it into reality, was the life's task of Tomo Geshe Rimpoche.

The great student of Eastern religions, T.R.V. Murti, makes the same point:

Everywhere the hold of tradition has loosened... The Christian world has been disintegrating for centuries, since the Renaissance. There is little hope that it could regain the lost ground and reassert itself... The present-day world lacks unity and goodwill; it has no soul or spirit to animate and unify it. The causes are not hidden. Western civilization, which has become the norm for all, has developed, since the Renaissance, along materialistic lines... Man has conquered Nature or is very near doing that; but he has not the rudimentary control over himself. The consequences are disastrous. Organized life with any pretense to stability and security has become precarious. We have gained the world, but have lost our soul...

We have to realize that the good of all is the good of oneself, and that there can be no room for the ego. In the last analysis, the transcending of the standpoint of the ego, or more positively, the attainment of the Universal, is the essence of the spiritual, and only the spiritual can provide the basis for the society and can be conducive for the realization of other values.

In this regard, Mahayana absolutism and the Advaita Vedanta are valuable as providing the basis on which a world-culture can be built... Both insist on the universality of the Real and transcendence of the ego-centric standpoint... The need is for the spiritual regeneration of the world... What we need is the realization of the spiritual, which is the bed-rock of all our endeavour. Only mystical religion, which eminently combines the unity of Ultimate Being with the freedom of different paths for realizing it, can hope to unite the world.

Pathetic voices. Mystical religion and the Path of Enlightenment are not included in the programming of terrestrial humanity's future, and the 'reassertion' of Christianity, given its ambivalent and tormented complicity in the career of Western civilization, is not an attractive, or even meaningful prospect. That future, rather, is in the hands of 'people' who, glued to their screens and poring over their printouts, pursue, or are possessed by, a decidedly different blueprint: one which, in their infantile interpretation, indeed celebration, is as much a fantasy as the global triumph of Mahayana absolutism and the Advaita Vedanta. It will prevail, of course, the 'technotopia'. The commodity-fetish science-fiction *Walpurgisnacht*, determined ineluctably by the interlocking agendas of technological development and Capital. Robots and zombies in the factories, marionettes and mannequins in the office buildings, couch potatoes in the family rooms, fingering the remotes: animated death in a synthetic environment—for Nature is already gone. Surreal delirium, high-tech phantasmagoria, Television World and the Net in which we have enthusiastically vanished as human presence, the Net we have become, the terminal trap. What is it? What is it all but a wail of exhausted expectations and baffled hope wrenched from the souls of beings imprisoned in a windowless Unreality, drowned out by the Commercial, mocked by the bland smiling faces of the News Team and the impenetrable electric oracle, unheard even by themselves? Celestial beings, made for heaven, the elect: envied even by the angels. They wail: because they can know suffering which is not of the body nor present in awareness—for they do not live by bread alone—and because they are deprived of their birthright, a joy that is not of this world.

It will prevail, the 'technotopia', self-ridiculing and triumphant at once. Nothing can hold back Progress. Its significance in human terms, however, is as inaccessible to the 'intelligence' of those who excitedly labor to bring it about as the collapse of a house to the 'minds' of the termites.

But those who affirm the Truth are the only hope in a hopeless world. For they have conquered that world, with its hopes and fears, and are 'of good cheer'. They have found, in that 'within' and 'without' which are one, the indestructible Reality of all the beautiful beings and things that appear perishable and perishing, they have found the Self. They can love truly, they can rejoice, they can know peace. They are compassionate. They know nothing has happened at all, yet they are still compassionate.

> *Empty yourself of everything.*
> *Let the mind rest at peace.*
> *The ten thousand things rise and fall while the Self watches their return.*
> *They grow and flourish and then return to the source.*

XVII

Taking Care of Business

The loss of inward Revelation, or of the eye of the Heart, shows that Eden was lost following upon a sin of outwardness or exteriorization... for the loss of Inwardness and its Peace proves a misdirected movement towards outwardness and a fall into passion. Adam and Eve yielded to the temptation of 'cosmic inquisitiveness', that is, they wished to know and experience the things of the outer world outside God, and independently of the inward Light... thus entering upon a path without end or escape... It is the path of exile, suffering and death; all errors and all sins retrace that first transgression and lead to that path endlessly renewed.
∾ FRITHJOF SCHUON, 'The Forbidden Fruit'

HELL FIRE IN THE PACIFIC. The West's arsenal of decaying chemical weapons is stored on Johnston Atoll in the middle of the Pacific. Paul Brown reveals how Nato is planning to ship out 7,000 tonnes of lethal nerve gases and the US Army, with little thought for the environment and in the face of growing opposition from neighboring states, is intending to set fire to the whole stockpile of up to 100,000 tonnes in an attempt to destroy it.
∾ From the GUARDIAN OF MANCHESTER AND LONDON, July 27, 1990.

Collective enterprise in the *Kali-Yuga* focuses on the deployment of techniques within an objective theatre of operations. What is 'out there' is alone reality, and 'out there' our drama unfolds. Out there: that is, History. That what happens 'out there' might be a reflection or manifestation of something 'within' is therefore a meaningless, or fruitless anyway, proposition. There is action; but no actor whose inner being—character traits, motivations, value system, self-conception, patterns of behavior, psychology, sense of reality, world picture, moral standards and standing, principles, 'case history', coincidence with or departure from a norm or propriety or *dharma*—might merit examination. Nothing exists but what is being done, what is happening.

There is an objective world, a human terrain, which presents us unceasingly with *problems*—budget 'crunches', environmental confrontations, urban violence, alcoholism, the spread of AIDS in the teenage population, unemployment, corruption, family breakdown, violations of the democratic ideal, falling SAT scores, child abuse, sluggish investment, etc.—and our task is to discover, invariably through the acquisition and analysis of 'information', and then implement the most efficient strategy to *solve* them. How to get from here to there, to transform this scenario into that scenario. And that's the whole story, the structure of things, the content of public discourse and public enterprise. That's 'what's happening', and 'what's happening', as the familiar phrase drives home, is all there is.

> Johnston Atoll should be a version of paradise: a coral island in the middle of the Pacific with silver sands and palm trees, untouched by modern civilisation. In reality this tiny island is the final resting place of a vast store of rotting chemical weapons dumped there by the United States and her allies, constantly guarded by soldiers with machine guns wearing gas masks and protective clothing. It is forbidden to approach within 12 miles of the island and passengers who try to get off civilian airliners which routinely refuel there are restrained at gunpoint. Only a few yards from the runway are bunkers containing thousands of tons of unstable chemical weapons.

When we consider, however, the damning testimony of the aberrations, outrages and insanities upon which technique and strategy are industriously brought to bear—wholesale extinction of species, endemic chemical addictions, pollution and demolition of the global habitat, vast sinks of 'toxic wastes', ubiquitous violence and a cult of violent 'entertainment', the feverish production of and secret traffic in unimaginably powerful instruments of mass destruction, institutionalizing a madness casually acknowledged as 'uncontrolled proliferation' and 'overkill', and so on—and their obvious and devastating implications about the nature of the protagonist, their interpretation as 'problems' must stand unmasked as a vast and transparent evasion, clearly rooted in a despair so deep beneath the surface, so inherent and 'natural', that it cannot be consciously experienced. This despair is nothing less than the soul of historical humanity in its terminal stage. Its secret inner self. A great Blindness, a protective ignorance, rooted in confirmed despair, insured by an insuperable shallowness, and dissembled by a relaxed arrogance, functions to shield the protagonist from inadmissible self-knowledge, from the 'moment of truth'. Progress can admit problems: but nothing more serious. It could also be said that no other mode of collective enterprise is possible, since the protagonist is merely a giant mechanism anyway, Mumford's Power System or 'megamachine', with no more selfhood or self-consciousness, no more capacity for repentance or conversion or sober self-confrontation and painful self-appraisal, than the network of computers which have been installed as its nervous system and brain. An 'artificial intelligence', as we have seen, limited in its 'operation' to 'procedural thought' or sequences of algorithms: 'thinking', for example, in the same way our car thermostats 'think' about how hot the radiator water has become. It is what our children are being trained to become by Turtle Graphics and Logo. And power is very much a part of the scene here, as well.

> Through Logo, Papert believes the child 'acquires a sense of mastery over a piece of the most modern and powerful technology.' Like many computer enthusiasts, he is much concerned with power; the word *powerful* appears prominently throughout *Mindstorms*. In one of the most developed Logo workbooks, Daniel Watt's *Learning with Logo*, the phrase powerful idea—taken from Papert—appears as a little flag that punctuates the presentation of each chapter' (THEODORE ROSZAK)

Recall Sherry Turkle's chapter title: 'The New Philosophers of Artificial Intelligence: A Culture with Global Aspirations.'

> The US now admit the atoll has been successively contaminated by fallout from unsuccessful nuclear weapons tests carried out in the 1960s and polluted from 1971 onwards by a series of spillages from deliveries of lethal chemical weapons. Parts of Johnston are still out of bounds because of an accident involving lethal doses of Agent Orange left over from the Vietnam War. This has not been washed away despite the fact that the island has been completely inundated twice by typhoons. Now Europe is to add to Johnston's appalling catalogue of chemicals. Nato has decided to unload its European chemical arsenal of 100,000 highly dangerous nerve gas warheads on the same island. It then intends to set fire to the whole lot—around 7,000 tons of highly volatile material. Preparations to move these warheads from a previously secret base deep in West Germany to Johnston started yesterday…

All incidents and situations, therefore, are dealt with either as isolated or related only through objective causal mechanisms, challenges to an equally mechanical strategy, since what actually relates and unifies them, in the final analysis, is *what we are*, what we have *become*. What Lewis Mumford, Lenny Bruce, Robinson Jeffers, Theodore Roszak, Joseph Epes Brown, T.S. Eliot, Jean Baudrillard, Aldous Huxley, Karl Marx, William Blake, Frithjof

Schuon, Huston Smith, Tom Wolfe, Helen Caldecott, Loren Eiseley, George Carlin, A. K. Coomaraswamy, Herbert Marcuse, Joel and Ethan Cohn, Siegfried Giedion, Gary Snyder, D. T. Suzuki, Joseph Heller, Peter Matthiessen, Marco Pallis, Hunter Thompson, Garrison Keillor, Tom Tomorrow, and many, many others, far too numerous to mention, in many many idioms and dialects, testify we have become. And this monstrous 'self' can never be admitted for the simple reason that we know full well nothing can be done for it. 'We are not the doctors, we are the disease', as the famous epitome goes, 'We have met the enemy, and they is us,' as Pogo happily reported. Our deepest collective conviction is that nothing can be done for us, that it's all over: the Sickness is incurable and terminal. Its complexity is too enormous, its inertia too stupendous, its origins too ancestral, too indigenous, our suicidal accommodations too ingenious. We can only submit stoically to 'future shock', consult the glowing extrapolations ('CAN COMPUTERS COME TO LIFE?') alternately admonitory and reassuring, of the 'futurologists' who write and think at about the same level, and in the same spirit, as advertising copy. Only 'ride it out', hoping that somehow it is Progress, or a series of temporary impediments or challenges to Progress, and fearing, knowing without *really* knowing — without, that is, realizing and accepting that the invalidation of Progress entails a reappraisal of our own lives — that it is not.

✳

And what we must face is that none of these 'problems' are any more than surface symptoms of the timeless placeless 'event', the supra-cosmic metamorphosis in the changeless Mind of God that is the *Kali-Yuga*, The Fall into Time, the Reign of Quantity, the Prison of Unreality, Separation from Spirit, Pride of Power, the End of Nature, the Mutation into Machinery… in a word, and down again onto the historical plane, that planetary apocalypse which has been judiciously celebrated by the renowned Oxford historian, J. M. Roberts, in his 1985 publication, as *The Triumph of the West*. He concludes that 'the most valuable gift' brought to the rest of the world by the West 'was the implanting of the idea that willed change was possible.'

It is this last which seems to me the essence of what was done by Western civilization. In principle, it brought into question everything that already existed on the spot — it forced people to think about their set ways and consider whether those ways could endure. Of course, it did not do so always and everywhere in the same way. Faiths and ideologies are changed by the world even as they change it. Nevertheless, Western civilization has been humanity's great champion; it is the greatest claim ever made for men's unique status among living creatures as a change-making animal.

'Animal'. As the distinguished Warden of Merton College wishes. And yes, the triumph of the West. A summarization (by a truly sinister intelligence, incidentally) as pathetically small-minded, given the fathomless profundity of cyclical unfolding, and as moronic in its blind ethnocentric bigotry, as it is, on its own level, absolutely accurate.

Johnston Island, once a nature reserve, has become the US Army's chosen disposal ground for weapons because they say the warheads and chemicals are too unstable and dangerous to be transported to the United States for disposal. The problem is that the weapons were created without any thought being given to how they were going to be dismantled and neutralized if they were not used in war…
Most of the stocks of US chemical weapons are held in bunkers on mainland America. There were fears that moving such munitions would be dangerous and the best way to solve the problem would be to incinerate them on the spot. As a result, the US military had already developed an experimental incinerator at the Aberdeen Proving Grounds near Washington. This was a tiny prototype which would have been developed to provide one large incinerator to destroy each of a further eight stockpiles of chemical weapons held on the mainland. Opposition to this so close to Washington and the prospect of one being built in various other states led to a revision of the plan. Instead the experiment was shifted to Johnston Island… All the information about the military's specific plans is classified… The army says it has produced an environmental impact assessment to cover the movement of the chemical weapons from Clauson in West Germany to Johnston Island but insists it cannot publish it because of fears of terrorist attacks.

Jacques Ellul's masterwork comes to mind. The *Technological Society* (1964), described by Robert Theobald, in 'The Nation', as 'one of the most important books of the second half of the twentieth century.' An incontestably prophetic work, even more 'important' now, over thirty years later, than it could have appeared to be then. ('Important', of course, to a microscopic handful of incorrigibly inquisitive people who cannot be at peace with themselves until they feel they have understood their world, and to no one else and in no other sense. To ascribe an 'importance' to Ellul's book or, for that matter, to any of the other books referred to in these pages, including the present volume, which implies in any way that their appearance will matter, make some difference, intervene in the course of events by attracting 'public notice' and generating 'public concern', would be ludicrous.) Also George Morgan, whose fine book, *The Human Predicament: Dissolution and Wholeness* (1968), apparently went unnoticed by the world (confirming, according to a Sufi master, that it was 'kept in heaven'); I've never seen it mentioned in any of the bibliographies where it ought to have appeared. And Neil Postman also, a passage from his *The Disappearance of Childhood*. None of these stubborn and insightful champions of humanity is aware of, and feels to the depths of his heart, the metaphysical background to their analysis; but they see quite clearly the waning of the human presence in this world.

✳

It's a challenge to try to summarize in his own words, although I shall soon try, Ellul's argument in *La Technique*, with its Hegelian methodology and style whose 'successive recantation and histrionic irony of statement must drive the literal-minded reader mad.' The translator, John Wilkinson, warns that 'it is only possible to approximate in English the mixed metaphors and the studied imprecisions.' Robert Merton writes in the Foreword:

> Enough of Ellul's idiosyncratic vocabulary has survived the hazards of transoceanic migration to require us to note the special meanings he assigns to basic terms. By *technique*, for example, he means far more than machine technology. Technique refers to any complex of standardized means for attaining a predetermined result. Thus, it converts spontaneous and unreflective behavior into behavior that is deliberate and rationalized. The Technical Man is fascinated by results, by the immediate consequences of setting standardized devices into motion. He cannot help admiring the spectacular effectiveness of nuclear weapons of war. Above all, he is committed to the never-ending search for 'the one best way' to achieve any designated objective.

That's us. Ourselves, in the age of science and scientific method. Merton is starting to get at it here, at Ellul's insight, but this is barely scratching the surface. Ellul (and, as we shall see, Morgan also) describes modes of behavior so characteristic, so fundamental and intrinsic to our modern world, so *automatic*, that we are unaware of performing them, *a fortiori* of their significance. Merton continues:

Ours is a progressively technical civilization: by this Ellul means that the ever-expanding and irreversible rule of technique is extended to all domains of life. It is a civilization committed to the quest for continually improved means to carelessly examined ends... 'Know-how' takes on an ultimate value... Doctrine is converted into procedure... The technicians form a closed fraternity with their own esoteric vocabulary. Moreover, they are concerned only with what is, as distinct from what ought to be... Purposes drop out of sight and efficiency becomes the central concern... Not understanding what the rule of technique is doing to him and to his world, modern man is beset by anxiety and a feeling of insecurity. He tries to adapt to changes he cannot comprehend.

The final stage of terrestrial humanity's career boasts a massive unprecedented power to *do* things, to *change* things, as the Oxford-based cheerleader for Western civilization explained, but... what? But no idea of how to employ that power to human ends and purposes? Not exactly; although that's the usual argument. The conquest of power, the *choice* of power, is already self-destructive, already inconsistent with the recognition and attainment of human ends and purposes. *Human ends and purposes are not attained through the exercise of power: that's the point.* They reside, in all their beauty and eternal fathomless simplicity, in the Reality itself, the Heart, the inwardness, the realm of Joy and Grace where power cannot even exist.

They are right before and within us all the time. If anything, they are attained through the relinquishment of power, its renunciation. It is difficult to imagine a more categorical error, or one more demonstrative of a terminal stage in the cycle. The argument that we now possess great power but don't know how to use it wisely is very much off the mark. Power *cannot* be 'used wisely', only in humble recognition of the visitation of some kind of fatality in human affairs and with a prayer for forgiveness and mercy, a *pardon* in response to a vow that we will do everything humanly possible to assure that such defection from propriety, such dishonor, will not occur again, and its existence as a value is already proof of a disastrous wrong turn; this is, indeed, the entire burden of Lewis Mumford's great life's work. And 'technique' is simply the ultimate refinement of power. Refinement, elaboration, dissemination, universalization. It is not neutral, but rather inherently corrosive of our capacity for discernment and discrimination, our spiritual probity, to the degree that it becomes an end in itself, a guarantee, a fetish, an 'answer'. In Wilkinson's words:

Now, Ellul's explanation of the technical takeover is based fundamentally on the fact that the material (that is, technical) substratum of human existence, which was traditionally not allowed to be a legitimate end of human action, has become so 'enormous', so 'immense', that men are no longer able to cope with it as means, so that it has become an end-in-itself, to which men must adapt themselves... Men in the past were not confronted with technical means of production and organization which in their sheer numerical prolif- eration and velocity unavoidably surpassed man's relatively unchanging bio- logical and spiritual capacities to exploit them as means to human ends.

The relationship goes both ways: separation from the divine wisdom that alone teaches us what are our proper ends engenders by default an imbal- ance, a fixation on enterprise in the material world and the feverish develop- ment of means or techniques, while a fixation on means further and progressively atrophies the knowledge and memory of proper ends. That is part of what happened in the West. Not all, to be sure, but one dimension of that great undertaking which finally emerged as the exemplary civiliza- tion. Where now at last, or so Ellul seeks to demonstrate, 'technique' alone remains.

And the process is a natural one: every part of a technical civilization responds to the social needs generated by technique itself. Progress then consists in progressive dehumanization—a busy, pointless, and, in the end, suicidal submission to technique. The essential point, according to Ellul, is that technique produces all this without plan; no one wills it or arranges that it be so. Our technical civilization does not result from a Machiavellian scheme. It is a response to the 'laws of development' of technique.

Wilkinson's summary, now, will take us one step deeper into Ellul's insight, at first elusive and then so luminous as to suggest that a finality has been reached, and provide the occasion for confronting a decisive question. For upon initial examination Ellul's thesis seems arbitrary.

Technique, the reader discovers more or less quickly, must be distinguished from the several *techniques* which are its elements. It is more even than a gen- eralized mechanical technique; it is, in fact, nothing less than the organized ensemble of all individual techniques which have been used to secure any end whatsoever. Technique has become indifferent to all the traditional human ends and values by becoming an end-in-itself. Our erstwhile means have all become an end, an end, furthermore, which has nothing human in it and to which we must accommodate ourselves as best we may. Technique, as the universal and autonomous technical fact, is revealed as the technological society itself in which man is but a single tightly integrated and articulated component. *The Technological Society* is a description of the way in which an autonomous technology is in process of taking over the traditional values of every society without exception, subverting and suppressing these values to produce at last a monolithic world culture in which all nontechnological difference and variety is mere appearance.

To the heart of the matter. It could be argued that Ellul has gone too far, that he exaggerates. Aren't there countless instances around us where technology is employed by human beings to human purposes, to the betterment and advancement of our lives? Consider our exemplary case. Johnston Island: dangerous chemical poisons are being carefully isolated from populated environments (European and American, to be sure), stored under strict military supervision and destroyed by state-of-the-art methods and with exacting precautions and contingency plans. Why doesn't this qualify as the employment of technology to a human end?

Because the whole thing is an affair of Technique. Civilization itself, 'the whole shooting match' if I may be permitted a homely figure of speech, is Technique. *Humanity* is now an evolving *ensemble of techniques.* An affair of Technique: from the initial ensemble, political, economic and military, in which the poison gases appeared, to the future ensemble in which their transfer will have been a contributory stage or moment. The technologies, or ensemble of techniques, that erected urban life engender the technologies, or new ensemble, which deals with the 'problems' it creates, and so on. One technical episode engenders another, one ensemble evolves into another, everywhere and at all levels, with no 'end' either causally implicit or proposed by human beings. We ride the back of an autonomously unfolding technological history *which is ourselves,* complacently pasting moral labels on, or imputing deliberate intention to, activities whose autonomous inner dynamic has no relationship whatsoever to choice or decision or judgement or morality or anything human whatever. We *are* Technique. The automobile, microwave oven, television, atomic bomb and computer, the factory, the work day, the suburbs, the insurance company, the stock exchange and the business administration faculty, disarmament conferences, the Olympic Games, the Federal Reserve System, interstate highways, trade unions, acoustical engineering and postage stamps, traffic signals, automatic tellers, email, fax machines, elevators, escalators, banks and the fire department, retail stores, range management and the city dump, innumerable acronym institutions such as IMF, OPEC, G7, EEC, EEOC, etc., *and the human identities, activities and relationships that produce, use and inhabit them,* all appeared among a passive, indeed hypothetical 'us' because the active autonomous 'ensemble of techniques' which we increasingly became *and now actually are*, produced them within itself, in response to itself, as 'our life'. Ellul is a heavyweight.

✳

Colonel Jerry Pate, US Army headquarters, said that the plans to remove the chemical weapons from Germany had been considered for four years... He said the army would be moving 100,000 artillery shells filled with chemical agents GB and VX. (One droplet of these gases causes paralysis, vomiting and diarrhoea and death usually occurs within ten minutes.) The shells, he said, have been stored in bunkers near the town of Clauson not far from Frankfurt in West Germany. They would be tied onto pallets placed in specially designed airtight secondary steel containers. These in turn would be placed inside a standard steel military container called a milvan. These milvans would be transported by road 20 miles from the storage site to the railhead at Miesaw Army depot. From there they would be transported by rail on a 13 hour trip to the port of Nordingham on the North Sea where they would be loaded into two ships which would take them to Johnston Atoll on a route and with a timetable that was to be kept secret.

The core of the argument can be extracted by skipping around in the eminent jurist's 'essentially dramatic work' (Wilkinson), and I shall quote verbatim rather than paraphrase. I have a stuffy compunction about quoting at length, which I shall overcome. A study such as the present one is inherently collective, as I said in the Introduction, and my debts are enormous; any pretense to 'originality' would be both shameful and absurd. We are all involved here, all implicated and summoned to account in our very humanity by the fate we share as witnesses to the final apocalypse of cyclical unfolding, and all relevant and sincere voices merit and demand our audience. Thoroughness is of the essence, the stakes are infinite. As far as possible, you must know everything that bears upon the great decision which—since you have read this far—you have resolved to confront. There is an assumption in academic communities that the scholar will have mastered and 'absorbed' his bibliography sufficiently to insure that its content will be implicit in his own discourse. I can't make that claim, meet that standard. The scenario, the scope, is too immense; the contemporary human condition in the *Kali-Yuga* is hardly an 'area of specialization' of the kind that makes such an absorption possible. And the *oeuvres* from which we can actually acquire something like an overview (Toynbee, Mumford, Marx, Eliade, Schuon, Baudrillard, Coomaraswamy) are too monumental: complementary angles or modes of perception rather than compatible analyses amenable to higher resolutions. Nor am I a scholar in any conventional sense; I am bound only by a commitment to thoroughness continuously menaced by my limitations. Nor do I write for people who are likely to pursue bibliographical references. What we're after here is a thrust in a certain direction of the whole life. Here's essential Ellul. I will interpolate comments here and there.

> 'The one best way'; so runs the formula to which our technique corresponds. When everything has been measured and calculated mathematically so that the method which has been decided upon is satisfactory from the rational point of view, and when, from the practical point of view, the method is manifestly the most efficient of all those hitherto employed or those in competition with it, then the technical movement becomes self-directing. I call the process *automatism*.

It's the feeling that we have escaped ourselves, trapped ourselves, outsmarted ourselves in a sense. We suspect the 'research and development' companies, the 'think tanks', but they are only Technique's behavior, not the 'being' itself. Everyone, and especially the technicians, is merely trying to 'keep track' of things, stay 'up-to-date' and not get 'left in the dust', in the remorselessly accelerating 'pace of change' that characterizes the *Yuga*.

It's History, the Fall into Time, the Myth of the Machine.

> Technique itself, *ipso facto* and without indulgence or possible discussion, selects among the means to be employed. The human being is no longer in any sense the agent of choice... He is a device for recording effects and results obtained by various techniques. He does not make a choice of complex and in some way, human motives. He can decide only in favor of the technique that gives the maximum efficiency. But this is not choice... Inside the technical circle, the choice among methods, mechanism, organizations, and formulas is carried out automatically. Man is stripped of his faculty of choice and he is satisfied. He accepts the situation when he sides with technique. We are today at the stage of historical evolution in which everything that is not technique is being eliminated... There is an automatic growth (that is, a growth which is not calculated, desired, or chosen) of everything which concerns technique.

Ellul, we should note, opposes *choice* to technique. He speaks often of our loss of freedom, of *liberation* from technique as our only hope. But where would this avenue lead? The only real 'liberation', the only real salvation from the tyranny of technique, is conformity to Divine Wisdom, to the immortal Dharma. Spirit. The Path. Obedience to the Law that follows from our deiformity, our fashioning in His Image, Oneness with the Tao of Heaven and Earth. This is the only meaningful 'choice'. And hardly likely.

Continuing with the concept of 'automatic growth', Ellul defines 'technical progression', which is 'of the same nature as the process of numbering.'

> What is it that determines this progression today? We can no longer argue that it is an economic or a social condition, or education, or any other human factor. Essentially. The preceding technical situation alone is determinative. When a given technical discovery occurs, it has followed almost of necessity certain other discoveries… Technique engenders itself. In this decisive evolution, the human being does not play a part. Technical elements combine among themselves, and they do so more and more spontaneously… A whole new kind of spontaneous action is taking place here, and we know neither its laws nor its ends. In this sense it is possible to speak of the 'reality' of technique — with its own substance, its own particular mode of being, and a life independent of our power of decision. It evolves in a purely causal way, the combination of preceding elements furnishes the new technical elements. There is no purpose or plan that is being progressively realized. There is not even a tendency toward human ends. We are dealing with a phenomenon blind to the future, in a domain of integral causality.

In Volume III of *The Americans: The Democratic Experience*, Daniel Boorstin saw the same thing:

> But how many Americans were haunted by fear that in the mushroom cloud over Hiroshima they had conjured a fifth rider of the Apocalypse? Along with Pestilence and War and Famine and Death, was there now a horse reserved for Science?… Oddly enough, the new instruments and evidences of American omnipotence brought a new sense of powerlessness about the future. Fate and Providence and Destiny were being displaced or at least overshadowed by a growing sense of Momentum: a deepening belief in the inevitability of continued movement in whatever direction the movement was already going. 'Momentum' described the new sense in many ways. By contrast with the notion of God's Will or the Economy of Nature or Progress or Destiny, it was neutral. It suggested a recognition of the force, a sense of powerlessness before it, and an uncertainty about whether it was good or evil. Perhaps never before in modern history had man been so horrified and bewildered by the threat of his own handiwork. A hint of the new way of thinking had been the theme of Anne Morrow Lindbergh's *Wave of the Future* (1940): 'The wave of the future is coming and there is no fighting it.'

You picture the cars and trucks creeping on the freeway, the hackneyed image of hysteria-inducing entrapment. You picture the laughing faces in the TV room, the whole family laughing together at the Cosby Show (then), at Seinfeld (today). There are unwritten protocols here, precepts and regulations and codes, unconsciously, punctiliously, innocently obeyed. Intricate webs, grids and networks traced by a million moving points of light, each a bright immortal soul, no more able to escape the gleaming circuitry than electrons in a wire. All the front covers of OMNI magazine show hybrid human-computer faces, screen faces, metallic faces with staring empty eyes, 'humanoids', transparent plastic skulls filled with the slick shit we are to imagine computers contain. The miraculous 'chips'. Terminator and Robocop, hundreds more in the Heavy Metal steeplechase nightmare netherworlds of the comix. Pre-fabricated articulations, response feedbacks and endless loops, passing through and composing the 'thoughts' of beings the angels envy, for they were made to realize their oneness with the Supreme. Folly; tragic and catastrophic. Waste, measureless waste. Lop-sided denouement, macabre metamorphosis into screaming impeccable logic. This is what it comes to, this is what it came to. This is us. Technique is only finally understood when we consider the stature of those upon whom it fell, who it became. This is sorrow, grieving, keening, this is head-shaking disbelief, this is grim resolve. Here we narrow our eyes and think seriously. Discard the ridiculous indulgences unrecognized as sentimentality. There's no room for it anymore, now. Our practice is detached compassion, the Buddhist perfection of manner. No fear. No regret. Nothing to gain, nothing to lose. It's a reeking terminal farce, alright: who could have predicted it? We minister to the wounded, and the bewildered, to each other, to what's left of us. And let no thought of the future diminish by an iota our love for the children.

In the world of Technique the very fabric of society seems to be made of injustice, gross unfairness, brutal indifference to suffering, outrageous neglect, against which decent people are constantly up in arms. A chronic moral imbalance, or vacuum, is constantly deplored: the 'problems'. We 'wage war' against it. Candidates for political office define themselves with respect to it. Political 'platforms' consist of techniques for coping with infamy. But it is Technique itself that has replaced morality, that is the absence of morality. Technique itself is the infamy.

> A principal characteristic of techniques... is its refusal to tolerate moral judgements. It is absolutely independent of them and eliminates them from its domain. Technique never observes the distinction between moral and

immoral use. It tends, on the contrary, to create a completely independent technical morality.

Ellul has referred here to 'its domain', but this should not imply a limitation of Technique's dominion. As he goes on to say,

Our technique, which is destroying all other civilizations, is more than a simple mechanism: it is a whole civilization in itself... Technique has progressively mastered *all* the elements of civilization. *Technical civilization* means that our civilization is constructed *by* technique (makes a part of civilization only what belongs to technique), *for* technique (in that everything in this civilization must serve a technical end), and *is* exclusively technique (in that it excludes whatever is not technique or reduces it to technical form)... Today, *technique has taken over the whole of civilization*... Henceforth, every component of civilization is subject to the law that technique is itself civilisation. Civilization no longer exists of itself. Every activity—intellectual, artistic, moral—is only a part of technique. This fact is so enormous and unpredictable that we are simply unable to foresee its consequences... The power and autonomy of technique are so well secured that it, in its turn, has become the judge of what is moral, the creator of a new morality. Thus, it plays the role of creator of a new civilization as well.

It negates and excludes Spirit:

The invasion of technique desacralizes the world in which man is called upon to live. For technique nothing is sacred.

And it negates and excludes Nature:

Technique is opposed to nature. Art, artifice, artificial: technique as art is the creation of an artificial system... The world that is being created by the accumulation of technical means is an artificial world and hence radically different from the natural world. It destroys, eliminates, or subordinates the natural world, and does not allow this world to restore itself or even to enter into a symbiotic relation with it. The two worlds obey different imperatives, different directives, and different laws, which have nothing in common. Just as hydroelectric installations take waterfalls and lead them into conduits, so the technical milieu absorbs the natural. We are rapidly approaching the time when there will be no longer any natural environment at all.

Spiricide, ecocide, and homicide as well, in the sense that our humanity resides in our depth and our wholeness. In our obedience to the immortal Delphic formula, the Socratic 'Know thyself' which is the central injunction, *command*, of the *Sophia Perennis* wherever it appears, and our only hope.

The superscription 'Know thyself' demands a knowledge of the answer to
the question, 'Who art thou?' and may be said, in the veiled language of the
mysteries, to ask this very question. The injunction, as Plutarch says, is
addressed by the God to all who approach him... 'Know thyself' is not a
'piece of advice' but the 'God's salutation to those who enter.'
～Coomaraswamy

Salutation, invitation, grace. Technological society, the whole modern
world, lies to us about who we are. What deeper damage? We are the impersonal hatred of ourselves. Our own demeaning.

There is the deep conviction that technical problems are the only serious
ones. The amused glance people give the philosopher; the lack of interest displayed in metaphysical and theological questions ('Byzantine' quarrels); the
rejection of the humanities which comes from the conviction that we are living in a technical age and education must correspond to it; the search for the
immediately practical, carrying the implication that history is useless and can
serve no practical ends—all these are symptomatic of that 'reasonable' conviction which pervades the social hierarchy and is identical for all social classes.
'Only technique is not mere gab.' It is positive and brings about real achievements.

❋

Finally, a few citations from the translator's Introduction, included here
because they situate in Ellul's context facets of our condition already noted
in these pages. Ellul is aware of universal quantification, Guénon's 'reign of
quantity' which announces the close of the cycle.

It is, in fact, the essence of technique to compel the qualitative to become
quantitative, and in this way to force every stage of human activity and man
himself to submit to its mathematical calculations. Ellul gives examples of
this at every level. Thus, technique forces all sociological phenomena to submit to the clock, for Ellul the most characteristic of all modern technical
instruments. The substitution of the *tempus mortuum* of the mechanical
clock for the biological and psychological time 'natural' to man is in itself sufficient to suppress all the traditional rhythms of human life in favor of the
mechanical.

(There's much good material on this subject in Jeremy Rifkin's *Time
Wars*.) And Ellul noted, even back in the early 50's, the central role of the
computer:

The reduction of everything to quantity is partly a cause and partly an effect of the modern omnipresence of computing machines and cybernated factories.

The relevance of Ellul's diagnosis to 'the style of collective enterprise in the *Kali-Yuga*' as I have examined it, focusing on the absence of any inner dimension, and of which I have taken the Johnston Island 'mission' to be representative, and to other portions of the analysis in these pages as well, should be obvious. Ellul is one of the great unconscious prophets of the *Kali-Yuga*, the first and greatest of whom was Karl Marx. There are lesser prophets, who cannot perceive 'the big picture' but have identified one of its aspects, one of the 'dangerous trends'; and, as I have tried to show, the whole society is pervaded by a prophetic foreboding: a generalized intuition of some kind of 'end of the world' to which just about everyone, in moments of candor, will wryly or sorrowfully or hesitatingly or belligerently confess, and which is most conspicuous, and penetrating and of course amusing, in its transformation into 'entertainment'. The great prophets, however, perseveringly direct our attention to a metamorphosis of humanity itself, always into some kind of mechanism, to which both Marx and Ellul, in the titles of their books, gave a name. *Das Kapital: La Technique*. For Ellul—the wealth of whose analysis and countless brilliant insights has scarcely been suggested here, in this desperate epitome—spontaneous life, or humanity, or collective responsibility, or consciousness, or the social infrastructure, call it what you will, becomes quantified and mechanized, or, more precisely, is gradually 'squeezed out' and replaced by a machinery that is as much intangible as material, by universal 'technique'. 'Technique' is humanity in the Age of Science and Technology, which is to say, in the *Kali-Yuga*. Or rather, it is the form assumed by the automatic activity (autonomous, automaton) of the empty husk (android; or, familiarly, 'droid') after the annihilation of humanity as its truth, its distinctive essence, its identity with the Intention of Grace. It becomes a terrifyingly alien shape on the landscape, a mindless implacable devastation making the world over into its own image, the incarnate 'Myth of the Machine'. Who else but we are 'the invaders' with a superior technology whose origin was projected into 'outer space'? What on earth is a 'cyberpunk'?

This sort of transformation, or I should say, humanity's metamorphosis in the *Kali-Yuga*, is quintessentially invisible, for it occurs everywhere, penetrates everywhere, within and without, between us, around us and beneath the surface. It's everything, as Ellul succeeds in making clear. Technique emerges from the mouth, and is implicit in the very existence, of the 'marriage counselor', the 'superintendent of schools' and the 'President of the United States'. All are technicians, all are interchangeable parts. Can we imagine a future in which Technique has been unmasked, recognized for what it is, and deliberately, with appropriate horror in the realization of an eleventh hour prevention of catastrophe, replaced by something else? Can we even imagine what that 'something else' might be? ('In the modern world, the most dangerous form of determinism is the technological phenomenon. It is not a question of getting rid of it, but, by an act of freedom, of transcending it. How is this to be done? I do not yet know.' Ellul, in his Foreword to the Revised American Edition.) Or, for that matter, a future without television? Without money, that universal 'measure of value' whose iron grip is called Capital and presence in our midst, *as ourselves*, is called wage labour? Can we imagine the recreation of *nature*, a natural *world*, pure and uncharted as it was in the timeless Beginning, the pristine primordial Setting, sacred, unreachable and inviolable by human powers, *unknowable*, which was taken for granted by the whole human race as recently as the turn of the century, *and which is implicit in our humanity itself*? The 'otherness' of Nature is implicit in our humanity: an essential dimension of our being human and the world being the world. And that 'otherness' has been abrogated, it's gone: that independent existence, erstwhile Nature, is now 'real estate' and 'natural resources', incorporated into the technological web, the Power System, the global 'economy', mapped and mangled, garnished and altered forever and continuously: *it is not itself anymore*. Which is the entire burden of Bill McKibben's restrained elegy, *The End of Nature*. The name of the Yuga is No Way Back. Irreversibility. Historical existence has swept across more than one threshold. *La Technique* is a brilliant and profound insight into our lives. As the author writes in the Foreword, 'At stake is our very life.' In the *Kali-Yuga* we 'get the job done', as never before; but 'we' are machinery, 'Technique', and machinery has nothing to say about itself, to know about itself, because there's no one left to know anything and to know: there's no one there, it's dead. Titanic, inexhaustible, ceaselessly moving, shaping, tearing down, building up, creating and achieving. But nobody's home. In more than one sense.

Human purpose is defined by Spirit. Spirit is our End, as it is our Origin and Truth. Rightly understanding ourselves, we follow the Tao of Heaven and Earth. Rightly understanding ourselves, we perceive and adore that cosmic interdependence or 'interbeing' of the Avatamsaka Sutra, which is the Buddhist Oneness and the consummation of the Noble Eightfold Path, and we practice mindfulness and non-injury and compassion, knowing that the highest good is a state of mind. Rightly understanding ourselves, we see the Self in all beings and things and all beings and things in the Self, and we know God became Humanity that Humanity might become God, and we love God with all our heart, all our soul and all our mind. We are to pray and meditate until we know from joyous direct experience that the Kingdom of Heaven is within us. We are, in a word, to learn what and where we are and behave accordingly, learn it from Revelation, the Eternal Word, and from the Teacher in our heart.

The installation was called JACADS, the Johnston Atoll Chemical Agent Disposal System. The incinerator had four parts to perform different tasks and each one would have four months of test burns with different kinds of munitions from nerve gas to mustard to check it worked efficiently. Each of the four incinerators had its own scrubbers, de-misters and quenching towers. Lastly the solid waste would be collected and shipped to the United States for burial in an approved site. The weapons would be dismantled by remote control in an operations room built to withstand blast if any of the weapons went off accidentally. The four incinerators would have different functions. One would burn the propellants and charges from the rockets, shells and landmines, another the nerve gases and mustards, a third the metal parts from the projectiles and the fourth the packaging material, protective clothing and other materials which had been in contact with the munitions.

✴

George Morgan, in the book I referred to above, identifies 'an orientation of mind that stamps our civilization, an approach men take to the world that I shall call the prosaic mentality.' Science and 'technology in the widest sense,' which for Morgan includes our daily practical activities of all kinds,

have in common certain interests and attitudes, and they jointly promote a basic orientation, or approach to the world. It is this convergence of the two chief activities of our time that accounts for the nature and dominant position of the prosaic mentality.

Morgan then defines the prosaic mentality in detail. That he is describing, from a different perspective, the same condition that compelled Ellul's remorseless analysis is quite obvious. I shall quote at length, as I did from *La Technique.* Morgan's style and content are a unity, with a refreshing down-to-earth incisiveness, well worthy of being presented and appreciated in the original. And his book is almost certainly long out of print; you are not likely to find it anywhere. I feel honored in acknowledging his wisdom and seriousness here, and in offering them to readers who might not otherwise have had the opportunity to benefit from them. He also unknowingly chronicles the *Yuga*.

> The prosaic mentality is characterized by a cluster of attitudes and interests that it raises to supremacy over others, which are ignored, denied, or suppressed. It is this suppression that constitutes the fallaciousness and perniciousness of the prosaic mentality...

The prosaic mentality is one dimension of what might be called the 'mind of the *Yuga*'. Morgan defines and accords priority to a sensibility rather than an errant tendency, social order or value system. It's a personality type, familiar to us all, by which the readers of this book are likely to have been affectionately patronized, and chided. It's the people who conceived and undertook the Johnston Island mission, and their predecessors who made it necessary.

> The prosaic man is interested in abstractions, in groups of properties that can be abstracted from people, objects, events, and so on, and used to deal with them. Often the abstracted properties are what the prosaic man calls facts. To 'get all the facts' and to 'stick to facts' are typical prosaic requests. The prosaic man believes in facts.

The scope of what is excluded, invalidated or called into doubt here encompasses an enormous range of human experience, indeed everything that makes life worth living and human birth 'that most precious thing', and its assertion has provoked the desperate but understandable colloquial exclamation, 'Don't bother me with facts, my mind is made up!'

> One kind of abstraction, or fact, is of especial interest—that to which numbers can be assigned. Numbers have sureness and clearness: when you have hold of a number you know precisely what you have; it is the most solid and reliable kind of fact. Dates of events, duration of processes, numbers of objects, sizes and weights and speeds of things, since they are countable or measurable, constitute an abstractable property that can be readily and dependably dealt with and so seems especially real. We want to know the number of rooms in a house, the size of a shirt, the weight of a parcel, the volume of flour in a recipe, and most important, the price... The interest in abstracted properties of things or in facts, especially in quantitative facts, is

evidenced in all sorts of behavior, from looking at one's watch to tell the time, to the most complex process of manipulating, producing, or organizing.

✳

We've already talked about quantification as the hallmark of the *Yuga*. Let's go into it more deeply. Try to gather up some threads.

The world *in divinis* is qualitative. That's the real world, Reality, the heavenly Archetypes. The world in our hearts, the world we love, the world which *is* Love. The world in the infinite Mind of God. Qualitative. But 'I was a hidden treasure, and I wanted to be known, so I created the world.' (*Hadith qudsi*) The Sovereign Good, by its very nature, radiates. There was Manifestation. 'Thou hast manifested!' is our mantra of praise. Manifestation: and the greater the proximity, chronological and ontological, of the Manifestation to the Source, of Earth to Heaven, of our world to God, of Humanity to Spirit, the more the Manifestation reflects and partakes of the Origin, of Reality, of Quality. The more fully we inhabit and experience Eternity, rather than Time, and all things appear eternal, as they are in heaven, rather than temporal, as they are on Earth. But the *Yugas* unfold, *Krita*, *Treta*, *Dvapara* and *Kali* (the names of *dice throws* in an Indian game), in the traditional nomenclature, which merely means that the distance between the Manifestation and the Principle, from which it was breathed forth, becomes greater and greater. The Reality is changeless, the world *in divinis*, in our hearts, indestructible, the Archetypes eternal. But in the accelerating inexorable separation of the Earth from Heaven, the world from God, the Manifestation from the Principle, quality gives way to quantity in the Manifestation, and things are relentlessly drained of their being, of their very *reality*, because reality is quality, and quality is rooted in the Divine Beatitude, in the Archetypes, in that transcendent Reality or Origin or Center from which the Manifestation grows increasingly remote — although never absolutely separated because it would then cease to exist at all: rather, it returns, and is reborn. This world is faded and dead indeed, compared with what the Hopi saw. What remains, then, is quantity: a world drained of its being. Numbers. The world becomes unreal because, among other reasons we have touched upon, its 'reality', its *unreal reality*, is pure quantity. Quantity becomes the basic 'reality'. The basic *language*, reaching its ultimate state, its ultimate emptiness, becomes computer 'languages', mathematical conceptions and procedures, the *language of numbers*. Science, progressively and inherently quantitative, culminates in the creation of 'thinking machines' to replace, and bring to perfection, their human prototypes. *Money* becomes the *language of society*. So the Beatles sing 'Nothing is real'. And the front page of every newspaper on earth is filled with numbers. And Nature, Creation, becomes dollars, and pounds sterling, and deutschmarks, and francs, and yen: the 'currency' of the front runners among historical societies, Western, or 'Westernized'—a term of unsurpassable gravity. Quantity follows upon the Fall into Time—also a Western affair. The clock measures, indeed produces, nothing but our imprisonment in the unreal. Quantity, as astrophysics, the 'physics of consciousness' and everything in between, is language and reality. In the *Kali-Yuga*.

✳

Back to Morgan. He establishes another link.

> Interest in quantitative facts is intimately connected with the devotion of the prosaic mind to a particular abstractable property—progress. Whenever achievement can be stated in numbers, then progress is an easily ascertainable fact. Increases in size, speed, precision, production, salary, circulation, and membership are goals the prosaic man pursues, confident that he knows when and how much progress is being made.

'Progress', in other words, is actually the measure and language of our degradation, our debasement. Our descent from heaven, from the sacred to the profane, from eternal beauty to transient ugliness. The language of quantity, the language of Progress, the language of the *Kali-Yuga*: one language. From grant applications to industrial production to social standings, to the records broken in the Olympic Games. Tests, polls and statistics. One language. The 'prosaic mind' is the mind of the *Yuga*. Like the computer, it thinks in quantities.

The link between mechanism and quantification is sufficiently obvious.

> The mechanization of most activities through the application of science has given enormous impetus to this stress on a few abstractable properties, especially quantitative ones. The making and use of machinery requires attention to timing, dimensions, speeds, output, power, and efficiency—all quantitative properties. The machine's products also are viewed in terms of a group of quantitative specifications. Thus, interest in time, size, number, and so on becomes ever more dominant as mechanizal processes are instituted.

From facts, numbers, and machinery to method, reminding us of Ellul. And, piece by piece, the Johnston Island mission in the minds of its executors.

Another prosaic interest is methods—means, techniques, and procedures. The prosaic man is intent on practicing a method, busy with a procedure, involved in a technique, immersed in a program. He clarifies and systematizes existing methodological schemes, extends and refines them, or develops new means and techniques. Whatever he does, the method, procedure, or program is the center of attention... Much daily activity is routine. The best way to get things done is to be methodical. A proven procedure closely adhered to allows us to accomplish things with a minimum of error and confusion. Also, since we are always trying to 'save time', 'speed up', and 'increase efficiency', we are always intent on 'improving' and 'streamlining' methods and on developing new ones.

The emphasis on method, on an exclusively objective reality or theatre of operations presenting us with tasks, problems and 'challenges'—on action, what is 'out there', what is *happening*—is both a cause and a consequence of our inability to think deeply about anything. Our inability any longer to *know truth* and *be human*. Truth, meaning and meaningfulness, reality and authentic human selfhood, human identity, are all *inner* things, and are pure quality, purely qualitative, without a trace of quantitative dimension. 'Inability to think deeply' is descriptively accurate, but slightly misleading: the depth and its contents are already there, in the nature of things, before and whether or not we 'think' about them. It's more like a blindness, or an imprisonment, or a mutilation. We just can't see it, can't get there, lack the faculties. Nor do we any longer have access to the categories, religious and philosophical, upon which depth of thought depends—a calamity quite sufficient in itself to eradicate depth from our lives. These also are invalidated; to the prosaic mentality, actually meaningless. And there's an element of fear here as well. Fear, guilt, bad conscience, bad faith: *mauvais foi*. Hypocrisy. We don't want to know this damning truth about ourselves, which means that on some level we *do* know it. The computers don't know it, the 'strong A.I.' guys don't know it, Technique doesn't know it, Capital doesn't know it, and Progress, of course, can't know it, but wherever our humanity survives we know it. Know it, and deny it. Because, as I have suggested, we know full well that nothing can be done. Quantification, emphasis on methods, efficiency and objectivity, on facts and action, all are a flight from reality. From direct confrontation with... what? What should we call it? Truth? Hopelessness? Ourselves? It makes perfect sense that we should become 'prosaic'.

The prosaic man is interested in what I shall call clear-cut boundaries. He wishes to have things sharply defined. He wants to know exactly what is meant, exactly what the facts are, exactly what constitutes his rights and

duties and exactly how to proceed. He hates what he calls blurred boundaries and sees them as a source of misunderstanding, confusion, inefficiency
and conflict. He is determined to find out where to 'draw the line'.
Clear-cut boundaries are another chief concern of much of practical life. We
want to know whether a certain train runs or doesn't; we want a shoe that is
Size 9 to have definite dimensions; we want to know, if we have business with
an institution, which department to apply to and which officer has certain
responsibilities; we want to know exactly what our insurance premium is and
exactly what the company will pay in each clear-cut set of circumstances...
Operating an automobile is a far more clear-cut affair than driving a horse
and carriage. Preparing a meal from pre-cooked, frozen foods is a much
more clear-cut procedure than most real cooking. The duties and activities of
a person employed by a modern organization that is steeped in the principles
of technical efficiency, 'scientific management', applied psychology, sociological surveys, economic analysis, and 'human engineering' are infinitely more
clearly defined (or are meant to be) than were those of men working in earlier
times.

And what lies beyond the world of clear-cut boundaries, what does *not*
have clear-cut boundaries? What is being excluded and invalidated, and
indeed slandered here? I run the risk of becoming repetitious. Quantification, method, 'clear-cut boundaries'—all serve the same purpose, reflect the
same condition and achieve the same end. Things 'tighten', congeal, crystal-
lize, geometrize, 'flatten', in the *Kali-Yuga*. There is the feeling of a last-ditch
defense. The desperate invention of ways to 'hold out', 'keep it together',
'carry on'. *Fill the time.* When the inner life is gone. The true purpose, the
true goal, the joy, the great inexpressible divine Joy that we and the universe
actually are in our Oneness: gone. When the inner life is gone, when there's
something inadmissible beneath the surface, an emptiness, and we still can
faintly, or acutely, or bitterly or nostalgically remember what should be, and
once was there, and we just can't face it, can't face what happened. Clear-cut
boundaries are at least reassuring; something we can hold on to, something
we can talk about with a show of confidence. Manuals, regulations, rule-
books, all the countless 'contracts' lawyers deal with; the forms we scrutinize
with furrowed brows and a vague combativeness and finally, as we always
knew we would, sign and date and put in the mail, satisfied, and subtly
relieved, that things have been taken care of and responsibilities been fulfilled. These hold our world together. They are our bravado; aspects of that
magnificently orchestrated whistling in the dark with which we preserve our
self-respect in the *Kali-Yuga*. Our image, and our nobility. It's right that we

do it. For beings like us, degradation and self-defense coincide, appearing as creativity. We are inescapably profound.

✳

The prosaic man stresses literalness. Whatever is to be understood and communicated he wants to see spelled out in explicit statements. He thinks that stark, literal prose is the only instrument of expression and communication, and sees deviation from such bare, denotative prose as leading to error, miscommunication, and emotionalism… To deal with clear-cut facts and properties, to set out a definite method, to mark sharp boundaries, we need literal prose. We want to avoid all ambiguity, vagueness, and indefiniteness. We want no non-prosaic elements of language to interfere with statements of the facts, rules, methods, regulations, and instructions that occupy our attention.

So whatever cannot be 'pinned down', 'spelled out', 'boiled down' to one simple sentence, reduced to an immediately plain, exhaustive and specific 'point' or 'bottom line', is meaningless.

Earnestness is the path of immortality, thoughtlessness the path of death.
Those who are earnest do not die, those who are thoughtless are as if dead already.
⁓Dhammapada II.21

Anything that eludes literalization, precise formulation, one-to-one correspondence with verifiable empirical data, is meaningless.

The Tao that can be told is not the eternal Tao.
The name that can be named is not the eternal name.
The nameless is the beginning of heaven and earth.
The named is the mother of ten thousand things.
Ever desireless, one can see the mystery.
Ever desiring, one can see the manifestations.
These two spring from the same source but differ in name; this appears as darkness. Darkness within darkness.
The gate to all mystery.
⁓Tao Te Ching, I

Anything that demands reflection, cogitation, figurative interpretation, self-examination and introspection, musing and pondering; that can't be 'put into words', such as, for example, the lessons we have learned from suffering, loss, defeat, endurance, faith, the contemplation of beauty in Nature and tragedy in human affairs—from living the life, in other words: meaningless.

But the Comforter, which is the Holy Ghost, whom the Father will send in my name, he shall teach you all things, and bring all things to your remembrance, whatsoever I have said unto you. Peace I leave with you, my peace I give unto you: not as the world giveth, give I unto you. Let not your heart be troubled, neither let it be afraid.

⁓JOHN 14:26–27

Which means that all the great Answers our humanity inherits, the Answers to those great Questions whose asking defines our humanity, are meaningless, as our failure to ask them, or to need them answered, is proof of our extinction. What is all this? Who am I? Why am I here? What must be accomplished before I die? What is the truth, and how can I know it? Meaningless questions now. When the Answers were invalidated, so were the Questions. And the Questioner.

For the man of the intellectual type, on the contrary, the contingent facts of existence are immediately apparent as such, they are as it were transparent; before asking 'what do I want?' he will ask 'what is the world?' and 'what am I?', which determines in advance a certain detachment with regard to forms and desires. It is true that he may have attachments in virtue of heavenly realities which shine through their earthly reflections; the most contemplative child can be strongly attached to things which, in the human desert with which destiny may have surrounded him, seem like reminders of a Paradise both lost and immanent. However that may be, it is the Invisible which is the reality for the deeply contemplative man, whereas 'life is a dream' (*la vida es sueno*); in him the Platonic sense of beauty takes the place of brute passion.

⁓SCHUON

In the effulgent lotus of the heart dwells Brahman, who is passionless and indivisible. He is pure, he is the light of lights. Him the knowers of the Self attain. Him the sun does not illumine, nor the moon, nor the stars, nor the lightning, nor, verily, fires kindled upon the earth. He is the one light that gives light to all. He shining, everything shines. This immortal Brahman is before, the immortal Brahman is behind, this immortal Brahman extends to the right and to the left, above and below. Verily, all is Brahman, and Brahman is supreme.

⁓MUNDAKA UPANISHAD, II.10–12

All the great Answers: meaningless. And the Questions also. And the Questioner.

Specific answers are complemented by specific actions. Hence, in the prosaic mentality the only questions concerning the world that are considered to have meaning are questions that admit of answers leading to, or provided by, clear-cut, definite actions... Questions that do not lead to clear-cut operations in the physical world are meaningless—and this renders meaningless most of our mental life.

Action, what is happening: that is reality. We speak approvingly, admiringly, of a 'man of action'. Sylvester Stallone, Arnold Schwartzenegger, Bruce Willis, Chuck Norris—to mention only the brightest lights in the current wave of descendents of the immortal John Wayne—these are all men of action. (The first three of these engaging two-fisted fictions have just opened a restaurant in New York called 'Planet Hollywood', which is as perfect a name for the hyper-real world of the *Kali-Yuga* as could be conceived. Marvelously incisive, a truly brilliant inspiration. The *Yuga* in two words.) *Action solving problems*: that's what life is, that's what it's all about. The ongoing story of historical society, the philosophy of the *Kali-Yuga*. Its symbolic form, its 'art form', is professional sports, our supreme spectacle; the great athletes, specialists in solving problems by taking immediate action, are our idols, our 'real-life' heroes. Their staged exploits are transmitted and choreographed with matchless technical virtuosity—split screen, instant replay, slow motion, interspersed film clips—their personalities and drama created, and their statistics unveiled, on television, where alone their world exists, and alone they are real.

Insistence on explicit answers and clear-cut actions has a far-reaching effect on everyday life. It means that one must always have a definite project, a clear program or plan. Hence the prosaic man is forever incapable of considering issues in depth. He stays at the surface; he remains with things that permit readily specifiable action. He entertains no questions with respect to life, man, or society that do not obviously lead to specific things to do. Everything else, it seems to him, is mere words—idealistic, not realistic; sentimental, not practical. Confronted with a difficulty, the prosaic man gets busy: he works at one thing and works at another; he changes, modifies, and manipulates; he institutes projects and programs; he raises funds, erects buildings, forms societies, appoints committees, holds meetings, collects data, writes reports, develops techniques, and makes rules. And he does all this without ever asking a single fundamental question, without ever attending to such basic things as the aims, underlying assumptions, values, or justificatin of what he is dealing with and what he is doing. Therefore all his busyness—restless, nerve-wracking, and exhausting—*is at bottom only a tinkering and an accelerating of what already exists.* (emphasis added)

This is finely said. No depth, on a one-way trip. In the *Kali-Yuga*, 'understanding the situation' and 'spelling out your agenda' are synonymous, and not by violence or fiat but genuinely so, in the nature of things. Reality has been squeezed to the surface, restricted to the domain of activity, reduced to the quantifiable externals, to *the problem*; in such a universe, it's really true that understanding means devising and executing a plan of action. They are one and the same thing. Ideally, we 'take the bull by the horns'. Those who have no opinion about what should be done quite simply have no conceivable relationship to the issue at hand. They are 'out of it'. To assume that there is some contemplative or spiritual 'solution to the problem' which is being invalidated or excluded from consideration by incorrigible activists would be an error. Once reality has been defined as the arena of action, once action alone is real, the circle has been closed, 'it's a whole new ballgame', where to perceive things in their depth is to disqualify oneself from participation in the affairs of the world. The prosaic mentality reflects and perpetually reproduces a prosaic world. There are sincere partisans of social causes—we've all known them, and many of us been one—who choose wilful blindness in this situation. 'Oh, I don't look into it that deeply. What would be the use of it, what would be the point? I'd be paralyzed.' To argue that contemplative modes of action, such as the *karma-yoga* of the Gita or the *wu-wei* of Taoism are called for here, in the *Kali-Yuga*, would be a misreading of the tradition. The first is a means of sustaining an inner disengagement, preserving detachment and a sacrificial devotion to God, a means of defending oneself against contamination by worldliness; the second is precisely a doctrine of non-interference—going with the grain, trimming sails to the wind, swimming with the current, stooping to conquer—aiming at the preservation of harmony, or extinction in the Tao. Neither is anything like a technique for attaining ends, or 'solving problems'. Religion, as genuine spirituality rather than a temporal institution, has never been a strategy for influencing the course of events, or for achieving worldly success in any interpretation of the word. The saints and sages bear witness to the immortal Dharma; what follows is out of their hands. Love is the Answer, Compassion is the Answer, Charity is the Answer, of that there is no doubt: but not to problems. Problems are perceived and 'tackled' by the prosaic man.

His orientation toward the world is epitomized in a question he is always asking: 'What's the problem?' And a problem, for him, is something that can be plainly stated, got hold of, and solved. He looks at the world as if he were studying Euclidean geometry, going from problem to problem—either dealing with those that present themselves or, often, looking for new ones to apply his method to. Since he reduces everything in the world to a problem, his awareness is extremely superficial and narrow.

And when nothing stands in the way, no reason why it can't be done, when we can cheerfully proceed with the job, when God's in his heaven and all is right with the world, we say 'No problem!' Action alone is real, motivated with equally heartening clarity by both the presence and absence of problems. Like Ellul's 'technique', Morgan's 'prosaic mentality' is one of the many faces of the *Kali-Yuga* that are invisible to us because they are our own.

One problem the Americans admitted they had not taken into account was the effect of the extra corrosion caused by the salt water on the efficiency of the incinerator. There were also doubts about what would happen to the emissions from the incinerator's smoke stacks which contain dioxins and furans, another toxic chemical. The army took the view that any dangerous quantities would disperse before they reached Hawaii 680 miles away. (Subsequently test burns of the incinerators during this month have gone wrong after a series of mechanical failures and the programme has been delayed.)

Collective enterprise in the *Kali-Yuga* focuses on the deployment of techniques in an objective theatre of operations, as I said at the opening of this discussion. More specifically, it deploys those techniques to solve a *present problem*, the key word here being *present*. The actual roots of the 'problem', which can only be inner, and only identified through self-examination in the light of wisdom—just as the 'problem' can only be 'solved' through a penitential transforming experience—do not exist in the objective theatre of operations, the world of action and technique, which is alone real to the protagonist, and are therefore non-existent as the protagonist defines reality A *self*, the protagonist's *self*, is non-existent. There is only the 'problem', and 'the one best way'. Even the details of the problem's objective history only 'enter into the calculations' insofar as knowledge of them contributes to the selection of the best, most efficient, most 'cost-effective' solution. I find a parallel to this approach, a societal and technological background, in the following observation, by Neil Postman, about the relationship of television to time:

Television cannot communicate a sense of the future or, for that matter, a sense of the past. It is a present-centered medium, a speed-of-light medium.

Everything we see on television is experienced as happening *now*. The grammar of television has no analogue to the past and future tenses in language. It amplifies the present out of all proportion...

The present alone is vivid. We must *act*, and the only time and place we can act is the present. This is 'The Now Generation'. Television 'news' presents reality as *what is happening today*. TODAY is, or was, I believe, the name of a television news program. I think TONIGHT also. The protagonist in the *Kali-Yuga* lives in the instantaneous speed-of-light world of television, 'telemanity' is 'telereality', and perceives itself as it would appear on television, as 'news'. In varying degrees and circumstances, it 'swings into action' in order to be 'chosen' by television and win the magic transfiguration into present reality. Through its ubiquity and its 'present centered' nature, television casts yet another light on the spirit of collective enterprise. For just as only a living consciousness has a self, so only a living consciousness has a past, a depth in time, that presence of biography we call experience. Machinery, however, the ensemble of techniques, because it is insentient, pure objectivity, because it is simply matter in motion, like any physical machine, because it is *dead*, has neither. No self, no past. Mumford's Megamachine, Ellul's Technique, Morgan's Prosaic Man, collective enterprise in the *Kali-Yuga* stands frozen in the icy unyielding objectivity of the present technological moment, staring resolutely into the 'challenge' of the present problem. Limited forever to the mental space between the 'problem' and the 'solution'—the space where projected contingencies (the future), information gained from previous experiments (the past), and scientific knowledge (the facts) are transformed into the data that will enable 'the one best way' to be determined—and achieving there its successes which always reveal themselves to be another problem. Insofar as we are television reality, insofar as we are mechanism, the Power System, we have no past, no future and no self.

What, then, are we? The News. The ensemble of techniques. The current spectacle, *cause celebre*, 'burning issue', 'topic of conversation'. The furious transience, the circulation of commodities, money. ('Money thereby directly and simultaneously becomes *the real community*...' [MARX, the *Grundrisse*]. This is one of Marx's most important sentences, by the way. Tucked away back in there on page 225. Absolutely fundamental to our self-understanding, a dazzling illumination.) Statistics, percentages, Dow-Jones, GNP, the genetic code, the print-out, the website. Motorists, users, shoppers, consumers, viewers, and fans. All these things. But basically, we are the absence of our selves. Our truly human Self. And although that sounds final, we can go even further on this: one step further: because we are separated from Reality, which is *inner*, what we are is incomprehensible. It's something like nothing. The *Kali-Yuga* is a volition of God, Lord of the Universe, Eternal Truth. Our Creator. Like Him, it is Absolute. 'Mind and speech return baffled from That.'

> The worst case accident with the nerve gas that the Americans envisaged was if a civilian aircraft missed the runway and hit one of the dozens of munitions bunkers. A single breached bunker would cause a poisonous cloud up to 200 miles out to sea but it would be sublethal before it reached any populated islands, the environmental impact study says. In normal circumstances, says the US Army, the exhaust from the incinerator would have a negligible effect because any toxins would be dispersed. The Pacific islanders do not accept that because they fear the effect on the food chain.

✳

Now I have been leading up to something here, and occasionally hinting at it. To the name of the vacuum, as it were. Johnston Island and collective enterprise in the *Kali-Yuga*, the insights we gain from Ellul, Morgan and Postman: we haven't grasped their full import until we have given its proper name to what is missing. The name of what comes to mind immediately—or *should* come to mind!—as conspicuously absent in the Johnston Island affair and in all collective enterprise in the *Kali-Yuga*, and which alone provides meaning, substance and cause for hope to actions addressed to the rectification of things, to all acts of restoration, mending, correcting, curing, healing, setting aright. Specifically, to confronting and dealing with unanticipated destructive consequences of one's own actions. That what's missing is the inner dimension of life, which is where our humanity resides, is of course obvious and has been a central theme from the outset. But it's a particular property or potential of that inner dimension that wants to be named here. When it is, and the picture is complete, we'll be able to add one more to the list of snares, devices and misrepresentations with which the *Kali-Yuga* seeks to deceive our hope, but can no longer.

On the day-to-day level, the name of the vacuum is remorse, regret, 'feeling sorry' or 'feeling bad'. The experience of rue, of 'recognizing the error of one's ways', and the resolve to 'turn over a new leaf', and never do anything like that again. Humility. Chagrin. These emotions are assumed normal and appropriate, and we are expected to admit and be instructed by them, and to make such resolutions, to examine ourselves before, during and after making amends, if our setting things aright is to have any durable significance. If, on the other hand, we simply try to set things back in place with a mechanical diligence, without any 'inner work'—and even worse, with the nonchalance, breezy self-assurance and mindless macho pluck that characterize contemporary large-scale projects such as Johnston Island and their prototypes on television—that would indicate that we haven't really understood or learned anything from the episode, and, remaining therefore the same person, will only go on to do the same kind of mischief in the future. 'Soul-searching', not the repairing or replacing or cleaning up, is the essential thing.

But the scale of 'unanticipated destructive consequences' of collective enterprise in the *Kali-Yuga* calls for something rather more serious and deeper reaching than the familiar sequence beginning with regret and ending with a determination to 'change one's ways.' We're talking about genocide and ecocide here. The worship of Mammon, and a patronizing contempt for the 'notion' that there might be a God somewhere, or a Law, a Truth. Extinction of species and irreversible defilement of the atmosphere and oceans, the wanton pillage of a whole world in an orgy of greed and power-celebration: all-out war against a planet and its life. Against Creation. Madness. (How cliche these incredible truths have become! The Judgment sounds like a string of platitudes!) True, Capital and Technique are impersonal mechanisms; but on the other hand, there's nobody here but us. Capital and Technique are what we made of ourselves.

The adequate term is *metanoia*, from the Greek, and the classic exposition is in Coomaraswamy's essay, 'On Being in one's Right Mind'.

Metanoia, usually rendered by 'repentance', is literally 'change of mind' or intellectual metamorphosis. Plato does not use the word, but certainly knows the thing: for example, in *Republic*, 514F, the values of those who have seen the light are completely transformed, and, in *Laws*, 803C–804A, we are told that those who have realized their true relation to and actual dependence on God will be 'thinking otherwise than they do now'… and the *Shepherd of Hermas* is certainly not misinterpreting the real meaning of metanoia when he says that 'Repentance is a great understanding' and, in fact, a transformation from the state of the fool to that of one possessed of intellect… Metanoia is, then, a transformation of one's whole being; from human thinking to divine understanding… To repent is to become another and a new man.

Metanoia, as Coomaraswamy goes on to point out, implies the existence of another 'voice' within us, a higher Presence; it implies that there are two selves, a higher Self and a lower self, that *duo sunt in Homine*.

> The mind is said to be twofold:
> The pure and also the impure;
> Impure—by connection with desire;
> Pure—by separation from desire.
> ⁓Maitri Upanishad, 6.34

> God compacted (man) of... two substances, the one divine, the other mortal.
> ⁓Hermes

> Two men are in me: one wants what God wants;
> The other, what the world wants, the devil, and death.
> ⁓Angelus Silesius

In Coomaraswamy's words:

> Metanoia is a 'change of mind' differing only in its larger implication from the change of mind that has taken place when we repent of any intention. When we do this, it is because we feel ourselves to be now 'better advised' and so able to act, 'advisedly'. Whose advice are we taking? Who gives counsel when we 'take counsel with ourselves'?

Coomaraswamy then catalogs some of the many names of the 'counselor' within us, as these names appear in the various spiritual traditions. From Plato, the Leader, Reason, Mind, Genius: the best, most divine, ruling and eternal part of us: the Immortal Soul which 'is our real Self' (*Laws* 959A) and of which 'we' are to be the servant. 'How otherwise, indeed, should "thy will be done on earth as it is in heaven"?' The 'immanent divinity' which is Philo's 'Soul of the souls', Hermes' 'Good Genius' and the 'Shepherd' of Hermas. The Scholastic 'Synteris', Meister Eckhart's '*Funkelein*', and our own Conscience, 'however attenuated.' Paul's 'Yet not I, but Christ within me' (Gal. 2:20). The Vedic 'Self of the self, called the Immortal Leader' (*Maitri Upanshad*), 'Inner Controller' and 'Self and King of all beings' (*Brihadaranyaka Upanishad*), 'immortal incorporeal Self' (*Chandogya Upanishad*), and 'That' of the famous dictum, *mahavakya*, 'That art thou.' And, we might add, Buddhism's 'Big Mind' or 'Zen Mind', or simply 'buddha-nature', the Taoist 'Stillness' or 'Virtue', 'True', 'Perfect' or 'Sacred Man', and the Heart-Intellect of pure metaphysics. The angel on your shoulder, the inner Presence or Light, the 'still small voice'. Your 'original Face before your mother and father were born.' All these are hypostases of God.

I am in all hearts.
I give and take away
Knowledge and memory.
I am all that the Vedas tell.
I am the Teacher,
The Knower of Vedanta.
⌁BHAGAVAD GITA

Coomaraswamy concludes:

> To resume: in the first part of this article our intention was to show that
> what 'repentance' really means is a 'change of mind', and the birth of a 'new
> man' who, so far from being overwhelmed by the weight of past errors is no
> longer the man who committed them; and, in the second part, to outline the
> doctrine of the duality of mind on which the possibility of a 'change of mind'
> depends, and to demonstrate its universality; to point out, in other words,
> that the notion and necessity of a metanoia are inseparably bound up with
> the formulations of the *Philosophia Perennis* wherever we find them.

It was Coomaraswamy's essay that first came to my mind when I read the
article on Johnston Island in the *Guardian*. It seemed to me that the absence
of metanoia was the whole deep invisible truth of the matter, and indeed of
all the seemingly conscientious collective enterprise in the *Kali-Yuga*, civic or
environmental, with which our apprehension is repeatedly sedated. Following that, the relevance of Ellul's 'Technique' and Morgan's 'prosaic mentality', and of the other vantage points I have suggested here, seemed clear
enough.

Now it could be argued that the expectation of a collective metanoia is
misplaced, that metanoia only occurs within the individual soul. That a
metanoia on the part of historical humanity is impossible, both for the reason just given and because, even granting the theoretical possibility of
'cumulative' metanoia, the sum of countless individual transformations, the
present condition of terrestrial humanity, as it has been diagnosed here and
elsewhere, makes such a proposal laughable.

But that is precisely the point.

Drive it home. Absence of metanoia: absence of anyone at all.

Those who have never wept for the Earth will not save it, for they never
loved it. How could they have loved it if they never wept for it? Could we
claim to have loved a daughter who died, if we never wept for her? Mercifully, they'll never know it's gone, never know it's lost forever, because for
them it was never there. Never know they are lost forever either. They've

been watching television, and now they're indistinguishable from television, and they'll go on watching television, where 'nature programs' and 'natural scenery' are breathtaking on the imperishable film. Hyper-reality, the world in which everything is simulated and only the simulated is real, is here. This is it. And none of this matters because Technique, technological humanity, is at one with its new state, its 'New Age', its final transformation labelled, with an unintentional precision and significance of which its blissful celebrants are blissfully unaware, the Omega Point. No one is damaged because the damage measurement doesn't exist in television society, information society, entertainment society. The humanity which can be damaged by television and Technique is rendered extinct, every day, by television and Technique themselves, by the merciful stupefaction of the screens: no one suffers. By videos, by the instant replay, by the Sales Effort and the data merchants, by the identification of human beings with their commodities. A new being, Capital, the Megamachine and the Worldwide Web, Technique and Telemanity, Planet Hollywood, is produced and reproduced. It cannot mourn or resurrect a Nature it never knew, or a Self it has forgotten. This is the *Kali-Yuga*. Hear the music! The Dance of Siva molto crescendo! The glorious cycle is fulfilled. The stars and the pine trees, the surf and the red dawn and the bright eye of the housecat. The hawks and the butterflies, the wild horses and the whales and the sailfish and the little minnows, the wind in the leaves, the shadows on the grass, the sound of the rain and the streams, the snow on the mountains, and all the flowers, the flowers, the incredible flowers. The colors. All that infinite Beauty, that Glory, that ineffable Joy, that leap in the heart. The rainbow and the lullaby, dixieland, cabaret and bluegrass rock 'n roll, the music, the singers, and the smile of love that fills the waiting world. It cannot be named or known, it is myriad, measureless, unutterable in every instant: our Life in that Garden, our Oneness in that Truth, that Divinity, that Beatitude. Fulfilled. That boundless Grace, for 'I was a hidden treasure, and I wanted to be known, so I created the world.' Fulfilled.

I believe that it is only in the context of cyclical unfolding that the insights of the writers I refer to in these pages, and all the truly serious and profound commentaries on our times, acquire their full and final meaning.

And you know what it is? You know what it is? The *Kali-Yuga* happens to people you love. You see the inner shape, the real one, when they're just walking away across the room with their backs to you, you see their secret faces when they're alone, and you see that they're trudging, their shoulders hunched and rounded under the burden, their faces baffled and bewildered, almost muttering, but still defiant, still determined, because they're human, and their demand, their consciousness of birthright, is ineffaceable, ineradicable. The divine imprint. His image. And you think they haven't got a chance, but then again you can't really know. God alone knows their fate. It happens to the people you love. That's what breaks your heart. Breaks your heart.

Environmental groups have also expressed concern for the 1,100 personnel involved in the operation at Johnston. Currently soldiers have been drafted in to construct a wharf on the island to take the Nato shipments. It is being built in an area already contaminated by agent orange. It also contains plutonium dust from the three aborted test missile shots of 1962 which brought live nuclear warheads crashing down on the island. Details of this disaster had never previously been revealed. For the Hawaiian islanders Marsha Joyner gave evidence at a meeting with the US military claiming that the interests of one million Pacific people, the whales, monk seal, green sea turtles, fish of all kinds and a food source for most of the world had been ignored.

XVIII

Remember What the Dormouse Said! Feed your Head! Feed your Head!

∽ With Thanks to Grace Slick

I would like to gather together at this point some brief reflections and commentaries on aspects of our lives in the *Kali-Yuga* which, given the ground we have covered, should not require elaboration. They follow: indications, implications, interpretations, links, 'Signs of the Times'.

Few people, if any, actually experience 'our collective guilt' over the genocide of the Native American, or the West's genocide of the whole world's indigenous humanity. This 'guilt' is a media event, paraded out at indicated intervals and occasions, and is simply another lineament, a rather minor one, in the composite identity which historical humanity has no choice but to assume and doggedly transmit to succeeding generations. History must be a part of every child's education, for, as we have seen, in the absence of transcendence, of Truth, of initiation into the sacred knowledge that we are immortal souls and the divine wisdom that sets us out upon the immortal Path, only the transient, only the perishable and ambivalent, define us. Define us, and bind us: to illusion, to mortality, to the ego with its anxious inconclusive biography and its faithful shadow of fear.

But when people do think about it, about 'native peoples' and their fate, I believe the feeling is not guilt—'How can I be guilty of crimes I never committed? That all happened before I was ever born'—but something like a haunting intuition of racial suicide. Not genocide, but suicide.

Because we know that we ourselves don't count: that, incredible as it sounds, we must be regarded as the descendants of the humans, ourselves not human, or not *quite* human: because we're losing it, 'losing the secret of how to make ourselves human', as Mumford put it. They were fully human, we are not. They were real, we are not. They were simply what they were: we are some kind of freak which is neither this nor that. They were part of Nature, the Earth, Creation, they were 'natural', fitting into the landscape like the trees and the mountains: we are strangers, invaders, unpredictable and fearsome, destroyers of Nature. They were essential good with acciden-tal evil, we are essential evil with accidental good. (Genocide was suicide, and ecocide is matricide. The Earth is our Mother: this is a fact, a great spir-itual truth, and in what remains of our authentic humanity we all know it.) The *Kali-Yuga* is the age of racial suicide. That is what we have been discuss-ing here, what it's all about. Suicide.

✳

We become aware of the horrified, futile and tireless urgency with which we try to awaken people to their situation, their condition. Try to make them see, for example, that 'Judge Thomas' and 'Anita Hill', 'O.J. Simpson' and 'Princess Di', 'President Clinton' and 'Monica Lewinski', do not exist and should not pollute their consciousness, 'Thomas' and 'Hill' and all the many millions. Human pseudo-events. Try to make them conscious—I think of the 'tactful teaching' concept, the 'artful methods' ex-pounded in the Threefold Lotus Sutra—of the innumerable ways they are being manipulated, administered, deceived, degraded, misdirected, assassi-nated… Aware of the futility, but never resigned.

Primary grade school-children now write their letters to Santa Claus on computers, send him email. Santa Claus, the closest thing to Christ we could come up with in these trying times. Computers: the mind-less magical mechanism that replaced collective self-confidence and self-respect, collective dignity, intrinsic prestige. In each case, shallowness replac-ing depth, death replacing life: Life Eternal, for that matter. So we teach them 'boot up' and 'return' and 'escape', with misgivings, sinking hearts. How can they think anything but that this is 'rad'? We guide their fingers. Or they guide ours. What's the difference? The clumsy hand-written letters left on the kitchen table or trustingly handed to parents were 'closer to the bone', that's all, closer to what we were long before Santa Claus was activated. Every little thing counts.

The ferocious emphasis on action, on doing, and on speed, cannot but have a corrosive effect on the opposite approach to life's opportunities and challenges, which is thoughtfulness. And the dispraise and effacement of thoughtfulness must, in turn, contribute to the ubiquity of violence, which is mindless by definition. Two-fisted Bruce Willis 'thinks on his feet'. He thinks with his fists. Among all the myriad characters we are offered by the media—as fiction or hyper-reality—are there any contemplatives? Any who are not defined solely by what they (generally violently) do or have done to them? Actions, and the passions which generate them: this is what we are made of, 'the passional humanity of the Iron Age' (SCHUON), our lives in the *Yuga*. Withering away of the inner, the contemplative, limitless development and elaboration of the possibilities latent in the outer, one of which is violence. The *Kali-Yuga explodes*.

Paralleling this, the tremendous fixation upon physical culture, on the *body*, statistics and measurements associated with its feats of prowess and endurance, its records, the procedures, practices and preparations that will enhance its desirability and prestige. ('The Vedanta expressly mentions the conviction, 'I am the body', as being the doctrine of the demons', Schuon remarks in *Stations of Wisdom*. And the latest miracle pharmaceutical, Viagra, of course, *prolongs identification with the body!* Our hand is unerring.) The fascination with all the things that can be done with and to *bodies*. 'LIFTS, LASERS AND LIPOSUCTION: THE COSMETIC SURGERY BOOM. We have seen the face of the future, and it is wrinkle-free.' (*Newsweek*) 'It's not only in your dreams that you can look like a movie star… Cosmetic dentistry can whiten, straighten, lengthen, shorten and completely reshape teeth… Cindy Crawford: People are paying big bucks for a radiant grin like hers.' (*San Francisco Chronicle*) 'The whole key in life is to make your body look great, whether by exercise or fashion. Give me a good line body-wise, and I'm fearless.' These words, from *Seventeen* or *Young Miss*, are attributed to 'Donna-Karen', who is perhaps the nude young girl shown back-view waist-deep in same kind of soapy blue foam, arms raised in spontaneous transport and looking back at us over her shoulder laughing with sheer joy, in the accompanying, and presumably confirming, illustration. (The *Taittiriya Upanishad*, I might point out, questions her claim regarding the roots of fearlessness. 'When one realizes the Self, in whom all life is one, changeless, nameless, formless, then one fears no more. Until we realize the unity of life, we live in fear.') Here, in all the things that can be done with bodies, are fun and excitement, ecstasy and awe, success, admiration, envy, rewards and glamour. In the *Kali-Yuga* we are, with terminal vengeance, our bodies. 'What we eat', what you see in the photograph or video, what showed up on the CAT-scan and the MRI. The instant replay, the lightning-speed kaleidoscope of disconnected sequences in the television commercials, the abrupt jumpcut to the line of dancers: bodies too *explode* in the *Kali-Yuga*.

In what follows we should recall that 'the contrast between past and present' is always a metaphor. 'Traditional' means a human norm, the *Kali-Yuga* its repudiation, disintegration, surrogate, perversion: its absence. Which all the ingenuity of technological propaganda cannot prevent us from feeling, suspecting, fearing. And knowing.

In traditional societies there was a reciprocity, a continuous dialogue, between 'the individual' and the sacred norms and forms originating in *illo tempore*, outside of time: the archetypes, mythical or scriptural. The proven and permanent models of restraint, propriety, responsibility, deference, courage, correct procedure, etc., which composed the constellation of forms and relationships that insured societal coherence and harmony and an unbroken fidelity to heaven. Received or revealed Wisdom. Recollection of the Origin, the Center, the Supreme Cause. Individualism, meaning deviation or innovation, was discouraged as a threat to the community and the Way.

These archetypal roles and patterns, ideally — for everywhere we are imperfect — offered opportunity for growth, reward and spiritual realization to everyone (if not immediately in this life then in the next, of whose existence they had no doubt) in just measure on the basis of merit accrued, and certainly the prescription for attaining peace of mind: they led 'upward'. There, in the dialogue between individualist rebellion, which in the dialect of this humanity was simply immaturity, or 'the passions', and archetypal fulfillment, the drama of life and character unfolded. Upon this background, democracy and egalitarianism cannot but appear 'progressive' to our modern minds, as the hierarchical social structures that characterized these traditional constellations can only appear unjust, oppressive or corrupt. But such is the paradox. As belief in their divine sanction and prototype faded, and alternative interpretations breached the walls, discontent and skepticism were born, and the shattering of the now oppressive stabilities was determined: this is History. The Tibetan 'peasants' didn't know they were being exploited by their 'landlords', and didn't hate them, until the Red

Army taught them this most fundamental truth of Marxism-Leninism and they acquired that zenith of Self-Realization called class consciousness. 'Their eyes were opened', they were recruited into the great global 'war of liberation', and they 'tasted freedom.' But even irony is simplistic here, in 'the relative world'. As I said earlier, we are inescapably profound: our name is paradox.

At any rate—for I have in mind a parallel here—in the *Kali-Yuga* there is also a reciprocity, a dialogue: in this case between 'the individual' and the degraded, moronic constantly changing images of the media-commodity world which is our reality. These images compose an incoherent chaos and are even, very often marginally, anti-social in themselves. They are not human, their promise is always false: they are empty and identification with them always makes us feel empty (or nervous, phoney, competitive, suspicious, estranged), and they lead 'downward'. Individualism, meaning anything totally self-centered, is encouraged as a means to and evidence of 'fulfillment'. Here, in the maneuvers of a suspicious and covertly desperate conversation between self-centeredness (the individual) and emptiness (the images), the videos and their viewers meet on equal terms.

Another angle on it.

In traditional society the Way or Truth, composed of the cultural forms and the natural environment as well, 'thought' in everyone's mind. It was a changeless instructive and salvific background, a permanent reference and framework of accountability, indeed it was Reality itself, to which the individual and the society appealed for reorientation into rectitude and confirmation of identity. Here too, in the *Kali-Yuga*, there is a background, which 'thinks' in people's minds—for we are everywhere social beings—but that background is history, 'progress', now above all technology, forever in flux, forever changing. In the absence of tradition, of cosmic invariables, celestial guidance, eternal truths and the enduring landmarks, at once physical and spiritual, of a home in Nature, it 'thinks' transience and uncertainty, 'excitement' and anxiety, innovation and obsolescence, and provides no basis for coherence of personality, rootedness, confidence, meaningful or even intelligible inter-generational relationships, or a sense of the content of life's stages. As the Yuga unfolds, with ever-increasing velocity, the question young people must face, 'What will I be when I grow up?' becomes increasingly problematic, harrowing, quite agonizing for some, and now begins to border on the absurd. The economic vicissitudes, technological 'developments' and ecological twilight which contribute to this travail, and which are freely admitted by official voices (they are 'problems'), are merely a subcategory or consequence of the dynamic background transience, the historical mode itself, which is fundamental.

✳

We assume in our innocent good will, indeed in our right minds, that there is a 'primary reality' out there, autonomous and independent, beneath the feverishly erupting megatons of tapes, videos, films, photographs and the deafening gibberish of the non-stop verbal reports. This is not true. The most important person at the wedding now, and everywhere else, is the one making the video and the wedding is organized and choreographed for the video. (The video of it? Of the wedding? That's just the point. There is no 'it'. There's only the video.) Everything is posed now. Counterfeit. Nature itself is made to 'pose', through the selection of time of day and angle, lighting and filters and shutter speeds and openings, editing and musical accompaniment. By Ansel Adams no less than Walt Disney. And the juxtapositions of trillions of these images, these simulations, these soundbites and marketing gambits and movie and television fantasy worlds, in trillions of combinations and settings, is precisely our 'reality'. What we talk about with each other. Our minds. Baudrillard's hyper-reality. Planet Hollywood. The terminal carnival macabre, the *Kali-Yuga*, escape-proof Prison of Unreality. Age of Racial Suicide. Age of Universal Bullshit.

PHOTOGRAPHY IN THE AGE OF FALSIFICATION
The wildlife photography we see in films, books and periodicals is often stunning in its design, import and aesthetics. It may also be fake, enhanced or manufactured by emerging digital technologies that have transformed— some say contaminated—the photography landscape... Mankind has lived through ages of stone, iron, bronze, exploration, enlightenment, the atom, space. Our own times is, as much as anything else, the Age of Falsification. The nip, the tuck, the face-lift, the silicone implant. The fascination with virtual reality in a world teeming with real realities... The Michael Jordan shoe... The blockbuster movie in which story line and plausibility are sacrificed to digital effects and Dolby Sound... The 'Do people care?' Chevron ads, which have now suckled a whole generation. White female blues singers singing on National Public Radio in exactly the style of old black men from the Mississippi Delta... Nature photography is one part of our culture where authenticity might make a stand. It is dispiriting to see its practitioners turn and go with the flow.
⁓KENNETH BROWER, *Atlantic Monthly*, May 1998

What is experienced in these times, in the *Yuga* we call home, what makes up most experience—and what are our lives but our experience?—are things which are not actually happening and which, furthermore, and most importantly, never happened at all. The world in which 'things happen' in the simple innocent sense that the words imply, in which there is a genuine unfabricated spontaneous reality, is on its way out. And we 'experience' these unrealities at different times, in different places, or many times, or piecemeal; we 'see it again' or 'hear it again'. And someone else also saw it. But not where you saw it, and not when you saw it. And what was 'it'? The terrain of our experience is no longer human, no longer humanly intelligible, no longer terrestrial. We inhabit and are inhabited by an electronic delirium. Terminal labyrinth, hall of mirrors, mad laughter. 'And mere oblivion, sans everything.' (More on this aspect of our fate in the Appendix Technology Update.)

The world came to an end by becoming unreal. That's how it turned out. Who would have guessed it? 'The end of the world'—prefigured in our grinding relentless subterranean apprehension, confessed in the collective desperation crouching with a pounding heart beneath the desperate cheerfulness—doesn't mean (necessarily) that everything blows to smithereens and is gone, the familiar scenario of nuclear holocaust and rubble-strewn radioactive wasteland. There was another way the world could 'come to an end.' It's the Prison of Unreality. Totally invisible, of course, precisely because it's what we see.

Only the Sacred is Real. As all traditions unanimously affirm. Desacralize the universe and humanity, deny God, Divinity, a Creator, Truth, an Absolute both transcendent and immanent, and you lose contact with Reality. You become unreal, and the 'creators' of the unreal. Cheap death. Crap death.

It goes one step further—at this point only technically, but the possibilities are incalculable. I refer to 'Virtual Reality', the current still clumsy cutting edge of computer technology. This is where they put a helmet on you... but there's a first-hand description in the December 12, 1991, San Francisco Chronicle. Alice Kahn was there:

> Coming soon to a mall near you: reality! Well. kind of, sort of... virtually.
> Reality in the '90s is a computer-generated cartoon where you can kill people·

It comes in the form of a game… 'the recreation vehicle of the '90s' in which 'players experience a uniquely realistic artificial world.'

The Virtuality stewardesses place a large helmet with headphones and goggles over the head of each of four players. A joystick is placed in the player's hand from a mobile fannypack that allows the player to move around in the three-dimensional virtual — computer-simulated — space. The game is called 'Dactyl Nightmare', and the object is to find people and shoot them while avoiding being shot or carried away by a pterodactyl. Meanwhile you are still in a nightclub with flashing lights from the psychedelic era… It is the atmosphere of overstimulation and confusion that this younger generation has learned to regard as normal… Dr. Winkie, trendmeister and DV8 owner, slinking around in black Spandex and a Captain Lizard shirt, talks about how the machines represent a phenom he calls 'cyberpunk', where the '60s meet the '90s.' Virtual reality is what kids are looking for when they go to nightclubs to escape reality', says the doctor… 'At malls in England they're already taking in $3,000 a week', says Andy Halliday of Horizon Entertainment.

And from *ELLE Magazine*, February 1992:

THE BRAVE NEW WORLD OF COMPUTER SEX.
SEX IN THE COMPUTER AGE.
From the moment virtual reality was invented, there was speculation about its erotic potential. Can computers be used to create the most exciting sexual partner ever dreamed of? Can technology make all your wildest dreams come true?
You are entering the brave new world of virtual reality (VR to those who are already in the know) — a computer technology in-the-making that is so advanced it almost defies imagining. Virtual reality makes use of the computer to create a simulated three-dimensional environment — one you experience as though it were absolutely real.
IN AN AGE OF FEAR AND REPRESSION, teledildonics, the science of reaching out and touching someone via computer-simulated sex, may be the wave of the future. Techno-erotic trysts will be conducted in the extra-physical realm of cyberspace, giving 'safe sex' a whole new meaning… Part of the general uneasiness with VR may have to do with the fact that it suggests the brink of something we can hardly comprehend. Richard Kadrey likens it to the discovery of photography… 'The first time someone saw a photograph, it was like seeing God,' he says.

Sex and Violence, the two great rivers flowing through the media terrain, the Entertainment/Reality that has become our natural habitat. Science fiction becoming our lives, our lives becoming science fiction. The hollowness and treason of every technological premise and promise revealed without fail in retrospective disillusion. A decision is clearly demanded here. A choice confronts us. How much complicity is inescapable? How much disaffiliation is possible or morally justifiable? Or, going to the heart of the matter, and to the heart of metaphysics, *scientia sacra*, what *sacrifice* is called for here? How can I 'make sacred' my life? For only the sacred is real, and to the degree that I identify with the selves projected, generated and celebrated by this culture I am nothing, and 'To sacrifice is to be born, and it can be said, "As yet unborn, forsooth, is the man who does not sacrifice."' (AKC)

The *Kali-Yuga* is characterized, even defined, by humanity's increasing inability to receive spiritual knowledge, to learn its own truth: therefore its separation from Reality. When someone presumes to speak on this level, even to suggest it, intimate its existence, people become embarrassed or condescending, sometimes even angered, as if the broaching of this subject, the appeal to this depth, is unfair and perhaps a deliberate affront. They don't want to hear it. Even such comparatively simple notions as, for example, 'We ought to have respect for the universe, and therefore always think before we speak,' or 'We ought to feel infinite gratitude for the miracle of existence,' or 'Indulgence provides fleeting pleasures and makes us weak; austerity brings eternal joy, and makes us strong,' or 'The most important thing about you, the only thing you really have and your only source of enduring happiness, is who you are when you're alone,' or 'There's an infinite peace beneath the agitated surface of life,' or 'All this is not really what it appears to be,' or 'The silence within alone is real,' and so on, all that sort of fairly obvious fruit of serious contemplative inquiry, examined experience and 'deep thought', the suspicions, intuitions and private convictions, not to mention the injunctions we find in the Dhammapada, Proverbs, the Gita, the great Sermon of Love and Comfort at the closing of John's Gospel—all these are now sort of unintelligible, sounding vaguely odd or peculiar, 'ancient', antique, even queer: strange, in all that word's meanings. Because they imply truth. Because they are serious about truth. That's the real reason.

Absence of Spirit, absence of Knowledge. Not knowing what we are, we have no way, or motivation, to become what we are. ('The whole task is to

stop being what we are not, and become what we always and already are.')
Remove the veils, inner and outer. Hence the fading out of human presence,
the gradual disappearance of 'the recollected countenance'. Absence of the
Divine, absence of the Human.

With our loss of the sense of the sacred, we've lost the capacity for adoration, for reverence. We 'appreciate the beauty' of Nature—in one of the jit-
tery twitching snatches of time, which is all a 3-seconds-at-the-outside attention span will permit, one of the frenzied instantly-forgotten snippets of
sense impression into which we chop up clock-time, like a series of rapid-fire
discontinuous snapshots, on our desperate exhausting cranky 'vacations'—
but can go no further; in the absence of the Divine we can no more 'situate'
the beauty of Nature than we can 'situate' ourselves: we don't know what it
means, we can't discover its relationship to our own existence, where it fits
in, the common Source—Self, *sunyata*, Tao—in which Nature's beauty and
our moment of 'appreciation' spring into simultaneous existence and fulfill
each other in oneness. Creation was once—*al-an kama kan*, 'And it is now as
it was then', as the Muslim sages often abruptly add, confirming the identity
of the illusory historical 'now' with the Eternal Now of the Beginning—
transparent: we 'saw through it' to the timeless divine Reality, and the shimmering realities—the real world, the 'world in our hearts' with which we are
one—it manifests, for everything is a symbol; we experienced what has been
called 'the metaphysical transparency of things'. In the *Kali-Yuga* Creation
hardens, congeals, becomes *opaque*: mere 'matter', nothing but 'matter'.
Becomes opaque: or we become blind. There's a limitation now, a barrier,
erected principally by the scientific world-view. 'Knowing' the stars to be
'nothing but' balls of flaming gases, of known temperature, mass and volume
and at such-and-such a distance in 'light-years' (numbers, numbers, numbers!), 'knowing' a meadow or waterfall or prospect to be a guidebook feature, one of the 'sights' of a 'national park set aside for recreational purposes,
'knowing' the oceans to be 'H$_2$O' composing 71% of the planet's surface with
a total area of 126,407,000 square miles (335,190,000 square kilometers),
'knowing' the moon to be an 'airless lifeless satellite' with a mean diameter of
2,158 miles (3,473 kilometers) whose distance from the Earth varies between
221,460 miles (356,410 kilometers) and 252,700 miles (406,685 kilometers),
upon which Neil Armstrong and Edwin Aldren's abandoned urine bags
have been alternately freezing and sizzling since July 1969, 'knowing' all these
things and countless more just like them, we have, quite simply, lost the
world. And of course ourselves.

The Western hunt for knowledge, analytic and objective to its core, has violence built into it. For to know analytically is to reduce the object of knowledge, however vital, however complex, to precisely this: an object. This being so, the Western hunt for knowledge, anthropology not excepted, is in a tragic sense the final exploitation…
∼HUSTON SMITH, *Forgotten Truth*

It is domination: intimate, and without respect. Gained Power, lost the world. Blind to Holiness, blind to Reality—for only the Sacred is Real.

Discourse that, in grappling with anything serious, does not appeal either implicitly or explicitly to wisdom, humility, grace, truth, God, love, and their derivatives for its sanction and warrant, in other words to the verities that establish us in reality, is not actually human discourse. Loss of metaphysical intelligence, of our intuition of the Absolute, abandons us, by definition, to a wilderness of contesting relativities. To expedience and quantification, adversarial maneuvers, identification and pursuit of one's own advantage: how else to carry on? We use calculators: we make calculations. 'Computers' instruct our interpretations, priorities and decisions. And distinguish what is real from what is 'subjective'. Those who are called 'computer people' are now the sages. They know the secret of *information*, they understand the arcana of 'programming' and software, email and websites. Human experience, the virtues and values, age, received or acquired wisdom, the fruit of examined ordained suffering, the explanations and injunctions and proposals of Holy Writ, the Word, all count for nothing. The shiny new people with the key to the disk drive are now Intelligence incarnate, the 'change agents, digital thinkers, talent scouts, designers and dreamers who are creating *your* future.' ('Fast Company: The Ultimate Guide to Change', Spring 1999). They know how to use the Machine. Which buttons to push and when. How to give us Information.

Imagine what would happen if all of a sudden the electronic web fell apart completely. No radio, no television, no telephones. Nothing. We'd have to walk out the door and consult with our neighbors. In completely new identities, the identities we had previously assumed only in life-threatening emergencies. The social 'we' would appear, an actual human community.

Face to face, as it had to be at one time. We'd meet each other at last; our very facial expressions, posture, tone of voice and vocabulary would be altered. We would actually became real to each other, we'd have no choice. Actually exist for each other. Bullshit and bullshitters, solid people and 'good heads' would be identified. Our social being, our communal being, is yet another dimension of humanness expropriated from us by technology, in this case primarily by television and the Internet. And this disaster, of course, this tragedy (conceded, once in a blue moon, by the vague term 'alienation') is regarded as just another one of those regrettable but unimportant 'down-sides' of the great 'breakthroughs' (Oh those 'breakthroughs'! 'The Hunt for a CANCER CURE: The Hope—and the Hype—Behind the Latest Breakthroughs', NEWSWEEK cover, May 18, 1998), a disgrace perhaps, perhaps even a scandal, but certainly nothing more, just as drawing attention to it is regarded as mouthing platitudes, whining nostalgia, 'belaboring the obvious'.

> 'Today's British village is not a place but a set of communications systems,' says Robert Worcester, chairman of Market & Opinion Research International (MORI), and Eric Jacobs, a leader writer with Today.'What binds the British into a community with common concerns and anxieties is what they watch on television and read in newspapers.'
> ⌒GUARDIAN OF LONDON AND MANCHESTER, July 9, 1990

We live in the 'global village' of the smiling cheerleader technocrats; or we should say, since this formulation is not quite correct, there is a 'global village', the media and the Net, but it is not human beings who 'live' in it. No one 'lives' in it. The village, after a manner of speaking, 'alters' its unsuspecting inhabitants. Changes them into 'viewers' and 'users'. From 'made in His image' to 'couch potatoes' and 'MUD-players'. (MUD = multiuser domain: an on-line habitat.)

✳

Television is never received seriously, never conceded the respect or commanding stature we formerly granted to living human beings, and still occasionally do even today. At the same time, it is our common reality, and received, talked about, as such. What does this tell us? It tells us that a new 'thing' has appeared in our midst, supplanting a genuine reality but claiming its prestige, and that is *entertainment*. It is not an objective entity, 'out there', simply a technology, but a relationship to ourselves—like Capital, like Technique—in which both 'we' and 'our world' become what seems to deserve the name *trash*: as a metaphysical entity, an essential, and defining quality, *trash*. But perhaps it would be better to say that we and our world become something for which there is no word, since it is an unprecedented and unforeseen condition, for which we need a new word: 'hyper reality', Baudrillard's word, which I have already used here, is as good as any. 'Entertainment' is accurate in one sense, as a word for what has replaced us, but it's a word whose familiar meaning obfuscates its stupendous implications in this context, precisely because it leaves out the simultaneous metamorphosis of the 'audience'. So on the one hand television is simply a spectacle — because its audience, after all, are just viewers — before which we 'relax', a discordant heterogeneous avalanche of images and voices, like an endlessly dumping garbage truck. And on the other hand, it is the only 'reality' we share: through its insane and enormously complex logic it establishes a manipulative artificiality as our latest and final mode of existence, the hyper-reality of simulations that springs into being in all television-times, drones away beneath the surface of our lives between those times, and carves out humanity's latest and final archetype, 'telemanity'. The terrain of human inter-relationship, 'civilization', becomes phantasmagoria, a fever dream, in which this very indictment, like the others, is simply another cliche in the hyper-reality. Closed circle, clanging of the cell door. Not a horrendous revelation: a cliche. The cliche, the actual mindlessness, behind such simultaneously eye-catching and yawn-inducing magazine article titles as: 'IS TV RUINING OUR CHILDREN?' (TIME MAGAZINE, October 15, 1990).

Such are the times. Television has, indeed almost single-handedly, slain humanity. (The Internet, arriving in the nick of time, possesses and animates the corpse.) Nor can this any longer become an 'issue' since humanity's replacement, telemanity, cannot recall its former state and is 'at home' in the present one. No one can be proven damaged, as I have already suggested, because no damage measurement can exist; the inconclusive ambiguity of the numerous surveys is predetermined. Finally, in a completely administered collective reality the intentions of the administrators are irrelevant: the situation itself is a disease. Therefore there is no such thing as a good program: television creates and perpetuates the bad reality in which 'good programs' are shown, for the precise purpose of providing ammunition to its defenders. No one can 'hear' these arguments, they can never assume social relevance, because we all know that nothing is going to stop television, and nothing is going to stop television because no one can hear these arguments. In Ellul's language, the 'ensemble of techniques' is self-generating: *is* 'reality'.

Like the Computer, television is a technology whose import can only be fully grasped by metaphysical intelligence, for it is—again like Technique, like Capital, like the Internet—a metaphysical nemesis: invisible, inherently hostile, malevolent, anti-human and in that ultimate characterization satanic. It knows where the jugular is, and it goes for it. (Because, of course, it is we ourselves; there's nobody here but us, as I have observed already more than once. 'That the soul herself, our "I" or "self" itself, should be the Devil—whom we call the "enemy", "adversary", "tempter", "dragon",—never by a personal name—may seem startling, but it is very far from being a novel proposition… No one will deny that the battleground on which the psychomachy must be fought out to a finish is within you.' Coomaraswamy, in his 'Who is "Satan" and Where is "Hell"?' He quotes William Law: 'It is your own Cain that murders your own Abel…' 'Satan,' remarks Law, 'or which is the same thing, self-exaltation.') There is no way to understand what is happening to us here in the absence of this sober recognition. And if the tone here seems insufficiently sober, it would probably be appropriate at this point to hear how Neil Postman, with greater restraint, but, I believe, similar assessment of television's enormity, says the same thing. I know I have too often lapsed—although I hope understandably, and that allowances will be made—from that 'serenity of spirit' I promised on the first page of this excursion. Postman:

> In the early decades of the twentieth century… a new note had been sounded, and photography and telegraphy set the key. Theirs was a 'language' that denied interconnectedness, proceeded without context, argued the irrelevance of history, explained nothing, and offered fascination in place of complexity and coherence. Theirs was a duet of image and instancy, and together they played the tune of a new kind of public discourse in America.

Postman refers to this 'discourse' as 'the electronic conversation', an ensemble of electronic techniques which 'called into being a new world, a peek-a-boo world, where now this event, now that, pops into view for a moment, then vanishes again, a world without much coherence or sense.' (Postman was writing before the Age of the Internet, the *interactive* 'peek-a-boo world' in which 'the audience' collaborates with its alter-ego assassin, the societal mechanism which is the enemy of its membership: suicidal climax.) This 'peek-a-boo world' came into existence in the late nineteenth and early twentieth centuries,

> But we did not come to live there until television. Television gave the epistemological biases of the telegraph and the photograph their most potent

expression, raising the interplay of image and instancy to an exquisite and dangerous perfection. And it brought them into the home...

To put it plainly, television is the command center of the new epistemology... There is no subject of public interest, politics, news, education, religion, science, sports—that does not find its way to television. Which means that all public understanding of these subjects is shaped by the biases of television. Television is the command center in subtler ways as well. Our use of other media, for example, is largely orchestrated by television. Television arranges our communications environment for us in ways that no other medium has the power to do...

Television has achieved the status of ' meta-medium'—an instrument that directs not only our knowledge of the world, but our knowledge of *ways of knowing* as well.

Prophetic. Replace 'television' with 'the Internet'—the uppercut following the left cross—in the above citations and those that follow, and for that matter throughout the pages of this book, and admire the beautiful consistency of the electronic media's role in our lives.

But even this doesn't go far enough. Television is more than the dominant epistemology, by the very fact that we are unaware of its dominion.

At the same time, television has achieved the status of 'myth' as Roland Barthes uses the word. He means by myth a way of understanding the world that is not problematic, that we are not fully conscious of, that seems, in a word, natural. A myth is a way of thinking so deeply embedded in our consciousness that it is invisible. This is now the way of television.

And it is why we, telemanity, can never seriously ask how television is affecting us. The *Newsweek* article, 'TV's Twisted Reality Trip' ('Real patients! Real crime! Real slime! These shows all exploit their subjects' ordeals. What is it that so fascinates us?'), is not *alarming* to anyone, *and is not intended to be*, but rather passes like a current of air, without leaving the slightest register or imprint of its passage, through the same mindless glassy-eyed reverie the 'slime' flowed through the night before, and will continue to flow through until the end of the cosmic cycle. *Dear Mom and Dad*, a California PTA newsletter, features in vol. 2, no.3 an article titled 'Television—Curse or Blessing' (information gathered from Children and Television, Publication of the National PTA and Children and Television, Communique, Publication of the National Association of School Psychologists), in which three paragraphs are titled 'Television—The Curse' and three titled 'Television—The Blessing'; it concludes with a chart listing five ways to encourage 'Positive Viewing Habits'. The question of how television affects us cannot be seriously asked, and is 'as if one were to ask how having ears and eyes affects us.'

Again Postman:

> The question has largely disappeared as television has gradually *become* our culture. This means, among other things, that we rarely talk about television, only about what is *on* television—that is, about its content. Its ecology, which includes not only its physical characteristics and symbolic code but the conditions in which we normally attend to it, is taken for granted, accepted as natural.
>
> Television has become, so to speak, the background radiation of the social and intellectual universe, the all-but-imperceptible residue of the electronic big bang of a century past, so familiar and so thoroughly integrated with American culture that we no longer hear its faint hissing in the background or see the flickering gray light. This, in turn, means that its epistemology goes largely unnoticed. And the peek-a-boo world it has constructed around us no longer seems even strange.
>
> There is no more disturbing consequence of the electronic and graphic revolution than this: that the world as given to us, through television, seems natural, not bizarre. [Like the world given to us by the Internet.] For the loss of the sense of the strange is a sign of adjustment, and the extent to which we have adjusted is a measure of the extent to which we have been changed. Our culture's adjustment to the epistemology of television [and the Internet] is by now all but complete; we have so thoroughly accepted its definitions of truth, knowledge, and reality that irrelevance seems to us to be filled with import, and incoherence seems eminently sane...
>
> The phrase 'serious television' is a contradiction in terms... Television speaks in only one persistent voice—the voice of entertainment.

Television: voice of Entertainment. Internet: voice of Information. Our voice: Infotainment!

In 1989 the average American spent nearly half of his or her conscious life watching television. Robert Pittman, the founder of MTV (the state-of-the-art program in which lightning-fast clips of heterogeneous images have been spliced together to produce sequences accompanying the latest teen-age popular music), says of MTV (with what point of view, one wonders) that it has 'liberated television from orthodox meaning. The meaning of time, or narrative, or paradox, or necessity, or cause and effect... eliminated the sacred and the profane... and authority as represented by schoolteachers, policemen, clergy, and parents.' A recent poll of high school seniors, asking what they believed in, produced lists including 'everything from God, family, and friends to partying, rock and roll, and Camel cigarettes.' (Both citations from 'Social Education', January 1992)

Telemanity. The zero state. In the *Dear Mom and Dad* PTA newsletter previously referred to, it is consecutively pointed out that 'watching violence on television can increase children's aggressive behavior,' that 'children may become less sensitive to the pain and suffering of others,' 'may be more fearful of the world around them,' and 'may develop distorted views of society since women, young people and the elderly do not appear on the screen as often as they do in real life,' that 'children who grow up constantly entertained by these exciting rapid-paced programs may find listening to a teacher too much effort,' and, finally, that 'since television gives instant pleasure and requires little effort from the viewer, children can escape boredom without thinking, without talking to others, and without developing other interests'; the very next sentence, however, reads 'Television is probably one of the most valuable inventions of the 20th century.' Who writes these words? *What* writes these words? These words and words just like these, work of the same cosmically prolific Author of public discourse in the Age of Universal Bullshit. Who? Why, people, of course! Decent well-intentioned mothers and fathers simply doing their jobs, earning their livings, worrying about their children's grades and the chance of cancer. Our friends and neighbors. What a trip this is! Smile, shake your head and love them.

I have one more television reference to make here, the last one, which I can't resist including because it's about a judiciously choreographed pseudo-event which is fresh in many minds, at least at this writing (this book was written before 'O. J. Simpson' was produced), and it so clearly illustrates, in its obvious implications and extensions, much of what has been said. I may also be unable to resist because I'm always, in the back of my mind, in the basic burning resolve that sustains my tenacity, hoping that some last irresistibly eloquent piece of evidence will finally convince the skeptic: the straw that broke the skeptic's back. Not of some 'fact'—as I've said, proof is not my purpose here—but simply of the possibility that there is in the manifested universe—which means also in Humanity, for they are One—an inherent unfolding, a fundamentally cyclical nature, an inevitability of cosmic dissolution deriving from the fulfillment and exhaustion of potentials and the ever-widening separation from the Origin, the Principle, from God: a Last Age, consequent upon the irreversible Fall Into Time and History and the irreversible loss of the universal sacrality, and therefore of Reality Itself, to which traditional humanity everywhere bore witness, which we have now entered with simultaneous enthusiasm and despair. And further, suggest to the skeptic, *honnete homme*, that we are, in our true being which is the Self, the immortal Atman which is Brahman Supreme — or the buddha-nature, Vedantic *tad ekam*, the Original Face, the Uncarved Block, Christ within us, the Supreme Identity, the Sufic *barzakh* or Heart, or Universal Person, *al-Insan al Kamil, Adam Qadmon* of the Kabbalah, *Anthropos teleios, Fedeli d'Amore.* Taoist *Chun-Jen*, Nirvana, Absolute Absence: the Reality, the Truth, the Godhead with which our Humanity is eternally united in Love and identified in Enlightenment — untouched by that cosmic dissolution, untouched by any cosmic or temporal event whatsoever, utterly untouched: changeless, unreachable, invulnerable and forever free.

Furthermore, this final television reference is included not only as illustrative corroboration, but as evidence, by the simple fact of its casual and unremarkable public existence, of the irrelevance of scandalous or damning disclosure, indeed of discerning self-awareness, in the *Kali-Yuga.* Nothing means anything here. And not even irrelevance; revelation of the outrageous is, like everything else, a marketable item — meaning that in some way it induces people to spend or continue to spend money for something: a commodity, in all the profound meaning Marx gave to the word — and a form of entertainment or diversion, a spectacle, a conversation piece, something to raise eyebrows momentarily: no different from bizarre behavior in a public place or a slice of juicy gossip.

We're talking about the televised 'Clarence Thomas-Anita Hill hearings'.

The following article, by Scott Rosenberg, appeared in the *San Francisco Examiner* on Sunday, October 20, 1991 It is titled 'TV: THE NEWEST BRANCH OF GOVERNMENT':

> The Thomas hearings brought to fruition trial by camera and 'performance' value.
> If any doubt remained that American politics have become a branch of the performing arts, the Thomas hearings dispelled it. They represented the inevitable culmination of a process that began in the 1950s with the Amy-McCarthy hearings and came to full flower during the Reagan presidency. By bringing sexually explicit language and racially charged issues before the mesmerized national audience, the hearings demonstrated that there is no subject over which the court of television does not now hold jurisdiction…
> TV is no longer the 'medium' for American politics — it is the very substance of our public life. Decisions are not first reached and then communicated on

the screen; they are made on, through and by television itself according to its own needs and forms.

We learn a new word here: 'soundbite'. On television, meaning the hyper-real mental landscape within and without, the 'world' that 'has made entertainment itself the natural format for the representation of all experience' (another fine incisive phrase by Neil Postman) and whose 'reality' is presented to us, and implanted within us, 'with a face whose smiling countenance is unalterable' (Postman again), the world of telemanity, the 'soundbite' might be defined as 'that which instantly convinces.' It is 'proof'. Not to a human intelligence, but to something which defies isolation from the hyper-reality itself, from the universe of simulations: 'that which watches television'.

Thomas' *coup de theatre*, the commentators have concluded, was his declaration that the hearings constituted a 'high-tech lynching'. With a little help from his White House and Justice Department friends, the judge had come up with the perfect soundbite—a defining moment of emotional television that will probably be remembered as long as its famous forebear, the moment in 1954 when a lawyer turned to Sen. Joseph McCarthy and said, 'Have you no decency, sir?'

It seems that the metamorphosis into telemanity occurred between 1954 and 1991, which is where Postman places it also: in his terminology, the momentous transition from the Age of Print or Typography or Exposition to the Age of Entertainment or Show Business.

In 'Trial by Television', Michael Straight's account of the 1954 Army-McCarthy hearings—the televised proceedings that broke the back of the McCarthyite witch hunt—the author describes the difference in approach between McCarthy and army counsel Joseph Welch: 'McCarthy never forgot the vast audience. Welch seemed not to remember it... Welch seemed to be conversing respectfully with one individual, and so he gained the audience's devotion in the end.'
In the Thomas hearings, it was Hill who seemed oblivious to the 'vast audience'. She played to no electronic galleries; she didn't seem to realize she was playing at all. That was her undoing. The difference between 1954 and 1991 is that, today, the 'audience's devotion' could only be won by the performer who understood the need to win it.

In other words, the very foundations of reality had shifted, and therefore, of course, the nature of human perception and interpretation, the standards and criteria by which we discriminate between genuine and spurious, actual and apparent, admirable and debased, significant and trivial: real and unreal. It's very important to grasp both the sequence and the totality here: the objective shift in the nature of reality, created by television, occurs *first*, generating a new experiential totality in which discrimination—discernment, judgment, the capacity to weigh and evaluate, draw distinctions—of the types I just mentioned, and all others of any importance, becomes a meaningless term. Not impossible, but meaningless; hyper-reality is, if I may again employ a ringing colloquialism, 'a whole new ballgame'. Where reality itself is a uniform contamination, not contaminated *by* something but *itself* contamination, corruption, derangement, what within that 'reality' is there to choose between? Who within that 'reality' is a human being making choices? And to what end, within that 'reality', will choices be made? The TV audience saw nothing real in the hearings, and never does. It 'sees' its own degradation, its own annihilation as human, there in that very moment in the 'TV room', as in a mirror, and is 'entertained'.

> We say that authenticity is what we value in our public figures—that what we respond to is the moment when a human being drops 'acting' and is 'sincere'. The hearings demonstrated the treacherousness of that wish. The TV camera does not help us distinguish between authentic feeling and dissembling. It simply gives the edge to the performer most capable of simulating authentic feeling, of reproducing the set of signals we've come to associate with honesty.

The actual message of this article is a cynical, 'hard-headed and realistic' submission to the electronic sickness, and can be nothing else insofar as it is a public statement, *insofar as it will be intelligible.*

> You can despise TV for its distortions of political process if you like, but you can't ignore its power. And entering the television courtroom without proper counsel today is as reckless and foolhardy as entering a traditional courtroom without a lawyer. No one knows instinctively how to convey integrity to a video camera—it's a learned skill.
> Thomas' backers railed against Hill's 'handlers'. But all that really meant was that the handlers on his side were savvier than those on hers—they knew that complaining against handling was a good tactic.
> They understood that, on television, you must plan ahead if you want to appear spontaneous. You must control your image if you want to appear genuine. And you must construct a simulacrum of honesty if you hope to convince people you're telling the truth.

The writer uses the phrase 'on television', as if there were somewhere else. But television, known with familiar and affectionate license as the 'boob tube', is collective reality itself. The community. There is no 'somewhere else'. As Postman said it, television 'is a way of thinking so deeply embedded in our consciousness that it is invisible.' Television is our minds.

There's something like a final blinding insight here, in the confrontation with television, in taking its measure. Blinding, rending. It's that television's damage, ultimately, where it really counts, is not inflicted on the children; the hackneyed 'issue' of television's effect upon children is actually a smoke-screen, a red herring, in military terms a diversionary tactic. It's an emphasis that, given a moment's thought, couldn't make sense anyway. Television is a destruction human beings *grow into*: it's the 'adults' who are deformed, who become telemanity, and precisely by never becoming adults, by being pre-vented from receiving what was promised to them at the foundation of the world. Telemanity can profess concern for the welfare of its children, and with that pretext—pretext, for Telemanity is devoid of all substance: it is pure deceit, corruption incarnate—profess concern about the *content* of television, but it is always invisible to itself, which is simply another way of say-ing that television itself is an inviolate institution that can never be seriously examined because there's no one there to examine it. Indeed, the emphasis on children is a device to insure telemanity's invisibility. Television is, as it were, a deforming mold, which is too large for children; in which, while they are certainly being habituated, 'set up', they still have 'room to move around', to 'be themselves': it hasn't yet shaped them. Television deforms the human potential, the promise of human birth, only later in life, gradually, relent-lessly, insidiously throughout the life, in the stages when that potential is supposed to be realized: until it's too late, and time has run out, and there's no hope of recovery.

And yet, as television begins to render invisible the traditional concept of childhood, it would not be quite accurate to say that it immerses us in an adult world. Rather, it uses the material of the adult world as the basis for projecting a new kind of person altogether. We might call this person the adultchild. For reasons that have partly to do with television's capacity to reach everyone, partly to do with the accessibility of its symbolic form, and partly to do with its commercial base, television promotes as desirable many of the attitudes that we associate with childishness—for example, an obses-sive need for immediate gratification, a lack of concern for consequences, an almost promiscuous preoccupation with consumption.

⁓POSTMAN

Television is 'pitched for' and molds a childish sensibility—shallow, incoherent, excitable, restricted to immediacy, indiscriminate, uncritical, 'moronic' on an adult scale—which is why children are not *essentially* damaged by it. But also why—for the procedure is clinically methodical, satanic in its thoroughness, and now fully automatic—they are drawn to it. Again, closed circle, perfect trap. Television and telemanity are one.

Television performs this infamy upon the people we love. Before our crumbling disbelief, our growing horror. It breaks your heart; you feel the familiar sour helplessness. At the time of 'watching', when the television is 'on', between telemanity mesmerized and humanity nauseated there is no common language. Love alone bridges the rift. The love that is *karuna* and *mudita*, Buddhist compassion and sympathy—two of the four *Brahmaviharas*, or Illimitable Sublime Moods—defined by Ananda Coomaraswamy in Walt Whitman's words:

> I do not ask the wounded person how he feels, I myself become the wounded person…
> I am the man, I suffered, I was there…

Krishna, the Lord of Love, enjoins nothing less:

> Who burns with the bliss
> And suffers the sorrow
> Of every creature
> Within his own heart,
> Making his own
> Each bliss and each sorrow:
> Him I hold highest
> Of all the yogis.

This is where we walk with them, arm around their shoulders. Calling them back. Back to the two of us here and now, in the world love makes real.

There's a deeper level, however, a deeper Heart, which nothing of this world can reach. This is the level—among other expressions of it, in other traditions—of the Paternoster, 'Thy Will be done.' We still walk with them; but in the Peace that contains and transfigures all. The Peace that is both infinite detachment and Oneness. Nothing 'here below' is what it appears to be, and nothing here is final. Finality is beyond, and unknowable. We are all in the hands of heaven. There is our Peace. The theistic Peace of the Abrahamic monotheisms corresponding to the metaphysical Peace, *moksha*, *ananda*, *nirvana*, *shantih*, of the Eastern revelations. 'Verily in the remembrance of Allah do hearts find rest.'

And so much for the screen.

✳

Time speeds up in the *Kali-Yuga*, the cosmic substance flows ever faster. Electric cities, electric lives, it's a speed-of-light nanosecond cyber-world now, the minutes close like clamps upon our blurred hurrying, step on it, it's getting late; wires and grids, unintelligible techno-terms acronymized so you can say them faster, the Great International Telecommunications Web, the super-charged ground and air humming and writhing with pulses of money, money and information, money and information racing the digital clocks through the metallic voids, through the intercontinental cyber-space: the goal is always instantaneous. Time is money and money is people and people are the money moving through the wires and relays and the fiber-optic cable from computer to computer at the speed of light, and their world is dying, their Earth devastation, they drown in invisible water. The Information Age, Age of Electric Death.

We know it. Our figures of speech prove that we know it. We say: Always on the run, keeping busy, running late, the pace of life, the pace of events, the jet set, I have no time for, tight schedule, the rat race, always in a hurry, the rush hour, try to squeeze it in, speedy, fast-paced, I need to slow down, easy does it one day at a time, no time to relax, time flies, time to unwind, fast lane, fast food, pedal to the metal, I want it yesterday, just a sec, snatch a moment, hurry up, time's a wasting, get moving, just can't fit it in, never a dull moment, get the lead out and on the double.

> Your schedule is busy. There are just not enough hours in the day. Staying informed is important to you, so you catch your news on the run. The Christian Science Monitor is your news source of choice... So how can it be, you don't have a subscription? Time out! Grab a moment to take advantage of this special offer...

The 'news' is history, fast-breaking events, the 'news' is hyper-reality, a fever dream. The accompanying photograph shows a well-dressed 'career woman' in a bus or railroad waiting room. She is standing up, alert, poised for action, reading the Monitor; behind her a variety of 'loser' types are pictured slouching on the benches. They gave up long ago, they are going nowhere, left in the dust, and are sprawled in postures of resigned defeat, inert dirt-bags. She has no time to sit down. She's going places, in a hurry.

I'd like to conclude this section on the speed-up of time in the *Kali-Yuga* with some passages from Jeremy Rifkin's excellent study, *Time Wars*. Thorough and insightful. He is another 'unconscious prophet of the *Kali-Yuga*.'

From a chapter titled 'The New Nanosecond Culture':

The modern world of streamlined transportation, instantaneous communication, and time-saving technologies was supposed to free us from the dictates of the clock and provide us with increased leisure. Instead there seems never to be enough time. What time we do have is chopped up into tiny segments, each filled in with prior commitments and plans. Our tomorrows are spoken for, booked up in advance. We rarely have a moment to spare. Tangential or discretionary time, once a mainstay, an amenity of life, is now a luxury... As the tempo of modern life has continued to accelerate, we have come to feel increasingly out of touch with the biological rhythms of the planet, unable to experience a close connection with the natural environment... Today we have surrounded ourselves with time-saving technological gadgetry, only to be overwhelmed by plans that cannot be carried out, appointments that cannot be honored, schedules that cannot be fulfilled, and deadlines that cannot be met. Strangely enough, even as society finds itself incapable of catching up with the time demands of the modern age, a new and faster time technology is being introduced into the popular culture—a technology that threatens to accelerate our sense of time beyond anything we experienced during the short reign of the modern age. It is likely that within the next half-century, the computer will help facilitate a revolutionary change in time orientation, just as clocks did several hundred years ago...The new computer technology is already changing the way we conceptualize time and, in the process, is changing the way we think about ourselves and the world around us...Never before has time been organized at a speed beyond the realm of consciousness...

Consider, for example, the LOGO program, perhaps the best-known educational software for young children. With LOGO, a child can program a flock of birds and then put them in motion on the screen. The child follows the motion of the birds, carefully scrutinizing the way they flap their wings, the way they move. But as John Davy observes in his critique of the LOGO program, this is not the same experience the child would gain from watching a flock of birds in nature. On the screen the temporal orientation of the birds is determined by the program. The child fuses with an artificial set of sequences, durations, rhythms, and synchronized activities and patterns. As Davy points out, there are 'no smells or tastes, no winds or bird song, no connection with soil, water, sunlight, warmth, no real ecology...' All of the environmental cues so essential in the formulation of everyday temporal skills are completely absent... Computer time bears no relationship to the rhythms of nature. It is an arbitrary temporal marker willed into existence by human ingenuity. Computers reduce time to numbers and turn duration into uniform segments that can be added, subtracted, accumulated, and exchanged. While the computer turns time into a purely manipulable commodity, programs turn human beings into instruments to serve the new efficiency time frame. With the computer and program, each person's immediate future can be predetermined down to the tiniest artificial time segments of milliseconds and nanoseconds. Computers and programs represent a new form of social control, more powerful than any previous means used to marshal and regiment human energy…

The nanosecond culture brings with it a new and more virulent form of reductionism. The clockwork universe of the industrial age is being replaced, in fast order, by the computational universe of the postindustrial age. For several hundred years Western culture has defined mind and matter in mechanistic terms, reducing all of reality to the operating principles of clockwork technology. Now, a new journey begins. In the coming century our children are likely to redefine their environment using the language of information theory and cybernetics as they attempt to conjure up a view of nature that conforms with the operational principles of the new computer technology. We are entering a new temporal world where time is segmented into nanoseconds, the future is programmed in advance, nature is reconceived as bits of coded information, and paradise is viewed as a fully simulated, artificial environment.

Time Wars brims with such converging insights. (I'm saving some for a later chapter.) Recall that the five hallmarks of the *Kali-Yuga* are: The Fall into Time, The Mutation into Machinery, The End of Nature, The Reign of Quantity and The Prison of Unreality. Clearly not watertight compartments. What a triumph, the Computer!

✳

The *Kali-Yuga* has a taste. Pre-eminently, bitter. This section's 'brief reflections and commentaries on our lives in the *Kali-Yuga*', as I referred to them in the beginning, leave that taste, and I would like to conclude it otherwise. Scarcely 'on a happy note', or even more absurdly, 'on a positive note', but with a reminder of the Transcendence which always has the last word. *Vincit omnia veritas.*

Our basic and ultimate posture in the universe, insofar as we still experience ourselves as separate and temporal beings, must always be one of humble gratitude—for the miracle of existence, for our lives, for the world called Earth, for flowers, music, and surf, for the laughter of our friends and the light in the eyes of our daughters, for love, beauty, and intelligence: for all the gifts of the infinite Grace, and in the knowledge that 'All is Thy Grace'—and humble adoration of that for which we are grateful. No small-mindedness, no disaffection, no resentment at our dispensation. No thralldom to the transitory, but rather worship, until Identity is realized, of the Eternal in whose Light of Splendor the transitory is revealed as illusion, or is transfigured into timeless archetype—for 'Eternity is in love with the creations of Time', and knows them as its very Self—or is unveiled, when our original sight is restored, when the Eye of the Heart is opened, as the Face of God.

> And we know
> that the enormous invulnerable beauty of things
> Is the face of God, to live gladly in its presence, and die without
> grief or fear knowing it survives us.
> ∼ROBINSON JEFFERS

The *Kali-Yuga*, in other words, is nothing. When all is said and done, nothing. It is the 'end' of what is after all only the Great Dream suspended in the Eternal Now, where all 'moments', the 'past' and the 'future' and the whole parade of Time, are simultaneous and ever-present: the Eternal Now which is the Reality, where everything always 'was' and 'we' always are. Dante's 'point whereto all times are present... where every *where* and every *when* are focused.'

We are beyond the orbit of the *Kali-Yuga's* claims, as we are beyond the manifested universe itself. We are the Eternal Witness, the Pure Consciousness: the Blissful Atman. And since Atman and *Maya* are One—*Kham Brahman, Sarvam khalvidam Brahman*, 'All this is Brahman'—the unitive vision, granted to us in meditation or ecstasy and verified throughout Scripture and of which our tears of joy are *known in the moment without possibility of doubt as absolute and glorious proof*, reveals that we *are* the manifested universe—only not as it appears to our earthly eyes, not as an object, but as it is in the Self, *as* the Self: as it is eternal Bliss, for 'From Bliss all things arise': as it is God. We are the universe, suspended in the infinite Radiance of the Void we become in Silence. 'The Silence within alone is Real.' In the I-Consciousness of the Universe, which is Siva. And *I am Siva, I am Siva, Sivo 'ham.*

The real world, the world in our hearts, is not redeemed, for it was never reprobate, never separated from Grace, from the Origin, from God: it is eternal, without beginning, without end, timeless and forever. Nor is the world of the *Kali-Yuga*, the world 'out there', redeemed, for there is nothing 'out there', it was never real. There is only the Self. *Rama Rama sat hai*: God alone is Real.

When a person knows the Truth, he

thinks yet he does not think. He thinks like the showers coming down from
the sky; he thinks like the waves rolling on the ocean; he thinks like the stars
illuminating the nightly heavens; he thinks like the green foliage shooting
forth in the relaxing spring breeze. Indeed, he is the showers, the ocean, the
stars, the foliage.
〜D.T. Suzuki

This world that we are is the real one. *Find it.* How? 'Die before ye die.'
That's how you'll find it. The only way.

> One autumnal eve I was wakeful,
> Took a staff, and went out of doors;
> The crickets were singing under the ancient tiles,
> The dead leaves were fast falling off the shivering trees;
> Far way the stream was heard murmuring,
> The moon was slow to rise above the high peak:
> All conspired to draw me on to a deep meditation,
> And it was some time before I found my robe heavily wet with dew.
> 〜Ryokwan, 1758–1831

When the cherries begin to bloom, Let me know at once': The mountain-
man has not forgotten my word; I hear him come. 'Saddle the horse, quick!
〜Minamoto No Yorimasa, 1104–1180

> Looking for a place to settle out
> Cold Mountain will do it
> fine wind among thick pines
> the closer you listen the better the sound
> under them a man his hair turning white
> mumbling mumbling Taoist texts
> he's been here ten years unable to return
> completely forgotten the way by which he came
> 〜Han Shan (legendary, c. 730)

> I come humbly to the bamboo grove
> Each day hoping to embrace the Way.
> Going and coming, there are only mountain birds.
> In the profound dark, there is no one.
> Alone I sit within the dark bamboo
> Strumming my lute, whistling along
> In the deep grove no one knows
> The bright moon, how we shine together.
> 〜P'ei Ti and Wang Wei (700–761)

Since I came to this T'ien T'ai temple
how many Winters and Springs have passed
the mountains and the waters are unchanged
the man's grown older
how many other men will watch those mountains stand...
I laugh at myself, old man, with no strength left
inclined to piney peaks, in love with lonely paths
oh well, I've wandered down the years to now
free in the flow; and floated home the same
a drifting boat
　⌒Shih Te (legendary, c. 730)

We carved our names in a courtyard near the river
when you were youngest of all our guests.
But you will never see the bright spring again,
nor the beautiful apricot blossoms
that flutter silently past
the open temple door
　⌒Chang Chi (768–830)

A thousand mountains. Flying birds vanish.
Ten thousand paths. Human traces erased.
One boat, bamboo hat, bark cape—an old man.
Alone with his hook. Cold river. Snow.
　⌒Liu Tsung-yuan (773–819)

Flock of peaks hunched up
and colored cold. Path forks
here, toward the temple.
A falling star flares behind bare trees,
and the moon breasts the current of the clouds.
To the very top, few men come;
one tall pine won't hold a flock of cranes.
One monk here, at eighty,
has never heard tell
of the 'world' down below.
　⌒Wu Pen (779–841)

Refusing worldly worries,
I stroll among village strollers.
Pine winds sing, the evening village
smells of grass, autumn in the air.
A lone bird roams down the sky.

Clouds roll across the river.
You want to know my name?
—a hill, a tree. An empty drifting boat.
⌒ Hsu Hsuan (dates unknown)

things of the past are already long gone
the things to be, distant beyond imagining.
The Tao is just this moment, these words:
plum blossoms fallen; gardenia just opening.
⌒ Ch'ing Kung (d. 1352)

I have more on my list, can hardly resist going on. They're taken from *A Drifting Boat*, edited by Seaton and Maloney, White Pine Press, 1994. There's more in *The Chinese Translations* of Witter Bynner.

By modern 'standards' the men who wrote these words had nothing. But in reality it is we who have nothing. They had everything. And what they had is eternal, eternal *now*. Oil spills, acid rain, clear-cutting, genetic erosion, Time itself, and the whole arsenal, physical and spiritual, of the *Kali-Yuga* can't touch it. Eternal in the Heart of the Universe, which is our own Heart. The Heart of the Universe is the Heart of my Heart.

And this Knowledge of the nature of things, with the mode of apprehension invisible behind it, though 'hard to understand', is a Knowledge that can be realized, directly experienced, a mode of apprehension inherent in all of us. Unmistakable as a 'fruit in the palm of the hand', as the saying goes, and understood, comprehended, *recognized*, with a kind of understanding, an absolute certainty, never known in knowledge which is merely of this world. We were intended to know divine things, divine truths, to become divine ourselves, to realize a divinity always and already present within us, and that Intention is indestructible. Nothing can touch it. It's the whole reason we're here.

XIX

One Way

When the great Tao is forgotten,
Kindness and morality arise.
When wisdom and intelligence are born,
The great pretense begins.

When there is no peace within the family,
Filial piety and devotion arise.
When the country is confused and in chaos,
Loyal ministers appear.
~Tao Te Ching, 18

THIS chapter comes often to mind. The smiling *Tao*, the shrewd implacable gaiety. It is never deceived.

'Parenting'. Let's start right out with that one, because it's so obvious. When people become confused, at a loss, about how to rear their children, the young of their own species, the 'Parenting Classes' appear. *Scission*: oneness with the stages of our own life, our own growth and development, is no more; oneness of 'inner' and 'outer' is no longer. There was one and now there are two: ourselves, and something new 'out there' which we do not understand: we must be taught a 'skill'. We must now be trained to do something we formerly assumed everyone would do simply by virtue of being human, being at one with an immemorial 'internal tradition': not identically, not *correctly*, but in one of the countless variations and moments, the 'give and take', whose dynamic interplay told the story and composed the spontaneous equilibrium of the commonweal, unplanned, unpremeditated and 'unintentional' -- just as the interaction of innumerable entities, elements and events composes the immense harmony, the perfection, of Nature: individually and collectively neither 'right' nor 'wrong', neither for better nor for worse, neither happy nor unhappy, neither 'correct' nor 'incorrect', neither 'progressive' nor 'reactionary', neither structured nor unstructured, neither wise nor foolish, but 'as it is', 'as things go', the Will of God, the fall of the dice, *karma*, Fate, the wheel of fortune, the Way. The Way that is beyond and prior to our judgments or discriminations or partisanships, the Way, the ancient *Tao* we once were, once saw, once recognized, once adored, as our own, our Self. (Having and not having arise together, To yield is to overcome, Accept misfortune as the human condition, Observers of the *Tao* do not seek fulfillment, High winds do not last all morning... and so on.) Now something has happened requiring that measures be taken, that a method or response be devised and taught, deduced and proposed, institutionalized, and, in its terminal form, programmed. By whom? Or what? How did it happen? Can what was innate, spontaneous, 'coming from the heart', like everything in the natural world, become a 'skill', a 'method', without our suffering, or having suffered, some sort of essential damage or alteration? What does it mean when things that formerly 'took care of themselves' have become 'skills', 'methods' and 'techniques'? (Recall Ellul!) A New Order. It happened. Irreversible.

John Blofeld puts it this way:

> It is taught that there is a Tao (Way) of Heaven, a Tao of Earth and a Tao of Man. This last is the way ordained by nature from which it is unwise and often perilous to depart. Nevertheless, human society began to depart from it at a very early date...
>
> A dedicated Taoist is one who seeks to live as closely in accord as possible with nature. From the outset, this involves contemplation of nature's ways, recognition of their fitness, and perception that all of them are 'good' in the sense of being essential to the pattern as a whole. Depart from them and chaos and destruction loom! To go along with nature effortlessly, as does a fish or a master artisan, is to swim with the current, to let one's knife slip along with the grain. When nature is taken as a guide, a friend, living becomes almost effortless, tranquil, joyous even. Care departs; serenity takes over. *Wu wei*, a cardinal principle of Taoists, literally means 'no action', but not in the sense of sitting all day like a dead tree stump or a block of stone; rather it means avoiding action that is not spontaneous, acting fully and skillfully by all means but only in accordance with present need, being lively when required but never over-strenuous and certainly not strained, eschewing artfully calculated action and every activity stemming from a profit motive.

To resume. The pattern is always the same; but our analysis is heading deeper. When life for many people no longer seems worth living, and, in the midst of millions, there's no one to turn to for comfort and heartening, the 'suicide hot lines' appear. When loneliness is endemic, again in the midst of millions, the singles' bars, encounter groups, 'chat rooms' on the Web, and a whole galaxy of facilitating subterfuges appear. When families are falling apart everywhere, 'dysfunctional', the 'marriage counselors' and 'family counseling' specialists appear. When animals are being widely tortured to death or subjected to chemical, biological and habitational outrages, 'animal rights activists' appear. When thousands are wandering the streets, rummaging in garbage cans and sleeping in doorways, the Salvation Army, the homeless shelters and indignant public advocates appear. When the very air we breathe is polluted, and urban 'normal life' can only be endured for fairly brief stretches of time before it becomes intolerable again, 'national parks' appear, recreational areas and 'facilities', and all the apparatus, paraphernalia and propaganda of 'getting away from it all'. When people's very minds have caved in or gone haywire, when the pain of sheer wretchedness has become so unbearable that 'breakdown' or 'crackup' seems inevitable, therapy, in its myriad forms, from powerful chemical agents to mastering the arts of screaming or laughing or crying or 'expressing your anger', rises to meet the challenge. Prozak, St. John's Wort, support groups, 12-step programs, magnets, you name it. When people are at a loss about how to give birth, make love and die, when fundamental dimensions of human biology present themselves as puzzling dilemmas and acute crises, experts, manuals of instruction and adult education classes appear. When the accustomed fare has turned out to be poisonous, 'health foods' appear, along with all the books and theories and special diets, an entire industry, (Or, when 'health food' appears, the fare has been poisoned. You can always say it either way.) When an 'environmental movement' of global scale appears, then it's really all over, the Earth will never again be what it was—which is to say it is no longer the Earth.

These are what might be called the 'disease and intervention' pairs, reflections of one another whose appearance confirms a new equilibrium or balance of forces; the two-sides-of-the-same-coin phenomena that always announce a new state of affairs: the end of a previous harmony (or a previous 'new equilibrium': we may have to trace several stages, or decades or millennia, backwards till we reach the harmony), the end of a prior spontaneous identity with the inner truth or nature of things and ourselves that was characterized by an absence not only of contrivance but of consciousness itself. Again, as in Nature—for the immortal Tao always refers us back to what is natural. This sort of end is the end of oneness with the Tao. Or the end of humility; the end of identities not bound to worldly contingencies. Or, introducing here a category from another context but which amounts to the same thing, the end of a traditional society. The cracks, divisions, makeshifts and stopgaps that gradually disfigure and corrode a spontaneous un-pre-meditated aboriginal unity and balance, the inherent un-administered 'nature of things'. The great prototype here, of course, is the Tree of the Knowledge of Good and Evil, whose fruit was forbidden: before yielding to that Primal Temptation, before that Primordial Disobedience, there was neither, neither Good nor Evil, afterwards both: therefore the Law. A threshold has been crossed in these instances, the cosmic cycle has advanced another notch, and there's no returning, no restoration, no going back, no re-establishment of the previous state. Only a coping, a holding at bay. The damage has always already been done, the wound inflicted, and the place where we were struck will never again be what it was, never be sound again. We limp, we suffer, we compensate; we're scarred, weakened. That's the real point: no return, a one-way trip; the apple's been bitten. Irreversibility.

A little digression here. I suggested, in the previous paragraph, that departure from the Way is analogous to departure from *tradition*. This bears further examination. In one sense the terms are distinct, in another synony-mous. Tradition, religion, may be seen as a Mercy extended to us after our defection, a path leading back to integrity and authentic humanity, to the lost Way or Truth; or tradition can be seen as a new offering of and access to that very Way, the Way itself, in which sense the terms are equivalent. There's an excellent examination of this very point in Chapter Two of Seyyed Hossein Nasr's magnificent *Knowledge and the Sacred*, titled 'What is Tradition?' He introduces the chapter with a quotation from the *Tao Te Ching*:

> By adhering to the Tao of the past
> You will master the existence of the present.

The usage of the term *tradition* in the sense understood in the present study came to the fore in Western civilization at the moment of the final phase of the desacralization of both knowledge and the world which surrounded modern man. The rediscovery of tradition constituted a kind of cosmic com-pensation, a gift from the Divine Empyrean whose mercy made possible, at the moment when all seemed to be lost, the reassertion of the Truth which constitutes the very heart and essence of tradition. The formulation of the traditional point of view was a response of the Sacred, which is both the alpha and omega of human existence, to the elegy of doom of modern man lost in a world depleted of the sacred and therefore, of meaning...

The reassertion at this late hour of human history of tradition which itself is both of a primordial character and possesses continuity over the ages, made possible once again access to that Truth by which human beings have lived during most—or rather nearly all—of their terrestrial history. This Truth had to be stated anew and reformulated in the name of tradition precisely because of the nearly total eclipse and loss of that reality which has constituted the matrix of life of normal humanity over the ages...

Normal humanities lived in worlds so impregnated with what we now call tradition that they had no sense of a separate concept called tradition as it has now been necessary to define and formulate in the modern world. They had an awareness of revelation, of wisdom, of the sacred and also knew of periods of decadence of their civilization and culture, but they had no experience of a totally secularized and antitraditional world...

As far as traditional languages are concerned, they do not possess, for reasons already mentioned, a term corresponding exactly to tradition. There are such fundamental terms as the Hindu and Buddhist *dharma*, the Islamic *al-din*, the Taoist *Tao*, and the like which are inextricably related to the meaning of the term *tradition*, but not identical with it, although of course the worlds or civilizations created by Hinduism, Buddhism, Taoism, Judaism, Christianity, Islam, or for that matter any other authentic religion, is a traditional world...

Tradition as used in its technical sense in this work, as in all our other writings, means truths or principles of a divine origin revealed or unveiled to mankind and, in fact, a whole cosmic sector through various figures envisaged as messengers, prophets, avataras, the Logos or other transmitting agencies, along with all the ramifications and applications of these principles in different realms including law and social structure, art, symbolism, the sciences, and embracing of course Supreme Knowledge along with the means for its attainment. In its more universal sense tradition can be considered to include the principles which bind man to Heaven, and therefore religion, while from another point of view religion can be considered in its essential sense as those principles which are revealed by Heaven and which bind man to his Origin... Tradition, like religion, is at once truth and presence... It comes from the Source from which everything originates and to which everything returns... Tradition is inextricably related to revelation and religion, to the sacred, to the notion of orthodoxy, to authority, to the continuity and regularity of transmission of the truth...

The relationship between tradition and the Truth is a subtle one because what we're really talking about here—Nasr almost makes this explicit, but not quite—is the relationship between time and timelessness, the *presence* of timelessness in time, the *transfiguration* of time by timelessness, the reentry of the Absolute into the relative world from which it was never really absent, and this is indeed an elusive domain, ungraspable by the discursive intelligence: a domain where definitive statements are definitively elusive. But statements are not really what life is all about. We can enter that domain, from which we were never really absent. It's within us. The Heart, the Self, Shiva.

Once again to resume. On a superficial first look it can appear that nothing is actually being said in these Taoist ellipses, that they are cases of circular reasoning or redundancy: of course we respond to 'problems', of course challenges are met with appropriate recourses, of course it's proper to schedule Parenting Classes when 'parenting skills', for very many reasons, seem to be falling drastically below grade level. But we've already unmasked the reduction of cyclic dissolution, in its many aspects, to a constellation of 'problems' amenable to technological intervention, and Taoist 'logic', here going deeper still—removing the mask beneath the mask, as it were—reveals a dimension of things invisible to Western rationalism and 'common sense'. It perceives, in every new strategy and in the 'praise' it receives—the social approval or validation, the complacent self-assurance, the satisfied sigh of relief that we've 'confronted the problem', 'handled the situation', or 'saved' the situation—an irreversibility of decline, an unrecoverable loss of original virtue and natural equilibrium: of the state before the strategy was initiated and before any such 'strategy', because we were living in spontaneous harmony with the Way, was even conceivable. New diseases, and their therapies, have appeared among us. Again, not a contrast here between past and present, but a departure from the Norm, the Path, the Intention, the 'Original Instructions' to which Native American critiques of Western civilization faithfully and imperturbably bear witness, from the divine Archetype, from *tradition*—formless in Itself, but capable of materializing or crystallizing in countless formal manifestations 'here below', and even at any time or place within the decadent structures of the *Kali-Yuga*, for 'the Spirit bloweth where it listeth'—in which our humanity originates and from which departure means decay; and though that departure is inevitable for historical humanity, though the consequences of defection and the interventions subsequently employed are inescapable, the resistance of individuals is inevitable as well, and not pointless, for we are summoned in defense of our humanity at all times: that summons and the hearing of it are a single event. And a proof. The atheists and relativists are wrong. There is a Truth. Witness to that Truth is defiance of their error.

So we read in the *Tao*, 'He who loses the Way feels lost.' And this is not a redundancy, a tautology, but rather an affirmation that everything hangs together, makes sense, is intended: that there is a Logos, a Truth: an Absolute. Our feelings of anxiety, panic, cynicism and despair in these times are definitely informed, and the billions we spend to reassure ourselves are both merciful—since there is no way out—and satanic—because we were made for the Truth. All this sounds 'odd' to modern ears only because we believe in Progress. That's the reason. In the perspective of Progress nothing in the *Tao Te Ching* makes any sense at all. But there is no such thing as Progress. There is only the cosmic unfolding. The succession of the great Ages or Yugas, the Fall into Time and the riveting drama it inaugurated in the eternal Stillness, the Harmony and Beauty, of our archaic residence in Nature. The cosmic unfolding which is actually *maya*, the Great Dream, beneath which the indestructible Truth, the Reality, shines forever—as it shines forever in all our hearts, our very Self.

Instances of *Tao Te Ching* chapter 18's applicability can be multiplied indefinitely in our times. All the 'healing' and 'caring' careers, the stress reduction and human development classes, the identification of and remedial proposals for 'compassion fatigue', the drug, alcoholism, child abuse and safe sex programs, the prisons and rehab centers and sanitariums and the proponents, theorists and facilitators of all these, the role models, and the 'praise' of it all. The 'humane responses', all 'progressive' movements and publications and demonstrations on behalf of oppressed and dispossessed minorities, defense funds and committees, trade unions, 'wars' on poverty, drugs and crime, exposes of corruption and infamy. The Citizens' Clearing House for Hazardous Wastes, The Cousteau Society, Earth First!, Fairness and Accuracy in Media, Friends of the River, Food First, National Audubon Society, National Coalition Against Misuse of Pesticides, Minority Rights Group Reports, Planned Parenthood Federation of America, Rainforest Action Network, National Wildlife Federation, World Resources Institute, the Environmental Protection Agency, Amnesty International, Oceanic Society, Union of Concerned Scientists, Worldwatch Institute, Zero Population Growth, and countless more. These responses, the protests, activist organizations and counter-attacks, the 'loyal ministers' we 'praise' with our vote, support and donations and upon whose claim we found our optimistic stances, the new strategies and ingenuities, from *ad hoc* rejoinders to entire ideologies, are invariably some form, no matter how intangible, of mechanism or artificiality: systems, philosophies, procedures, methods, programs, ordinances, legislation; materializing as organizations, Councils, 'funds', societies, coalitions, parties, alliances, committees; generating conferences, manuals, instructions, statements, policies, chains of command, 'skills' training, investigations, reports. In a word, *techniques*, Ellul's technique. Technique replaces inner communion, spontaneous empathy and collaboration, immediacy, affinity, understanding, directness, living presence: the Tao of Heaven and Earth. Ellul's brilliant insight is here metaphysically situated, consummated, in Taoist teleology. As Merton wrote in the Foreword to *La Technique*, technique 'converts spontaneous and unreflective behavior into behavior that is deliberate and rationalized.' Salaam Lao Tzu.

✳

Chapter 38, the first chapter of the second part of the *Tao Te Ching*. known as the 'Te Classic', sums up and analyzes the stages of the progressive decline intimated in Chapter 18 and here and there in the intermediate chapters, Here are the Feng/English translation of a passage from that chapter, the Lin Yutang translation of the same passage, and Ellen Chen's commentary.

> Therefore when Tao is lost, there is goodness.
> When goodness is lost, there is kindness.
> When kindness is lost, there is justice.
> When justice is lost, there is ritual.
> Now ritual is the husk of faith and loyalty,
> The beginning of confusion.
>
> Therefore:
>
> After Tao is lost, then (arises the doctrine of) humanity.
> After humanity is lost, then (arises the doctrine of) justice.
> After justice is lost, then (arises the doctrine of) *li*.
> Now *li* is the thinning out of loyalty and honesty of heart.
> And the beginning of chaos.

This chapter delineates

> the descending order from Tao (the creative ground) and *te* (nature), to the struggles and warfares of the moral sphere, through the stages of *jen* (universal humanity), *i* (group righteousness), and *li* (ritual or propriety). Entrance into the moral sphere is fittingly called *shih*, loss of Tao and *te*, the original carefree state of nature.
>
> When nature is perfect (high *te*), it is unconscious of itself. As soon as nature becomes conscious it falls below itself (low *te*)... Low *te* is indeed not nature

but virtue. In the *Tao Te Ching* virtue means the loss of nature's (high *te*) original perfection... A person of high *te*, at one with Tao and the movement of all beings, does not act or toil. There is no cause for action. A person of low *te*, standing apart to judge the world, relying on the self and doing everything consciously, is burdened with toil... The unconscious high *te* is distinguished from the conscious low *te* by its non-action *(wu-wei)*.
The moment human action is introduced into the world humans step out of nature into virtue. *Jen*... means humanity or human heartedness, in its high form, which, according to Wang Pi, is universal, benevolent, all-loving, impartial and selfless; *jen* transcends itself to reach the freedom of *te*. Thus, although we enter the sphere of morality with *jen*, in its high form *jen* reverts to *te*. The person of high *jen*, at one with the harmonious self-ordering nature (*te*), has no cause for action.
⁓ELLEN CHEN

High *jen*, I might point out, is clearly identical to the Four Illimitable Sublime Moods (*Brahmaviharas*) of Buddhism referred to earlier in this text: *metta, karuna, mudita,* and *upekkha,* or Loving-kindness, Compassion, Sympathy, and Impartiality. These are Vedantic virtues as well, and they can also be identified in the Abrahamic monotheisms where the distinction between high and low *jen* is perhaps not as clearly drawn as it is in the Eastern doctrines.

The next stage, *i* (righteousness), when the self is subordinated to the common good... is a more restricted form of morality. While *jen* stands for universal humanity or love, *i* is the morality of a group or the obligation between ruler and subjects. A person of high *jen* finds no cause for action. A person of high *i* finds much to do in the world...

That the person of high *jen* 'finds no cause for action' does not mean, of course, that such a person does nothing. It means just what it says: that he or she neither discovers nor conceives personal goals or purposes, but simply 'flows with the river', moving along in harmony with the unfolding of events in the great Life that is Nature, accepting with equanimity what comes unsought, at one with the All. The 'life-style' of all the Illumined, the 'liberated in this life'. The 'life-style' of grass, clouds, waves, and weeds.

The *Tao Te Ching's* overall attitude toward *li* is negative. In this chapter *li* as ritual coming after *jen* (universal human solidarity) and *i* (group solidarity) occupies the last stage of moral development such that it actually marks human alienation from the divine. Ritual behavior externally manifests an inner awareness of one's separateness from the divine... The religion of ritual is the religion of the Pharisees, bordering on irreligion.

Metaphysical intelligence knows that the *Kali-Yuga* must display *li* in its terminal form, and of course it does. Lewis Mumford's Megamachine, Jerry Mander's megatechnology, technological rationality, universal quantification, scientism, the mechanization of all aspects of life, the Power System, the Computer, the invalidation of subjectivity, Ellul's technique—our world is the triumph of *li*, its complete victory. Animated Death. The consummation of Ritual is the Robot. The Celebrity. Work and The Worker.

For Ellen Chen the passage twice translated above

sums up the progression from Tao (the creative ground), to *te* (the created world), to *jen* (humanity), to *i* (righteousness as group morality), and finally to *li* (ritual behavior), as the steady process of loss (*shih*), sacrificing a greater and more inclusive unity to a narrower and more restricted consciousness. Tao and high *te*, being unconscious, are reversive and harmonious. From low *te* down to *jen*, *i*, and *li* we fall from the reversive process of Tao and *te* (nature) to the non-reversive rigidity of conscious human actions. Moral consciousness as a permanent rupture from the world issues in actions aimed at changing the shape of the world. Human action is warfare waged by humans against nature... People in the state of nature are virtuous because they do not know what virtue is. Moral virtues are called forth due to the loss (*shih*) of nature. It is due to the loss (*shih*) of a more inclusive virtue (*jen*) that narrower forms of virtue (*i*, *li*) also become hard to maintain. The important thing is to preserve the original wholeness. Then all will be well.

Commenting on the same chapter, Chapter 38, Lin Yutang writes, 'Taoism lays great emphasis on unconscious goodness, goodness that is natural and without motivation. The moment goodness is motivated, it is regarded as a decline or deviation from Tao.' He quotes from Chuang Tzu:

To arrive there (in Tao) without realizing why it is so is called Tao. There is no greater injury to one's character than practicing virtue with motivation A man feels a pleasurable sensation before he smiles, and smiles before he thinks how he ought to smile.

'Original wholeness', oneness, harmony, unity, simplicity. Oneness with Nature, the Way, the unreflective, unintentional, un-purposive Way of the Earth where everything gets done but nowhere is there conscious intention to do anything. The Fall is *our fall from that state*.

Quite ironically, Man, who is by nature so made as to be able to become the most perfect embodiment of Virtue—and hence of the Way—is the sole creature that is capable of obstructing the full activity of Virtue. For nothing other than Man acts with 'intention'.
〜Toshihiko Izutsu, *Sufism and Taoism*

From that state, and into this one. Into activity, increasingly frenzied and with increasingly stupendous consequences, into a multiplying chaos of contested values and 'dubious battles', into divisions and divisiveness, the pulverizing of life into innumerable fragments and the elaboration of those fragments into a geometrically expanding and inexhaustibly ramifying network of mind-boggling complexities, 'requiring' an ever-growing regiment of 'specialists', equipped with an evergrowing arsenal of computers, who only breed more varieties of themselves: and all this in the context of an interminable identification of 'problems' and enterprises, proposals of ever-new 'solutions' and methods, and endless, fruitless, utterly specious 'debate'.

> Once the whole is divided, the parts need names.
> There are already enough names.
> One must know when to stop,
> Knowing when to stop averts trouble,
> Tao in the world is like a river flowing home to the sea.

The *Tao Te Ching* is full of these sparkling, pregnant, simultaneously cryptic and transparent, even roguish, slightly 'tilted' from our Western perspective (and in our languages) insights into life that characterized the ancient Chinese wisdom tradition, now replaced by nervously contested (by men who have good reason to be nervous) and almost unbelievably reductive 'sciences' such as Marxism-Leninism, (maybe) Mao-tse Tung Thought, the Law of Supply and Demand and Information Theory. They sound simple-minded, romantic, even meaningless, and 'the point' seems elusive, because they assume decline rather than Progress, the implacable menace of degeneration and decrepitude rather than evolutionary ascent, assume deterioration rather than victories, an eternal norm rather than universal relativity. Cyclical Nature—'Returning is the motion of the Tao': *fan*, to return to the world; *fu*, to recover, repeat, or return; *kuei*, to return to the ground or source; *chou*, to move round and round; *huan* to come back or to retribute (pay back, give in return, requite): 'The succession of growth and decay, of increase and diminution... each end becoming a new beginning' (Chuang Tzu)—rather than linear History ('the rhythm of universal decadence, that some call "History"' (Frithjof Schuon) is the Reality and the Good, and our unconscious participation in its immemorial life, the life of the Earth, and even more our infinitely respectful adoration of Creation's divinity, our love for the Great Way, is our state of grace: conscious intervention in the original Oneness announces a dichotomy between humanity and its primordial nature, Nature itself, and is the hallmark of the Fall. The Tao assumes oneness, harmony and contentment, not only as desiderata—it is not an idealism—but as fundamental realities—changeless, inherent in the cosmic Life, violable only at our peril and to our irrecoverable loss—rather than power struggles, conquest and enterprise, deeds of prowess, 'achievements'.

> The world is ruled by letting things take their course.
> It cannot be ruled by interfering.

Therefore 'Those who accept the natural course and sequence of things and live in obedience to it are beyond joy and sorrow. The ancients spoke of this as the emancipation from bondage.' (CHUANG TZU) Or, in Izutsu's penetrating formulation: 'The Way does not interfere with the natural course of things. Nor does it need to interfere with it, because the natural course of things is the activity of the Way itself.' We err, we suffer, because we forget the Truth, even denying that there is such a thing, and choose instead to 'live by our own lights'. It happened that way, and we must accept that nothing else could have happened, and here we are. In forgetfulness, here we are: in remembrance, nothing has happened at all.

Nevertheless, long live the ecology movement. That must be said. Long live the Greens, long live restorative and humanitarian endeavors everywhere. Their warriors are of the Covenant, their names engraved on the scroll of Love's witnesses and the planet's champions. Hats off to all of them, they're my friends and I love them. Everyone who's coping with our miseries or simply coping.

But—and this must also be said—these witnesses and footsoldiers, unsung heroes and heroines, are testimony to what has been lost forever. Shadow of that loss, and proof. I am reminded suddenly of James Agee's words:

> And some there be which have no memorial; who perished, as though they had never been; and are become as though they had never been born; and their children after them.
> But these were merciful men, whose righteousness hath not been forgotten. With their seed shall continually remain a good inheritance, and their children are within the covenant.

Their seed standeth fast, and their children for their sakes. Their seed shall remain for ever, and their glory shall not be blotted out.
Their bodies are buried in peace; but their name liveth for evermore.

The women too, of course.

✳

We began with the passage from Chapter 18. Ellen Chen writes:

The overall message of this chapter, just as in preceding and subsequent chapters, is that the unconscious state of nature is superior to the conscious state of virtue. Consciousness marks a lack. We are not aware of and do not pursue something until we have already become separated from it. Nature and virtue issue from the same origin. When virtue is perfect and rooted in Tao it is called nature (Tao and *te*); when nature opens and becomes conscious it is called virtue (*jen* and *i*). Nature, being unconscious, is effortless and successful; virtue, being conscious, struggles and fails. From this viewpoint the so-called progress from nature to virtue marks a movement toward strife, not peace... When moral ideas appeared nature had already suffered a loss. Only when humans had lost their original solidarity with the rest of the natural kingdom did they become conscious of the moral values of humanity (*jen*) and righteousness (*i*) exalting humans above other creatures... *Wei,* what is done by humans, means art or artificiality in contrast to the work of nature. The natural world is the work of Tao; art or artificiality is the work of human intelligence... According to the *Tao Te Ching* the realm of nature is holy and authentic; culture and civilization, the work of human intelligence, stands apart from nature and is the realm of great deceit... When human society was one with the great society of nature there was no need for loyal ministers.

It's all like an iron ball rolling down a flight of steps. Defeat after defeat, one last-ditch defense after another, one whirl-around rally after another, losing ground every time before the utterly impersonal remorseless advance that we ourselves have become. A desperate recourse, a defiant parry, hurried planning and mobilization; engagement, assessment and reports, new shape of the menace, regrouping, and counter-attack again. But always retreat, always loss: always slicing off something of the Spirit, something of the essence, something we always recall as 'simpler, more human, closer to Nature,' and replacing it with another component of the Machine, whose terminal incarnation is the Computer. Like an iron ball rolling down a flight of steps, each step a new ensemble of measures taken, of techniques and expedients, upon which the hope and despair are once again founded, and by which the bewilderment and cynicism, the gnawing sense of betrayal, are once again justified. A new instability, a new disposition of antagonisms, and increasingly short-lived as the ball rolls faster and faster. History, passing 'like falling rocks'. Civilizations, and the West. Science and Industry. Urbanization and Money. The Fall into Time.

✳

The question will inevitably cross our minds: doesn't Lao Tzu's familiarity with, and even focus upon the dialectic of degeneration indicate that it had already begun in his own time? (Which was around 600 BC. In the traditional scholarly consensus the shadowy author of the *Tao Te Ching* was an older contemporary of Confucius.) It does indeed. We are very far into the *Kali-Yuga*, It must never be forgotten that all revelations, the world religions, are addressed to a fallen humanity. Salvific Grace is by definition subsequent to Separation—to Ignorance, Disobedience, Rebellion, Sin—a subsequence actually ontological, 'vertical', of course, but 'translated' by the timebound mentality of our fallen state itself into a chronological or 'horizontal' succession which, while 'real' as *maya* can only be symbolic of the Reality: we are 'increasingly remote' from what is eternally present in the Eternal Now: our Truth, which is God, Who is the Self. The myths of native humanity—which are unanimous in their hearkening back, in a kind of 'holy nostalgia', nostalgia for Paradise (which is actually the entire motivation of the supremely misguided enterprise of the modern world), to a Golden Age or Sacred Time or 'time out of time' when people lived longer, and in peace, knew neither toil nor sorrow, were even contemporary with divine beings, were in a word 'closer to perfection', or to *the* Perfection—affirm the same ineluctable fatality: and in the profound spirituality that permeated every aspect of their lives—characterized always by a complementary opposition between Heaven and Earth, a reverence for the divinity in Nature, and by monotheistic and metaphysical doctrine as well—the same eternal Mercy. So the Tao often cites the example of 'the men of old'.

> The ancient masters were subtle, mysterious, profound, responsive.
> The depth of their knowledge is unfathomable.
> Because it is unfathomable,
> All we can do is describe their appearance.
> Watchful, like men crossing a winter stream.
> Alert, like men aware of danger.

Courteous, like visiting guests.
Yielding, like ice about to melt.
Simple, like uncarved blocks of wood.
Hollow, like caves.
Opaque, like muddy pools.

And in Chuang Tzu:

The pure men of old slept without dreams, and waked up without worries. They ate with indifference to flavor, and drew deep breaths… The pure men of old did not know what it was to love life or to hate death. They did not rejoice in birth, nor strive to put off dissolution. Unconcerned they came and unconcerned they went. That was all. They did not forget whence it was they had sprung; neither did they seek to inquire their return thither. Cheerfully they accepted life, waiting patiently for their restoration (the end). This is what is called not to allow the mind to lead one astray from Tao, and not to supplement the natural by human means. Such a one may be called a pure man.

Reverence. Circumspection. Dispassion. Contentment. The way it was, the way it's supposed to be. The way we can never stop wanting it to be. Whenever we seek peace and happiness, simple joy, the joy that is simultaneously oneness with everything and oblivion, we know it's a kind of return to something, to an original state prior to all human accretions and 'creativity', prior to any cultural tampering with our pure humanness, prior to history, civilization, literacy, the measurement of time and the knowledge of good and evil, and we know it's only found in Nature, in solitude, in stillness. 'Stillness and tranquillity set things in order in the universe.' We want to return to the original state, our true state, and *because* we know it is our true state, which is oneness with the immortal Tao of Heaven and Earth. The uncarved block. The No-Mind of Zen. The *So'ham* of Advaita Vedanta. In the language of theistic realization, we only want to be back with the Beloved we lose and find and lose again and again. ('There is only the fight to recover what has been lost/And found and lost again and again.' T. S. ELIOT) That Presence, our very Heart, the Self which is the Universe. It's always both 'back there' and within us, now. In the world of Time it is increasingly remote. In Itself, eternal in our hearts.

None of this, the Fall into Time, the one-way trip described in Chapter 18, the *Kali-Yuga*, is 'bad news'. It's simply the Truth. The message, the gift of Truth, is always Peace. Peace, Bliss, Emancipation: which is to say, you yourself, your very Self. You are the gift of Truth. And Truth is the Absolute, which is both 'within' and 'without'. It's visible right there, right before your eyes, in a single blade of grass. The way it sways in the wind, the way it holds and is held by your attention, your presence: the Cosmic Presence 'you' and 'all things' are. We say, 'the setting sun disappeared behind a cloud', but neither the sun nor the cloud know anything about each other, about that event we observed, and were just being what they are, what they eternally are. Can you see it? No one is here. Nothing has happened.

> The birds have vanished down the sky.
> Now the last cloud drains away.
> We sit together, the mountain and me,
> until only the mountain remains.
> ⁓Li Po, 701–762

> To those who know the secret,
> 'there's not a single thing'.
> They learn to give things up
> And simply practice stillness…
> Green mountains are white clouds
> In a passing transformation.
> ⁓Lu Yen

In John Blofeld's clear prose, referring here to Taoism and Buddhism:

Both systems stress the essential voidness of objective things, meaning that none of them is permanent nor can exist independently of other objective things, all of them being analogous to waves which, appearing on the surface of the ocean, have but a transient identity that is soon merged in the ocean that gave them birth. Just as there is no real and lasting difference between two sea waves, so is there no real difference between objects, since all arise from and revert to the universal 'non-substance' variously known as mind or spirit… distinctions spring from our minds; when false distinctions are not made, everything is as it is, neither good nor bad, neither this nor that… in order to attain to full realization, one does not have to *do* or to *become* anything whatsoever; what is needed is just to *be* what in fact one really has been from the first.

> From first to last there is
> No dying or being born;
> From a flash of thought a myriad
> False distinctions spring to mind.
> But when you know just where
> Those thought arise and vanish
> A radiant moon shines forth
> In the temple of the mind.

Then before you lies the truth
That there's nothing to be sought.
Of *themselves* the hills are green;
Of *themselves* the waters flow.
Let the mind by night and day
Embrace this single thought—
By thought wherein there's no thought
Must one cultivate the Way.
　～WANG CHING-YANG

Toshihiko Izutsu, in his marvellous *Sufism and Taoism*, puts it this way:

Being completely unified and identified with the Way itself, the man can
have no likes and dislikes. The man in such a spiritual state transcends the
ordinary distinctions between 'right' and 'wrong', 'good' and 'bad'. And since
he is now identical with the Way, and since the Way is constantly manifesting itself in myriad forms of Being, the man himself is 'being transmuted'
from one thing to another, without there being any obstruction, as if he were
moving around in the great Void... For he himself is, in this state, completely
identical with every one of these things, participating from within in the cosmic flux of Transmutation; or rather he is the cosmic Transmutation itself...
This is the moment when all things and 'I' become absolutely one. There is
no more opposition of subject and object—the subject that 'sees' and the
object 'seen' being completely unified—nor is there any distinction between
'this' and 'that', 'existence' and 'non-existence'. 'I' and the world are brought
back to their absolute original unity... At the stage of the absolute Oneness,
there is no more consciousness of the distinction between 'past' and 'present'.
There is no more consciousness of 'time'. We may describe this situation in a
different way by saying that the man is now in the Eternal Now. And since
there is no more consciousness of ever-flowing 'time', the man is in the state
of 'no Death and no Life'.

When no discriminating thoughts arise
the old mind ceases to exist.
When thought objects vanish,
the thinking-subject vanishes,
as when the mind vanishes, objects vanish.
Things are objects because of the subject [mind];
The mind [subject] is such because of things [objects].
Understand the relativity of these two
and the basic reality: the unity of emptiness.
In this Emptiness the two are indistinguishable

and each contains in itself the whole world...
words!
The Way is beyond language
for in it there is
no yesterday
no tomorrow
no today.
〜Hsin Hsin Ming, Verses on the Faith-Mind,
Seng Ts'an, (d. 606)

Blofeld, Izutsu, Chinese poetry. I've been trying to illustrate the point made above, in the paragraph where the setting sun disappeared behind a cloud. The *Kali-Yuga* is not 'bad news'. Nothing has happened. 'From a flash of thought a myriad false distinctions spring to mind.' Find the Eternal Now. Then all will be well.

XX

Zen and the Art of Cosmic Cycle Discountenance

WHILE writing the previous section on the keen Taoist insight I was constantly recalling, and locating, passages from D.T. Suzuki's great volume in the Princeton University Press Bollingen Series, *Zen and Japanese Culture*, especially from the concluding chapter titled 'Love of Nature'. (The Bollingen Series also includes fine books relevant to our discussion by Ananda Coomaraswamy, Mircea Eliade, and Henri Corbin.) There's a Zen Buddhist angle on our original state and its loss. In all traditions, for that matter, there's an 'angle' on our original state and its loss; all Revelations, as has been pointed out, are addressed to a fallen humanity. (Which is a *very* important thing to know about them.) There's an angle on it in your own Heart: an inner voice, drowned out, but never completely, by the racket in your mind, the *Kali-Yuga* roaring and gibbering, squawking and raving the internal monologue you think is your stream of consciousness. It's not yours.

How can we strike right through to it here?

Central to the Buddhist spiritual enterprise is a methodology, actually several methodologies, supported by its sublime metaphysics, the *prajna-paramita* of the Mahayana, for perceiving, for getting at and becoming one with, for realizing a pre-existing and eternal oneness with 'things as they really are': in their suchness which is their emptiness, *tathata* which is *sunyata*, emptiness of inherent or autonomous existence, *anatta*—words which are always defined only indirectly and with reluctance because 'defining' things, conceptualizing and objectifying, is precisely the way we *lose* the 'suchness' of things. Suzuki speaks of 'the mysterious Suchness that is beyond all comprehension.' He quotes the words of the 8th-century Master

Tenno Dogo: 'If you want to see, see right at once. When you begin to think, you miss the point.' Yet Suzuki tries; throughout all three volumes of the great *Essays in Zen Buddhism* series, in *The Awakening of Zen* and *Studies in Zen*, he tries his level best. Smiling, we can be certain, at the paradox; the smile of the Bodhisattva of Infinite Compassion, who has seen the serene invulnerability of Truth. Actually, there's a mysterious British fellow who writes under the name of Wei Wu Wei and publishes with the Hong Kong University Press—*Ask the Awakened, The Tenth, Man Posthumous Pieces,* among others—who comes about as close as language permits to elucidating the Buddhist *via negativa*; but his books are hard to find. (Well worth an effort, however.) Back to Suzuki:

> What Zen is most anxious to do in its own characterization is to reject conceptual mediumship of any kind… The epistemology of Zen is, therefore, not to resort to the mediumship of concepts. If you want to understand Zen, understand it right away without deliberation, without turning your head this way or that. For while you are doing this, the object you have been seeking for is no longer there. This doctrine of immediate grasping is characteristic of Zen… Zen leads us into a realm of Emptiness or Void where no conceptualism prevails.

Thus the Buddhist Realization, Zen's *satori*, unveils the world stripped of history and our lives of autobiography, of time and place and cultural accretions, of the illusory personality's illusory projections, of everything we plaster over immediate 'reality' and then assume to be 'out there'. There is no longer any separation between 'subject' and 'object', but a merging into the Oneness that has been Reality all along. 'It is better to say that there has never been any separation between subject and object.'

> Because of conceptualization our sense-experiences inform us with an incorrect picture of the world. When we see a mountain, we do not see it in its suchness, but we attach to it all kinds of ideas, sometimes purely intellectual, but frequently charged with emotionality. When these envelop the mountain, it is transformed into something monstrous… Instead of living in a world presented to the Primary Nature in its nakedness, we live in an artificial, 'cultured' one.

What remains when conceptualization is annihilated is the 'Void of Prajna' (translated by Suzuki as 'transcendental wisdom'), or Nirvana, which is not other than Samsara, daily life, transfigured through 'realization of emptiness' into what 'it' always was. I say 'it' in quotes because there is no 'it':

that's the whole point. Thus, this Realization, this Life in the Dharma which is Enlightenment, *reverses*, through a mental and sometimes physical disengagement from the conceptual mirages of civilization, through an attainment of 'no-mind', the dialectic of degeneration described in Chapter 18 of the *Tao*: it's a return, return to the Source, 'back to beginnings', to 'the Original Face.' 'Returning is the motion of the Tao.' This return is an option for any individual possessed of self-confident intuition, sound mind and indestructible resolve—or, more accurately, it is an answer to every life's questioning, it is the Truth which we are 'here' to realize,—but never for the collectivity, whose fate, as we have seen, was determined otherwise, at the foundations of the world, and which at any rate can never do what only individuals can do because it is metaphysically non-existent.

> The aim of Zen is thus to restore the experience of original inseparability, which means, in other words, to return to the original state of purity and transparency. This is the reason conceptual discrimination is discredited in Zen.

And, as we again recall, 'Returning is the motion of the Tao.'

Now Nature is the 'place' which is traditionally associated with Enlightenment and enlightened people, in Buddhism and the other traditions as well. The forest sages, holy hermits and anchorites, monastics in their mountain fastnesses, saints in remote *ashrams*, the 'God-possessed' ascetics and desert fathers. As recourse to a domain civilization has not yet polluted nor its attendant screen of conceptual mediations obscured and disfigured, a domain of purity, the 'return to Nature', or Creation—'the great "objectivation" of the "Divine Subject", the divine manifestation par excellence' (FRITHJOF SCHUON)—parallels the 'return' of individual consciousness to its primordial state, the enlightened mind or no-mind of Zen, and is therefore also a refuge, on the physical plane and as a 'life-style', from the Taoist dialectic of degeneration, from History: an escape from historical humanity and its fate which was always certain, and is not in the future—as those honest souls who issue urgent warnings and alerts, determined to keep the fire of hope -and-despair burning brightly, necessarily and ritualistically assume—but already present, here and now, the desolation we inhabit. The withdrawal from artificiality, decadence and deceit to the purity and, for some, experienced holiness of Nature ('where one can forget the world and its sad turmoils,' as Queen Victoria wrote, recalling with melancholy nostalgia a vacation in Scotland in 1847) has been a permanent rhythm among 'civilized' people, and is practiced today in various terminal forms such as the 'weekend', the 'vacation' and the 'suburbs' — strategies which, since they carry their own full cargo of irony, their own poignancy, require no comment. Suzuki, writing in the fifties — that is to say, when no one was yet aware that Nature as a planetary and cultural presence had been eliminated — discussed the recourse to Nature, 'the longing which most of us seem to feel in the depths of our hearts to go as far back to Nature as our human existence will permit and to be at one with her,' by defining the Japanese terms *wabi*, *sabi*, *fuga* and *kaminagara no michi*.

But before I proceed I want to explain why we are going into this, into the relationship between Zen and Nature, in Suzuki's exposition, as a response to Chapters 18 and 38 of the *Tao Te Ching*. It's a question that had been nagging me, a demand to justify what might be a misinformed compulsion, while I was putting together the material; it didn't seem, strictly speaking, to be germane. Actually it is; and for a reason deriving from that same Taoist intuition. The values that repudiate 'the rhythm of universal decadence that some call 'History', countering its insults, are themselves, as we have seen, a stage in its implacable unfolding, testimony, and proof. An anatomy of the *Kali-Yuga* would be incomplete without examples of the retorts it generates, the stratagems and affirmations with which the Protagonist, conscious of the threat and obliged both by self-respect and responsibility to its inner truth, retaliates. Furthermore, these values Suzuki identifies in the Zen dimension of Japanese culture are still, although admittedly decreasingly, options in our time. Even the last tree in the world would still be purely a tree, still the same evidence, the same transparency, the same perfume of 'that Bliss from which all things arise'. (For 'Bhrigu practiced meditation and learned that bliss is Brahman. For from bliss all beings are born, by bliss they are sustained, being born, and into bliss they enter after death.' — *Taittiriya Upanishad*). The stars — which are, to human eyes, in a human universe, a universe with primordial humanity as its Center, very Heaven, Beauty of God, Splendor of Truth, the Infinite Unknowable Glory, the Mystery to be Adored, 'the floor of heaven' (*Romeo and Juliet*), the Certitude of Spirit, Transcendent Joy, Ineffable Peace — are forever beyond the reach of the modern contamination, so long as we see them in their suchness, through human eyes, and not as the fictions (great big very heavy balls of very hot thermonuclear explosions) into which Science — meaning humanity, us, the original Being, transformed into instruments and equations, perceiving the world through instruments and interpreting the 'data' with mathematical equations, *and thereby creating that world as its new habitat*, the world of 'the physicist'—has slandered their inviolable attest. As I have insisted in many contexts, the *Kali-Yuga*, of which the Taoist dialectic of degeneration is one mode among others, is the fate of the collective but not of individuals who resist, for Mercy is eternal. 'I will not leave you comfortless: I will come to you.' (John 14:18) 'And, lo, I am with you always, even unto the end of the world.' (Matt. 28:20) *Patitapavana*, 'purifier of the fallen', is an epithet of Krishna, embodiment of redemptive Grace. I am reminded suddenly of the last page of *One-Dimensional Man* by Herbert Marcuse, another unconscious prophet of the *Kali-Yuga*, in which he used the phrase 'The Great Refusal'—thinking, in his day, of a radical political activism which, in its Hegelian ideology of 'negations', its urban setting and its purpose and purposiveness, could not be more distant from Japanese Zen, but which, nonetheless, in its instinct of rejection and disaffiliation, and its subsequent chastened reorientation toward more spiritual values, pacific solutions and an ecological perspective, has since matured, with the next generation of disaffection, into a sensibility considerably and consciously closer to the transcendent vision, detached compassion and awareness of unity with Creation that characterize the Eastern Wisdom. (As good old Wavy Gravy put it, in the 21st century we will learn 'how to duck with compassion.') Retorts, retaliations, refusals, apostasies, even rebellions—all necessarily distinguish the final stage of the cycle, for we remain human, we affirm the human, we bear witness.

So to resume. All four of the Japanese terms cited by Suzuki refer, with varying emphases, to turning one's back on History or Civilization or Society, on artificiality, 'Progress', the tormented 'creativity' of the *Kali-Yuga*, shaking that dust from your feet, and returning to the imperturbable reality, purity, simplicity and eternity of the natural world because there alone happiness and authenticity, peace and joy and our true humanity, oneness with Heaven, will be found.

> However 'civilized', however much brought up in an artificially contrived environment, we all seem to have an innate longing for primitive simplicity, close to the natural state of living... just to stay quietly content with the mystical contemplation of Nature and to feel at home with the world.

From an outer setting, the collective fraudulence, which corrupts or suppresses or confounds the inner being, to an outer setting, Nature, which awakens and nourishes its innate joy and self-sufficiency, its oneness with the All. For *Aham eva sarvam*: 'I myself am All'.

Suzuki introduces *wabi* by referring to the pensive feeling induced by the loneliness of autumn, giving one 'opportunity to withdraw the attention towards the inner life, which, given attention enough, spreads out its rich treasures ungrudgingly before the eyes.'

Here we have an appreciation of transcendental aloofness in the midst of multiplicities — which is known as *wabi* in the dictionary of Japanese cultural terms. *Wabi* really means 'poverty', or, negatively, 'not to be in the fashionable society of the time.' To be poor, that is, not to be dependent on things worldly — wealth, power, and reputation — and yet to feel inwardly the presence of something of the highest value, above time and social position: this is what essentially constitutes *wabi*. Stated in terms of practical everyday life, *wabi* is to be satisfied with a little hut, a room of two or three *tatami* (mats), like the log cabin of Thoreau, and with a dish of vegetables picked in the neighboring fields, and perhaps to be listening to the pattering of a gentle spring rainfall.

In our aboriginal humanity, prior to the introduction of any form of mechanization or inorganic power sources, our daily lives and labor kept awake in us a humble awareness and adoration of the Mystery in which we are contained and to whose Wisdom or divine prerogative we must submit, and we were rewarded, in this state, in this identity with our true stature in the universe, with the experience of the deep peaceful joy at the core of that awareness, and that humility. 'A life of *wabi* can then be defined: an inexpressible quiet joy deeply hidden beneath sheer poverty.' And 'Poverty is Zen'. Analogously, not 'knowing where we are', on the aerial photographers' maps or in the astronomers' radio-telescope universe, not 'knowing', according to Science's definitions, who we are or what we are or what anything whatsoever is, not having *any* of that crap in our consciousness, is *truly* knowing where we are, who we are and what everything actually is. Here too is Zen. A Japanese painting of the 12th century, showing 'a simple fishing boat in the midst of the rippling waters,'

is enough to awaken in the mind of the beholder a sense of the vastness of the sea and at the same time of peace and contentment — the Zen sense of the Alone. Apparently the boat floats helplessly. It is a primitive structure with no mechanical device for stability and for audacious steering over the turbulent waves, with no scientific apparatus for braving all kinds of weather — quite a contrast to the modern ocean liner. But this very helplessness is the virtue of the fishing canoe, in contrast with which we feel the incomprehensibility of the Absolute encompassing the boat and all the world.

This is *wabi*. A casualty of the *Kali-Yuga*. Yet immortal, yet eternal.

✳

Sabi, translated as 'loneliness', 'solitude', 'poverty', 'simplification', 'aloneness', is nearly synonymous with *wabi*, but stresses the objective aspect, that which 'evokes in one a mood to be called *wabi*.' It is found in 'antiquity or primitive uncouthness', in 'rustic unpretentiousness or archaic imperfection': everything that is the opposite of slick, streamlined, modern, expensive, efficient, and especially machine-made: all the state-of-the-art electric gadgets and megatons of electronic Information Age shit piled to the roof in the Radio Shack display windows. Remarking upon the crack in Rikyu's famous 'Onjoji vase' (the bamboo cracked in the drying), Lord Fumai (1751–1819), who 'had very fine taste for *sabi*,' reproved a complaining attendant with 'The *sabi* of this bamboo vase consists in the very fact of this leakage.' *Sabi* is whatever evokes an aesthetic appreciation of humility, of our obvious limitations and imperfections and the solemn depths to which our consciousness is ushered in dwelling upon them; it is an acceptance with a tranquil mind of whatever is given, or not given. '*Wabi* or *sabi*, therefore, may be defined as an active aesthetic appreciation of poverty.' 'Poverty' here is analogous to the distinctive trait of the 'poor in spirit' who are blessed, 'for theirs is the kingdom of heaven.' (For an insight into the meaning of 'poor in spirit' we are often directed to Isa. 66:2, 'But this is the man to whom I will look. He that is humble and contrite in spirit and trembles at my work.' In Eckhart's sense it means the emptiness of claim or pretension into which alone God may enter.) That poverty which is Zen, that 'philosophy of poverty, of *sunyata*, or Emptiness', is simply one man or one woman alone and consciously at one with the dispensation of God in that moment. '*Sabi*... is poetically defined by a tea-master thus':

> As I come out
> To this fishing village,
> Late in the autumn day,
> No flowers in bloom I see,
> Nor any tinted maple leaves.
> ⁓FUJIWARA SADAIYE, 1162–1241

As I have suggested, the return to Nature, to the richness of 'poverty' as opposed to the actual impoverishment hidden beneath material abundance and worldly 'success', parallels the 'return' from Ignorance to Enlightenment, to 'realization of Emptiness'. Suzuki points to the same parallel:

The poverty that permits no room for anything, even for the point of a nee-dle, is what is known in the philosophy of *Prajnaparamita* (*hannya, pan-jo*) as 'Emptiness' (*sunyata ku, k'ung*), and *sabi* or *wabi* is no other than the aes-thetic appreciation of absolute poverty.

To cling to things, to accept at face value worldly definitions and believe in the importance of worldly things, is to clutter the mind with hampering illusions, for there is no independent existence of anything at all: everything, preeminently the separate 'self', is empty of independent existence; to cling to *nothing*, and merely 'appreciate' it all as it goes by, kiss it as it flies (as I will at the San Francisco Blues Festival this weekend), 'rising and subsiding' in the Void of Prajna which we are and the world is, simply to live the given life without making any claims whatsoever upon the universe, imposing no alien standards, is the philosophy of poverty, here being equated elliptically with the Buddhist philosophy of Emptiness, whose discerning appreciation is *wabi* or *sabi*. 'Prajna' is the 'transcendental wisdom' or intuitive knowledge that directly perceives or 'realizes' the truth of Emptiness, or, more precisely, 'realizes' that 'Emptiness is in truth no less than the concreteness of reality itself.' When prajna-intuition is awakened, 'one has the enlightenment-expe-rience that constitutes the center of Buddhist philosophy.' It is being at peace. It is wonderful.

The Master—Suzuki is a Master—appeals again to autumn when he intro-duces the idea of *fuga*. 'In the beginning of autumn, when it begins to shower occasionally, Nature is the embodiment of Eternal Aloneness.' At this time, 'a lone traveler grows pensive over the destiny of human life. His mood moves with that of Nature.' When we enjoyed our true state—'once upon a time', in Eternity—we were all 'lone travelers' from time to time, maybe a good part of our time, and grew 'pensive over the destiny of human life.' (The modern parallel would be the alternating moods of anxiety, depres-sion, fear, regret, resignation, cynicism and despair experienced on the free-ways and upon awakening to the sound of the 'alarm' clock heralding another day at work.)

According to Basho, what is here designated as the spirit of Eternal Alone-ness is the spirit of *fuga* (or *furyu*, as some would have it). *Fuga* means 'refine-ment of life', but not in the modern sense of raising the standard of living. It is the chaste enjoyment of life and Nature, it is the longing for *sabi* or *wabi*, and not the pursuit of material comfort or of sensation. A life of *fuga* starts from the identification of one's self with the creative and artistic spirit of Nature. A man of *fuga*, therefore, finds his good friends in flowers and birds, in rocks and waters, in rains and the moon.

Two poems of the T'ang Dynasty (7th to 9th century), the golden age of Chinese poetry, embody well the spirit of *fuga*. It's strangely moving to read them; we feel clearly, drawn into a domain of immediacy and certitude where the irrelevance of dates and facts, the historian's 'reality', is too obvious even to remark upon, that these poets of long ago, or the dozens of others from whose poems these two were chosen almost at random, were the first, the prototypes, to express one particular sensibility's response to the grimly advancing obscuration of the unfolding cosmic cycle. Their voices reach out to us across the cloudy abyss that seems to separate us from that vague intemporal world of all the 'ancient sages' whose message and example always seem more urgent now than when we were young. The people whose character and world-experience were simultaneously innocent and profound beyond our capacity to reconstruct in imagination—so different from us!— and yet in whom we unfailingly recognize the image of our own deepest humanity. There is no time; only a greater or lesser proximity. The first poem is by Li T'ai-Po translated by our old friend, the fine Taoist scholar John Blofeld; the second is by Ch'ang Chien, translated by Witter Bynner.

> You ask me why I dwell
> Amidst these jade-green hills?
> I smile. No words can tell
> The stillness in my heart.
> The peach-bloom on the water,
> How enchantingly it drifts!
> I live in another realm here
> Beyond the world of men.

'At Wang Ch'ang-ling's Retreat':

> Here, beside a clear deep lake,
> You live accompanied by clouds;
> Or soft through the pine the moon arrives,
> To be your own pure-hearted friend.
> You rest under thatch in the shadow of your flowers.
> Your dewy herbs flourish in their bed of moss.
> Let me leave the world. Let me alight, like you,
> On your Western mountain with phoenixes and cranes.

✳

With *kaminagara no michi* the thesis of Zen comes closest to Taoism as discussed in the previous section. (Indeed in listing some of the old Masters' famous cryptic answers to the traditional question 'What is Zen?' Suzuki comments parenthetically, 'This is tantamount to asking "What is Tao?"') The *Kali-Yuga*, the harrowing experience of the Fall into Time, of History and 'Progress', the Reign of Quantity and the Mutation into Machinery, as we have seen from numerous perspectives, is characterized by a profound, and in its subsequent quest almost universally misdirected, sense of loss: stark chagrin, melancholy regret, helpless embitteredness, a nostalgia whose absence of clear content makes it only the more intense. We know we have strayed from something, something of our beautiful truth, our core of joy, strayed too far ever to return, and on a trajectory of ever-increasing velocity. *Kaminagara no michi* is one of the many forms this recognition of irreversible mishap, or incomprehensible destiny, assumes.

> There is in every one of us a desire to return to a simpler form of living, which includes simpler ways of expressing feelings and also of acquiring knowledge. The so-called 'way of the gods' points to it. Although I do not know exactly what signification the advocates of *Kaminagara no michi* want to give to this term, it seems to be certain to my mind that by this they wish to mean going back to or retaining or reviving the way in which the gods are supposed to have lived before the arrival of humankind. This way was one of freedom, naturalness, and spontaneity. How did we go astray from this? Here lies a great fundamental religious problem.

Great indeed. We think of the Fall from Grace of the Abrahamic monotheisms, *avidya*, or beginningless Ignorance, in the Eastern traditions, the Taoist dialectic of degeneration, and the unfolding of the great *Yugas, Krita, Treta, Dvapara and Kali*, in Hindu cosmology, the ever-widening gulf between the Principle and the Manifestation, Breath of the Eternal. This is our condition of suffering, *dukkha*, variously defined, to which the Mercy of Heaven, 'showing forth' as Truth and Presence — Incarnation and Atonement, Prophecy and Theophany, Revelation and Wisdom, Illumination and Realization, Divine Love and the Immortal Dharma — is addressed: waters of the eternal healing river. Here indeed 'lies a great fundamental religious problem.' For Suzuki, for Zen, 'its solution gives the key to understanding some aspects of Zen Buddhism and of the Japanese love of Nature':

> When we speak of being natural, we mean first of all being free and spontaneous in the expression of our feelings, being immediate and not premeditating in our response to environment, not making any calculation as to the effect of our doings either on others or on ourselves, and conducting

ourselves in such a way as not to leave room for thought of gain, value, merit, or consequence... When there is thus no crookedness in one's heart, we say that one is natural and childlike. In this there is something highly religious, and angels are represented sometimes as babies with wings.

'Going back to Nature, therefore, does not mean going back to the natural life of primitive and prehistoric peoples.' It means *becoming one* with Nature. Nature is the mirror that reveals, elicits, awakens our true selves, our authentic humanity; it is our Home. 'When we face nature, our whole being goes into it and feels every pulsation of it as if it were our own.' Nature remains what we were ourselves before the Fall, before we heeded the Serpent's arousal of suicidal inquisitiveness and the separate ego, *knew* we were 'naked', and were expelled from the Garden, the Paradise of Timelessness. (Naked: the knowledge that is shame, which has the same root as 'sham': we were separated from our unconscious, spontaneous, primordial state, no longer genuine, and *knew* it, although we were no different from what we had been before and always are: we were no longer 'at home', *at one*, with our true selves, no longer 'at home' in the Garden: in Creation. And remember: the Garden without the Serpent would have been Heaven, would have been God, Who is alone 'perfect'. Manifestation entails a 'hazard'.) Taoism and Zen Buddhism, of all the traditions, perceive most clearly the identity between the 'style' of Nature, unintentional, unconscious, purposeless, spontaneous—

there is no visible purpose in the waves rolling on from the beginningless past in the Pacific Ocean, and in Mount Fuji covered with ancient snow, standing absolutely pure high against the sky

—and the 'life-style' of the emancipated, which is to say, *the human norm.* They have a common Source.

Zen wants us to meet Nature as a friendly, well-meaning agent whose inner being is thoroughly like our own, always ready to work in accord with our legitimate aspirations... Zen purposes to respect Nature, to love Nature, to live its own life; Zen recognizes that our Nature is one with objective Nature, not in the mathematical sense, but in the sense that Nature lives in us and we in Nature.

But this identity and our departure from it, the schism between our essence and our existence, as we now understand, is perceived, noted with sorrow or anguish or alarm, only after the separation, prefigured in the Garden outside of Time, has already occurred, and only gradually, as the cycle

unfolds. Only after loss does recovery—Salvation, Redemption, Atonement, Sacrifice, Surrender, Submission, Illumination, Liberation—become
a project. In the words again of Ellen Chen, 'We are not aware of and do not
pursue something until we have already become separated from it.' And
'loss' is not quite the right word; our true nature, as all teachings agree, is
never actually lost; it is rather obscured, repudiated, paralyzed, ignored,
veiled, even fought. If damaged it can be healed, if tarnished cleansed, if
buried resurrected: for individuals. The sleeper can be awakened, the sinner
redeemed. The Buddha nature within us and within the universe, establishing our oneness, annihilating the subject-object illusion, is indestructible,
like the immortal Atman, like the Tao. It is the Reality: *tad ekam*, That
One. We've had glimpses (although only in words, of course) of what the
Buddhist understands by 'awakening'. Here's John Blofeld with the Taoist
experience:

> An immortal is one who, by employing to the full all his endowments of
> body and mind, by shedding passion and eradicating all but the simplest and
> most harmless desires, has attained to free, spontaneous existence—a being
> so nearly perfect that his body is but a husk or receptacle of pure spirit. He
> has undergone a spiritual rebirth, broken free from the shackles of illusory
> selfhood and come face to face with his 'true self', aware that it is not his per-
> sonal possession, being no other than the sublime undifferentiated Tao!
> With the vanishing of his seeming ego, he sees himself no longer as an indi-
> vidual, but as the unchanging Tao embodied in a transient cloud-like form.
> Death, when it comes, will be for him no more than the casting off of a worn
> out robe. He has won to eternal life and is ready to plunge back into the lim-
> itless ocean of pure being!

✳

Suzuki's exposition of 'returning to Nature' in Zen terms recalls a point
made more than once in these pages, namely that any contrast of the present
with the past should be construed as a metaphor, that it's really a matter of
conformity to or departure from the human norm; for historical humanity
the cycle unfolds in one direction only, away from that norm; there's no
returning to past ways of life closer to the Origin, and the comparisons serve
merely as an index of that unfolding. We shall not, as historical humanity,
re-enter the Garden; nor does the Garden exist anywhere other than where
it always existed and always exists: in our Hearts, in the Self, in Eternity.
The Buddha is your own Mind. The Taoist dialectic of decay, registering—

through successive 'ensembles of techniques', in Ellul's terminology—our progressive departure from spontaneous virtue, unpremeditated humanity, from Nature, from the Tao itself, unreels in the world-appearance only: it is *maya*, *samsara*, the round of birth-and-death, the transmigratory travail, the ever-flowing current of forms: the Cosmic Dream. Decadence is purely phenomenal. The Reality of things, their being *in divinis, sub specie aeternitatis*, is not subject to decay. In the language of Islam, the Names are forever, one with God. Nature, wherever it survives in the crevices not yet contaminated by humanity and History—and that contamination can be very subtle: a topo map or clock or calendar, in your mind or your backpack, is enough to do it—can reawaken in us the experience of the timeless present, the Eternal Now outside of Time, and the joy in the divine Beauty, the Beauty which is God or the Self or the ineffable Emptiness: and then there is no Fall from Grace, no Expulsion from Eden, no Taoist degeneration from the dawn in which we 'slept without dreams, and waked up without worries', no poignant appeal to *kaminagara no michi*. No *Kali-Yuga*. History vanishes into the Void of Prajna, like fog into the morning light.

✳

For Christians, to whom the world and events, History, were made real, objectively real, by the Incarnation, the descent of God into Time—as they were initially by the Voice from Sinai, the interventionism of Jehovah and the unwavering insistence of the prophetic writings, although this descent, restricted to ethnic Israel, could only be a prologue to its consummation, the universal radiation of Christ, Fulfillment of Israel—the miseries of History are overcome through our love of that very Event, our love of God in Christ, our Faith in Jesus.

> For I am persuaded, that neither death, nor life, nor angels, nor principalities, nor powers, nor things present, nor things to come, nor height, nor depth, nor any other creature, shall be able to separate us from the love of God, which is in Christ Jesus our Lord.
> ⁓ROM. 8:38–39

True; but the implications here—the subject is broached, at last, we'll have to deal with it at length later—give pause to even the most hesitant surmise. The suspicion that there might be a relationship between the Revelation of God in Christ—not the Christian religion as an historical presence and institution, not Western Christendom as the origin of Western

Civilization but the Revelation itself, the divine Initiative, the Incarnation—and the end of the cosmic cycle, the inescapable suggestion of causality, raises the gravest and most profound question the human mind can aspire, or presume, to address. (Our task in chapter XXIV) The Apostle's answer is definitive: definitive, true, metaphysically unimpeachable and glorious to contemplate in the oratory of the heart: it abolishes the question. 'Thy Will be done' is also definitive: it is the answer to 'Why?' Our own powers, summoned into play by our feeling that we have a right to understand our fate, and by an audacity enjoined, we hope condoned, by our extremity, are only adequate to answering the question 'How?' How did Bethlehem and Galilee, Golgotha and the Sea of Tiberias, generate and set in motion the stupendous forces that power the *Kali-Yuga*? How did Nazareth and Jerusalem, Olivet and Gethsemane, introduce, in Frithjof Schuon's words, 'the final decadence of the present cycle of humanity, this decadence being necessary for the exhausting of all the possibilities included in this cycle, necessary therefore for the equilibrium of the cycle as a whole and the fulfillment of the glorious and universal radiation of God'? How? Details of His unfathomable Providence: 'important' only to our curiosity, or to our detached thoroughness, our peculiar human impulse to thoroughness: 'for the sake of the record'.

✳

For Zen, on the other hand, History is overcome, the Taoist dialectic of degeneration annulled, by freeing oneself of conceptual interpretations and directly experiencing the 'isness' of Nature in the reality of the living moment. 'Have nothing left in your mind, keep it thoroughly cleansed of its contents. and then the mirror will reflect the images in their isness.' (YAGYU TAJIMA NO KAMI MUNENORI, 1571–1646, from the 'triple treatise on the sword'.)

> Zen is in close touch with Reality; indeed, Zen takes hold of it and lives it, and this is where Zen is religious... Reality or Suchness or Emptiness is taken hold of in the midst of the concrete living facts of the universe... The Philosophy of Zen consists in seeing directly into the mystery of our own being, which, according to Zen, is Reality itself.

> In Zen, in Reality, nothing is fixed and nothing is objective, as concepts are, but rather 'the living truth itself' is at once instantaneous and eternal in a realm, the Void of Prajna, where observer and observed are one: everything

inhabits that realm. Conceptualization, however, everything we *think* about the world, every interpretation or even every statement, separates us from its reality, which is always immediate, and from our own. In the words of the Master, 'But my solemn proclamation is that a new universe is created every moment Zen looks out from its straw-thatched four-and-a-half-mat retreat.' For a Zen adept, we are 'imprisoned in History', in the devastation described in these pages, the 'disaster' of the *Kali-Yuga*, only through an unexamined acquiescence, at once oddly casual and fanatically intractable, to definitions that are ultimately arbitrary, the captivating superimpositions ceaselessly erupting in our own minds. 'To reach maturity does not mean to become a captive of conceptualization. It is to come to the realization of what lies in our innermost selves.' We could recall here Suzuki's words quoted at the beginning of this section:

> Instead of living in a world presented to the Primary Nature in its nakedness, we live in an artificial, 'cultured' one. The pity is that we are not conscious of the fact.

Here, then, is the 'Zen Buddhist angle on our original state and its loss' to which I referred in the opening paragraph. 'The Primary Nature in its nakedness' is our original state; conceptualization and lives removed from the natural world, 'civilized' lives, are its loss. Yet this is not final, for it is itself conceptual: one step removed, one fatal step. On the one hand, all Revelations, in their esoteric core, as doctrines of Realization, are addressed to individuals 'capable of God' scattered among the doomed collective, individuals who are not 'pre-determined' but are potentially anyone who 'raises sails in the ever-blowing breeze of Grace': they can 'rise above' the *Kali-Yuga*; and on the other hand, all Revelations, Realizations, bondage and liberation, Ignorance and Enlightenment, individuals and the collective, are equally illusory: the Cosmic Dream. Buddhism knows itself to be an *upaya*, 'a saving mirage'. All Religions are *upayas*. 'In reality, the entire terrestrial existence of the Prophet passed thus, as a dream in a dream.' (Ibn 'Arabi, *Fususu 'l-Hikam*) Nirvana is Reality, and It is accessible—but only to no one.

> The point I wish to make here is that at the time Chiyo perceives the morning-glory early in the morning, which is the best time to see the flower, she is so absorbed in its unearthly beauty that the whole universe, including herself, is transformed into one absolute morning-glory blooming all by itself. This is the time, as Zen would declare, when Chiyo really sees the flower and the flower in turn sees the poetess. This is a case of perfect identification

between subject and object, seer and seen: the whole universe is one flower, one real flower that stands here defying all change and decay. There is no one seeing it and admiring it. It is the flower seeing itself, absorbed in itself. At this supreme moment, to utter even a word would be altogether out of place…

The *jnani*, sage, *jivan-mukta*, 'liberated in this life', affirms with calm bliss, 'I am the Self-Awareness of the Universe which is the Universe.' *Tat tvam asi*: That art Thou.

Now Capital (*Kapital*: which we will be examining very shortly) is really one particular embodiment of the *Kali-Yuga*—one of the forms it assumes, one of its faces. It screams and whispers, raves and gibbers, howls and lies to us in this form, incessantly. And among the myriad topics, whose totality composes (in both senses!) our entire so-called 'lives', upon which it offers commentary and clarification is the very topic we have been addressing: the withdrawal from civilization into Nature. Here it often aspires to the poetic, and the following may be profitably compared to the preceding samples from the T'ang Dynasty. It was selected from among the thousands available in the newspapers and magazines lying around anyone's home. Capital, of course, is we ourselves: our present state.

THE END OF CIVILIZATION
There you are. Beyond the last lonely outpost. Where civilization ends and nature takes over. Oops. It's getting dark. As the wind whistles down your neck and shadows begin to grow tall, you pull out your secret weapon: the Eddie Bauer turtleneck.
This is the quintessential item. The proven friend of mountaineers, travelers, poets and bohemians alike. It is simply the best.
With a premium cotton interlock body, spandex in the collar and cuffs to seal out the cold. and elastic-reinforced shoulder seams.
To want one is natural. To have one is nearly essential. It's in your genes. And it also goes with them. Women's: $15. Twelve solid colors. Nine sizes.
Men's: $15. (Slightly more for Tall and XXL.) Ten colors. Nine sizes.
Visit our stores or order now. 1-800-426-8020.
EDDIE BAUER
Each Piece is a Signed Original
⌒ATLANTIC MONTHLY

XXI

Three

THROUGHOUT this study (I just realized it this morning, just put it together in my mind) I have tried to convey the reality of what Eastern metaphysics calls the *Kali-Yuga* through the convergence and mutual confirmation of three bodies of testimony.

First, Tradition: the revealed Word, Word of God, *Hagia Sophia*, Divine Wisdom; that metaphysical Comprehension which is Knowledge Absolute, the Intellect, 'that in man which participates in the divine Subject: the Intellect is in the subjective mode what Revelation is in objective model' (Frithjof Schuon); *scientia sacra*, gnosis, esoterism; *Religio Perennis*, the Perennial Philosophy.

Second, the interpretations, analyses, and admonitions of serious secular thinkers, witnesses to the humanist perspective, from Karl Marx to Jean Baudrillard, whom I have referred to as 'unconscious prophets of the *Kali-Yuga*.'

And third, evidence drawn from the panorama of life in these times, the nature and quality both of our experience and our culture. In a word, the experience of the Protagonist, Historical Humanity. The experience of people living in 'the under-developed countries', what was once called 'the Third World', is of course different in many respects, as was the experience of people living in those anxious commonwealths whose 'leaders' identified their regimes as 'communist' or 'socialist' or 'mixed'; but what I describe in these pages is, with local variations, the future they are struggling to realize, the future they've been 'sold' and to which they aspire with fierce and quite understandable determination: it is the life they envy, it is called 'development', and it is the only 'fulfillment' conceivable to them. *Sunset Magazine*, Californialand, *Wired*. They cannot escape their identity with the Protagonist, nor can the inevitable dawning awareness of that identity, with all its implications, assume any form other than the baffling apprehension, cynicism, defensive anger and exhausted stupefaction, the 'escape' into the Prison of Unreality, I have been describing in these pages. They will become, they already are, *the transformation into technology* which is our final state, the True Death, the *rigor mortis*, Final Curtain. Their future is the drug to which they are already addicted.

It should be understood that the first of these three 'bodies of testimony' is not on the same plane as the other two, although they are indispensable to a thorough understanding. It 'stands without', casting Light on our lives in this world, situating the partial insights of secular thought and personal experience in their metaphysical foundation, in the Totality—in a word, in their position in the descending trajectory of cosmic time—but also affirming this world's ultimate unreality and therefore our independence, as individuals, from its fate: it is both Truth and Salvation, both Consolation and Emancipation.

XXII

Four

～No nod to Miles Davis intended

1. After 'Dover Beach'
Homage to Matthew Arnold

The sky is clear tonight.
The roof of stars, the Milky Way,
A dazzling splendor. Tall firs fringe the light;
Orion blazes. A night breeze murmurs down
The hill, circles the meadow, ascends again.
Stillness, peace, after a noisy day. I lie down in the grass. Men
And women with jet black hair, brown
Faces, lived here once. They may
Have walked this meadow; lay down in the grass
Like me, strung the Northern Crown
To Vega, Rigel to Capella—though
With their names. Watched the torn clouds pass
Across the moon. So long ago.

There ghosts are here: I feel
Them. Silent shadows staring at the stars.
The Sinkyone. We watch the diamond wheel
Of heaven turn, they lie
Beside me—ancient avatars
Of earth, my very soul. They cannot die.

You have to go
Further back, Matthew Arnold, my old friend:

Further back than the age of faith, to find
The measure of our fall.
You saw an end in Europe. We see an end
Also: you'll never know
What happened. Rest in peace. These ghosts are all
We have. You walk the land, they come to mind.

Still the stars; and still
The Deep humanity—it yet survives.
We're human: but we live inhuman lives.
And we don't pretend otherwise; we kill
Ourselves, the land, and know it. But tonight
The stars, the meadow and the ghosts; we dwell
Enough upon our pain. Here all is well.
They smile at me, their eyes gleam, cold and bright.
We drift, like dreams, into the deathless light.

2. Friends

There are certain expressions
That appear on our faces
When we meditate or pray
Whose decreasing incidence traces

The winding down of the cycle.
This is a very basic fact.
Their disappearance marks the eclipse
Of humanity: The Final Act.

Why? Because they reflect the states
Of mind and stations of the heart
In which we are fully human
And Truth unveiled. 'Things fall apart,

The Center cannot hold,' in the words
Of the poet, when the human face
Becomes a stranger to itself.
There are losses nothing can replace,

We're talking about oblivion.
Imagine the faces of your friends
Transfigured by the love of God,
By knowledge of their final ends:

How beautiful, how radiant!
That's who they really are, you know.
I always think of them that way,
Transfigured, radiant. Their eyes glow,

At peace at last, they know the Truth.
These thoughts can move a man to tears.
Absences, the fate of friends, the fate
Of us all. The gathering years.

3. EntryExit

There is no joy to equal the joy
Of knowing the 'me' does not exist.
Nothing even approaches it.
Miss that joy, that bliss, and you've missed

The whole purpose of life. You will
Have lived without ever knowing
The Truth: Buddha-Nature, Tao, the Self:
The Changeless in the Ever-Flowing.

Try to learn about these things.
Turn your back on the inane
Racket of the world, listen
To something real, like the rain,
Birds, anything, and tell yourself,
As if your whole life is at stake,
And it is, that you have the strength
Left, the will, to make the break.

But it's not an achievement.
Nothing is achieved. In all this
There's nothing personal anywhere.
You are Impersonal Bliss.

Impersonal, which is why
It's so wonderful. Why you'll know,
Without the slightest doubt,
That this was the only way to go.

4. Brief

To see things as they really are,
To know the Morning Star's a star
And not what telescopes proclaim,
To know what water was, and flame,
Before the chemists came along
And said we were completely wrong,
Said compassion, joy and dread
Were just secretions in the head,
To see the land, the sea and skies
The way they looked through human eyes,
The rainbow, river moon and sun
When we, the world and God were One.
Those days are gone, beyond recall.

There are two aspects of the Fall.
Two settings for the Fall from Grace:
Eternity, and time and space.
It happens in Eternity—
Eve and Adam, you and me,
The dialogue in paradise,
The snake, the apple and the price—
And Eternity becomes the world,
The Earth upon which we were hurled:
Where that rebellion of the blest
Is called the Triumph of the West.

And now we're blind. We lost our sight.
There's darkness where there once was light.
It's still the Garden, we're still there,
It lies about us everywhere,
But all we see now, all we find,
Are the facts and figures in our mind.
The given world was not enough:

We looked for more, discovered stuff
Behind, beyond what eyes could see,
And called that stuff reality.
The world that science says is real,
The world that instruments reveal,
A world we cannot see or hear,
Wonder, love, respect, revere,
That's where we live now: our reward.
The angel with the flaming sword,
The exiles in their maze of lies
Who feverishly specialize
In finding ways to numb their pain—
Both are us. We toil in vain.
What's human suffering but the price
Of discontent in paradise?

XXIII

What a Long Strange Trip It's Been

Rest in Peace, Jerry Garcia, and regards to
the Grateful Dead wherever you are

WE don't know what will become of our children, we who live in
the *Kali-Yuga*. As we don't know what will become of the world, the Earth.
We wish the best for them, but we don't know what that would mean, and
we know we don't know. We want them to be happy in their lives, because
we love them, but we feel, as they do, that they are entering, have already
entered, the last few hours of a ravaged and desecrated planet, upon which
the human race has become a cancer. We survey a scene unprecedented by
definition. All our thoughts are of the unknown and unknowable future.
We stare into the darkness as if mesmerized by a wondering dread. We are
reduced to the embodiment of one question: 'What will become of us? Will
we survive?'

That was one voice, one mind. A time-capsule voice, voice of our times.
Decent, noble, truthful, troubled: responsible: matured. It speaks of, and
believes in, 'our children', 'the Earth', a 'planet'. It envisages a 'future', the continued unfolding of historical time. From 'our children' to *the* children,
meaning all the children in the world, posterity, is a lightning leap in that
generous mind.

But that generous mind, as we should recognize by now, is trapped. In
History, and in a purely material 'reality'. Trapped in Time, trapped in Matter, trapped in its own error. Reality is not physical, we are not physical
beings, Humanity is not temporal, not a biological succession of generations. 'We' is an illusion and the Reality to which the pronoun refers does
not 'live on a planet'. All of this is Ignorance, of which the 'hope-and-fear
regard' is the very fountainhead.

Ignorance, however, within which certain observations can be made, as they always have, whose thrust is to turn our vision inward where the Truth may be discovered and our souls become free. The subject here is children. Children, childhood, parenthood, childrearing—the most 'personal', most emotional area of our lives, therefore where Truth seems most irrelevant, and our attitude towards it most defiant. Let's review at the outset our fundamental experience, we who are historical humanity at the closing of the cycle, as it has been evoked in many contexts.

We view nearly everything in the *Kali-Yuga* with a mixture of hope and fear. Apprehension, foreboding; expectations also: but always tentative, guarded, carefully circumscribed. Slightly forced. Because we never know what's going to happen next, what might be in store for us. Never sure what's really going on. Is 'the economy' going to collapse or is this just another 'budget crisis'? Are the algal blooms appearing everywhere natural or caused by pollution? Holes in something called the ozone layer, global warming, the greenhouse effect, endangered species, deforestation, desertification: what's it all about? Are the schools really going to be 'restructured' or is it just a lot of bullshit? Are we winning or losing the war against crime, the war against drugs, the war against AIDS, the war against cancer, the war against homelessness? Historical society: life always in flux, the invisible wheels always turning. nothing stable; behavior and consequences, decisions and outcomes, on every level are unpredictable, maybe even unconnected. Even the significance of what we see plainly, what has already happened, is never clear: this most recent and obviously revolting or alarming development in culture or life style, in our own family, may be nothing more than another new norm, a change of mode, perhaps even an advance or improvement, but probably neither better nor worse than last year's or last month's norm—or the norm we knew when we were young—and nothing to be upset about. Nothing to worry about or view through narrowed eyes. 'Don't over-react.

But the apprehension, the undercurrent of suspicious misgivings, is always there. It doesn't go away. Presentiments of trouble or a serious problem or jarring calamity have taken up permanent residence in the back of our minds; we're always wondering uneasily what it's all about, what might be going on 'behind the scenes', where it's heading. 'What does this mean?' Is this a portent or just the latest thing? Should I be doing something about this? Is it going to hit us personally? What's going on around here? In our own collective life, our collective self.

And nowhere does the 'hope and fear *regard*', that insistent continually resurfacing duet of feelings, turn more frequently and focus more intensely than upon our children. Through our children, through our struggles to guide or even understand their lives, we are identified with, possessed by historical humanity in its gathering darkness most completely, most automatically—without a second thought, as it were—we face ourselves as historical humanity most intimately, most passionately, face ourselves 'closest to home', and we suffer, suffer because we love, grapple with ourselves—arguing, pleading, reasoning, cajoling, scheming, lying awake at night, worrying and fighting endlessly about money—like wrestlers locked in struggle with their mirror images. The colossal thundering kaleidoscopic scenario exploding around them, the Great Spectacle, the Great Technotopia, society at this moment, the *Kali-Yuga* now, into which they fly away from our homes and arms and hearts whirling like leaves in the wind, the space so different from the one we knew, or thought we knew, appearing so full to them, so 'exciting', so 'challenging', abashes and confounds us: alien, unprecedented, indecipherable: clearly treacherous, clearly perilous, almost mockingly men-dacious—or simply 'crazy'. It mocks our most prudent decisions; foils our most conservative strategies. We are assured, we assure ourselves, that it's always been this way, that things have always seemed on the brink of falling apart but held, that there's always been a 'generation gap'. But we're not consoled.

Not consoled. What we forget, or never learned, which would console us—the point is not belabored; every way of saying it is another way of seeing it, therefore an opportunity to ponder it, to think about whether it's going to mean anything to us—is that humanity has not always been historical (there has not always been a 'generation gap') and in its truth, its Reality outside of Time, is not. Or, in other words, as humanity, the eternal spiritual being, is not historical, so historical humanity is not human, not where humanity is *found*. Or to be fully precise, fully fair to ourselves, History is the road along which we 'progressively' lose our humanity. The road out of Heaven and Eden, the road from Oneness, from the Origin and Center, from Nature, from the Great Tao, from ourselves. The road into the *Kali-Yuga*, the road called Progress.

Let's begin on a Foundation.

From 'our side of the river' the original and eternal Oneness, *Tad Ekam*, The One, *Ekam Eva*, The Only One, appears to divide into three: Heaven, Earth and humanity. These are, in Vedanta, *Atma*, *jagat* and *jiva* (which, incidentally, uttered as a single Sanskrit word, *Atmajagatjiva*, makes a powerful mantram), although one could substitute *Isvara*, God as Creator, for *Atma*, the Self, and we should keep in mind that *jiva* shifts the emphasis from Humanity, the collective being, to the individual soul.

> The *jiva*, *jagat* and *Ishvara* constitute the triple relative order. The individual experiencer (*jiva*), the world of experience (*jagat*), and their Supreme Ruler (*Isvara*) are the three main categories of the relative existence. These are acknowledged by most religious and philosophical systems…Truly speaking, *Isvara* is the Supreme Self (*paramatma*) that manifests and sustains all finite existences, conscious and unconscious, the animate and the inanimate… The Tripartite relative order vanishes when the Absolute (the unconditioned Brahman) is released.
> ⁓Swami Satprakashananda,
> *The Universe, God, and God-Realization.*

So, for a human child blessed with a human habitat, a traditional society, and by extension a human adult similarly blessed—for those, in other words, from whom we can claim descent: our progenitors, the humans—there are two great Realities in which we 'discover' ourselves (in both applicable senses of the word here), and they are Heaven and Earth (or Revelation and Creation, God and the World, Spirit and Matter, the Mystery and its Manifestation, *Atma* and *Maya*, Father Sky and Mother Nature or Mother Earth, *Magna Mater*) neither of which are brought into being by our own agency and therefore synthetic, artificial, manufactured, 'man made', easily explicable, amenable to modification and improvement or critical reevaluation and discard: 'beneath' us; but rather are 'found', prior, given, 'intended', 'for us': the inherent dimensions of our metaphysical being, our Truth: our inner and outer Reality, the elicitation and orientation of our love, reverence, worship, adoration, gratitude and apprenticeship and the Source both of our Knowledge and our Existence. Heaven and Earth, the eternal Setting, the irresistible enchantment, the thrill of joy leaping in our hearts when, *deo favente*, the veil is lifted in the silence of the candlelit shrine: the Great Tao: both 'the Hidden Treasure that wanted to be known' and the World It created to that end (*Hadith Qudsi*). To live thus, on Earth and under Heaven, is, and was, to be human. To realize their Oneness, and our Oneness with both—'Thou art the world in our hearts, I am the world in God'—is, and was, fulfillment, Realization: Illumination, Salvation and Peace. True, it had to be *received*: but it was *offered*. Reality is Grace, there is nothing but Grace, all this is Grace.

In contrast, the components of 'reality' for children of the *Kali-Yuga*, the 'reality' in which they 'discover themselves', assume their identities, and which they *become* as adults, are wall-to-wall man-made, actually machine-made, 'our work' as we construct the mechanism of which we are the components. Nor is the 'outdoors' any more genuine: supervised recreation in parks, camps and soccer fields is simply another technique, and even when children manage to escape supervision, the 'outdoors' is approached and experienced in social situations, and in prefabricated 'modern' mind-sets and identities, that transform Nature into 'instances' of media imagery, making its direct perception, as the original humans knew it, all but impossible. (This is *Bonanza* country! And Little Joe and Hoss are dead!) We know all too well what their world is about. The television programs and the non-existent 'reality' they imply, the media images and semblances, both visual and conceptual, the videos, sports spectaculars and their relentlessly fabricated 'super-stars', musical fads, the end-of-the-road brain-shattering unreality of MTV, computer games with their grotesque supremely *ugly* little cartoon people and animals, cars, gadgets, statistics, buzzwords, soundbites, cyborgs, commercials, innumerable brand names, Numbers and Money. Numbers and Money world without end. Circus Maximus, Universal Bullshit. ('Exciting', incidentally, our most positive adjective, *always* refers to the Universal Bullshit.) Something new in the world called 'sleaze', and all the bright pointless countless scraps of worthless junk that drift and flicker through our 'minds' in the 'Information Age' — in which 'information glut', by destroying the capacity to recognize irrelevance destroys relevance as well, therefore significance, coherence, usefulness, importance, meaning... and *things* in infinite variety, *things* in charge of society, *things* in the saddle, *things* tearing off and chewing up the shreds of human minds, the continuous volcanic eruptions of cultural sewage — in short, in a word, what Jean Baudrillard called 'hyper-reality'.

Hyper-reality. Let's seize this juncture as the occasion (finally) for an exposition of hyper-reality — the word Baudrillard uses to point at what has happened to us, our true honest-to-goodness condition, so bizarre it's almost impossible to describe or even perceive, our terminal catastrophe as historical humanity, the language-defying, invisible and all-pervading *unreality of our lives*, the supreme suicide made possible at last by the convergence of all technologies, and not as a digression here but as the currently most penetrating (most 'metaphysical', most 'far-out', most 'visionary', sounding often most crazy, as crazy as the mind-bending craziness, the omnipresent infinitely elusive madness it is determined nonetheless to identify, apprehend and dissect, to drag out into the open and thrust under your nose) examination of the 'reality' in which our children 'discover themselves' in the *Kali-Yuga*. Their, and our, intangible assassination. For we inhabit, and our children inherit—in the new 'technopoly' (Neil Postman's term), in the synthetic nether world of urban-industrial-vehicular-commercial-technological-pharmaceutical-electronic-'information'-spectator-entertainment-consumer society whose sole 'intention', since it is Capital, is *to use human beings as a machine uses fuel*, where they will discover the 'work-day' and will 'work', where they will discover advertisements and commercials and will consume, and where they will recuperate in 'screenworld', in that moronization of the mind and massacre of the spirit induced by 'entertainment' (and now also by 'infotainment', 'infomercials', and Blockbuster Video) and welcomed with a sigh of pleasure and relief, *earned*, as 'leisure': and since there is no one here but us, it is *we* who do all this to *ourselves*, which is what Marx meant when he called Capital a *social relationship*— inherit (picking up after that lengthy *parentithenai* the syntax here) inherit the ultimate polar opposite, the ultimate negation, of the human Norm, that vanished-in-History yet ever-present-in-potential 'triple relative order' composed of the human soul, facing no other enemy of its eternal promise than the hazard of freely-chosen error, the true Earth, divine, unfettered, unpolluted and unexpropriated, and the Creator, Who is infinite Love, of both: Humanity on Earth and under Heaven. Reality. *Nara, Sakti*, and *Siva* as One in the great mantra *Hamsah* of the Yoga of Supreme Identity. The basic 'nature of things' which was, and remains, and is forever the inheritance of human children. We've come a long way, a very long way.

'Man-made': it begins as a thin film, transparent, its future unforeseeable, over Nature, containing only what is necessary for survival of body and soul, for continuity without change, a mirror of the observed Order, the great Tao. As the cycle unfolds, as 'civilizations' develop, it thickens, becomes thicker and thicker, increasingly opaque and ever enriched, drawing its raw material from the Nature it is inexorably replacing, transforming this material into a fascinating living screen, a new world, articulate, irresistibly captivating and joyously self-aware, the world of 'culture', which, plastered over

Nature, pushing it ever further into the background, exploiting it for ever greater triumphs of 'culture', decreeing its increasing marginality, irrelevance, obsolescence, and eventually, in its terminal incarnation as Technology, eliminates it. Expels it: as we were expelled, the fulfilment in Time of our own Expulsion *ab origine*, the fulfillment prefigured in Eden. And as Nature disappears, so also Heaven: for we are sufficient unto ourselves. We, ourselves, the Power and the Glory, the Source and the Purpose, Alpha and Omega, Arche, and Eschaton, the Goal and the Way—and the Explanation. This is the way it goes, and that was the way it went.

✳

Baudrillard's work follows upon Marx's. The Marx of commodity circulation and fetishism, reification, alienation, that great masterpiece *Capital Volume One, The Economic and Philosophical Manuscripts of 1844, The Poverty of Philosophy* and the *Grundrisse*. He describes the stages in capitalist development following upon the stages seen and foreseen by Marx, and announces the transcendence of those stages, their yielding of centrality. I would like to go into Marx here, into the unhuman 'universe of exchange value' which we inhabit and have come to accept as normal, the notorious 'social relationship of the commodity form' in which people are transformed into 'workers', or 'labor power', and in their social dimension, like the things they produce, are actually 'commodities', or forms assumed by 'money'— 'Above all the worker can only become conscious of his existence in society when he becomes aware of himself as a commodity' (Georg Lukacs, 'Reification and the Consciousness of the Proletariat'): that is, when our children finally decide in what guise they will enter 'the job market'—since this condition, this transformation of Humanity into Capital, was already terminal and its shattering recognition therefore and potentially a profound spiritual event for certain individuals, a basis for vigorous spiritual incentive.

(In a nutshell: 'The worker' is both producer and consumer of the 'life' by which he or she is degraded and dehumanized, in the labor process and in consumption. Capital, that 'social relationship of the commodity form', is as indifferent to the product of labor, 'whatever sells', as it is to the producer, a 'factor of production' no different from raw materials and machinery, as it is to the consumer, the 'point' where the circulation of commodities is completed, consummated: *The Accumulation of Capital through Conversion of Surplus-Value into Capital* [*Capital* vol. 1, pt. VII, chaps. 23 and 24], the great god 'economic growth', alone matters, and for its own sake, because it is the engine of the whole system, the *sine qua non* and *raison d'être* of capitalism. The world of things, of commodities, and the closed universe it erected for and within itself—all of it our 'work', all of it our 'enterprise'—the entire synthetic urban-industrial environment within which the inferno of production and consumption rages, Marx's 'immense workshop', supplants Nature and Humanity, while the successful sale of oneself in the labor market, as well as the 'problem of unemployment'—which, incidentally, is inherent in the system—assume that being a producer and consumer of one's own degradation is a 'good', indeed the sole good, the very meaning of life, and to be excluded a harrowing mischance if temporary, a disaster if prolonged. We call all this Freedom, and a recent planetary consensus seems to suggest that it's the best we can do for ourselves in the *Kali-Yuga*.)

But the bibliography here, the Marxian intellectual archive, is sufficiently immense, and the structure of this essay sufficiently determined, to make such an excursion into Marx ill-advised, to say the least. I am thinking, of course, that if you, whoever you are, could see the world as Marx unveiled it in *Capital I* and the *Grundrisse*, meaning see your society for what it really is, in its truth, 'get the idea', you'd have yet another basis, and a compelling one, for laying down the burden of worldly hope that binds you to historical humanity and choosing instead to 'consider' Spirit. (I am always, in enthusiastic collaboration with the world, provoking you to this end!) But I just can't do it. It's too much, tempting as it may be. And anyway, at the present moment in this essay the question of 'overkill' is starting to enter my mind from time to time.

As is the question of academicism. (Am I an academic? Up here in these rolling dope-growing hills, so remote from academies?) Marx's work—not the 'brilliant but shallow' *Communist Manifesto* crap of his youth but the profound 'Critical Analysis of Capitalist Production', as *Capital I* is subtitled, of his maturity—is the deserving subject of respectful, almost reverent appreciation by European and American (North and South) university intellectuals, and nothing more than that: it has no social relevance or even presence, and what Martin Nicolaus says of the *Grundrisse* in the Foreword to his translation is certainly equally applicable to the writing of Baudrillard today:

> In 1858, not a single person in the world understood the *Grundrisse* except Marx, and even he had his troubles with it. It was an altogether unique and in every sense *strange* product of the intellect, and must have appeared like the reflections of some man from a distant planet.

Nonetheless, both men saw truly. So let's take a look at Baudrillard's work—as brief as possible, and always remembering the context here: the world, or absence of a world, that our children inherit, and the journey in our hearts that knowledge of that inheritance demands of us. Throughout, unless otherwise indicated, I will be quoting from Douglas Kellner's study, *Jean Baudrillard: From Marxism to Postmodernism and Beyond* (Stanford University Press, 1989), and all quotations within Kellner's text, unless otherwise indicated, will be from Baudrillard himself.

During the 1980s Jean Baudrillard has been promoted in certain circles as the most advanced theorist of the media and society in the so-called postmodern era. His theory of a new, postmodern society rests on a key assumption that the media, simulations and what he calls 'cyberblitz' constitute a new realm of experience and a new stage of history and type of society. To a large extent Baudrillard's work consists in rethinking radical social theory and politics in the light of developments in the consumer, media, information and technological society. Baudrillard's earlier works focus on the construction of the consumer society and how it provides a new world of values, meaning and activity, and thus inhabit the terrain of Marxism and political economy. From the mid-1970s on, however, reflections on political economy and the consumer society disappear almost completely from his texts, and thereafter simulations and simulacra, media and information, science and new technologies together produce what Baudrillard calls 'implosion' and 'hyper-reality'. These novel phenomena become the constituents of a new postmodern world which in—Baudrillard's theorizing—obliterates all the boundaries, categories and values of the previous forms of industrial society, while establishing new forms of social organization, thought and experience.

Baudrillard traces three stages, three 'centers of the dynamic', ultimately three defining centralities of human experience, three inner and outer landscapes or life styles or ways of dehumanizing ourselves in the grim unfolding of Capital's dominion to its final consummation in our times: production, consumption, and finally, now, hyper-reality. The transition from the first object of classical Marxian analysis, to the second took place in the 1920s, from the second to the third in the last four decades of this century. All 'stages' remain, however; no previous stage is annulled, but rather a new center of emphasis emerges. 'Whereas capitalism focused its energies on developing a system of mass production during the nineteenth and early twentieth centuries, beginning in the 1920s the issue of mass consumption and the management of consumer demand became an issue of paramount importance.' In Baudrillard's own words:

We don't realize how much the current indoctrination into systematic and organized consumption is *the equivalent and the extension, in the twentieth century, of the great indoctrination of rural populations into industrial labor, which occurred throughout the nineteenth century.* The same process of rationalization of productive forces, which took place in the nineteenth century in the *production* sector, is accomplished, in the twentieth century, in the *consumption* sector... We are surrounded today by the remarkable conspicuousness of consumption and affluence, established by the multiplication of objects, services and material goods, all of which constitutes a sort of fundamental mutation in the ecology of the human species. Strictly speaking, these affluent individuals are no longer surrounded by other human beings as they were in the past, but by *objects*... Just as the wolf-child becomes a wolf by living among them, so we are ourselves becoming functional objects. We are living the period of objects: that is, we live by their rhythm, according to their incessant succession. Today, it is we who are observing their birth, fulfillment and death... We have reached the point where 'consumption' has grasped the whole of life...

What else do we ever see, wherever we look, but *products* and their *names* and the inflammation of a consumer appetite? Want This Now! we are ordered.

What we are talking about here in the restricted language of political economy—although with Baudrillard that language is clearly challenging its limitations, threatening to 'burst its bounds'—is, in the total, 'infinite' and ecstatic vision of cyclical apprehension, the 'thickening' of the world into pure matter, its increasing 'heaviness' and opaqueness to Spirit, as everything transcendent, the Unseen, the Divine, the human Truth, ceases to be real, and the consequent loss of Reality altogether. *Tadeva Satyam Tat Brahma,* That alone is Real, That is Brahman. 'Brethren, our ancestors have left us a legacy in the form of the holy wisdom but our modern children want to imitate the West in its worship of matter.' (Shri Dada Sanghita, recalled by Hari Prasad Shastri.) The greatest contribution here, of course, is in the work of René Guénon. (It's amusing to imagine an encounter between him and Marx: 'Are we actually seeing the same thing here? That creep, and me?') He writes:

It is quite natural that in the course of cyclic development both the cosmic manifestation as a whole and also human mentality, which is of course necessarily included therein, together follow the same descending course, the nature of which has already been specified as consisting in a gradual movement away from the principle, and thus away from the primal spirituality inherent in the essential pole of manifestation. This course can be described in terms of current speech... as a sort of progressive 'materialization' of the cosmic environment itself, and it is only when this materialization has reached a certain stage, by now already very marked, that the materialist conception can appear in man as its correlative, together with the general attitude which corresponds with it in practice... In order to reach the stage which has been described man must have lost the use of the faculties which in normal times allowed him to pass beyond the bounds of the sensible world, the loss being due to the existence of 'materialization' or 'solidification', naturally as effective in him as in the rest of the cosmic manifestation of which he is a part, and producing considerable modifications in his 'psycho-physiological' constitution... In order that it might take place, man had first of all to be induced to turn all of his attention exclusively to sensible things; the work of deviation had necessarily to begin in this way, the work which could be said to consist in the 'manufacturing' of the present world, and it clearly could not 'succeed' in its turn except precisely at this phase of the cycle and by using, in 'diabolical' mode, the existing conditions of the environment itself.

⁓THE REIGN OF QUANTITY AND THE SIGNS OF THE TIMES

Solidification, then, accompanied by the dissipation, dispersion, of consciousness and experience, life and selfhood, into things, objects, the sluggish or hectic flux of material substance, into consumption as a way of life, and the appearance in the world of a new 'self', even lower than the traditional 'lower self', consisting of identifications with objects and their properties and claims, with *merchandise* and its 'statements of selfhood': a new 'self' whose components are selected in the showrooms of the 'shopping mall' and carried piecemeal in boxes out into the parking lot where they are dropped into the trunk or back seat of the most eloquent and 'valuable' component of all: and our children, 'hanging out' where selves are purchased, are called 'mall rats'.

This 'solidification' of the world that Baudrillard called 'the period of objects', where 'consumption has grasped the whole of life', is also characterized, as we have seen, by universal quantification: Guénon's 'reign of quantity' jibes with Marx's identification of 'exchange value' as the hallmark of the commodity form and relationship. Capital's 'entire basis is labor as exchange value and as the creation of exchange value.' (*Grundrisse*) Witnesses as spectacularly diverse as Lukacs and Mumford also agree on it:

We are concerned above all with the *principle* at work here: the principle of rationalization based on what is and *can be calculated*.
⌒Lukacs

Quantity is all. To question the value of mere quantitative increase in terms of its contribution to human well-being is to commit heresy and weaken the system.
⌒Mumford

Hence the Computer as the center of life, *because information, access to information, is a quantitative affair, a quantitative conception, innovation and celebration, quantitative in its essence and to the core*, and the calculators in everyone's desk drawer and pocket, and the numbers, always money or its translation, in everyone's life and mind and hopes and fears. Beyond Marx's and Guénon's wildest dreams? I don't think so.

Nor do our witnesses fail to agree on the triumph of mechanization, what I have called the 'mutation into machinery', as a third pillar, along with solidification and quantification, in Baudrillard's 'period of objects' where, in Kellner's epitome, 'consumption has become the center of life.'

Guénon first:

This direction has been designated as that of the 'solidification' of the world, conferring on all things an aspect corresponding ever more closely (though never really corresponding exactly) to the way in which things appear according to quantitative, mechanistic or materialistic conceptions. The 'solidification' of the world has yet other consequences not mentioned hitherto in the human and social order: it engenders therein a state of affairs in which everything is counted, recorded and regulated, and this is really only another kind of 'mechanization'.

And Mumford:

All living forms must be brought into harmony with the mechanical world picture... For the machine alone was the true incarnation of this new ideology... To be redeemed from the organic, the autonomous, and the subjective, man must be turned into a machine, or better still, become an integral part of a larger machine that the new method would help to create... From Descartes' platform it was easy to take the next step; and that was to outline a set of principles favorable to a political order that would deliberately turn men into machines... I have now to show how the new ideas of order and power and predictability that dominated the new mechanical world picture made their way into every human activity. Within the last four centuries the older tradition of polytechnics was replaced by a system that gave primacy to the machine, with its repetitive motions, its depersonalized processes, its abstract quantitative goals. The later enlargement of these technical possibilities through electronics has only increased the scope and coercive absolutism of the system.

And finally Marx, the Old Master, bent over an old wooden table in the British Museum, still crankily cranking away in Notebook VI, p 694, of the *Grundrisse*:

> In machinery, objectified labour itself appears not only in the form of product or of the product employed as means of labour, but in the form of the force of production itself. The development of the means of labour into machinery is not an accidental moment of capital, but is rather the historical reshaping of the traditional, inherited means of labour into a form adequate to capital. The accumulation of knowledge and of skill, of the general productive forces of the social brain, is thus absorbed into capital, as opposed to labour, and hence appears as an attribute of capital, and more specifically of *fixed capital*, in so far as it enters into the production process as a means of production proper. *Machinery* appears, then, as the most adequate form of *fixed capital*, and fixed capital, in so far as capital's relations with itself are concerned, appears as *the most adequate form of capital* as such.

All three of these guys are seeing and saying the same thing, in different ways. And corporations, as a matter of fact, our fundamental economic institution, are themselves machines, as Jerry Mander demonstrates in a chapter of his excellent *In the Absence of the Sacred* titled 'Corporations as Machines'. They are aspects of the increasing 'organization' or 'inorganicism' of society, the intensifying ubiquity of 'management', control, supervision. administration: technological rationality.

So, to summarize and resume, Baudrillard's 'period of objects', in which 'we have reached the point where "consumption" has grasped the whole of life,' is actually a perception of the *Kali-Yuga*, of the end of the cosmic cycle, seen however in the narrow, and shallow, focus to which political economy, and the historical view as a whole, is fatally restricted. But not without merits and usefulness, if the larger picture is kept in mind, which is why we return to its scope. The era of consumption whose implications are exposed by Baudrillard marks the replacement of Nature by a world of manufactured things — 'an immense accumulation of commodities,' as Marx put it: 'Our investigation must therefore begin with the analysis of a commodity' (both quotes from *Capital*, vol. 1, bk 1, pt. 1, chap. 1, sect. L, p 1) — a world which is quite literally worshipped, hymned, adored. Look anywhere, and mull over the synergistic convergence of the testimony that has here been cited. Back to Baudrillard.

> Thus, 'Marketing, purchasing, sales, the acquisition of differentiated com- modities and objects/signs — all of these presently constitute our language, a code with which our entire society *communicates* and speaks of and to itself.' The consumer, therefore, cannot avoid the obligation to consume, because it is consumption that is the primary mode of social integration and the pri- mary ethic and activity within the consumer society. The consumer ethic and 'fun morality' thus involve active labor, incessant curiosity and search for nov- elty, and conformity to the latest fads, products and demands to consume... In the consumer society, consumption thus replaces production as the cen- tral mode of social behavior from which standpoint the society can be inter- preted and critically analyzed. Baudrillard thus conceives consumption as a mode of being, a way of gaining identity, meaning and prestige in the con- temporary society.

Thus in the *Kali-Yuga* we refer — blandly, casually, mindlessly — to the abstract prototype of human beings as 'the consumer' (exactly as Marxists, in the era when production was central, appealed to an abstraction called 'the worker', always forgetting that although social classes may be defined by their relationship to production, human beings cannot: in other words, it is not 'workers' who are alternately, even simultaneously, heroic and degraded, but human beings: a slave rebels not because he is a slave, but because he is *not* a slave: History is the locus, indeed the generator, of false identities), and we keep track of and receive daily, even hourly (it probably changes, in the computer brain, in nanoseconds), reports of a number called 'the consumer index' (among innumerable other numerical indices), a measure of *faith*(!) whose fluctuations, to the second decimal place, are of vital importance not only to the 'business community' but to the strategies and reputations of 'presidential candidates', a number which actually refers to nothing objective whatsoever but is rather, like everything else in the 'broadcast news', like all the disseminated quantifications that claim to illuminate us about ourselves, an instance of the manipulation of consciousness inherent in the media: it refers to nothing at all. The ubiquitous jive.

People saw all this coming, back in the thirties, this bizarre invisible transformation of human beings and human life into numbers and objects, this 'alienation' from each other and ourselves when direct relations between human beings were replaced by the sale and purchase of labor power and the circulation of commodities:

> The essence of commodity-structure has often been pointed out. Its basis is that a relation between people takes on the character of a thing and thus acquires a 'phantom objectivity', an Autonomy that seems so strictly rational and all-embracing as to conceal every trace of its fundamental nature: the relation between people,
> ⌒ LUKACS

when no type or category of human affairs could resist its transformation into exchange value:

> The dissolution of all products and activities into exchange values presupposes the dissolution of all fixed personal (historic) relations... Activity, regardless of its individual manifestation, and the product of activity, regardless of its particular make-up, are always *exchange value*, and exchange value is a generality, in which all individuality and peculiarity are negated and extinguished

into something that had a price and could be bought and sold *and therefore was no longer itself.*

> Money represents the general exchange value of all commodities. On one side, it is possessed as their exchange value; they stand on the other side as only so many particular substances of exchange value, so that it can either transform itself into every one of these substances through exchange, or it can remain indifferent to them, aloof from their particularity and peculiarity. It is the *'precis de toutes les choses'*, 'the epitome of all things', in which their particular-character is erased... All commodities are only transitory money; money is the permanent commodity. Money is the omnipresent commodity; the commodity is only local money... Money is therefore the god among commodities,

and the goal of 'human' existence became the production and realization of surplus value and the Accumulation of Capital.

The only utility whatsoever which an object can have for capital can be to preserve or increase it. The goal-determining activity of capital can only be that of growing wealthier, i.e. of magnification, of increasing itself... it is therefore the constant drive to go beyond its quantitative limit: an endless process.

And people had no choice but to become components of this machine, 'workers':

In fact, of course, this 'production' worker cares as much about the crappy shit he has to make as does the capitalist himself who employs him, and who also couldn't give a damn for the junk.
⌒ Preceding four citations from *Grundrisse*, the author's weariness apparent in the last.

Capital is a social relationship, not an economic abstraction. It is what we are, *we are it*. This is what blew him away sitting there in the British Museum, staring into space, totally alone in his brilliance. What did he see?

The positing of the individual as a *worker*, in this nakedness, is itself a product of *history*...The exchangeability of all products, activities and relations with a third, *objective* entity which can be re-exchanged for everything *without distinction*—that is, the development of exchange value (and of money relations) is identical with universal venality, corruption. Universal prostitution appears as a necessary phase of the social character of personal talents, capacities, abilities, activities...The individual carries his social power, as well as his bond with society, in his pocket...Activity, regardless of its individual manifestation, and the product of activity, regardless of its particular make-up, are always *exchange value*...All commodities are perishable money; money is the imperishable commodity...Exchange value expressed as money, i.e. equated with money, is *price*...to the degree that money develops in its various roles, i.e. that wealth as such becomes the general measure of the worth of individuals, there develops the drive to display it...Through the exchange with the worker, capital has appropriated labour itself; labour has become one of its moments...Money then exists as the exchange value of all commodities alongside and outside them. It is the universal material into which they must be dipped, in which they become gilded and silver-plated, in order to win their independent existence as exchange values...Money thereby directly and simultaneously becomes the *real community*...

And so on through 893 furiously tormented pages of the *Grundrisse: Foundations of the Critique of Political Economy*.

Back in the thirties, then, roughly sixty years after the *Grundrisse* is believed to have been drafted (Winter 1857–58), Marx's insight, what he had
seen and struggled so desperately to articulate, because he realized it was
'over the top', incredible, *utterly invisible*, was becoming the general property
of European intelligence: the quantification of all life, the transformation of
Humanity into Capital. He expressed it most powerfully in human terms in
The Poverty of Philosophy, in a passage which, according to Kellner, Baudrillard quoted in his own work.

> There was a time, as in the Middle Ages, when only the superfluous, the
> excess of production, was exchanged. There was again a time, when not only
> the superfluous, but all products, all industrial existence, had passed into
> commerce, when the whole of production depended upon exchange...
> Finally, there came a time when everything that men had considered as
> inalienable became an object of exchange, of traffic and could be alienated.
> This is the time when the very things which till then had been communi-
> cated, but never exchanged; given, but never sold; acquired, but never
> bought—virtue, love, conviction, knowledge, conscience, etc.—when every-
> thing finally passed into commerce. It is the time of general corruption, of
> universal venality, or, to speak in terms of political economy, the time when
> everything, moral or physical, having become marketable value, is brought to
> the market to be assessed at its truest value.

But neither Marx nor any 'marxist', nor any analysis for which history's
claim to exhaust reality is uncontested—the claim that we are historical
beings and beyond historical determination, conditioned existence, *there is
nothing*—could suspect that what was being perceived here, the invasive
quantification of all aspects of life, marked something as preposterous, to
the secular perspective, as 'the end of a cosmic cycle'. But it does. For quantification is the disappearance of reality. The abrogation, usurpation, destruction, termination of reality. The created world is the ecstasy of its qualities:
their manifestation, theophany, epiphany, of that infinite Beauty, that ineffable Majesty, that is God. *Jalal* and *Jamal*. 'His signature is the beauty of
things.' (Robinson Jeffers) So, alongside Marx's characterization in *The Poverty of Philosophy*, Guénon's in *The Reign of Quantity*.

> This characteristic is chosen in preference to any other, not solely or even
> principally because it is one of the most evident and least contestable, but
> above all because of its truly fundamental nature, for reduction to the quanti-
> tative is strictly in conformity with the conditions of the cyclic phase at which
> humanity has now arrived; and also because it is the particular tendency in

question that leads logically to the lowest point of the 'descent' which pro-
ceeds continuously and with ever-increasing speed from the beginning to the
end of a *Manvantara*, that is to say, throughout the whole course of the manifestation of a humanity such as ours… in our world, by reason of the special
conditions of existence to which it is subject, the lowest point takes on the
aspect of pure quantity, deprived of every qualitative distinction.

But quantification, although certainly fundamental, is, in a sense, indirect, impersonal: something like a disease or corrosive disintegration
of reality. What followed—as we shall see, and as neither even Marx nor
Guénon could have imagined—was a direct assault on reality. But this is to
anticipate.

Those who determined to oppose Capital, whether they perceived, as some
did in the thirties, its true and awesome nature or simply saw an oppressive
'ruling class'—the 'bourgeoisie' exploiting the labor of the 'proletariat', the
'workers of the world' who needed only to organize and unite to break their
chains—who were determined to *do* something about it, could discover no
better solution (and to the secular intelligence there really wasn't any) than
the communist or socialist fantasy of a 'liberated society', achieved by the
'further development of the forces of production' which, by 'aggravating the
contradictions between the forces and relations of production', would lead
to a 'revolutionary seizure of power' on the part of 'the working class' guided
by a Leninist 'vanguard party' culminating in 'the dictatorship of the proletariat'. This vision became History: with a vengeance, and with the results
we now all know. Those who envisioned other, less scientific (!) fantasies
were, in the eyes of the makers of history, utopian idealists or petit-bour-
geois individualist collaborators with the ruling class, out of touch with historical reality which 'scientific socialism', 'historical materialism', alone could
grasp. And in the wake of all this, in virtually every biography, disillusion-
ment, 'party line' doctrinal optimism or cynical despair. Again, the entrapment within a perspective where nothing is real but History: the Fall into
Time. 'In rejecting or losing celestial values, man became the victim of
time… time is the decadence which carries us away from the origin.'
(Schuon). We are, in other words, when 'celestial values' are rejected, nothing but what the accidents of mechanical causality within empirical existence make of us, nothing beyond our material 'factual' life in a world where

everything is relative, contingent, conditioned without exception by physical circumstances, where 'truth' and 'transcendence' are antiquated words. Beyond biography and history, beyond 'the facts', there is nothing.

> For over a century, the greater part of the scientific and philosophical effort of the West has been devoted to the factors that 'condition' the human being. It has been shown how and to what degree man is conditioned by his physiology, his heredity, his social milieu, the cultural ideology in which he shares, his unconscious—and above all by history, by his historical moment and his own personal history. This last discovery of Western thought—that man is essentially a temporal and historical being, that he is, and can only be. what history has made him—still dominates Western philosophy.
> ⁓ELIADE, *The Myth of the Eternal Return*

Marx, it will be recalled, perceived immediately and with alarm that Hegel, with his 'Universal Spirit', was upside-down, and wasted no time in turning him right side up. (The figure of speech, if I remember correctly, was 'standing on his head'.) 'With Marx, history cast off all transcendental significance; it was no longer anything more than the epiphany of the class struggle.' (ELIADE) Baudrillard and his Frankfort school predecessors, Marxists all, for whom neither God nor Truth nor any absolute whatsoever had *ever* been real, for whom 'the revolution' was *no longer* real, and for whom History was *alone* real, had therefore no choice but to defend their fated dead-end opinion: *no way out.* Baudrillard

> describes a situation in which alienation is so total that it cannot be surpassed, because it is the very structure of the consumer society. His argument is that in a society in which everything is a commodity that can be bought and sold, alienation is total. Indeed, the term 'alienation' originally signified 'to sale', and in a totally commodified society in which everything is a commodity, alienation is ubiquitous. Moreover, the conclusion describes 'the end of transcendence', a phrase borrowed from Marcuse, a state in which individuals can perceive neither their own true needs nor another way of life.

And they are correct, *within History: for historical humanity:* and for any individual who cannot see, and adore (or at least admit, at least pursue, for 'Seek and ye shall find'), beyond biography and History, the divine Reality within which all that happens here below is but a dream of the instant— *maya, samsara, al-wahm,* 'the phantom flux of life'—the divine Reality which is the Self of all, and the eternal Truth. 'Think no more of this night's accidents / But as the fierce vexation of a dream.' (*Midsummer-Nights' Dream*)

They are *correct*, because this is the *Kali-Yuga* and the *Kali-Yuga* is indeed a one-way trip; and they are *wrong*, wrong eternally, because God alone is real and dwells, Life Eternal, within the hearts of all. We wear 'a crown of uncreated light.'

✳

Back to consumption. Baudrillard's perception of the displacement of production by consumption as the central dynamic in capitalist society is expressed initially in his concept of *sign value* and *sign fetishism*. 'To Marx's analysis of the commodity in terms of use value and exchange value, Baudrillard thus proposes adding the further feature of sign value.' Sign value and fetishism is an extension of Thorstein Veblen's familiar 'conspicuous consumption' (*The Theory of the Leisure Class*), and states, essentially, that consumption victories confer and define 'human' identities, and the 'creation' of these identities, their perpetual replacement through the introduction of new commodities, is now the motor force of society. In a word, we purchase not the commodities themselves but what the commodities and their acquisition 'signify'. 'Sign value' is what is actually purchased and actually advertised; we aspire to 'be' the 'people', increasingly athletes or simply athletic, or youthful and enthusiastic, or tastefully vain, 'glamorous', adventurous, carefree, victorious, or simply 'cool', shown reveling in their objects and experiences in magazine ads and television commercials; the commodity is really a 'sign' of that consumer identity, that 'happiness' and 'success', and actually is that consumer's identity on the subjective plane: it is felt within as the true person, the true self. Selves are purchased, entered and displayed. People are transformed into images, generated as images, generated as 'fame' or 'success', as *enviable*, *purchased* as *models* and *produced* as themselves *commodities*, in order to sell *other* commodities, to *be* the images which potential consumers, 'ordinary people', will admire, identify with, and purchase. And those original people, the famous and successful who became images, became images because they themselves identified with them, pursued them, believed them. (A glimpse here, but only a glimpse, of the hyper-real!) They're not paid to model the shoes: they're paid to *be* the people who *wear* the shoes, and they themselves, in the person of their 'agents', pursue and compete for this commodity-identity sale of themselves.

Children, of course, are not excluded from these vistas of opportunity:

THEY SEE THEIR PRO KIDS AS MEAL TICKETS: The Pushiest Tennis
Parents: Jennifer Capriati is pulled out of her junior high school classes,
flown to Europe, told at 14 to endorse a skin-moisturizing cream because her
father wants to wrinkle a few thousand dollar bills… What ails professional
tennis most in the 1990s?… the weasel-like agents who mold a player's image
into whatever's marketable at the moment, the obscene gobs of endorsement
money that have forged an entirely different Grand Slam for this era. (Nike,
Ellesse, Ray-Ban, and Yonex)
〜SAN FRANCISCO CHRONICLE

I can't resist sharing the article (not an ad, an 'article': *news*) that appears
right next to the one about the tennis parents:

CHIC GLASSES MAKE AGING LESS PAINFUL.
Wild half-glasses for reading in frames of vivid colors are beginning to
appear, including recent entries with designer labels such as Christian Lac-
roix and Gianfranco Ferre… frames for half-glasses in patterns of hot pink,
purple, black, and bright green… 'The whole idea of bifocals said "old man",
he said… So his optometrist gave him a pair called Lifesavers… "They are
very funny glasses," Currie said. They happen to look great." He figures he
can get away with an eccentric look because "I'm a bit of a nonconformist"…
When the need for glasses could no longer be denied, she began searching
for something that would not make her look old. "I had a certain style I
liked," said Kealy, who used to work in the fashion business. "I didn't feel like
turning into Ben Franklin.'"

'Under the reign of sign value, consumption and display become a central
locus of value, and are as important as production in determining the logic,
nature and direction of social processes.' Commodification, in other words,
is inching, carving, chewing its way deeper and deeper into the personality,
into the self. The 'economic person' of Marxism, 'labour as exchange value
and as the creation of exchange value', although still present, has reproduced
itself in new variations, mutations, and defined new targets of usurpation;
commodification is thereby expanding its dominion, expropriating more
and more of what used to be called 'private life' or 'inner life', refining its techniques, replacing the aspects, potentials and properties that compose a
human person as cancer cells replace the healthy ones, and is gradually
becoming the whole person. The inner citadel is being stormed, the circles of
defenses breached. Humanity is *becoming* Capital, ever more deeply, more
intimately: what Marx saw was only the beginning. The core, *identity*, has
been reached.

Baudrillard's argument is that the 'conspicuous consumption' and display of commodities analyzed by Veblen in his *Theory of the Leisure Class* has been extended to everyone in the consumer society... Baudrillard sees the entire society as organized around consumption and display of commodities through which individuals gain prestige, identity and standing... For Baudrillard, the crucial feature of the consumer society is the proliferation of commodity signs through which commodities take on ever new and ever greater significance for those for whom consumption is a way of life.

It's very important to recognize the gravity of the implications here, to resist the natural tendency to become blind to the significance of what we have grown to accept as 'normal'; we must *see*, directly and in identification with our theomorphic being, how far we have 'progressed' into the corrosion of everything human and therefore divine, divine and therefore human, that fundamentally characterizes the *Kali-Yuga*. Within the social relationship called Capital people are inserted into a closed self-referring system devoted solely to *purchasing*, to the purchasing of objects and experiences which confer the 'identities' dreamed up in order to 'sell' those very objects and experiences. No area of human and planetary life escapes the reverberations of this catastrophe. It's not just a matter of the 'inner person'.

CONSUMERISM BLAMED FOR MUCH OF DAMAGE TO PLANET. Growing Fixation on Shopping Malls Ripped in Study. The richest fifth of the world is ruining the planet by consuming too much, says a Worldwatch Institute study that blames the 'consumer class' for ozone-depleting chemicals, greenhouse gases and acid rain. The study released Saturday concludes that only rapid population growth causes more environmental damage than rampant consumption.
The study—entitled 'How Much Is Enough?'—comes down particularly hard on the global spread of shopping malls. It recommends curbs on advertising... and it deplores the yearnings in poorer countries to adopt the consumer lifestyle. It says the world's consumer class is responsible for releasing virtually all ozone-depleting chemicals and two-thirds of greenhouse gases and pollutants that cause acid rain. Similarly, the consumer class produces a large share of everything from pesticides to radioactive waste.
Author Alan Durning, in the book-length report, attacked the construction of a giant shopping mall and indoor amusement park in Bloomington, Minn. The complex, to be called 'The Mall of America', is projected to attract more visitors than Mecca or the Vatican, he said. 'All of the United States seems to be remaking itself in the image of the mall', writes Durning. He said the boom in consumerism is also taking place in Europe, Japan and other rich

countries... In addition to the spread of malls, the study blames the world-wide availability of television... and the widespread belief that ever-increasing consumption is the only way to create jobs. 'Over a few short generations, we in the affluent fifth of humanity have become car drivers, television watchers, junk-food eaters, mall shoppers and throwaway buyers', said Durning.

The report also cites studies showing that Americans visit their neighbors less, have fewer family conversations and even eat less together as a family than they did in 1950. And what about all those modern appliances that are supposed to make life so much better? The study says most of the time saved by Americans, at least, seems to be used up watching television.

⁓ SAN FRANCISCO EXAMINER, sometime in 1992

None of this, of course, is 'news', or can even be surprising, to anyone who hasn't been in a coma in recent decades. I might only add that the 'rapid population growth', which alone surpasses consumerism as a cause of environmental damage, is as evident and decisive a manifestation of 'the reign of quantity' as Capital itself, no matter how 'inhumane' it may sound to say that; overpopulation, 'the population bomb', announces, quite simply, quite incontrovertibly, that *humanity as a sheer quantity* is among the gravest 'problems' we face. I might also add that the Worldwatch study, at least as it was summarized in the *Examiner*, is as shallow in its rhetoric and indictment, in pointing the finger at the resulting 'damage to the planet' as the essential evil of consumerism and the reason it ought to be discouraged (by whom?), as all the rest of the environmentalist analysis and literature which views Creation as something like a rented apartment and Humanity as something like an irresponsible tenant. (You know, at the end of the day—as they say in Merry England—it wouldn't be too far from the truth to say that the disease of which Humanity died, in the final analysis, was shallowness: through the centuries, millennia, the unfolding of the *yugas*, we became shallower and shallower, like a gradual inexorable falling of the water level, the drying up of an ocean, and finally died of sheer insuperable terminal shallowness.) Only voices from that 'past' in the illusion of chronological time which is actually the divine Eternal Present, the Truth outside of time within us, go to the heart of the matter. Like Sextus the Pythagorean (dates unknown; 'probably the same that Seneca so greatly extols'):

Everything which is more than necessary to man, is hostile to him.

Or APOLLONIUS OF TYANA to the King of Babylon:

Superfluity distresses wise men more than deficiency distresses you.

AL-GHAZALI (d. IIII):

> The knowledge which results in renunciation consist of the realization that what is renounced is of little value in comparison with what is received.

TSO SSU (3rd century AD):

> The bird in a forest can perch but on one bough, And this should be the wise man's pattern.

YOGA-VASISHTHA:

> It is only after the disappearance of all worldly interests that the universality of the transcendental Spirit is known.

And the *Tao Te Ching*:

> He who has little will receive.
> He who has much will be embarrassed.

It should be noted—a final irony here—that neither Marx nor Baudrillard, nor any of the great theoreticians of their school who flourished between them, believed or believe that there is anything fundamentally (or 'essentially', as they would say) *human* that is being violated or replaced in the commodity universe of production and consumption, exchange value and sign value, shopping malls and television commercials, 'the capitalist system'. (The activists, the footsoldiers of 'the revolution'—virtually all of them, incidentally, very wonderful loving people indeed—may have felt differently about that; their theater, nonetheless, was History, their battles planned by the ideologues.) For them, for all those for whom reality is history and nothing more or beyond, everything is a 'stage' in the temporal unfolding, aspects of the pitfalls and triumphs which characterize 'progress,' everything is relative to what preceded and might follow: something like the career of an incorrigibly optimistic adventurer whose pursuit of a dream, forever frustrated, repeatedly sabotaged, continually betrayed by explosive and unforeseeable circumstances, eventually replaces the dream itself, even the memory of it. For secular thinkers there is nothing 'essentially' human. No human norm or Law or Path or Way with respect to which individuals and societies may be interpreted and assessed. 'The essence of man does not possess any true reality', as Marx wrote in his Critique of Hegel's *Philosophy of Right*, just as, for Baudrillard, 'there is no such thing as pure use value or a pure subject with essential needs for whom objects have essential uses.'

On the one hand, then, the ideal of the right to vote, a steady job, and television, information, and merchandise for everyone—the ideal that has finally swept the world—and, on the other, the ideal of those who clearly perceive the hell beneath the shopping mall, or suspect it, smell it, but scoff at the idea that there is any such thing as a Truth to pursue, or recover, and a Wisdom, of transcendent origin, by which we may be guided: ultimately, that there is any such thing as Spirit: that humanity is or can be anything more than—to recall Eliade's words—'this historical moment… what history has made him.' The 'liberals' among this microscopic academic community, in their ephemeral, heartfelt and well-intentioned books and articles, appeal to secular humanism in various emphases. The 'critical thinkers' of the Marxian school, in turn, perceiving no present strategy with plausible claims to lead toward that 'revolutionary transformation' which is their 'scientific' version of Progress, no present evidence that the famous 'solution to the riddle of history which knows itself to be the solution' is 'latent' in society, courageously seek, in books and articles equally heartfelt, well-intentioned and ephemeral, 'a renewal of the Left': 'new maps of the social world and new political strategies to produce a better world,' new forms of 'resistance', 'rebellion', and 'revolt': because, as Kellner continues (he is one of them), 'I, for one, am not ready to throw in the towel and declare that our projects were illusions and not worthwhile.'

> I would suggest that a major task for critical social theory today is a critique of conservative ideology and politics in order to prepare the way for a renewal of the Left. To be sure, the Left has labored under many illusions in the past—including a revolutionary proletariat, the certainty of socialism and a belief that socialism will automatically produce disalienation. But it seems too early to surrender belief in the socialist project and the Left…

As I have suggested, repeatedly I suppose, the historical consciousness is doomed to oscillate back and forth between hope and despair with respect to a future 'new dawn'—or at least, in Neil Postman's hope, a new 'curriculum', embodied in the witness of 'the loving resistance fighter': 'a serious conversation that will allow us to distance ourselves' from the thought-world of Technopoly. Kellner, like Postman, Roszak, Jeremy Rifkin, Bill McKibben, Ivan Illich, et. al., clings to hope. Baudrillard cheerfully testifies to the other alternative. In the modern world, where 'it is impossible to distinguish between media and reality', in our 'totally cyberneticized, rationalized society

> resistance and revolt are a 'mirage', and social transformation is an 'illusion' (two of Baudrillard's favorite terms). Thus, consistent with this bleak picture, Baudrillard no longer poses *any* social alternative, resistance, struggle or refusal.

✳

Picking up the thread again! (We go with the flow here. It was either digressions or footnotes: I chose digressions.) We've covered the transition from Stage 1 to Stage 2, from production to consumption as the central dynamic in modern, or postmodern, society. The transformation of commodities into signs, and of social life into the enactment of 'codes', is, in Baudrillard's vocabulary, the bridge from Stage 2 to Stage 3, from consumption to hyper-reality. 'Code' is perhaps a misleading translation ('he uses the word 'code' in a sometimes confusing multiplicity of ways,' as Kellner laments), but the concept is so subtle that probably any word would have caused trouble; we're on the border of 'unreal realities' here, approaching 'hyper-reality', where the capacity of language begins to be stretched to the breaking point, where humanity, both as a being and a concept, undergoes an unprecedented science-fiction metamorphosis: where we 'lose our bearings' and the task of regaining them becomes central and critical. Hyper-reality is a precision of what I have referred to earlier, in proposing a 'translation' of the Sanskrit *Kali-Yuga*, as The Age of Universal Bullshit — 'bullshit' being a word which both indicates the hyper-real nature of our lives and, as indictment of an all-pervading bogusness or fraudulence, expresses the appropriate human attitude towards it, a salvage of our self-respect.

While Baudrillard does not define 'code' with any precision here, he will soon equate the concept with a series of 'simulation' models, and will increasingly move to what I would call a *semiological idealism*, whereby signs and codes becomes the primary constituents of social life… his model of the code seems to be the DNA which programs various directions and constraints on behavior in an individual but which itself is not perceived… All dichotomies between appearance and reality, surface and depth, life and art, subject and object, collapse into a functionalized, integrated and self-reproducing universe of 'simulacra' controlled by 'simulation' models and codes…

Let's define the terms one by one: *Simulations* are the 'images, spectacles and the play of signs' which surround us: television, commercials, videos, ads, pop music, radio voices, 'public relations', politics, sports, fashion, style, photography in all its ubiquity, fabrications and copies of all kinds, all things mass-produced, generated from models or prototypes, anything acted, 'played', portrayed, clichés and stereotypes, and by extension, because this is what it's all about, anything making *claims*, *aiming* at us, 'pushing our buttons'; and, perhaps now most importantly, 'computer-generated' images of *events that never happened at all*—the technique unveiled in that marvellous and macabre sequence in *Wag the Dog* where we saw how it's actually done! Such images now envelop our lives.

Codes are constellations, groupings, gestalts, outside us or in our minds, of simulation models whose 'language' is the sign or 'sign value': '"code" refers to the rules, laws and structures of the political economy of the sign', i.e. the rules, laws and structures by and within which we are manipulated, which we enact without our being aware of them; as puppets of the code we are hypnotized into accepting our society, capitalism, technocracy, the Market-place, screenworld, mallcondo, as a human place, a real place, an OK place, where things hang together and make sense, refer to each other in a natural way: the tone of voice and funny anecdotes of the sportscaster and the cryptic captivating images on the passing billboards and our daily commute in intermittent gridlock and our designer sunglasses and all the rest of the megatons of crap and our unconscious assumptions about the whole mind-fuck all hang together, all signify coherence and normality; *the code is the pattern of our mutated lives: the cultural DNA that makes us what we have become in postmodern society.*

Simulacra are 'reproductions of objects or events', the output of industrial machinery, of the system of mass production instituted with the Industrial Revolution, 'exact replicas, infinitely produced and reproduced by assembly-line processes and eventually automation': 'a game played with signs'. *And hyper-reality is the totality of signs, codes, simulacra and simulations:* 'Digitality is its metaphysical principle… and DNA its prophet.' (BAUDRILLARD)

But listen: the words aren't important, English translations of a French-man's desperate attempt to dissect a seamless fiendish transmutation of human experience. The thing is to get the idea, to see it with your own eyes, out there and in your own mind, our psychic environment, psychic habitat, our new selves and their relationships to each other. And to detest it.

All of this seemingly groping and tormented vocabulary is a deadly serious and determined struggle to describe something mind-boggling, a society in which, as the Beatles sang, 'Nothing is real' (that was 'Strawberry Fields Forever'), employing the discourse which developed precisely as a response to that eerie 'situation' we found ourselves in: the science of semiology, 'semiotics', whose subject is the pervasive 'significations' or signifying functions in modern society and whose most brilliant exponent was Michel Foucault. It's a way of 'seeing' things formerly invisible, seeing things from a new angle. Baudrillard's work is described as 'a universal semiotic of technological experience', a true picture of what's actually happening here, 'the totality of experience in contemporary society, in which "the whole environment becomes a signifier, objectified as an element of signification.'"

We have entered a new era in which radical semiurgy—that is, the production and proliferation of signs—has replaced production of objects as the center of social life and as a new mode of social control... We are not aware how we are channeled into certain forms of class behavior, consumer behavior, conformity, sex role behavior, ethnic behavior and the like which are being controlled by the code... we have entered a new stage in history, in which sign control is almost complete and totalitarian... the sign no longer designates anything at all. It approaches its true structural limit which is to refer back only to other signs. All reality then becomes the place of a semiurgical manipulation, of a structural simulation.' The entirety of Baudrillard's subsequent work to the present explores this situation, and draws out its implications.

⁓KELLNER

What is at stake is always 'reality'. Heaven and Earth were and always are the only Reality for beings such as ourselves, created beings, the central Consciousness of a Manifestation, *imago dei*, and therefore the only Origin and Foundation of our being human and the only sanction, the only 'appeal' in all meanings of the word, of our cultures. When we become separated from Reality, from Heaven and Earth, *the words and the world are simultaneously drained of their only possible human meaning and we ourselves become separated from the only possible wellspring of our humanity.*

✳

Photography, simple innocent wonderful photography, long before signs and codes, had already made the first incursion.

The effects of the mechanical reproduction of images were first explored, in the context of visual art, by Waiter Benjamin, and later investigated by Daniel Boorstin in his analysis of the mid-nineteenth-century 'graphics revolution' in *The Image*. For our purposes, it is sufficient to note that there was a time when sacred images, the iconography of religions, were only found in sacred places, and therefore only rarely seen and always in an atmosphere of sanctity, and when rivers and mountains, trees and snow-covered fields, birds and animals, all of Nature, were only seen in their actual real presence, with all the immediacy, life, actuality of existence and attendant drama of biographical episode and spiritual rapture, *ekstasis,* that would accompany the event. Now the innumerable reproductions of sacred art and the countless photographs of Nature on postcards and posters, and with almost invariable insistence in the backgrounds of magazine ads and television commercials (Now why might that be so?), have, to say the very least, altered our relationship to Heaven and Earth out of all recognition. The first mode has all but vanished from human experience; in the second we have, to use the blunt appropriate figure of speech, 'lost it'. If it's not the real thing it's not real at all, its just nothing: it's trash. Coffee-table books are not the encounter with God, or His Presence in Nature. But we've gone far beyond simple innocent photography, and the 'ingenuity', the 'creativity' with which we 'advance'—from the steam engine to the chain saw to the cunning little chip—is the motor of our demise, the parade disappearing over the brink. Science and Technology, Progress and Economic Growth: J.M. Roberts' 'Triumph of the West'. What is at stake is always reality, and in the *Kali-Yuga*

> Signs and modes of representation come to constitute 'reality', and signs gain autonomy and, in interaction with other signs, come to constitute a new kind of social order in which it is signs and codes that constitute 'the real'. Baudrillard is arguing that commodity signs, for instance, refer to and gain their significance in relation to other commodity signs within the code of a 'structural law of value', rather than to any external referents or ground of value, just as media representations refer primarily to other media representations rather than to any outside world... In the society of coded simulation, urban planners, for example, modulate codes of city planning and architecture in creating urban systems, in much the same way that television producers modulate television codes to produce programs. Models and codes thus come to constitute everyday life.

In the 'society of simulations'—*es decir*, the *Kali-Yuga* in *one* of its 'presences' which we are, *one* of its 'faces' which are our own—there is no longer anything real, *external to our own fabrications*, to which social 'realities' refer, anything real, *independent of our 'creativity'*, in which they are rooted; this society is totally self-referential, totally created, synthetic, 'a new artificial environment' totally (blithely, ferociously, idiotically) *independent* of Heaven and Earth and the universe of truths, values and meanings with which they bless our humble petition—and in which, I might add, as if it were necessary, human identities, we ourselves, must also be artificial, 'artifices' of our own rootless, feverish collective imagination: *for if our world is not real, how then can we be?* It's not only that we identify with the sign values or 'who I

am' pronouncements of our commodities, innocent rubbish-adorned gro-
tesques dancing attendance upon Capital without the faintest notion of
what's actually going on here, performing the codes without the slightest
inkling of the presiding Puppetmaster which is our own collective being, *our
work*: it is that we are playing roles in a drama that wasn't written by or for
human beings, in which we *cannot* be human. Therefore nothing is real.
'Civilized, crying how to be human again,' as Robinson Jeffers entreated our
wretchedness, we now inhabit, and our children inherit,

> the stage of 'simulation proper,' the end result of a long historical process of
> simulation, in which simulation models come to constitute the world... we
> live in a 'hyper-reality' of simulations in which images, spectacles and the play
> of signs replace the logic of production and class conflict... The era of simu-
> lations by contrast is an era of information and signs governed by models,
> codes and a system of 'general economy'... In the new postindustrial, post-
> modern era, the model or code structures social reality, and erodes distinc-
> tions between the model and the real. Using McLuhan's cybernetic concept
> of *implosion*, Baudrillard claims that in the contemporary world the bound-
> ary between representation and reality implodes, and that, as a result, the
> very experience and ground of 'the real' disappears... Whereas in a previous
> stage of the philosophy of language and metaphysics, words referred to
> objects and things, and representations were believed to refer to a 'real', this
> era of thought and discourse has now come to an end... In this universe of
> radical indeterminacy, it becomes increasingly difficult to distinguish true
> from false, good from bad, for in the society of simulations it is impossible to
> gain access to a real or to perceive what is determining or constituting various
> events and processes... Individuals are so caught up in a world of commodity
> signs, media spectacles, representations and simulations that there is no
> longer any access to a 'real'... We thus now live in a radically relativistic, ideal-
> ist and imaginary universe.

Where nothing is real nothing *is*, nothing is *anything*, and we are condemned, in Baudrillard's words, to total relativity, to groundlessness of life
and bleak hollowness of soul, and not as an ideology or world-view originating in secular historicism but as the very structure of society. (Enter
Prozak.) Here, in this consummation of Western trends converging over
centuries, we may appreciate the accuracy and fullest validation of Schuon's
oft-repeated identification of the crux of the modern decadence: loss of the
intuition of the Absolute, which is the Divine. The long and blessed morning, the corrupted 'best-that-we-are-capable-of' shimmering autochthonous

(autochthon: one sprung from the ground which he inhabits) childhood of human existence, in which there was a Reality, a Heaven and Earth and a Meaning and a Truth, when 'The days as they succeed one another do but repeat always the same day of God; time stops in a single blessed day, and so is joined once more to the Origin which is also the Center' (Schuon), when Krishna said (as He says now, in Eternity) 'I am the Truth and the Joy forever' and Christ said (as He says still, in Eternity) 'I am the Light of the World, 'when every man and woman knew that what we see and where we are is a miracle and divine and eternal in our hearts,

> all this is surpassed by the other stage of value, that of total relativity, of generalized commutation, which is combinatory and simulatory. This means simulation in the sense that from now on signs will exchange among themselves exclusively, without interacting with the real... The emancipation of the sign: released from that 'archaic' obligation that it might have to designate something, the sign is at last free for a structural or combinatory play according to indifference and a total indetermination which succeeds the previous role of determinate equivalence.
> ∼Baudrillard

✳

The media of mass communication—need it be said?—especially television, play center stage in this brave new unreal world ('which has moreover, owing to its 'mechanical' character, something 'artificial' about it... which is not such as to inspire confidence in its duration' (Guénon), the electric 'global village', and, since this world is the *Kali-Yuga*, acquire a metaphysical stature and significance. Television *is* 'reality' here, and the very few people who don't own a set, or don't watch it (You mean you didn't see the final episode of Seinfeld?), are considered impoverished if their 'deprivation' is involuntary—their deplorable fate, their forlorn inadmittance to 'watching', being tantamount to a national disgrace—and simply 'oddballs' or 'wierdos', marginally sinister, if 'deprivation' is voluntary. ('What need of so much news from abroad, when all that concerns either life or death is all transacting and at work within us?' William Law, 1686–1761.) The 'TV Object' (Baudrillard's phrase) is securely enthroned at the center of the modern household, the very definition of 'the family room', and constitutes the essential proof that the owner is a genuine member of society.

The escalating role of the media in contemporary society is for Baudrillard equivalent to THE FALL into the postmodern society of simulations... it is the media themselves which abstract from the concreteness of everyday, social and political, life and provide abstract simulacra of actual events which themselves become more real than 'the real' which they supposedly represent... The rise of the broadcast media, especially television, is an important constituent of postmodernity for Baudrillard, along with the rapid dissemination of signs and simulacra in every realm of social and everyday life. By the late 1970s, Baudrillard was interpreting the media as key simulation machines, which reproduce images, signs and codes which in turn come to constitute an autonomous realm of (hyper) reality and also to play a key role in everyday life and the obliteration of the social. This process constitutes a significant reversal of the relation between representation and reality. Previously the media were believed to mirror, reflect or represent reality, whereas now they are coming to constitute a (hyper) reality, a new media reality, 'more real than real', where 'the real' is subordinate to representation thus leading ultimately to a dissolving of the real... the 'hyper-reality of simulations' in the media are more real than real, and come to produce and define a new reality.

Meaning, the concept and pattern of a meaningful life, even meaningful*ness* as a meaningful *word*, all collapse when 'the medium and the real are now in a single nebulous state whose truth is undecipherable' (Baudrillard). We have been described, I believe by Lewis Mumford, as beings whose essential quality is the discovery and enactment of meaning: the pursuit of meaning, the identification of and with meaning: beings whose inherent calamity, innermost pain, is 'to live without meaning, the ultimate negation of life itself' (Postman). We are made for meaning by the simple fact of possessing intelligence, the power to think and the inescapable constraint to think—just as we are 'made for' the Absolute, for God, by the simple fact that we contain, that we are, at the center of our being, the Heart-Intellect or 'cardiac intelligence', the *buddhi, intelligentia spiritualis*, the *takhayyul mutlaq* or Theophanic Imagination of Sufism: *imago dei*, candidate for deification, apotheosis—a faculty whose only function is the display of meaning, the 'world of light,' as it were, which is the home of meaning; the relation between intelligence and meaning is no less mutual and intimate than the relation between vision and the visible. The essence of our present state, however, is the suicidal sabotage of this function, which is literally our salvation, our hope and our joy, our very humanity; the only image of intelligence now, the only image of 'mind at work', is a person seated before and staring at a computer screen: this means thinking, this means knowledge: 'access to information', 'figuring' it out: Power. ('ACCESSIBLE INFORMATION. THE POWER TO MOVE A SOCIETY. AND AT GTE, THE POWER IS ON.') But it's a Lie. Intelligence is the divine Mind, the Self which is the universe, the Logos, Cosmic Intellect, and it exists — here below, as an indestructible potential — fully only in that being which is deiform, which 'knowing itself, knows its God', only in the living human being: for *meaning* is the world 'falling into place' around the divine Center which we are and thereby becoming Real: the world as Truth. 'This belief in the transcendent Intellect, a faculty capable, and alone capable, of direct contact with the Real, is common to all Traditional doctrines, of all ages and countries.' (MARCO PALLIS, *Peaks and Lamas*). The man seated before a computer is a prisoner in the network of false promises, seductive perfidy and universal exploitation which is our present hell: a gewgaw which a vicious hoax of history has condemned him to marvel at and emulate, to sit before and rot. The collusive partnership of Capital and Technology, our malevolent transpersonal identity, our collective despotism, transforms the entire human race into chumps.

✳

There is in man something which must become conscious of itself; which must become itself, which must be purified and liberated from all that is foreign to itself; which must awaken and expand, and become all, because it is all; something which alone should be: it is the soul as knowledge, namely the Spirit, whose 'subject' is God and whose 'object' is likewise God.
〜SCHUON

The Computer and the Internet, the megatons of software, Roszak's 'cult of information', television world, Hollywood world, video world, shopping malls and superbowls, the polls and the fads and the superstars and the styles, reach their nadir in their marketing of themselves called 'advertising'—instantly dumbfounded and gagged when anything genuine is presented before its stupefied dismay, it is a language whose essence is *lying* and which knows no idiom other than conniving and imbecilic vulgarity: can you imagine an ad for the *Dhammapada*?

One of the fundamental processes of the contemporary age involves the absorption of all modes of expression by that of advertising, 'because it is without depth, instantaneous and instantly forgotten... the triumph of superficial form, the smallest common denominator of all significations, the zero degree of meaning…

Sex and hype, violence and freeways and credit cards and fuel injection and election campaigns and the 6 o'clock news, the entire electric commodity-consumption discourse of spectacle, all adds up to something like a perpetual nuclear explosion in our midst and minds, what Baudrillard calls 'cyberblitz'. All of it, each element and in totality, is *saying* something to us, *signifying* something, sending a *message*, and what is being said to us by all this, by our culture, is what Baudrillard means by *sign*. And what is it saying, what's the message? *Believe in me, believe in all this, embrace the happiness I offer you.* Semiotics, in a way, is the perception of culture, its artifacts and institutions, as *propaganda*. Commodities and technology are propaganda, propagation of a world-view, the elements of which are, in Baudrillard's terminology, 'signs'. It's not a good word; but it will have to do.

The proliferation of signs and information in the media obliterates meaning through neutralizing and dissolving all content, a process which leads to both a collapse of meaning and the destruction of distinctions between media and reality. In a society supposedly saturated with media messages, information and meaning 'implode', into meaningless 'noise', pure effect without content or meaning. Thus, Baudrillard claims, 'information is directly destructive of meaning and signification, or neutralizes it. The loss of meaning is directly linked to the dissolving and dissuasive action of information, the media and the mass media… Information devours its own contents; it devours communication and the social… information dissolves meaning and the social into a sort of nebulous state…' Baudrillard uses here a model of the media as a black hole of signs and information that absorbs all contents into cybernetic noise which no longer communicates meaningful messages in a process in which all content implodes into form.

The vacuum of reality and meaning does not occur *around* us, hyper-reality is not *around* us, an environment, it is within us as well, both within and without, or more precisely *we are it*.

In the same invisible intangible way that *we are Capital*—commodities, money, exchange value, the commodity called labor power, a factor of production, both the pipes through which exchange value flows in the circulation of commodities and the exchange value flowing through the pipes, creating, through our labor power, our 'work', the marvellous added quantity called 'surplus value' which we alone, human beings, can create, making us the source, therefore, the fountainhead, of the precious, sacred and implacable Accumulation of Capital which is the 'meaning' of our lives, the *economy*, which is either sluggish or vigorous, ailing or healthy, stronger than Germany or weaker than Japan, *perhaps not growing fast enough*: for the production and realization of surplus value is the secret reason why everything happens here, the very purpose, essence and indestructible dedication of the social relationship of the commodity form, Capital, which we are.

And in the same invisible intangible way that *we are Technique*—the components, interchangeable parts, of autonomously unfolding ensembles of techniques, for

> when technique enters into every area of life, including the human, it ceases to be external to man and becomes his very substance, it is no longer face to face with man but is integrated with him, and it progressively absorbs him... it has analyses him and synthesized a hitherto unknown being.
> ⌁ELLUL

And in the same invisible intangible way that *we are the Megamachine*— first crudely constructed, tested out, in the Egyptian and Mesopotamian communities of the Pyramid Age, the 'marmoreal' civilizations, and now finally, and with a quantum leap, reassembled, fulfilled, in 'the great technical transformation that took place after the sixteenth century' which 'provided the frame for a depersonalized world picture within which mechanical activities and interests took precedence over more human concerns':

> And it was this world picture, not individual mechanical inventions alone, that contributed to the final apotheosis of the contemporary megamachine... All living forms must be brought into harmony with the mechanical world picture... for the machine alone was the true incarnation of this new ideology... To be redeemed from the organic, the autonomous and the subjective, man must be turned into a machine, or, better still, become an integral part of a larger machine that the new method would help to create... Ultimately, organization Man has no reason for existence except as a depersonalized servo-mechanism in the megamachine... In plain words, the religion of the megamachine demands wholesale human sacrifice, to restore in negative form the missing dimension of life...The ideology that underlies and unites the ancient and the modern megamachine is one that ignores the needs and purposes of life in order to fortify the power complex and extend its dominion. Both megamachines are oriented toward death.
> ⌁LEWIS MUMFORD

Can there be any doubt that the Computer, *as finally the mechanization of mind*, is the consummation of the megamachine? Mumford knew it already in the sixties: 'The new megamachine, in the act of being made over on an advanced technological model, also brought into existence the ultimate 'decision-maker' and Divine King, in a transcendent electronic farm: the Central Computer.' But it's gone much further: 'Carla's analogies and Dennis' theorizing are not isolated examples of what happens when people meet up with computers. They are taking first steps towards playing with the idea of mind as machine, personality as program. This kind of play with computation and models of the self is very much a part of what the adult world is doing with computers.' (SHERRY TURKLE, *The Second Self*) Carla is a fifth-grader; Dennis is fourteen. Bureaucracies and programs, corporations and input, information and statistics, cognitive science and artificial intelligence, genetic engineering, space technology, satellites, nanotechnology, military lasers, 'computers are at the base of them all... because of computers, all of these technologies are intertwined with one another' (JERRY MANDER). We inhabit now not a biosphere but a technosphere. The mission of the EPCOT Center in Orlando (Experimental Prototype Community Of Tomorrow), in the Center's own words, is to 'help people who are unsure about these changes, or feel intimidated by futuristic environments and seemingly complex systems; the exhibits are aimed at making us feel comfortable with computers and other implements of high technology': comfortable being the machinery, the animated death, we are becoming.

In this same invisible way *we are Hyper-reality*.

There's no one here but us, no one here but us. 'We have met the enemy, and they is us', as Pogo reported. Marx, Ellul, Mumford, Baudrillard—the brilliant, unintentional and irrelevant prophets of the *Kali-Yuga* who, in the pathetic microscopic communion of obsolete print, of fat 'hard' non-fiction books, identified, out of desperate commitment to us all, commitment to the great Protagonist whose integrity they so passionately respected, the stages of historical humanity's blind descent into the final darkness, the final dissolution of the cosmic cycle: phantom doctors of humanity, 'intellectuals', recording the sequence of morbidities, the simultaneously frenzied and somnambulistic suicide, of the simultaneously oblivious and horrified Protagonist—these four and many others are voices which mercifully cannot be heard because, for the collective, there is simply no point, nothing to be gained, in dwelling upon the hopeless. Only a very small minority can ever see -– though, paradoxically, nearly everyone *suspects*—the 'big thing' that's going on and, interpreting the phrase in every possible sense and with the unrestricted generosity it deserves in this context, 'face it'. There's a vague malaise, a general uneasy bravado or suppressed misgiving, something like a metaphysical moment of absentmindedness, and then attention is quickly directed to 'little things': inequities of gender, class or ethnicity, moral issues, 'quality' of television programming, 'dangers' of technology getting 'out of control', 'pitfalls' of materialism, 'defects' in the scientific worldview, the 'price' of Progress — not 'little' in themselves, of course, but in the gigantic setting, the cosmic panorama.

✳

So: returning to Baudrillard. Methodical exposition here, punctuated by illuminating, urgent and necessary asides, but always resumed: I never lose the thread of the 'argument', and I know where we're heading. Trust me. Returning to Baudrillard and the postmodern 'media-world' we live in — what Kellner calls 'The Postmodern Carnival' and Neil Postman 'The Age of Entertainment' or 'The Age of Show Business' and technocrats 'The Information Age' and hippie or yuppie air-heads 'The New Age' or 'The Omega Point' — we discover the human person 'transformed into an object as part of a nexus of information and communication networks.' ('*Sports Parents*: How to Help Your Kids Get the Most out of Sports. Parent & Coach: Can You be Both? 'Sports Parents' is now On-Line! Visit our Website!' September, 1998) People become 'terminals of media and communication networks', they 'internalize the media and thus become terminals within media systems, 'they "plug into various communication systems and participate in television, radio, telephone, computer and other communication and information networks" and "in this way individuals become terminals in communication matrices": "the mass and the media are one single process."'

For Baudrillard all the media of information and communication neutralize meaning, and involve the audience in a flat, one dimensional media experience, which he defines in terms of a passive absorption of images or resistance to meaning, rather than an active processing or production of meaning... Television is viewed as a media 'which suggests nothing, which magnetizes, which is only a screen, or is rather a miniaturized terminal which in fact is found immediately in your head — you are the screen and the television is watching you'... The interiorization of media transmissions within the screen of our mind obliterates, he claims, the distinction between public and private, interior and exterior space, both of which are replaced by media space... Once again, Baudrillard projects a cybernetic imaginary, which sees people as becoming more and more like machines, like information processing... On this analysis, the social — taken as interpersonal relations, as a specific sphere mediating between the public and private spheres — is literally 'electrified' in media and computer networks which relate and organize individuals through electronic circuits rather than libidinal or face-to-face social relations.

We don't pause to examine exactly what our children are talking about, when they talk about what they saw on television, because there's no reason for the question to arise, no space in the brain for it; nor does it seem odd to us when they, or we, chat and chuckle about fictional movie and television characters and events as if they were real; nor does it seem peculiar to us that we 'know' the television set is an 'idiot box', 'boob tube', and refer to it contemptuously as such, and yet flop onto the couch in 'the TV room' every night with a sigh of relief and anticipation. Media-reality, hyper-reality, has become normal for us, has *become* reality — a reality which, moreover, has definite plans for us, which knows all about us, knows us intimately, as a matter of fact knows *everything* about us, because it has *created* us, because it *is* us. Our keenest intelligences, trained in the great universities, are, right now as you read these words, adjusting the 'fine tuning', 'ironing out the bugs', exploring 'the exciting potentials', and 'making the breath-taking breakthroughs'.

Our children's enchanted enthusiasm for television, videos and electronic games clearly testifies to the insight and ingenuity of the numerous professionals whose collective labor led up to and culminated in the final transport of consumption, to the accuracy of the deliberately addictive elements conceived for and incorporated into those technologies, while for adults the media-world, especially now the Internet, functions as something like a giant pharmacy of sedatives and 'maintenance' drugs, with 'something for everyone'. The point, however, is that we know this and cannot care. Cannot care, don't have the strength to care, don't know what it would *mean* to care. Because the trajectory of historical humanity is fixed, and we know it. That's what we really know. That's why we cannot care.

Some of my students seem to be looking for the same stimulation and entertainment in class that they find in television. As one of them remarked, 'Young people have a TV attitude toward school, like it is there to give you a good program and all you have to do is watch, complain, and turn the channel now and then.' Kids talk in class, another girl explained to me, the way they talk at home during a TV commercial, ignoring the teacher as if he or she had no more feelings than a Sony Trinitron...

There was a time when many young people would curl up with a good book when they were bored. Today, they are more likely to rent a movie at a video store, or turn on their Nintendo or Sega home video games, or simply pick up the remote control of their TV and 'slum around' its dozens of cable channels until they find something that distracts them. This past spring I had kids sneak their pocket-sized Nintendo video games into class; others were wired with special Walkmans that are very hard to detect. Several girls told me that before they leave for school in the morning they set their VCRs to record the soaps from 12:30 to 4:00. Said one: 'When I get home from my after-school job around five, I go to my room and start watching my regular programs like 'Laverne and Shirley'. I'll grab a quick dinner and then pick up my night shows like 'Cosby' until about 9:30. Then comes the best part. I turn on the VCR and get caught up in my soaps. At about midnight I fall asleep.' Stories like that, chilling though they are to a teacher, are not uncommon... (Patrick Welsh, English Teacher 'for the past twenty years' at T.C. Williams High School in Virginia)

⁓ THE WILSON QUARTERLY, Summer 1991

Was this kind of 'life' planned for our children by human beings, by Technology, or by Capital? Trick question! Human beings *are*... but you know.

And we like it, we dig it. It's a 'turn-on'. Armed with the magic wand, the 'control', often scuffling over its possession or protesting someone's monopoly, we channel-surf and graze, click and switch; happy, powerful, and at peace. There was a time (really not very long ago) when we talked about 'escape literature', literature in which we immersed ourselves to escape the harshness or tedium of reality, which meant that we could and did distinguish it from other literature which reflected or examined reality, brought us toward rather than away from reality. This distinction has become not impossible but meaningless, and not because (as one might think) *everything* is now a technological version of 'escape literature' but because *there is no longer any 'reality' from which to escape.* We are, after a fashion, permanently 'woozy' as we lurch and straggle through our days, 'intoxicated' across the whole spectrum of meanings attached to that word: befuddled, elated, disoriented, captivated, stupefied, delighted, as we move from one media experience to the next, in an endless series, with scenes from the experience immediately preceding, or from the immense archive of stored-up media imagery we carry within us, perpetually rising and subsiding in our minds, lingering, erupting, suddenly *there*, insistent images, favorite images meticulously cultivated, luscious images, invigorating images, even unfathomable images, passing in dreamlike parade through our minds, along with the 'blips', the 'facts', the senseless disconnected fragments of 'information' that are never retained, that mean absolutely nothing to us, clickety-clacking by like car after car of a train with no end. And all this we pursue; we don't accommodate to it, we actually go for it. Because it is powerful. It is definitely what's happening. Because it is *seductive*. We *made* it seductive: so that it could successfully, triumphantly, distract us from the haunting terror, the incomprehensible absence… of what? Heaven and Earth.

> Baudrillard sees the function of television and mass media as prevention of response, by isolating and privatizing individuals, trapping them in a universe of simulacra in which it is impossible to distinguish between the spectacle and the real and in which individuals came to prefer spectacle to 'reality'… Baudrillard thus views the mass media as instruments of a 'cold seduction' whose narcissistic charm consists in a manipulative self-seduction, in which we enjoy the play of lights, shadows, dots and events in our own mind as we change channels or media and plug into the variety of networks — media, computer, information — that surround us and allow us to become modulators and controllers of an infinitely variable panoply of sights, sounds, information and events.

It must be understood, however, that Baudrillard is most emphatically *not* describing something that can be isolated as a media experience, going on solely 'in our heads', an addiction to television or the Internet. He has referred earlier to 'the destruction of distinctions between media and reality': 'the model or code structures social reality, and erodes distinctions between the model and the real', 'simulation models come to constitute the world', we live in 'media space', an 'imaginary universe', where 'all reality then becomes the place of a semiurgical manipulation.' When we walk through an airport, for instance, we are actually walking through an *image* of 'airport' created by media; the glamour, romance, excitement, importance, imperturbable bank accounts and awesome invisible power whispering, rippling and surging through the circuits and neurons of the ambience were components built into the image and, translated here, are experienced as direct perception: as reality. It takes real effort to 'shake off' the media-experience and perceive the truth: the tawdriness, unrelieved artificiality, vulgarity of values and sheer ugliness, the commercial trying to 'sell us' on high-tech success, victory, prestige and power; we're supposed to perceive the calm and absolute command of technological self-confidence, the current 'state-of-the-art' eminence of scientific and managerial achievement, but actually this glitz is nothing but a shed-ful of merchandise, reeking of 'sign' and 'code', a charade of stressed-out unhappy victims fueled by Prozac, nursing their secret moans of exhaustion as they struggle to experience the 'excitement' they've been told is here and now theirs, being shunted from city to city, almost invariably under direct or indirect orders from money, dressed up to look on top of it, in the technosphere, the great advertisement, the living lie that has replaced a human habitat.

But 'airport' is even more; it is itself a node, a terminal, in a giant global communications grid composed of video, telephone, and computer relays, the great 'International Telecommunications Web', where not only information but humans themselves, transfixed by the pulsing geometric patterns of colored lights and the ecstasy of take-off, tranquilized in the cabins of the sleek jets purring and rearing on the runways, are processed, transmitted, pampered and debriefed. And this whole scene is media, media within media; there are screens everywhere, movies in the air, flight attendants looking just like flight attendants, executives looking just like executives, and we are there: genuine passengers with our genuine boarding passes. Men are virile, as men are supposed to be, women are exciting, as women are supposed to be. Clothing and accessories, luggage especially, voices and mannerisms are intriguing, irresistibly interesting, actually thrilling, speaking volumes to us, because we have seen all this before somewhere: we 'remember' it: we knew it would be like this because this is what we knew it was. *We saw it all on television and in the movies!* On which program? In which movie? In all of them. That's the secret. All the programs, all the movies, all the computer technology, all the screens are saying the same thing—because the medium is the message, remember?—saying, if I may paraphrase the inexpressible (to make certain aspects of the *Kali-Yuga* visible it is often necessary to resort to verbal or literary strategies that may seem forced or unseemly): 'We are the amazing electric, we are the arrival of the electric saints, the cyberplastic-good-life the whole world slavers for, we are the flawless, the slick and the victors, the speed-of-light fix and the magical fax, porno-perfecto, your own PC, the miraculous holograph gleaming on the credit card and the instant replay of the turn-around jump shot. We've snared the lust of an entire planet, all eyes are upon us, our argument unanswerable. And all *you* have to do is *look!* We're all yours, and you want us, *because this is where it's at and you know it!*'

In the ecstasy of communication, a promiscuity of information and communication is circulated and disseminated by a teeming network of cool, seductive and fascinating sights and sounds which are played on one's own screen and terminal. With the disappearance of exciting scenes (in the home, in the public sphere), passion evaporates in personal and social relations; yet a new fascination emerges ('the scene excites us, the obscene fascinates us') with the very universe of media and communication. In this universe we enter a new form of subjectivity, in which we become saturated with information, images, events and ecstasies. Without defense or distance, we become 'a pure screen, a switching center for all the networks of influence.' In the media society, the era of inter-subjectivity, meaning, privacy and the inner life is over; a new era of obscenity, fascination, vertigo, instantaneity, transparency, and overexposure begins: Welcome to the postmodern world!

And so: the name given to all this, this world, our world, is *hyper-reality*. Can you believe it? Say it isn't so, Shoeless Joe! (But he couldn't, could he? Couldn't look the kid in the eye, and shuffled away.) Is Baudrillard 'right'? Is semiology for real? Those aren't the questions, for people like us, anymore than the question, debated by the academicians and pivotal for Kellner, of whether or not Baudrillard's 'theory' actually supersedes Marxism or neo-Marxism or 'critical theory'. The question is: Does it ring true? Can you smell the coffee? Or, Have you been to Disneyland?

✳

Disneyland provides an example of Baudrillard's difficult and crucial concept of hyper-reality. For Baudrillard, the hyperreal is not the unreal but the more than real, the realer than real, as when models of the United States in Disneyland appear more real than their instantiations in the social world, as the United States becomes more and more like Disneyland. On this theory, 'the very definition of the real' has become 'that of which it is possible to give an equivalent reproduction,' and the 'hyperreal' is 'that which is always already reproduced,' that which perfectly instantiates its model: 'the real is produced from miniaturized units, from matrices, memory banks and command models—and with these it can be reproduced an infinite number of times.

It should be clear why, as I suggested earlier, the task of regaining our bearings is central and critical. It would also seem clear that all attempts to interpret our lives in the twentieth century that do not admit, at least as a possibility, the hyper-real nature of things, or something like that, of the society they seek to analyze, run the risk of missing the rather main point, really missing the forest for the trees, and reducing themselves to another blip in the cyberblitz. We're on treacherous ground; or, as we have seen, maybe there *is* no ground: people who seek to 'interpret our lives' in the *Kali-Yuga* run the risk of interpreting not 'nothing' but a new 'something', the hyper-real, whose mode of existence, whose ontological status, is utterly different from anything we have previously and comfortably regarded as 'real', *or as unreal*, defying, as it does, the distinction between the two. Mumford warned us in 1970:

> What is involved if the human race is not to lose its grip on reality entirely is something like a profound and ultimately planet-wide re-orientation of modern culture, above all the formidable recent culture of 'civilized' man... How long, those who are now awake must ask themselves, how long can the physical structure of an advanced technology hold together when all its human foundations are crumbling away? All this has happened so suddenly that many people are hardly aware that it has happened at all: yet during the last generation the very bottom has dropped out of our life; the human institutions and moral convictions that have taken thousands of years to achieve even a minimal efficacy have disappeared before our eyes: so completely that the next generation will scarcely believe they ever existed.

And even earlier, in *The Transformations of Man*, he wrote, 'In some degree, as I have already suggested, man has lost the secret of how to make himself human.' But the desperation of the great old humanist seems quite pathetically outdated. We've gone a long, long way since we lost that secret. And the warning, in its irrelevant reiterations, has become a cliché. *Transformations* appeared in 1956. *Technopoly*, by Neil Postman, appeared in 1992. Its reviewer in the *Christian Science Monitor* wrote, 'Postman believes people are becoming less and less what we were meant to be: human beings.' Less human beings and more what? In Postman's words, 'From the proposition that human beings are in some respects like machines, we move to the proposition that humans are little else but machines and, finally, that human beings *are* machines.' The same thing Mumford was saying so long ago, the classic humanist warning of the modern period. But it's obsolete. It still packs a punch, of course; but we've done something to ourselves that makes mere mechanization, 'turning ourselves into machines,' look like a minor alteration, a marginal accommodation, reveals it as merely a rudimentary beginning, the first crude groping experimentation with racial suicide whose final dazzling consummation requires a new vocabulary to describe it, an unqualified defection, irreversible apostasy, to perceive it.

The fact is, the proposal of hyper-reality, like the divine, no matter how plausible or 'satisfying', is ultimately unverifiable by reason or demonstration, and, again like the divine, must somehow be directly experienced, and this through an instinctive spontaneous revulsion originating in identification with and 'recognition' of our authentic humanity, our uncorrupted intelligence, our wholeness, dignity and self-respect, an identification itself originating, and necessarily, in an intuition of the Reality: Heaven and Earth. Heaven and Earth, the Soul, the Heart, Nature, Love, Wisdom. Humility… those things. And this intuition will genuinely present itself as a memory of 'the way things used to be' — 50 years ago, 100 years ago, and all the way back, in vaguely tormenting nostalgia, to the archaic dawn of time, to what we now call 'primitive' — which will be synonymous with 'the way things ought to be': because 'the past' we remember is always simpler, saner, closer to the heart, closer to Nature, closer to our Truth, closer to the Origin; for this 'memory', this intuition of purity, this intuition of 'the beginnings', the Great Beginning, is actually Plato's famous *anamnesis*, the cancellation of our amnesia, our inveterate forgetfulness, which unveils the 'fabulous pleromatic *illud tempus*, which man has to remember if he is to know the *truth* and participate in *Being*' (ELIADE): anamnesis, or knowledge through recollection, in recalling to mind what we actually are in the Eternal Now of God, traces our departure, identifies its rhythms: our departure from the Garden, our descent into Time, into History and Trouble and Loss and Sorrow, into the titanic phantasmagoric darkness of the final *yuga*, when all our 'possibilities' are realized. (Aspects of anamnesis are discussed most fully in Ananda Coomaraswamy's beautiful essay, 'Recollection, Indian and Platonic'.) But 'full-blown' anamnesis, which is equivalent ultimately to Enlightenment, is not required here; any intuition of human integrity, dignity and self-respect, any memory of times before the era of electronic media, any traces of what we acquired from an old-fashioned humanist education, and especially the simple gut feeling that 'all this is bullshit', any of these identifications with our basic humanity is sufficient to awaken, if only episodically, that contemptuous revulsion for the contemporary 'scene' which is the mode of perceiving hyper-reality. Or, if all else fails, you can go to the movies and see 'Sneakers'! (Or, now in 1998, 'The Truman Show', starring Jim Carey of 'Pet Detective' fame. Hollywood Knows!) This 'up-to-the-minute story full of computers and megabytes,' a film with 'a sassy political

message tagged onto the tale,' was reviewed in the September 14, 1992 issue
of the *Christian Science Monitor*. 'Despite all its high-tech gadgets, though,
it's a deliciously old-fashioned movie at heart, with glamorous stars romping
through a classic example of the familiar caper-comedy genre.'

> Along with suspense and humor, 'Sneakers' has a tantalizing awareness of
> how images, electronic circuitry, and endlessly proliferating information are
> waging a battle with facts, experience, and reality itself in the contemporary
> world. One character suggests that there's no such thing as reality anymore —
> tilting the movie toward French philosopher Jean Baudrillard's theory that
> today is a 'hyperreal' time when the image 'bears no relation to any reality
> whatever' and has become 'its own pure simulacrum', to quote his influential
> book 'Simulations'. 'Sneakers' doesn't pursue such notions deeply, but they
> lend substance to what's otherwise an exercise in pure entertainment… This
> is one of the year's most enjoyable pictures, and I'll be surprised if it doesn't
> became a major hit. Rarely has the hyperreal been so much fun.

So much fun. *So much fun!* But actually this is the Archfiend himself,
invisible behind the scenes and playing here his final trump card, the one
that can't be beat, that disarms us completely *because it transforms our identification of him into his 'entertainment' of us*, dangling a funny caricature of
himself before us — it's a 'caper-comedy'! — and making us laugh — for 'the
suspense grows, and so, to the movie's credit, do the laughs' — and teasing,
luring, coaxing, cajoling us once again and for the millionth time and forever
into that inexhaustibly fascinating Carnival, that inner and outer Never-
Never-Land, that Supreme Altered Consciousness called *Entertainment*:
but our response would be quite otherwise if we could see the frozen murderous hatred of humanity which is his only and real face. The film reviewer
is not an idiot, not a conspirator, nor are the makers of the film. They are
simply earning their livings, and playing by the rules. Simply communicat-
ing. There is no 'space' in which they can speak to us seriously, and both the
film *and* the review are entertainment, for 'it is not merely that on the television screen entertainment is the metaphor for all discourse. It is that off the
screen the same metaphor prevails.' (POSTMAN) There is no social exit from
all this. Only the disaffiliation, the apostasy of individuals who, in their love
for the real, their intuition and love of humanity *sub specie aeternitatis*, enter
upon one of the great Paths to that Reality which is the Truth: the Truth
and the Joy forever, the Way and the Truth and the Life. The cards are on
the table.

For hyper-reality is *perceived* as real and *is* 'real'; it is nothing less than a contamination or systemic disease of reality itself, an invisible metamorphosis, mutation, of the social foundation: a collective mask behind which there is no one. It is, in the *Kali-Yuga*, the ultimate stage of *maya*, defined by immemorial doctrine as 'the relative world', 'the world-appearance', 'neither real nor unreal' and therefore indescribable (but not incomprehensible; it is 'comprehended', although in an indescribable manner or mode of apprehension and *as* indescribable, in meditation, in God-Realization — but I digress), 'knowable' only by contrast with the changeless Absolute, the Reality that is God, Bhagavan, Paramatman, Brahman Supreme. This Reality is *first*; and Its Manifestation, Creation, is also *first*: they are Heaven and Earth, the Word and the World It uttered, and back to them must be traced anything whatsoever we would claim as real or meaningful or authoritative for us insofar as we are serious about being human. A transcendent Origin and a sacred Creation define what we are and are our only appeal. We discover ourselves only when we stand beneath the infinite sky, and on the holy ground: or when we *know* that. But all this has changed.

In a hyper-real world, 'the model comes first,' and its constitutive role is invisible because all one sees are instantiations of models (while one reproduces models of thought and behavior oneself). For Baudrillard, the entire facade and ecosphere of neo-capitalist societies are hyperreal, in that more and more areas of social life are reproductions of models organized into a system of models and codes. Such a hyperreal society of simulations includes such things as interstate highway and urban freeway transportation systems, fashion, media, architecture and housing developments, shopping malls and products which are reproductions of models, instantiations of codes: 'today it is quotidian reality in its entirety — political, social, historical and economic — that from now on incorporates the simulatory dimension of hyper-realism'. Everyday life thus becomes more and more hyperreal as hair, teeth, fingernails, food, flowers, grass and houses constitute a new hyper-reality that is 'more real than real'. Thought and behavior are likewise determined by codes and models which are reproduced in everyday social interactions and the presentation of the self in everyday life… There is no 'reality', or even potentiality, in the name of which oppressive phenomena can be criticized and transformed, because there is nothing behind the flow of codes, signs and simulacra.

Nothing behind them. Nothing there. It just happens. *La Technique.* Brain fever, shifting medley of our collective derailment, our societal 'mind' whose family name is Capital, or Science, or maybe Pride, Europe, the West. Disneylands are everywhere now, in Japan, Paris, our brains. 'Baudrillard claims that Disneyland presents itself as an imaginary space so as'

to conceal the fact that it is the 'real' country, all of 'real' America, which *is* Disneyland… Disneyland is presented as imaginary in order to make us believe that the rest is real, when in fact all of Los Angeles and the America surrounding it are no longer real, but of the order of the hyperreal and of simulation… It is meant to be an infantile world, in order to make us believe that the adults are elsewhere, in the 'real' world, and to conceal the fact that real childishness is everywhere…

⌒BAUDRILLARD

Baudrillard's writings, full of references to black holes, entropy, DNA and genetics, digital codes and information theory, satellites and cybernetics,

constitute perhaps the first radical high-tech, new wave social theory. They also involve what is perhaps the first self-consciously produced science fiction social theory to project futuristic anticipations of the world to come, the world right around the corner.

The world our children inherit. 'What Jean Baudrillard called hyper-reality', recalling here the phrase that initiated this journey, pages ago.

❋

The world our children inherit: the theme of this section, as you will recall, the heart of the matter. A few remarks, however, a few final points, before we turn our attention to that heart of the matter. That is to say: to the same situation we have just explored, only now not as an object of the analytical intelligence but as an event in our hearts, in the Heart of Humanity.

But first:

The hyper-real media world originating in the integrated economic and technological systems of the 'Western democracies', and especially in the United States, is not restricted to their boundaries but is exported with tireless industry to the whole rest of the planet, and is, in the cyclical perspective as well as their own, their most significant export. American intellectuals, well aware of this, 'have been pondering the immense world-wide impact of American popular culture.'

On March 10, a host of thinkers—few of then quite as overwrought as the French antagonists of Mickey Mouse—gathered at the American Enterprise

Institute in Washington, D.C. for a conference (with papers to be published as a book later this year) on 'The New Global Popular Culture: Is it American? Is it Good for America? Is it Good for the World?' Conference organizer and AEI Senior Fellow Ben J. Wattenberg's answers to those questions were 'Yes', 'Yes', and 'Yes', and he added, for good measure, that 'what's happening in this realm is the most important thing now going on in the world.' This last sentiment, both ardent fans and gloomy critics of American popular culture agreed, was not merely a reflection of the undying American penchant for superlatives.
⁓from 'The World in Our Image?',
WILSON QUARTERLY, Summer 1992

Wattenberg's 'for good measure' is, of course, right on the mark, since it identifies—unbeknownst and unknowable forever to a 'mind' such as his—a central 'movement' in the closing of the cycle. And at the same conference, sociologist Seymore Martin Lipset—in what is apparently, from the excerpt quoted, a classic of self-serving and imbecilic *petitio principii* – argued that 'It is not that the world is becoming Americanized. Rather, it is that we all like the same kinds of candy, ice cream, automobiles, computers, movies, detective stories, TV sitcoms, comics, music.' (A remark so literally thoughtless and utterly stupid defies credibility; it wasn't ironic, however, as one almost hopes: he meant it.) Todd Gitlin, on the other hand—again, like nearly all our unconscious prophets of the *Kali-Yuga*, bearing witness to the humanist tradition—was eloquent in his indictment:

The Rambo grunt, the Schwarzenegger groan, the 'Die Hard' machine-gun burst, degrade the human spirit.' Todd Gitlin insisted. 'If the export of... the vicious, the blatant and stupid is 'good for the world', to use the conference organizers' phrase, then all values have been sacrificed to the bottom—and I do mean bottom—line.' Hollywood, he said, 'is in the grip of inner forces which amount to a cynicism so deep as to defy parody. The movies are driven by economic and technological incentives to revel in the means to inflict pain, to maim, disfigure, shatter the human image.'

In the same vein, French novelist Jean-Marie Romart, responding to the opening of Euro Disneyland near Paris, warned, 'If we do not resist it, the kingdom of profit will create a world that will have all the appearance of civilization and all the savage reality of barbarism.' (The words 'Civilization' and 'barbarism' of course, both bear closer scrutiny; but his point is clear.)

We are developing and rapidly exporting a new material culture, a mallcondo culture. To the rest of the world we do indeed seem not just born to shop,

but alive to shop. Americans spend more time tooling around the mallcondo—three to four times as many hours as our European counterparts—and we have more stuff to show for it... This burst of mallcondo commercialism has happened recently—in my lifetime— and it is spreading around the world at the speed of television.
⌒JAMES TWITCHELL, *Wilson Quarterly*, Spring 1999

And in the same vein again:

And the emerging US Dominated global culture, far from reflecting a regard for human dignity and other liberal values, is 'the culture of Hollywood, rock and roll, and Madison Avenue... a culture of hedonism, cruelty, contempt, and cynicism.
⌒From a review of CHRISTOPHER LASCH's 'The Fragility of Liberalism', *Salmagundi*, Fall 1991

Finally we may read in a *Christian Science Monitor* (July 10, 1992) report from Kejaman Lasah, Malaysia:

Many young men have already left this vast longhouse, stretching along a riverbank in interior Borneo, for the city... Modern life and the lure of the city are changing longhouses, the pristine jungle hamlets that time, it seemed, had forgotten... Change is encroaching. Many longhouses, except the most remote, are lit by generators and tube lights. Air-conditioned motor launch taxis, featuring kung-fu movies and videos of American professional wrestling, growl up and down the rivers. At the Long Geng festival, music from the *sape*, a four-string, lute-like instrument, reverberated through an amplifier. The crowning point of the festival was a Rambo movie shown on the chief's video-cassette recorder.

This destruction of tradition, its replacement by merchandise, by technology, by hyper-reality, by filth, is global, of course. And, also of course, a cliché. An educational television program. The suicide of the human race in the *Kali-Yuga* appearing before your eyes as an 'educational TV special report' introduced by a real live movie star right there 'on location'. Can you untangle that? Can you see through the screen?

Hyper-reality, predictably, presents a serious challenge to novelists who wish to fulfill their historic mission. A *Wilson Quarterly* article (Spring 1992) by critic Sven Birkerts, titled 'Mapping the New Reality', is introduced: 'If the novel is, in Stendhal's words, a mirror moving along a highway, what is the fate of the novel in our time, when highways are turning 'smart' and electronic gadgetry defines the fabric of human communities? Depicting our elusive reality may prove impossible.' In a *Christian Science Monitor* review (August 17, 1992) of Birkerts' *American Energies: Essays on Fiction*, we read:

> As a reflection of an American culture spun into confection by technology, he argues, mostly lightweight novels are being written now… He offers a partial lineup of novelists who 'reached artistic maturity' just before technology and the sonic boom of media communications swept the globe… He compares them with a current list of novelists he calls 'children of the media culture…' Is the latter group a purveyor of lightweight excellence?… No, if you are a member of that generation and accept the world of sudden pulses, quick images and 'circuit processes', as Birkerts calls it.

Like Baudrillard, Ellul, and many others, Birkerts recognizes that a radical and all-pervading metamorphosis of humanity has occurred here. He perceives, as this essay and the writers quoted in it have contended, that the 'electronics revolution', Information Technology, Internet and OnLine, broadcast media, computers and all they carry along with them have erased the familiar boundaries and landmarks in every area of our lives and in our very consciousness. Because people are no longer quite people in the way they used to be, and human experience is no longer quite human in the way it used to be, a basic assumption of novelists, that there is an objective reality out there, real people in a real world, and therefore a viable literary strategy called 'realism', must be reexamined. Birkerts confines himself to the impact of the electronic metamorphosis in his field of expertise, the writing of fiction; but that metamorphosis, as we have seen, is but an aspect of the rending, cosmic, irreversible separation from Reality altogether, from Heaven, from Earth and from our own Humanity, that marks the end of the great terrestrial cycle.

> There is nothing intrinsically wrong with the realist procedure, and in skilled hands the results can still be persuasive. The problem lies elsewhere. It lies in the fact that our common reality has gradually grown out of the reach of the realist's instruments. We live our late-century lives less and less in the foursquare world of surfaces and bounded events that realism evolved to depict. Our business is increasingly with a new experiential hybrid. We live among signals and impulses and processes that our language has a hard time capturing. Our consciousness is mapped to a new field, and the contours of that field are determined by the way we spend our days. We don't talk over the fence but over the phone—worse, we leave messages on machines and check in to see if our messages have been returned. Our professional lives are likewise shorn of clear boundaries—most of us interact more with buttons and digits than with people. We drive, park, drive again, surrounding ourselves

during bubble time with a distracting environment of music or talk-show barking. Dinner? Often as not we nuke it in the microwave, before kicking back for a well-deserved night in front of the VCR.

And in striking resonance with one of the basic themes of the present essay, singling out John Updike as one of the very few writers who 'have the narrative gifts and perceptual resources to make readable fiction out of the real stuff of our daily experience,' Birkerts writes, 'the power and poignancy of *Rabbit at Rest* arise less from his evocations of the present and much more from their constant often implicit contrast to the way things used to be. Rabbit's appetite for nostalgia is mighty; it is what makes him a poet':

> Rabbit feels betrayed. He was reared in a world where war was not strange but change was: the world stood still so you could grow up in it. He knows when the bottom fell out. When they closed Kroll's, Kroll's that had stood in the center of Brewer all those years, bigger than a church, older than the courthouse, right at the head of Weiser Square there, with every Christmas those otherworldly displays of circling trains and nodding dolls and twinkling stars in the corner windows as if God Himself put them there to light the darkest time of the year.

The Knight of the Woeful Countenance, incidentally, addressing the generous mystified goat-herds who 'fed heartily and said nothing' shared the same sentiment—for it is universal in the *Kali-Yuga*, universal ever since the Fall into Time—four hundred years ago. He, too, recalled 'the way things used to be.'

> And now Don *Quixote* having satisfy'd his Appetite, he took a Handful of Acorns, and looking earnestly upon 'em: O happy Age, cry'd he, which our first Parents call'd the Age of Gold! not because Gold, so much ador'd in this Iron-Age, was then easily purchas'd, but because those two fatal Words, Mine and Thine, were Distinctions unknown to the People of those fortunate Times; for all Things were in common in that holy Age: Men, for their Sustenance, needed only to lift their Hands, and take it from the sturdy Oak, whose spreading Arms liberally invited them to gather the wholesome savory Fruit; while the clear Springs, and silver Rivulets, with luxuriant Plenty, offer'd them their pure refreshing Water... All then was Union, all Peace, all Love and Friendship in the World: As yet no rude Plough-share presum'd with Violence to pry into the pious Bowels of our Mother Earth, for she without Compulsion kindly yielded from every Part of her fruitful and spacious Bosom, whatever might at once satisfy, sustain and indulge her frugal Children.
>
> ⁓ PT. I, BK II, CHAP. 3

(Notice how both Cervantes' immortal hero and the cosmological symbolism of far-away India refer to this as the 'Iron Age'. Coincidence? Evidence of cultural contact? Attribute of iron?)

Recalled that Age—which, the reader will surely remember, is none other than the Way, high *te* of the Tao of Heaven and Earth, is it not? 'When virtue is perfect and rooted in Tao it is called nature (Tao and *te*)... Nature and virtue issue from the same origin...' (ELLEN CHEN)—and, later on in the glorious recounting of his incomparable exploits, defined his destiny, his immortal sallying forth into the world, as the vehicle of its restitution:

> Know, *Sancho*, cry'd he, I was born in this Iron Age, to restore the Age of Gold, or the Golden Age, as some choose to call it. I am the Man for whom Fate has reserv'd the most dangerous and formidable Attempts, the most stupendous and glorious Adventures, the most valorous Feats of Arms. I am the Man...
>
> ⁓PT. I, BK III, CHAP. 6

And so on. He was the Man. Updyke's Rabbit, Cervantes' Knight and all the rest of us: where is our orientation, our point of reference, our standard, touchstone and appeal, but in some kind of 'past' that rings true in our hearts? A past when 'the world stood still so you could grow up in it.'

When I reached this point in the final editing of this text I couldn't help recalling Erich Auerbach's beautiful and profound masterpiece, one of the truly illuminating great books of the twentieth century, *Mimesis: The Representation of Reality in Western Literature*. Surely there would be additional insights here, a prefiguration or premonition of what was to come, an analysis of the stages preceding the present one where, in Birkerts' words, 'our common reality has gradually grown out of the reach of the realist's instruments.' And we are rewarded. The last writer whose work (*To The Lighthouse*) Auerbach explores is Virginia Woolf.

> The writer as narrator of objective facts has almost completely vanished: almost everything stated appears by way of reflection in the consciousness of the *dramatis personae*... In our passage...there actually seems to be no viewpoint at all outside the novel from which the people and events within it are observed, any more than there seems to be an objective reality apart from what is in the consciousness of the characters...

Confidence in an objective reality, then, in the enterprise of Western writers, was the first casualty. States of mind, the celebrated 'stream of consciousness', alone remained. A common, therefore objective world had disintegrated, or traveled beyond the reach of language. Auerbach continues:

As recently as the nineteenth century, and even at the beginning of the twentieth, so much clearly formulable and recognized community of thought and feeling remained in those countries [the countries of old European culture] that a writer engaged in representing reality had reliable criteria at hand by which to organize it. At least, within the range of contemporary movements, he could discern certain specific trends; he could delimit opposing attitudes and ways of life with a certain degree of clarity. To be sure, this had long since begun to grow increasingly difficult. Flaubert already suffered from the lack of valid foundations for his work; and the subsequent increasing predilection for ruthlessly subjectivist perspectives is another symptom. At the time of the first World War and after—in a Europe unsure of itself, overflowing with unsettled ideologies and ways of life, and pregnant with disaster—certain writers distinguished by instinct and insight find a method which dissolves reality into multiple and multivalent reflections of consciousness. That this method should have been developed at this time is not hard to understand. But the method is not only a symptom of the confusion and helplessness, not only a mirror of the decline of our world. There is, to be sure, a good deal to be said for such a view. There is in all these works a certain atmosphere of universal doom... Let us turn again to the text which was our starting-point. It breathes an air of vague and hopeless sadness...

Mimesis was written between May 1942 and April 1945 in Istanbul, where Auerbach had relocated after being discharged from Marburg University by the fascist sickness then in power. ('I may also mention that the book was written during the war and at Istanbul, where the libraries are not well equipped for European studies.' Testimony to a heroic devotion fruitful to ponder.) It was published in 1946. Respect for his witness demands that we read the final paragraph of his Epilogue:

With this I have said all that I thought the reader would wish me to explain. Nothing now remains but to find him—to find the reader, that is. I hope that my study will reach its readers—both my friends of former years, if they are still alive, as well as all the others for whom it was intended. And may it contribute to bringing together again those whose love for our Western history has serenely persevered.

And there is something about it we can love. Despite all. I confess.
Finally, hyper-reality colonizes our measurement of time.
First to review: Following upon the Fall into Time, when we became History, historical humanity, the linear time that then came into being was measured, of course, by sequences of events; especially those that subsequently turned out to have been, in the consensual judgement, 'important'. They

were History with a capital H. And History, as we have seen, is our fundamental and exhaustive identity. History in the macrocosm, biography in the microcosm.

In our derivative identity as Capital, the significant events are the prices of things, and by them we mark time: what a gallon of gas, a loaf of bread, a ticket to the movies, a pair of shoes, a down payment on a house, used to cost. Our 'history' as Capital is the history of commodities, of fashions in the world of commodities, and of the appearance on the market of innovative appliances and technologies: the vicissitudes of merchandise and exchange value.

In our present identity as Entertainment, the significant events by which we measure time are television constellations, the careers of media personalities and entertainers, musical styles, movies and movie stars, and the highlights, records and milestones in the world of spectator sports — 'the main events', as it were. We measure time increasingly now, however, principally by what we watched on television, *both as 'programs' and as the current 'reality'*. And the new wrinkle introduced by what we now understand as hyperreality, of course, is that we can't separate the two. The past we 'remember', remember as *real*, is often actually the hyperreal world of the media. In a San Francisco *Chronicle* review of *The Way We Never Were* by Stephanie Coontz, we read:

> According to Coontz, when most Americans mention 'family values', they are thinking of 1950s and 1960s TV shows such as 'Leave It to Beaver' and 'The Adventures of Ozzie & Harriet', or combining elements of those sit-coms with vague concepts of late 19th and early 20th century life that ignore the facts.

Hyper-reality (and there aren't any 'facts', of course, in a hyper-real world: or, more precisely, no 'fact' can survive in it), in other words, dissolves into itself not only our present 'reality' but the past as well. Which can only mean that the projection of a 'real' future for ourselves is, to say the least, unlikely. Upon what could it be based?

That was the third and final 'remark'. Time now to begin circling in on the landing field: on our children's inheritance of a hyperreal world as an event in our hearts, in the Heart of Humanity.

✳

I suppose it should be said that nothing we became conscious of in an analysis like this — hyper-reality, historical humanity, urbanism and secularism, mechanism and quantification, the entire 'anatomy' of the *Kali-Yuga* I am seeking to exhibit—has the slightest practical relevance to the raising of our children. (Which isn't to say that this essay is not about the real lives of real people, you and me: it most emphatically is.) We love them, deal with the problems as they arise and as 'society' defines them and creates them, and hope for the best without looking too narrowly at what that could mean. The whole and sole thrust of cyclic awareness is toward Spirit; the only 'answer' to the *Kali-Yuga* is Enlightenment, the only decision it enjoins is adoption of a spiritual Path.

But there is something else here: something else, something elusive, something beyond those deformations of childhood and childrearing, many of which are obviously implicit or derivative in our exploration or have been treated explicitly, whose origins can be readily traced to the cyclic situation. Absence of respect for older people, or absence of the social relationship in which 'elders' exist, for example, are obviously rooted in perpetual innovation and the continual obsolescence of knowledge, as well as in the impossibility of maturation into Wisdom in secular historical societies where Wisdom has been superseded by the Computer, by 'information' and its claims. Hence 'old fogeys', 'old farts', and 'old-fashioned ideas'. Pedagogical theories which urge that grade-school children be encouraged—'Be creative! Use your imaginations! Brainstorm!'—to 'create' their *own* myths (Myths! Explanations, instructions and directives from heaven, from the depths of our identification with the divine!), their *own* Native American legends, to 'invent' civilizations and languages, are not intended simply as instructive reenactments but clearly originate in and reflect humanity's self-conception in the *Kali-Yuga*—powerful, progressing, perpetually cancelling and transcending the past, autonomous, independent of law or nature, self-creating—as well as in a sort of patronizing sense of superiority to anything merely given, merely found. And ultimately, of course, originating in Ignorance, Darkness, Separation. It's a surrender, a defeat, at once innocent and abject. And, if we continue to view human affairs in their whole span, as we must in the context of cyclic unfolding—recalling the aphorism of James Woods quoted by Ananda Coomaraswamy in his 70th birthday address, 'From the Stone Age until now, *quelle degringolade!*'—it could be argued that the perpetual 'crisis in education' is rooted in the very existence of 'schools', social institutions integral to the functioning of atomized production-oriented mass societies organized by techniques of social management and according to principles of technological rationality. Literacy, urbanism, the stupendous accumulation of 'knowledge' and its infinitely ramified subdivisions, the division of labor and the specialization of human beings, the new social meta-institution called 'bureaucracy', with its perfected central instrument of regimentation through reductive mutilation, the 'form' (Who composes those forms we fill out? Who sits down and thinks like a form?), government and administration, the 'functionalization' and 'instrumentalization' of the human person and the ideology and formulas of citizenship, all these are surely among the great milestones marking our Progress out of the tiny 'primitive' communities in which each boy became what his father was and each girl her mother and the immemorial Way of Life hung suspended time out of mind in the Eternal Now of Nature... and there were no schools.

Progress: into the present, where screens now have incomparably more power than people to hold the attention of my typical second graders in the local elementary school, while the nature of the 'attention' television programs foster and 'hold' is the direct cause of the drastically reduced concentration spans and increasingly common 'attention deficit disorder' (ADD) children display in 'the real world'. 'Best of all—you have fun, while Fantavision does most of the work'—as we read in an ad for primary-grade software.

> American society tends to create ADD-like symptoms in us all. We live in an ADD-ogenic culture. What are some of the hallmarks of American culture that are also typical of ADD? The fast pace. The sound bite. The bottom line. Short takes, quick cuts. The TV remote-control clicker. High stimulation. Restlessness. Violence. Anxiety. Ingenuity. Creativity. Speed. Present-centered, no future, no past. Disorganization. Mavericks. A mistrust of authority. Video. Going for the gusto. Making it on the run. The fast track. Whatever works. Hollywood. The stock exchange. Fads. High stim. It is important to keep this in mind or you may start thinking that everybody you know has ADD. The disorder is culturally syntonic—that is to say, it fits right in. ⁓ From *Driven to Distraction*, 1998, advice to teachers

Keep in mind that the authors define the effects of this admittedly ADD-ogenic environment as 'pseudo-ADD', not the real thing, because they are not traceable to the putative genetic or chemical 'syndrome' whose alleged identification poses no questions about society: they are, in other words, normal. This sort of subtle twist in mainstream self-analyses is characteristic in the *Kali-Yuga*. What is remarkable is not the twists themselves but the fact that such obvious dishonesty, even manifest illogicality or outright stupidity, goes unremarked. The explanation is that everyone is simply doing the work for which they are remunerated, and no one is about to jeopardize their social standing or annual income by raising uncomfortable questions or suggesting that there might be more here than a 'problem'; the contradiction between the acute intelligence displayed in the above list of 'hallmarks' and the flabby mindlessness of its interpretation will not be noted. The show must go on. *Progress* into the present, where the question 'counselors' hear most frequently from desperate parents of 'dysfunctional families' is 'What's *normal?*' Where

> growing up, to paraphrase an old song, is so very hard to do. And plenty of shows on television these days describe just how tough it is. The tribulations and trials of the young as they confront all the temptations and dilemmas of this society make a mixed bag of weekly drama and melodrama.
> ⌒ 'Coming-of-Age Dramas Crowd TV', CHRISTIAN SCIENCE MONITOR, September 25, 1992)

TV drama and melodrama: the kids will be entertained by images and attitudes they will unconsciously emulate and strive to realize in 'their own lives', thinking they are their own, and the parents will be reassured that responsible people are 'on top of all this' and 'know what's going on.'

> The daily misery around us is, I think, in large measure caused by the fact that—as Paul Goodman put it 30 years ago—we force children to grow up absurd. Any reform in schooling has to deal with its absurdities. It is absurd and anti-life to be part of a system that compels you to sit in confinement with people of exactly the same age and social class… It cuts you off from your own past and future, sealing you in a continuous present much the same way television does… Think of the things that are killing us as a nation: drugs, brainless competition, recreational sex, the pornography of violence, gambling, alcohol, and the worst pornography of all—lives devoted to buying things, accumulation as a philosophy. All are addictions of dependent personalities and that is what our brand of schooling must inevitably produce.

> What can be done to improve education?

> First, we need a ferocious national debate that doesn't quit, day after day, year after year, the kind of continuous emphasis that journalism finds boring. We need to scream and argue about this school thing until it is fixed or broken beyond repair, one or the other… We've all had a bellyful of authorized voices on television and in the press. A decade-long, free-for-all debate is called for now… (from a speech by John Gatto, New York City's Teacher of the Year)
> ⌒ UTNE READER, Sept/Oct 1990

A sincere man: a hero.

But the point is not to select from the interminable monotony of indict-ments: diatribes, laments, theories, diagnoses and proposals addressed to the permanent tribulation of rearing successive generations in the *Kali-Yuga*. The *Kali-Yuga*, where the word most commonly heard is 'breakdown', where megatons of 'information' and analysis addressed to the solution of an end-less 'menu' of problems and originating in every 'field' from bio-engineering to penology rake across our brains in every medium of communication like a perpetual monsoon. For all the 'problems' we face—all the sadness, the anxi-ety, the sense of emptiness and loss that resists definition or attribution of cause, and the certainty, ineffaceable, that *something is wrong*—are rooted in the irreversibly advancing cyclic structures we have been exploring through-out this essay: in the hyper-real, incessantly mutating, foundationless and substanceless, sizzling petrodollar shopping-mall superscience megatechnic grid the human world, historical humanity, has becomes in the absence of Heaven and Earth, the absence of everything upon which our recognizable humanity and the rearing of human children depend.

Something else here, something elusive. We can approach it through an exami-nation of role models, the acquisition of identity.

The role models for children at the close of the cycle, for whom Heaven—the inner transcendent Source, time out of time, in which archetypes, arche-typal patterns, exemplary models and eternal values originate—and Nature—the 'purposeless' Beauty, Majesty and Purity in which we discover our own eternal presence, discover we are already *there*, where alone we can become human—no longer exist, are neither *whole* people nor even *real* peo-ple, but are instead human pseudo-events: bullshit images, fragments, pic-tures in magazines, poster people, fashion people, movie, television and sports idols, never 'seen' except as the simulations without originals which is all they are, cardboard nothings perpetually replaced by new improved mod-els: the hyper-reality into which the cycle has exploded. Disneyland phan-tasms, rock stars, rap stars, 'Spice Girls', 'Teen-age Mutant Ninja Turtles' named after Italian painters of the Renaissance: more real than their own parents, and certainly more interesting. Whereas, in a contrast almost stupe-fying in the grimness and unmistakable import of its message, the role mod-els for children born into a human setting—a spiritual communion in a natural habitat—are the cultural paradigms or mythical archetypes of virtue and rectitude, humility and serenity, obedience and fulfilment, aspiration and honor, task and skill, and the adults, especially their own parents and kinfolk, as they strive to embody them. The traditional, normative, permanent ideals and the people who strive to realize them, or refuse to so strive and thereby manifest the negative archetypes which inevitably 'prove' their affirmative counterparts. Inevitably: because the Reality in which they originate and cohere, Nature, Spirit and their Unity, is changeless, perfect and our own Truth: the human Truth: the Truth that is the Way and the Life: God's Will does not contradict Itself, or, the same thing put differently, His Decree that we be given freedom of will was simultaneously a Decree that each life would be a moral drama within a just and inflexible Legislation: Pascal's 'necessity of the wager'. To this great Law the entire *Dhammapada* bears witness, every page. (I open it at random: 'The foolish man who scorns the teaching of the saintly, of the noble, of the virtuous, and follows false doctrine, bears fruit to his own destruction... Not in the sky, not in the midst of the sea, not if one enters into the clefts of the mountains, is there known a spot in the whole world where if a man abide, he might be freed from an evil deed... Whosoever offends a harmless, pure and innocent person, the evil falls back upon that fool, like light dust thrown up against the wind.') And the *Tao Te Ching* as well, every page:

> Oversharpen the blade, and the edge will soon blunt; amass a store of gold and jade, and no one can protect it; claim wealth and titles, and disaster will follow... He who is self-righteous is not respected; he who brags will not endure... Easy promises make for little trust; taking things lightly results in great difficulty.

We reap what we sow, a violent man will die a violent death, the chickens always come home to roost. The role models for children in a human, i.e traditional setting are other humans, real people, who though they walk the Earth are at the same time superhuman, 'beyond themselves'. Characters in the timeless cosmic Drama, whose lives are instruction in, and proof of, the Truth that guides and saves—and loves us.

But a contrast like this is still an object of the analytical intelligence—and a contrast which, as a matter of fact, hasn't gone far enough. It's not enough to say that we are, or should be, revolted by the degradation of role models into media-generated hyper-real slime: our requirements in this area, because we are drawn always, *bon gré mal gré* and by the eternal magnetism of heaven, to identify somehow with our eternal humanity, humanity *in divinis*, are inescapably stringent: we cannot comfortably tolerate even relativity here. We cannot identify ourselves, our humanity, with an uninterrupted series of historically or biographically conditioned images. Relativity here cannot be assimilated, we know in our hearts it's a lie; we know humanity is an absolute, a truth or essence that does not change (Marx was *dead* wrong) without ceasing to be itself, without departing from a human Self that is eternal and independent of all empirical change: Humanity is *there*, in an absolute realm, which can be conceived as 'out there' somewhere in the world of Archetypes or changeless Ideas, or 'within us', an immutable essence, a Purity, while change, mutability, insubstantiality, is *here*, in History, in this *mess*. Therefore we are always searching for, and reassured in invariably discovering, the common and universal humanity behind the countless and inexhaustibly beautiful faces of humankind unveiled for us by geography and anthropology, and our own journey through the world.

✳

It begins with identities; but we must go deeper. Imagining what it was like.

Once upon a time, when I looked at my son or daughter I saw myself, and I felt great joy; I melted into the eternal nature of things, the timelessness that is Heaven and human reality. I knew myself as the manifestation in time of something that is timeless, exemplary, a celestial Form, like my son or daughter, and I knew that all was well and all is well in this universe. I 'saw that it was good', as God did in the Beginning. The generations of humanity spoke to me of eternity, of Heaven. I saw that we need only keep the faith with the Original of ourselves, the divine Form, identify ourselves with the immortal Person, the Pattern of Humanity, need only discover that we were that Person: achieve that identity and be immortal ourselves. All this is eternal, I knew, this great Life, this world, this Earth and we upon it, it never ends, it will never end, its repetition in time is but the recurring images of its eternity in Heaven, birth and death, joy and sorrow, summer and winter, the sun and the stars, the rain and the rainbow, myself and the rest of us, there is eternal return.

And this last phrase, these intimations, summon to mind now the great work of Mircea Eliade. But before enlisting his luminous attendance, I want to evoke the contemporary counterpart to this 'remembrance'. You already know it.

Now, when I look at my son or daughter, I do not see myself: I see my end, myself as an end, without sanction, affirmation or validation of archetype, purely contingent, connected to and deriving from nothing but arbitrary inorganic circumstance, 'cut off' from something I can sense but cannot name, glimpse but cannot grasp. In my son or daughter I see something increasingly inscrutable, novel, of unknown destiny; I look through narrowed eyes, bemused, increasingly indifferent as the distance between us widens, feeling sometimes bad about that but recognizing with sober resignation that since their world is not mine I really haven't much to offer them other than a 'positive attitude' toward their unreachable unprecedented lives and an uncritical love that seems trapped in the past, the same kind of love I loved them with when they were children, and therefore increasingly formal. The proper unfolding of the stages of inter-generational relationship depends upon the continuity and invariability of identities and setting, until in my son or daughter I see and love myself: and what that love felt like, what that unfolding felt like, we can only guess. When I was archaic, when I was human, I was exemplary: I was one with changeless Being, with the Real, with the simple invulnerable rock-bottom nature of things, and perceived as such by my children, or as reprehensible for departing from that proper nature, and as such I saw them, and trained them, and taught them the immemorial ways and means, the initiatory secrets, the answers, and as we each unfolded according to the same pattern we were like two people walking along the same Path, one ahead of the other, a Path trodden by all since the Beginning, the good and true Path, and looking back and forth at each other as we walked, one for guidance and one with encouragement, from the same eternal landmarks and milestones: our relation to each other was itself a Path, one that we walked together, side by side. But now I am a moment in serial transience, as they are, having no relationship with what preceded or follows other than through a mechanistic, hence meaningless, causality; or even less: I am, as they will be, a 'part' which is no longer being manufactured, obsolete, like something that simply appeared, 'popped into view', then vanished, 'popped out of sight': like one of the countless split-second images that flash across the screen in the twenty seconds of a high-tech television commercial: as meaningless, as disconnected, even as contemptible, and nothing more, because there is nothing more, because in the career and lifestyle and experience of historical humanity there is nothing behind the transience, no exemplary celestial pattern, no sanctified archetype, and nothing within it, no ecstatic self-recognition of the immortal soul, and no one home, because only the timeless is real. And yet we are still saved, even now, in this state, still the immortal Self, even here, because Mercy, we are taught and know in our hearts, is infinite and eternal. 'The Reality that pervades the universe is indestructible, O Arjuna,' be it Brahman Supreme, or the Void of Prajna, or the God of the Faiths, be it the Word which was in the

Beginning, the Name which is hallowed, or OM, the Pranava, the Supreme Syllable of Mandukya, be it Nirvana, Paramatman or the Tao of Heaven and Earth, be it Satchidananda which is Existence-Consciousness-Bliss Absolute, or Love or the Eternal Beloved or the One that is the All that is the Truth, be it the Immortal Dharma or the Light of Lights or the Heart: 'Truth is One: the sages call it by many Names.' And Tat Tvam Asi: That art Thou. We cannot sink below the reach of Grace. What we lose on Earth is recovered in Heaven. But until that recovery our loss was real, and we were estranged, and we suffered.

✳

Eliade writes, in *The Myth of the Eternal Return* subtitled *Cosmos and History* (and you might be remembering here that 'returning is the motion of the Tao'):

> For archaic man, reality is a function of the imitation of a celestial archetype... What he does has been done before. His life is the ceaseless repetition of gestures initiated by others. This conscious repetition of given paradigmatic gestures reveals an original ontology. The crude product of nature, the object fashioned by the industry of man, acquire their reality, their identity, only to the extent of their participation in a transcendent reality. The gesture acquires meaning, reality, solely to the extent to which it repeats a primordial act... For the traditional societies, all the important acts of life were revealed *ab origine* by gods or heroes. Men only repeat these exemplary and paradigmatic gestures *ad infinitum*.

And it is in the definition and nature of human identity, of selfhood and 'role model', that we find the most far-reaching and significant consequence of this 'original ontology', indeed its true *raison d'être*.

> An object or an act becomes real only insofar as it imitates or repeats an archetype. Thus, reality is acquired solely through repetition or participation; everything which lacks an exemplary model is 'meaningless', i.e., lacks reality. Men would thus have a tendency to become archetypal and paradigmatic. This tendency may well appear paradoxical, in the sense that the man of a traditional culture sees himself as real only to the extent that he ceases to be himself (for a modern observer) and is satisfied with imitating and repeating the gestures of another. In other words, he sees himself as real, i.e., as 'truly himself', only, and precisely, insofar as he ceases to be so.

Ceases to be that ego, that precious 'personality', that precious 'individual' who first began to appear in the European 'renaissance' and has now seized center stage with a vengeance, a veritable Colossus of Misery, in the uncontested, unanswerable and all-pervading dominion of 'psychology', erected and unassailably established on the granite foundation set in place by the great Viennese scientist (his initials are S.F., his name and its derivative adjective a household word) who delivered, to the relief and satisfaction of so many, the revelation of humanity's truly contemptible nature. But enough of irresistible irony. The point to notice here is that the archaic person's 'real identity' as a transcendent archetype or paradigm, a *divine* Person, an identity in that Dawn or Golden Age spontaneous and woven into the entire fabric of daily life, is identical to the goal of the *sadhanas* or spiritual practices enjoined by the axial religions later addressed, out of His infinite Mercy, to a fallen humanity upon whom the darkness of the final Age, the *Kali-Yuga*, was implacably descending: *jivan-mukta*, Wayfarer, *bodhisattva*, Microcosm, Imago Dei, Taoist *sheng jen* (sacred man or woman), Islamic *insan kamil* (perfect man or woman): 'I live, yet not I but Christ lives within me.' As Eliade remarks, 'It is interesting to observe that the state of beatitude itself, *eudaimonia*, is an imitation of the divine condition, not to mention the various kinds of *enthousiasmos* created in the soul of man by the repetition of certain acts realized by the gods *in illo tempore*.'

As I have suggested throughout this essay, the relationship of the archaic Way to *the potentiality of becoming historical*, the haunting possibility of 'falling into time', was not only inherently preventive, through the Way's inflexible rootedness in the timeless realities of Heaven and Earth, but must be regarded as a legitimate premonition since that was indeed the cosmic Fate. It is 'a second aspect of primitive ontology':

> Insofar as an act (or an object) acquires a certain reality through the repetition of certain paradigmatic gestures, and acquires it through that alone, there is an implicit abolition of profane time, of duration, of 'history'; and he who reproduces the exemplary gesture thus finds himself transported into the mythical epoch in which its revelation took place... Archaic humanity, as we shall presently see, defended itself, to the utmost of its powers, against all the novelty and irreversibility which history entails.
> ∼ELIADE

Repetition of the exemplary model, then, identification with an archetype, with humanity *in divinis* as I have termed it in these pages, situates the archaic personage — or *homo religiosus*, any 'spiritual' person, anyone on a

Path; or even anyone in the 'timeless' moment of a fleeting dazzling insight, for, as the Buddhists smilingly point out, one is in that instant enlightened, because enlightenment is not anyone's property, there being no one here to gain it. Suzuki *roshi* always warned us against those 'gaining thoughts'!—in Reality, which means in the Sacred, for only the Sacred is Real. Divinity, Reality, Humanity and the Universe are One here. Heaven and Earth and Humanity are One here. In archaic Humanity we perceive that inexpressible and ecstatic unity of Being whose absence in our time is our absence as human, our presence as History and Hyper-reality, machinery and money, television and computers, Science and Technology, shopping malls and freeways and alcohol and 'work', and all the rest of it, the measureless rest of it, all the megatons of crap and caverns of emptiness, all the rest of the pitiful wreckage we writhe in and call Progress. Yes: we live longer now (a statement whose meaninglessness is easily demonstrated). And we have orthoscopic surgery for our bad knees. And hot showers. Cellular phones and refrigerators. Eyeglasses, anesthesia, watches, blenders, cordless drills, palm pilots... I could go on forever. *You name it, we have it! Make me an offer!*

> This faithful repetition of divine models has a two-fold result: (1) by imitating the gods, man remains in the sacred, hence in reality; (2) by the continuous reactualization of paradigmatic divine gestures, the world is sanctified. Men's religious behavior contributes to maintaining the sanctity of the world... As we saw, the sacred is pre-eminently the *real*, at once power, efficacy, the source of life and fecundity. Religious man's desire to live *in the sacred* is in fact equivalent to his desire to take up his abode in objective reality, to live in a real and effective world, and not in an illusion... The man of the archaic societies tends to live as much as possible *in* the sacred or in close proximity to consecrated objects. The tendency is perfectly understandable, because, for primitives as for the man of all pre-modern societies, the *sacred* is equivalent to a *power*, and, in the last analysis, to *reality*. The sacred is saturated with *being*... The polarity sacred-profane is often expressed as an opposition between *real* and *unreal* or pseudo-real. (Naturally, we must not expect to find the archaic languages in possession of this philosophical terminology, *real-unreal*, etc.; but we find the *thing*.) Thus it is easy to understand that religious man deeply desires *to be*, to participate in *reality*...
> ⌐ELIADE, *The Sacred and the Profane*

The contrast between this world, the world of archaic humanity or *homo religiosus*, and the hyper-real world of our technological distopia, takes your breath away! *Quelle degringolade* indeed! We are reminded of Zen's *kaminagara no michi*:

To wish to integrate the *time of origin* is also to wish to return to *the presence of the gods*, to recover the *strong, fresh, pure world* that existed *in illo tempore*. It is at once a thirst for the *sacred* and nostalgia for *being*... For those who have a religious experience all nature is capable of revealing itself as cosmic sacrality. The cosmos in its entirety can become a hierophany.

⁓ELIADE, ibid.

The consequences of irreligion are not restricted to diminished church attendance and a defence of abortion; they go 'across the board' indeed, and it is essential that we identify ourselves on their terms, for 'this nonreligious man descends from *homo religiosus*' and it is only by the contrasts I have been drawing in these pages that we can grasp, and assess, what we have become and how, as individuals, we might respond. Here alone is illumination — 'light on the subject', as Wei Wu Wei wittily remarked. There is, quite simply, no context other than these contrasts — here between the 'original ontology' which identifies the *real* or sacred and the degenerate 'ontology' of hyper-reality and the profane — within which individuals can correctly interpret their experience and make meaningful decisions about their lives.

Homo religiosus always believes that there is an absolute reality, the *sacred*, which transcends this world but manifests itself in this world, thereby sanctifying it and making it real. He further believes that life has a sacred origin and that human existence realizes all of its potentialities in proportion as it is religious — that is, participates in reality. It is easy to see all that separates this mode of being in the world from the existence of a nonreligious man. First of all, the nonreligious man refuses transcendence, accepts the relativity of 'reality', and may even come to doubt the meaning of existence... Modern nonreligious man assumes a new existential situation; he regards himself solely as the subject and agent of history, and he refuses all appeal to transcendence. In other words, he accepts no model for humanity outside the human condition as it can be seen in the various historical situations. *Man makes himself*, and he only makes himself completely in proportion as he desacralizes himself and the world. The sacred is the prime obstacle to his freedom. He will became himself only when he is totally demysticized. He will not be truly free until he has killed the last god... Profane man is the result of a desacralization of human existence.

⁓ELIADE, ibid.

The richness of Eliade's elaboration on these themes throughout his work knows no parallel. He's the one who did it. (I must mention here that Eliade has devoted an entire book, and a great one, *Myths, Dreams and Mysteries: The Encounter Between Contemporary Faiths and Archaic Realities*, to the contrast or confrontation we have been examining in this section, and indeed, after a fashion, throughout this essay. You should read it! It's a beautiful book!) His contribution to our self-understanding in these times is invaluable. And he is not among the 'unconscious prophets'.

> As the end of the cycle, that is, the fourth and last *yuga*, is approached, the darkness deepens. The *Kali-Yuga*, that in which we are today, is, moreover considered to be the 'age of darkness'... The conception of the four *yuga* in fact contributes a new element: the explanation (and hence the justification) of historical catastrophes, of the progressive decadence of humanity, biologically, sociologically, ethically, and spiritually. Time, by the simple fact that it is duration, continually aggravates the condition of the cosmos and, by implication, the condition of man. By the simple fact that we are now living in the *Kali-Yuga*, hence in an 'age of darkness', which progresses under the sign of disaggregation and must end by a catastrophe, it is our fate to suffer more than the men of preceding ages... On the other hand, the sufferings that fall to him because he is contemporary with this crepuscular decomposition help him to understand the precariousness of his human condition and thus facilitate his enfranchisement... and this by the very fact that he is conscious of the dramatic and catastrophic structure of the epoch in which it has been given him to live.

Conscious of it. The whole purpose of this essay. The reason I write.

✳

But to return. Examining the inter-generational regard now from the other direction, from the younger protagonist's point of view, imagining again the intemporal Norm, what it was like for us before the Fall into Time, before we became History. Aiming at a mutual illumination of experience and analysis: the former 'proving' the latter, making it real for us, 'putting flesh on the bones', the latter situating, interpreting and universalizing the former: examined life, the one worth living. And always the contrast: 'Life' in the Hyper-real and Life in the Real, or Bullshit and Truth: the Profane, which is profanity, and the Sacred, which is Humanity. History, and Heaven and Earth. Circling in on the heart of the matter.

Once upon a time (which always means, as Coomaraswamy or Seyyed Hossein Nasr pointed out somewhere, in *illo tempore, ab origine*, the time out of time, the place where truths and values came from as apples come from trees), when I looked at my father or mother, I saw what I was going to be when I grew up; what they did I would do, what they knew I would know; I would sing the same songs, dance the same dances, laugh at the same stories, acquire the same skills, fear the same dangers, welcome the same good fortune, walk and sleep in the same land under the same sky, and love that land and sky as they did; when they became old I would care for them as they cared for my grandparents now: and in all of this I knew that the world we lived in was our home, and that the way we did things here, the way we lived, was the way we were supposed to do things, the way we were supposed to live, because the way we lived was clearly a part of the way everything in the whole world happened, inseparable from the world. What I saw and heard was real. I was one of the people, the humans, as were my mother and father, exactly as clouds were clouds and rivers were rivers, there was a way to be one of the people, one of the humans, handed down from generation to generation all the way back to *illud tempus*, the time of the gods, the sacred time when the Pattern was created, when the world was being born, *in statu nascendi*, and all of us were that Way, walking in holiness, learning to walk in holiness. I loved the humanity I was going to become, and I loved the world it was my gift and blessing to inherit. But in a sense I didn't really 'know' any of this; I never thought it, never 'saw' it, never even 'took it for granted', which implies, if only a shred, some awareness of what is being so 'taken'. I just lived. I was human, without 'knowing' that fact, and because I didn't 'know' it — as the clouds were clouds and the rivers were rivers. I 'respected' elders without knowing I 'respected' them, I 'learned the Truth' without knowing I was 'learning the Truth', the way we maintain our balance while walking without knowing we are doing so. My world was real without my even knowing the word, the concept, and therefore everything 'showed' me what it was, everything was transparent, revealing and identical with its sacred meaning, a hierophany, a doorway to the Infinite. I was contained in and part of a glorious Mystery, the miracle of Existence, the great visible Manifestation of the great invisible Truth, the Spirit, which was capable at any moment of speaking to me of Itself, and nothing was clearer or more obvious than that the entire meaning of my life originated in an Intention at the Beginning of all this, the same Intention that created the world and everything in it. My fidelity to that Intention guaranteed the harmony and coherence of Creation and of my social world, and I would be taught, as my parents had before me, and before them their parents, and before them theirs, all the way back to that Beginning, how to keep that faith.

The sun was near to setting when Black Elk said: 'There is so much to teach you. What I know was given to me for men and it is true and it is beautiful. Soon I shall be under the grass and it will be lost. You were sent to save it, and you must come back so that I can teach you.' And I said: 'I will come back, Black Elk. When do you want me?' He replied. 'In the spring when the grass is so high' (indicating the breadth of a hand)...

They returned, in May 1931, and Black Elk recounted his Great Vision.

After the conclusion of the narrative, Black Elk and our party were sitting at the north edge of Cuny Table, looking off across the Badlands ('the beauty and the strangeness of the earth,' as the old man expressed it). Pointing at Harney Peak that loomed black above the far sky-rim, Black Elk said: 'There, when I was young, the spirits took me in my vision to the center of the earth and showed no all the good things in the sacred hoop of the world. I wish I could stand up there in the flesh before I die, for there is something I want to say to the Six Grandfathers.'

So the trip to Harney Peak was arranged, and a few days later we were there...

'Right over there,' said Black Elk, indicating a point of rock, 'is where I stood in my vision, but the hoop of the world about me was different, for what I saw was in the spirit...'

Having dressed and painted himself as he was in his great vision, he faced the west, holding the sacred pipe before him in his right hand. Then he sent forth a voice; and a thin, pathetic voice it seemed in that vast space around us:

'Hey-a-a-hey! Hey-a-a-hey! Hey-a-a-hey! Hey-a-a-hey! Grandfather, Great Spirit, once more behold me on earth and lean to hear my feeble voice. You lived first, and you are older than all need, older than all prayer. All things belong to you... Day in and day out, forever, you are the life of things.'

'At the center of this sacred hoop you have said that I should make the tree to bloom.'

'With tears running, O Great Spirit, Great Spirit, my Grandfather — with running tears I must say now that the tree has never bloomed. A pitiful old man, you see me here, and I have fallen away and have done nothing. Here at the center of the world, where you took me when I was young and taught me; here, old, I stand, and the tree is withered, Grandfather, my Grandfather! Again, and maybe the last time on this earth, I recall the great vision you sent me.

We who listened now noted that thin clouds had gathered about us. A scant chill rain began to fall and there was low, muttering thunder without lightning. With tears running down his cheeks, the old man raised his voice to a thin high wail, and chanted: 'In sorrow I am sending a feeble voice, O Six Powers of the World. Hear me in my sorrow, for I may never call again. O make my people live!'

For some minutes the old man stood silent, with face uplifted, weeping in the drizzling rain.

In a little while the sky was clear again.

⌒from BLACK ELK SPEAKS, as told through John Neihardt

Now, when I look at my mother or father, I see people whose lives prior to my appearance are so remote from and irrelevant to my own that I scarcely think to inquire about them, am only scarcely aware that they had any lives at all, and their story would only bore or amuse me if I was tricked into being their audience: if it holds my interest at all, the tale of their exploits and travails, it is only through its oddness, and as temporary entertainment, never as instructive, never as having anything to do with me and my life, for their world, their reality, is gone, utterly gone; 'gone with the wind': 'it's history'. They are people, furthermore, whose present lives seem to be enmeshed in some sort of permanent apprehension, crisis or anguished debate, sometimes concealed sometimes out in the open, who are comical, pathetic, weird, and unfathomable by turns, who speak with exasperated uncertainty or hollow-ringing conviction, forced self-assurance or painstaking tentativeness, carefully chosen words or snapped commands, about the decisions I must face, leaving me always feeling uneasy or insulted, shaken or desperate. My parents mean well, but they're out of it. They don't know what's going on. I keep many things secret from them because they're old-fashioned and wouldn't understand. They worry about me for no reason. Only my friends know who I really am, only my friends know about my real life. My mother and father don't live in the real world.

Yes. It's always been a question of reality, hasn't it?

And the elusive 'heart of the matter'. 'Our children's inheritance of a hyper-real world as an event in our hearts', as you will recall. Hyper-real and all the rest. That was the heart of the matter here, as it is the heart of the matter everywhere, because the heart, as Wisdom unanimously affirms, is where everything real happens. It came to me this morning, in meditation. Much simpler and more down-to-earth than I thought it would be.

The whole thing centers around *innocence*. The word, its flavor and associations, all the poignant potent cargo it carries: their innocence. Our children's inheritance of all this deformity is an 'event in our hearts' roughly when they're between the ages of eight and fifteen. Before that the bullshit hasn't really hit them, 'taken them for a ride', 'swept them off their feet', inflamed their innocent zeal, hasn't became the substance of their social reality, of what is irresistibly important to them. And after about fifteen they're at least starting to become aware of something called 'defining themselves', no matter how imprisoned the definitions may be, at least starting to develop the capacity for suspicion, objective evaluation, and cynicism. They're not totally passive anymore, it's already hit them, just as it hit the rest of us; the *onslaught*, as it were, when we watched their helpless innocence being totally overwhelmed, relentlessly victimized, is over now. I mean they're a little hardened. They've begun to enter the stage of life when there's at least the possibility of looking at the world through narrowed eyes. (That's the figure of speech I always used. I illustrated it for them literally.) Between when it hits their innocence and when they lose their innocence: that's when the *Kali-Yuga* is an event in our hearts, those of us who are parents. From first massive socialization—when they've swallowed it hook, line and sinker, the whole spectacle, the whole sports/fashion/pop music/celebrity/television/hightech/commodity culture: Hyper-reality: the Disney-land—to first tentative individualization, when they begin to select and reject in the great cornucopia of treacheries. For we are several million miles from suggesting, as I'm sure you knew, that the first disengagement from blind and total conformity is an escape from anything: it means only that they are joining the rest of us, entering the adult world, where alone they have a chance, where you can start talking to them, or at least try, where there's actually the possibility of identifying menace to our humanity and taking measures. Our experience of the *Kali-Yuga* as parents is not confined to this particular period in our children's lives; but it's most intense there—at least, I think, for most of us. There where our false and murderous world first seizes their full attention, confiscates and captivates their vitality, enthusiasm, and aspirations, takes possession of their drama, and becomes everything to them: becomes *their world*. And they are held, temporarily, in thrall.

But the themes and scope of the preceding commentary on 'reality', which might be reality, or maybe hyper-reality, or maybe even Reality, and on other subjects which presented just demands for a digression, call for a commensurate finale. One that is addressed neither to our sentimental and enforced identity as parents, nor to its expansion into our mistaken and suicidal identity with historical humanity, where 'our children' become 'posterity'. Both identities are illusory; as are, consequently, the two fictions, 'our children' and 'posterity', that 'descend' from them: from our sentimentalism and our mistake.

We must always return. That is the motion of the Tao. And what we must always return to are Heaven and Earth, for they are the Foundation, they are Reality. It was only from this Foundation that we could set out to investigate contemporary 'reality', and only by repeated referral back to it that we could recover our bearings along the way. Returning to Heaven and Earth we become human, become Humanity. Become Real. Capable and viable, faithful to ourselves and to the Intention. This is the lesson we learn, and this is the unanswerable Answer to whatever confuses, exploits or insults us. Which will always be we ourselves, because there's no one here but us. We ourselves, as History. We ourselves, in our stupendous, invisible and malevolent mutations. We ourselves, in the *Kali-Yuga*.

So I'm going to cite here, in conclusion, Black Elk again, the Robinson Jeffers poem whose first line I already quoted, a passage from Rumi, and, finally, the great invocation to *Brihadaranyaka Upanishad*. They are voices that speak to our hearts: to our intimations, to our deep silent reflections upon our experience, to the ineffaceable aspirations of our humanity, and to our indestructible spiritual intelligence, the Knowledge within us, the Self. We always welcome voices like these, as if we've been awaiting them, because we recognize ourselves: the Truth.

We should understand well that all things are the works of the Great Spirit. We should know that He is within all things: the trees, the grasses, the rivers, the mountains, and all the four-legged animals, and the winged peoples; and even more important, we should understand that He is also above all these things and peoples. When we do understand all this deeply in our hearts, then we will fear, and love, and know the Great Spirit, and then we will be and act and live as He intends.

⁓ Manderson, South Dakota; from THE SACRED PIPE)

Black Elk speaks from the past buried within us, the archaic humanity called 'primitive' now nearly vanished from the Earth, and which is now appreciated far more as a measure of our loss, of our own decadence, than our guilt as genocides. He is what we were: originally, in the Intention — which means what we still are, for the Intention is eternal. 'The great imponderable in all spiritual work is: how to be what one is, and how to cease being what one is not' (WHITALL PERRY). Robinson Jeffers is, or was, one of us. Black Elk's is the voice of what we were and are meant to be: Jeffers' voice is our awareness of what we have become. The voice of our own torn and violated heart, the voice of our exile and our wild fierce passion to return. Loren Eiseley, in his beautiful Foreword to *Not Man Apart: Lines from Robinson Jeffers*, wrote:

I have never again encountered a man who, in one brief meeting, left me with so strong an impression that I had been speaking with someone out of time… Something utterly wild had crept into his mind and marked his features… The sea-beaten coast, the fierce freedom of its hunting hawks, possessed and spoke through him… He felt in his bones man's transience and the looming disaster contained in the sciences upon which man placed his hope… Man himself will descend into the night he has decreed for other creatures… Of an old rancher who had spent his life under the open sky, Jeffers remarked that his was an existence all of our ancestors since the ice age would have known and appreciated… He saw humanity as the destroyer of a world it could not live without and remain human. He pleads with us to be, not fractional, but whole men; partakers and enjoyers of the natural world outside ourselves, not trapped in men's 'pitiful confusions.' The wise, he says, seek solitude, 'the splendor of inhuman things,' which give value and meaning to our lives. Jeffers is gone now, and so many years and miles lie between us that I do not care to ask the fate of the trees he loved to plant, nor of those who stood with us on that summer afternoon at Carmel.
⁓ Written in Wynnewood, Pennsylvania, June 10, 1965)

And now to Jeffers.

> Civilized, crying how to be human again: this will tell you how.
> Turn outward, love things, not men, turn right away from humanity,
> Let that doll lie. Consider if you like how the lilies grow,
> Lean on the silent rock until you feel its divinity
> Make your veins cold, look at the silent stars, let your eyes
> Climb the great ladder out of the pit of yourself and man.
> Things are so beautiful, your love will follow your eyes;
> Things are the God, you will love God, and not in vain,
> For what we love, we grow to it, we share its nature. At length
> You will look back along the stars' rays and see that even
> The poor doll humanity has a place under heaven.
> Its qualities repair their mosaic around you, the chips of strength
> And sickness; but now you are free, even to become human,
> But born of the rock and the air, not of a woman.

He also wrote, in *The Broken Balance,*

> I remember the farther
> Future, and the last man dying
> Without succession under the confident eyes of the stars.
> It was only a moment's accident,
> The race that plagued us; the world resumes the old lonely immortal
> Splendor…

And finally:

> Integrity is wholeness, the greatest beauty is
> Organic wholeness, the wholeness of life and things, the divine beauty
> Of the universe. Love that, not man
> Apart from that, or else you will share man's pitiful confusions,
> Or drown in despair when his days darken.

Jalal al-Din Rumi (1207–1273) was the founder of the Mevlevi Order of dervishes and Persia's greatest Sufi poet. His and Jeffers' are the same ladder—as you probably will have noted.

> Every form you see
> has its archetype in the divine world, beyond space;
> if the form perishes what matter,
> since its heavenly model is indestructible?
> Every beautiful form you have seen,
> every meaningful word you have heard—
> be not sorrowful because all this must be lost;
> such is not really the case.
> The divine Source is immortal
> and its outflowing gives water without cease;
> since neither the one nor the other can be stopped,
> wherefore do you lament?…
> From the first moment when you entered this world of existence,
> a ladder has been set up before you…

All that capitalism and its ecocidal technology pollute and destroy, everything that the reign of quantity transforms into numbers and the hyper-real media roar poisons or replaces altogether, are but images of an eternal archetype in Heaven, reflections of their indestructible reality in the Reality, in your own Heart, for you are the blissful immortal Atman, the Self. This truth can be directly perceived in meditation. The *Kali-Yuga*, when all is said and done, and understood, is an event in the world-appearance, the end of the Great Dream, and therefore an Awakening, or the occasion for it.

✳

The Path of non-dual Vedantic realization is sometimes traced in four stages, and epitomized in four Sanskrit statements. They may serve to introduce the invocation which will conclude this essay and solicit our emancipation from the decadence it seeks to expose, and from the cyclic unfolding in which that decadence was inevitable: from the Illusion itself.

The transient nature of this world is obvious, and that the transient is also the unreal becomes equally, indeed blindingly obvious following upon direct perception, in meditation, of That which is alone and incontrovertibly Real and Eternal: Real because Eternal, Eternal because Real: the Divine, the Presence, the transcendent Spirit. Hence *Brahma satyam jagan Mithya*: Brahman is Real; the universe is unreal.

The next stage of traditional Vedantic contemplation is the realization of unity in diversity, the realization that Brahman is the Absolute Truth behind the universal transience, the ineffable 'One without a second'. Hence *Ekam-evadvitiyam brahma*: There is only one Brahman without second.

In the third stage the Absolute Reality is worshipped, meditated upon and finally discovered within our own hearts, our very Self: Atman is Brahman, and we can know, in the wordless rapture of the extinguished ego, the truth of the *mahavakya*, or Great Saying, *Aham brahmasmi*: I am Brahman.

In the fourth stage we realize that Brahman, the impersonal Absolute or Self which is also the personal God, the Beloved Who is One with His devotees, is everything: all-pervading, both within and without, the Light and the World: God is everything, the Universe is God, the One is the All. *Sarvam khalvidam brahma*: All this is Brahman.

And so to conclude:

This Grace, this Realization, awaits us, here in the *Kali-Yuga* and forever, eternal Truth of eternal Humanity, and in anticipation of its bestowal by the Infinite Benevolence we repeat the invocation to *Brihadaranyaka*—and may our prayer be from the heart.

Asatoma sadgamaya,
Tamasoma jyotirgamaya,
Mritiorma mrtangamaya.
Lead me from the unreal to the real.
Lead me from darkness to light.
Lead me from death to immortality.

XXIV

Christ &
the *Kali-Yuga*

*To this end was I born, and for this cause came I
into the world, that I should bear witness unto the truth.
Everyone that is of the truth heareth my voice.*
~JOHN 18:37

Prefatory Remarks

WE are near the end of our journey now, end of the Head Trip to Reality. Journey's End in sight. Landfall. Calm seas not quite; prosperous voyage I hope.

And though it's impossible not to feel a certain reluctance or exhaustion, even foolishness, at the prospect of going into the present subject, Christ and the *Kali-Yuga*, we really have no choice. It looks us right in the face. It is Christ Who broods over the world.

Reluctance. Partly because there's clearly no definitive statement here, and that because there's nothing definitive 'out there'; the water's over our heads, this is not a subject that can be grasped by the finite mind or encompassed within its categories or made amenable to its procedures of elucidation and systemization: it is beyond us, not merely beyond articulation but beyond our direct experience, beyond the limits of what is knowable to us. There is nothing, to say the least, we will ever be able to 'nail down'.

But even more. Reluctance because there's an unavoidable imputation of intentionality when we seek to discern a Divine Plan in our analysis of the cosmic unfolding, when we pursue the question *as if* there were a 'Divine Plan' (there isn't: the cyclic unfolding, or simply misfortune, suffering, tragedy, death and 'blind fate', *evil*, waste, promise unfulfilled, perceived and experienced on our side of the river is an 'affair' of the Impersonal Absolute; it originates in the very structure of universal Reality: *Infinite, Manifestation,*

Imperfection—'the explanatory formula for all that can seem 'problematic' to the human mind in the vicissitudes of existence', as Schuon put it—not in any 'scheme' of the Personal God: anthropomorphism, though inescapably implied, is not where it's at here), trying to 'make sense' out of it as we do when we employ inference and deduction in analyzing the initiatives of human agencies. This imputation, this programmatic ascription of motive and method, inevitably carries with it the uneasy suspicion that we have gone too far, over-stepped our bounds: that we are guilty of a folly or arrogance or curiosity ('In a certain sense, Adam's sin was a sin arising from inquisitiveness'... SCHUON) bordering on presumption. Pride. Something for which we'll need to pray for forgiveness, and not afterward, because we knew full well what we were about, but in advance. For we are interrogating not only Christianity—a clearly perennial and reliably, even ferociously popular responsibility which has rarely been prefaced with apologies—but the Christ, Who is God.

And yet, on the other hand, 'we really have no choice.' Really don't. We are made for the Truth. We are Immanent Revelation, the Intellect.

> The sufficient reason for the existence of the human creature is the capacity to think; not to think just anything, but to think about what matters, and finally, about what alone matters. Man is the only being on earth able to foresee death and to desire survival, the only being who desires to know—and is capable of knowing—the why of the world, of the soul, of existence. No one can deny that it is in the fundamental nature of man to ask himself these questions and to have, in consequence, the right to answers; and, further, to have access to them, precisely by virtue of this right, whether through Revelation or through Intellection.
> ⌁SCHUON

We cannot, without impugning the divine gift that shines at the core of our humanity, not want to know our story. And where the Truth is inexpressible, or unintelligible to us, or beyond language or discursive reason, we want anyway to think about it, dwell upon it, muse over it, meditate on it. Feel its inarticulate depth within us, and within the heart of humanity. It cannot fail to be glorious, to lead us heavenward, for it is of God, it is the Glory of God, and must be adored as we adore Him, as we adore His Creation, His Sovereignty, His Perfection and Wisdom. Our truth is 'understood', as a matter of fact, in precisely this manner: through adoration. 'To love is to know Me, My innermost Nature, the Truth that I am' (BHAGAVAD GITA, 18.55).

But the format in this section must be appropriate to the subject. As our nearly completed collective terrestrial biography is not a coherent account, so neither will be its exploration; as the elements that compose that biography—insofar as we can discern them at all, or believe we have discerned them—are independent, episodic, thematically parallel rather than systematically interrelated, so will be the remarks that follow. In other words, pieces there are: but not that can be 'pieced together'. Therefore insights, speculations, glimpses, citations from the work of those Masters who've been most tenacious and illuminating on this matter. But never a thesis, and never a synthesis: only fragments which do not fit together, and are themselves of ambiguous import. If a 'big picture' seems to be emerging, think of it as an *upaya*, a 'saving mirage'. There is no pattern in the landscape, no logic, no intentionality, in the story of the meadow from sunrise to twilight. The Great Tao of Heaven and Earth is simply what is, what happens of itself right then and there without forethought, afterthought or knowledge of itself; what flows. This is the style of God. Everything added to it is our own invention: the deed for which we pay the price.

The Fall Into Time

With regard to the drama of the *Kali-Yuga*, the central role of the Revelation of God in Christ is conceded.

Behind that, the Fall from Grace.

Behind that, Eternity.

For the Fall from Grace was, among other things equally momentous but peripheral in this context, the Fall into Time, and the Fall into Time was the separation from our Eternity in God, from our Humanity *in divinis*. The basic cosmic fatality in the unfolding of the *yugas* is the inexorable transition from Eternity to Time.

> That indescribable Reality which the Vedas speak of as ever beyond apprehension, being the Uncaused Cause, the Limitless Vast, the Light of Consciousness, the Non-qualified, the Changeless, Pure Being, Attributeless, and Actionless—That Vishnu Thou verily art, as these eyes behold Thee: and Thou art, too, the Illuminer of all faculties. When at the end of the two halves of the life of Brahma the phenomenal universe vanishes, the gross elements get merged in the subtle, and these and all other evolved entities are retracted into the unmanifest by the impetuous onset of Time, Thou alone remainest.

Time the Destroyer of the Worlds. Invoked in the words of Devaki extolling Krishna in bk 10, pt. 1, chap. 3 of the *Srimad Bhagavatam*, 'The Birth of Krishna'. 'I am come as Time, the waster of the peoples, Ready for that hour that ripens to their ruin', declares the Bhagavan in Chapter XI of the *Gita*, 'The Vision of God in His Universal Form'.

In the life of archaic humanity the destruction represented by Time was always foreseen, always recognized hovering on the horizon, and feared, and always forestalled or annulled by ritual identification with a timeless archetypal Reality: specifically, by 'the faithful reproduction of paradigms' and the 'ritual repetition of mythical events'. (ELIADE) Until the pressure became too great and the line of defense broke at its weakest point. Or a People was chosen.

The Jews and History

The historical drama, History as a new mode of existence, this life we live, begins, as we have already noted in these pages, with the Jews of the Old Testament. The Judaic elite were the first human beings to become aware of, directly experience and, in obedience to God, actively embrace the new situation of humanity consequent upon the Fall into Time. That is to say, they were, as they were instructed to attest, *chosen*: chosen to become the receptacles of this awareness: the Chosen People. And since this awareness 'occurred' in their relationship to God, to Jehovah, since they 'received' it there, it is, being divine, absolute: final: irreversible: the destiny of the world.

Compared with the archaic and paleo-oriental religions, as well as with the mythic-philosophical conceptions of the eternal return, as they were elaborated in India and Greece, Judaism represents an innovation of the first importance. For Judaism, time has a beginning and will have an end. The idea of cyclic time is left behind. Yahweh no longer manifests himself in *cosmic time* (like the gods of other religions) but in a *historical time*, which is irreversible. Each new manifestation of Yahweh in history is no longer reducible to an earlier manifestation. The fall of Jerusalem expresses Yahweh's wrath against his people, but it is no longer the same wrath that Yahweh expressed by the fall of Samaria. His gestures are *personal* interventions in history and reveal their deep meaning *only for his people*, the people that Yahweh had *chosen*. Hence the historical event acquires a new dimension; it becomes a *theophany*... Yahveh is the divine Person who reveals himself in *history*; therein lies his great novelty. Elsewhere, God had been revealed as a

Person; we remember the terrible epiphany of Krishna in the *Bhagavad Gita* (9.5 *et seq.*): but this revelation of the Supreme Being under the form of Krishna occurs in a mythical locality, Kurukshetra, and in a mythical time— that of the great battle between the Kauravas and the Pandavas. In contrast to this, the fall of Samaria actually did occur in history, and it was an event willed and provoked by Jahveh: that was theophany of a new type, hitherto unknown—the *intervention of Jahveh in history*... Thus, for the first time, the prophets placed a value on history, succeeded in transcending the traditional vision of the cycle (the conception that ensures all things will be repeated forever), and discovered a one-way time... For the first time, we find affirmed, and increasingly accepted, the idea that historical events have a value in themselves, insofar as they are determined by the will of God... It may, then, be said with truth that the Hebrews were the first to discover the meaning of history as the epiphany of God, and this conception, as we should expect, was taken up and amplified by Christianity.

⁓ELIADE

History, however, does not *abrogate* cyclic time: it is the *final stage* of cyclic time: the *Kali-Yuga*. Krishna's announcement in *Gita* XI, already quoted, 'I am come as Time, the waster of the peoples' (Or, in another trans-lation, 'I am the mighty world-destroying Time...'), is necessarily a reference to *historical* time, the corrosion of an increasingly inescapable linear tempo-rality *sensed* in the traditional society of the East as the cyclic unfolding, of which it was well aware, approached the final stage and *instituted* in the West with, ultimately, the Incarnation.

The Jews, Jesus, and the West

Christianity, the Revelation of God in Christ, continues and decisively ful-fils the initiative of the Chosen People: He is the Fulfilment of Israel. The Incarnation of our Lord in Time, the Word become flesh—'the doctrine of incarnation which marks the entrance of the truth into history' (SEYYED HOSSEIN NASR)—confirms and inaugurates the ultimacy of the historical mode, the ultimacy of one-way Time, and not as a 'point of view' or a mode of human experience merely but as a divine decree, a 'decision' of God.

Christianity goes even further in valorizing *historical time*. Since God was *incarnated*, that is, since he took on a *history-conditioned human existence*, his-tory acquires the possibility of being sanctified. The *illud tempus* evoked by the Gospels is a clearly defined historical time—the time in which Pontius

Pilate was Governor of Judea—but it was *sanctified by the presence of Christ.*
When a Christian of our day participates in liturgical time, he recovers the
illud tempus in which Christ lived, suffered, and rose again—but it is no
longer a mythical time, it is the time when Pontius Pilate governed Judea...
The Incarnation establishes a new situation of man in the cosmos... This is
as much to say that history reveals itself to be a new dimension of the presence of God in the world.
　⁀Eliade

And where else, other than history, *could* 'He'—the Word, the Logos,
The Avatar of Redemptive Grace—incarnate? Jesus appears in Time because Time had finally forced itself irreversibly upon us, definitively and
inescapably upon us, as it must *in and as* the cyclic unfolding; because there
was no other 'place' for an Avatar to appear. Where else does God 'find' us, in
His blessed Mercy, but where He has placed us?

Where He has placed 'us.' Forced itself irreversibly upon 'us'. Who is this
'us'?

A portion of humanity that resided in what we call Biblical Lands, in
what we call Biblical Times. Why them? Because that humanity, it would
appear, was possessed by a very sharp, visceral, urgent and absolutely certain
apprehension of separation from its primordial state, its Origin *in divinis*, a
devastating intuition of some primordial terminal disgrace, a decisive Event
in the very heart of existence, definitely involving Disobedience, even inso-
lence, or in theological terms Pride, and an equally devastating premonition
of the consequences. It knew of Eden: of Transgression and Expulsion.
Knew Sin and the Fall, the beginning of Time, a new Presence, an omniscient infinitely powerful Scrutiny which was anything but disinterested,
glaring down and passing instant judgment upon every instant of a night-
marishly unprecedented situation: knew a tremendous tension gripping
every episode of what was now a one-way drama, a dialogue with the relentless inescapable Agenda of an Omnipotence capable of jealousy and wrath: a
definitive end, once and for all and forever, of that eternal repetition of
archetypal patterns in human affairs which was Paradise. That humanity
was the first to realize what had happened. Or was going to happen.

And in that humanity was born a Saviour, and His Legacy became a
Church, and that Church became Western Christendom, and Western
Christendom became Europe, and Europe, in full flower, became the West.
And the West became the world.

J. M. Roberts, the eminent Oxford historian whom we have met before, celebrates this 'victory' with judicious naivete. He knows how it all began:

> It is literally true that we could none of us today be what we are if a handful of Jews nearly two thousand years ago had not believed that they had known a great teacher, seen him crucified, dead and buried, and then rise again to live a little while on this earth before going to dwell in glory everlastingly with their Jewish God, his father.

He knows, here reaching the pinnacle of his magnificent innocence, the secret of the West's 'success':

> Nonetheless, to put it briefly and crudely, I believe that two central myths can be found at the heart of the Western view of history. One is the idea that men are, in some sense, able to take charge of their own destinies: they are autonomous. The other is the idea that history is meaningful because it has direction; it is going somewhere.

(It certainly is 'going somewhere'.) And he is relieved that the 'victory' is final:

> This is the age of the first world civilization and it is the civilization of the West... the day of its creative role can hardly be thought to be over; Western civilization has evidently not lost a shaping power. Paradoxically, we may now be entering the era of its greatest triumph, one not over state structures and economic relationships, but over the minds and hearts of all men. Perhaps they are all Westerners now.
> ∼ This reassurance appearing in 1985

When we consider these sentiments in the context of the entire preceding text of the present study... but words fail me.

'Christianity', writes Schuon,

> has a dramatic quality about it; it has the sense of the Sublime rather than of the Absolute, and the sense of Sacrifice rather than of Equilibrium... European humanity has something Promethean and tragic about it. It therefore required a religion which could surpass and sublimate the dramatism of the Greek and Germanic gods and heroes. Furthermore, the European creative genius implies a need to 'burn what one has worshipped,' and from this comes a prodigious propensity for denial and change.

And this mutuality of a religion and a humanity has 'provoked historical disequilibriums that are both disastrous and providential.' As we shall see.

Historicity of Jesus

All the contradictions of Christian life, all the soul-searching breast-beating doubts and torments experienced by Christians embracing the salvation offered by Christ, reside in the historicity of Jesus and of the humanity whose situation He assumed and thereby transformed forever. For the Incarnation was a very great religious revolution—too great, indeed, to have been assimilated even after two thousand years of Christian life. Let us explain why. When the sacred made itself known only in the Cosmos it was easily recognizable: for a pre-Christian religious man it was, on the whole, easy to distinguish a sign that was charged with power—a spiral, a circle or a swastika, etc.—from all those that were not; easy, even, to separate liturgical time from profane time. But in Judaism, and above all in Christianity, divinity had manifested itself in History. The Christ and his contemporaries were part of History.
⁓Eliade

And since God, by Incarnation, 'had accepted existence in History,' the Christian now confronts the agonizing dilemma presented by a fundamental, radical and entirely new 'administrative' distinction selecting among historical events and assigning personal incumbencies. 'Certain events were theophanies… while others were merely secular events.'

And this, for the true Christian, creates an exceedingly difficult situation: he can no longer repudiate History, but neither can he accept it all. He has continually to *choose*, to try to distinguish, in the tangle of historical events, the event which, *for him*, may be charged with a saving significance.
⁓Eliade

Recall this 'confusion' later on: it is yet another, and very basic, 'descendant' of the esoteric/exoteric blurring in the Christian tradition, consequent upon the rending of the Veil of the Temple, which we will be exploring at length. Drawing distinctions in high-stake situations is very close to the heart of the Christian life.

We know how difficult it is, this choice… For we live in an epoch when one can no longer disengage oneself from the wheels of History, unless by some audacious act of evasion. But evasion is forbidden to the Christian. And for him there is no other issue; since the Incarnation took place in History, since the Advent of Christ marks the last and highest manifestation of the sacred in the world—the Christian can save himself only within the concrete,

historical life, the life that was chosen and lived by Christ. We know what he must expect: the 'fear and anguish', the sweat like great drops of blood', the 'agony' and the 'sadness unto death'. (Luke 22:44; Mark 11:34)
〜ELIADE

We've all known, and some of us are, and some of us have been sincere Christians, followers of Christ. Not an easy road.

Incarnation and Faith, Surrender as Salvation

The Incarnation is the *salvific finality* of the Fall into Time.

Christianity arrives, not at a *philosophy*, but at a *theology* of history. For God's interventions in history, and above all his Incarnation in the historical person of Jesus Christ, have a transhistorical purpose—the *salvation* of man.
〜ELIADE

This then is the pattern. The divine mercies *consequent upon or accompanying* the Fall into Time are also *stages* of that Fall, ecstatic states and experiences *defined by* and *responding to* that Fall. This is the *style* of it, the compensatory 'response' of the Personal God to the inexorable spontaneous unfolding of the *yugas* implicit in the structure of universal Reality, the breathing forth and withdrawing of Manifestation inherent in the Impersonal Absolute, the changeless Principle Which is alone Real: 'This universe comes forth from Brahman and will return to Brahman. Verily, all is Brahman.' (*Chandogya Upanishad*) It is God's 'methodology', if you will—a very important point to note. Each divine Initiative, archetypally the Incarnation, is genuine, as of course it must be, each is a vehicle of salvation: as the cycle unfolds He must offer salvation to those who cannot but identify themselves with the new cyclic situation, i.e. with themselves as temporal beings conditioned more and more pervasively by History, by Time. But always His offering of salvation (which is simultaneously, by His Grace, our *pursuit* of salvation) the moment of personal entry into the historical drama under the sign and in the inspiration (the 'breathing in') of sacrificial love, Christ's hallmark, *is itself a stage of the Fall into Time, a stage in the unfolding*, an initiation into Realization bestowed in recognition of the new 'situation' so urgently demanding transcendence, the unfolding which is that new 'situation' called History.

For the Hebrews, Salvation resided in fulfilment of the historical role God had willed for them, in *obedience*; hence their drama, their 'stubbornness' at war with compliance, their resistance at war with submission, their refusal or inability to recognize the new form of salvation, their desperate and repeated flight from the terrifying demands of historical existence back to the archaic cosmic theophanies, 'the Golden Calf', the 'mystery religions', the orgy of purification and renewal, *the rituals that were always the same, that annulled Time.*

We are saved, then, as we are carried onward in the unfolding of the cycle, rescued from the corrosive annihilation of temporality, by voluntary response to an Initiative from Heaven which is itself a dynamic of that unfolding, and this paradox, subsequent to the divine influx, is perpetually repeated, enacted, through *the salvific state of mind, inaugurated by Abraham, called 'faith'.* The 'specificity' of Christianity

> is guaranteed by *faith* as the category *sui generis* of religious experience, and by its valorization in *history*. With the exception of Judaism, no other pre-Christian religion has set a value on history as a direct and irreversible manifestation of God in the world, nor on faith—in the sense inaugurated by Abraham—as a unique means of salvation... One might say that the discovery of faith as a religious category was the one novelty introduced into the history of religion since neolithic times.
>
> ⌒ELIADE

Faith, 'a new formula for man's collaboration with the creation,' i.e., *for the making of history,* is 'a freedom... which has its source and finds its guaranty and support in God.' The paradox is repeated perpetually in that the Christian's infusion of creative energy into the temporal unfolding, into the making of history, the unfolding of the cycle, is a participation in the 'direct and irreversible manifestation of God in the world', and *guaranteed* as such by the self-surrender implicit in their faith that this is indeed the case, that they are carrying out the will of God. History *is* the *Kali-Yuga* and *is* that divine manifestation, simultaneously, and the Christian is saved from spiritual dissolution into a merely profane sequence of events by an accompanying self-sacrificial 'interiorization of worship' called *faith.* Faith reconciles the two realms—Eternity and Time, inner and outer, esoteric and exoteric, Cosmos and History—succeeds in nullifying their 'confusion' precipitated when the Veil of the Temple was rent in twain. Fallen into Time, the Christian reaches upward, identifying himself, through his faith, with the Will of the Eternal. Fallen: but saved through Faith. The *Kali-Yuga* flows into the radiant Void

on a river of Faith. Such is our glory. Incarnation: salvific finality of the Fall
into Time.

And this dispensation was, obviously and *par excellence*, a two-edged
sword. As it had to be. For it meant *freedom*. It was the secret of the West's
success, as good old Roberts would have it, the source of 'the idea that men
are, in some sense, able to take charge of their own destinies.'

The horizon of archetypes and repetition was transcended, for the first time,
by Judeo-Christianism, which introduced a new category into religious experience: the category of *faith*. It must not be forgotten that, if Abraham's faith
can be defined as 'for God everything is possible', the faith of Christianity
implies that everything is also possible for man. 'Have faith in God. For verily
I say unto you, that whosoever shall say unto this mountain, be thou
removed, and be thou cast into the sea; and shall not doubt in his heart, but
shall believe that those things which he saith shall come to pass; he shall have
whatsoever he saith...' Faith, in this context as in many others, means absolute emancipation from any kind of natural 'law' and hence the highest freedom that man can imagine: freedom to intervene even in the ontological
constitution of the universe. It is, consequently, a pre-eminently creative freedom. In other words, it constitutes a new formula for man's collaboration
with the creation—the first, but also the only such formula accorded to him
since the traditional horizon of archetypes and repetition was transcended.
Only such a freedom (aside from its soteriological, hence, in the strict sense,
its religious value) is able to defend modern man from the terror of history—
a freedom, that is, which has its source and finds its guaranty and support in
God. Every other modern freedom, whatever satisfactions it may procure to
him who possesses it, is powerless to justify history... We may say, furthermore, that Christianity is the 'religion' of modern man and historical man, of
the man who simultaneously discovered personal freedom and continuous
time (in place of cyclical time)... In this respect, Christianity incontestably
proves to be the religion of 'fallen man': and this to the extent to which modern man is irremediably identified with history and progress, and to which
history and progress are a fall, both implying the final abandonment of the
paradise of archetypes and repetition.
~ELIADE

A Master at his most profound: prophetic in retrospect. We know what
that 'freedom', that collaboration, has meant. What it released. 'Disequilibriums that are both disastrous and providential', as Schuon stated it. Saved,
as we are carried onward and downward: as we 'make history'. Faith in
Progress, the career of historical humanity, the unfolding of the cycle, the

Kali-Yuga: all one. It's all the same thing. Christendom, Europe, the West, the World. Men of good will reach out to Him in faith, and He is there. As He promised. How else could it be? 'I am with you always, even unto the end of the world.'

But recall Sri Krishna: 'I am come as Time, the waster of the peoples, Ready for that hour that ripens to their ruin.' Live in gratitude from day to day. Find peace in 'Thy Will be done.'

Legacy of Atonement

After Disobedience we were offered the Mosaic Law. Rules to obey. 'We' meaning the 'Chosen People', representatives of humanity in its 'outer' life and the prefiguration of historical humanity, the doomed collective. (Some people might want to argue that the Holocaust, and the militant worldliness and disproportionate influence of Zionism and the modern State of Israel, are symbols or 'proofs' here, even heralds of The End, 'full circle'; but that is mechanistic thinking. The Holocaust—as the great 20th-century apostle of the *via negativa*, 'the terrible Wei Wu Wei,' says of Christianity itself—is 'our own personal affair.') Our repudiation of this dispensation, and its sobering consequences, are documented by the Prophets.

And then we were offered Christ.

This was the limit, the maximum, there is no going beyond it. What more could He do for us? What greater proof of His love for us? What more beyond assuming Himself the human condition? Because He incarnated, consented to conditioned existence in Time, He is *here with us*, in History, walking along with us, accompanying us, sharing our suffering and making it endurable, *meaningful*. How many millions have found His Comfort, the Paraclete, Holy Spirit, and continue to find it every day of their lives? 'He walks with me, and He talks with me, and He holds me by the hand...' Walks among us 'full of grace and truth'—Light of the World, Wisdom of the Father, Fulfilment of Israel: 'God became Man that Man might become God', in the famous patristic formula, for 'the function of the historical Christ is to awaken and actualize the inward Christ', to usher us 'into a mystery of inwardness, sanctity, and Divine Life'—teaching us to adore God 'in spirit and in truth', dying in agony on the Cross and forgiving us 'for they know not what they do.' This was truly 'the last plank of salvation' for the West, as Schuon somewhere remarks.

But Pilate saith unto them, What shall I do then with Jesus which is called Christ? They all say unto him, Let him be crucified. And the governor said, Why, what evil hath he done? But they cried out the more, saying, Let him be crucified.' (Matt. 27:22–23) Or, as we find it in John, 'And he saith unto the Jews, Behold your King! But they cried out, Away with him, away with him, crucify him. Pilate saith unto them, Shall I crucify your King? The chief priests answered, We have no king but Caesar.'
⁓JOHN 19:14–15

Then and now, always and forever: 'And the light shineth in darkness, and the darkness comprehended it not.' (John 1:5) The Atonement on the Cross and our repudiation of the Atonement was a single event, the same event. The Redemption and our rejection of the Redeemer, a single event. Eternal, here and now and forever, the dark radiance of our estate.

Still fall the Rain—
Dark as the world of man, black as our loss—
Blind as the nineteen hundred and forty nails
Upon the Cross…

Still falls the Rain—
In the Field of Blood where the small hopes breed
And the human brain
Nurtures its greed, that worm with the brow of Cain.

Still falls the Rain—
At the feet of the Starved Man hung upon the Cross.
Christ that each day, each night, nails there, have mercy on us—

Still falls the Rain—
Still falls the Blood from the Starved Man's wounded Side:
He bears in His Heart all wounds—those of the light that died,
The Last faint spark
In the self-murdered heart,
The wounds of the sad uncomprehending dark…

Still falls the Rain
⁓EDITH SITWELL, 1942

He fell three times when He carried the Cross—a fine subject for meditation. It invites and enables us to focus upon, and directly experience, the grief, the pathos and bitterness, the helpless almost wild remorse, woven into the ragged fabric of our post-Edenic penalties; and if the meditation is confirmed by Grace, we may be rewarded with 'the gift of tears', and a more determined, grimmer spiritual resolve: to keep the faith—with Him, with Him forever.

The Messiah was tortured to death. It's rarely put that way, because it's so horrible to say it. But it's true. The Messiah: the Love of God.

> He is in agony till the world's end,
> And we must never sleep during that time!
> He is suspended on the cross-tree now
> And we are onlookers at the crime.
> Callous contemporaries of the slow
> Torture of God.
> Here is the hill
> Made ghastly by His spattered blood.
> ⁓from *Ecce Homo*, by DAVID GASCOYNE

He was mocked.

The Crucifixion was a supernova. One that would explode uninterruptedly, with ever-increasing energy and violence. A legacy of insupportable guilt, which could only be purged through an eruption of inexhaustible self-affirmation.

The comparison may be unfair, but this passage in D.T. Suzuki's *Zen and Japanese Culture* comes to mind:

> I cannot help making reference in this connection to the Nirvana picture of the Buddha... It is certainly in Japan that it has entered deeply into the religious consciousness of the people. The picture has came to be intimately connected with the Buddhist life of Japan, especially with Zen. There must be something in it which appeals powerfully to us all. The one prominent feature of the Nirvana picture is, naturally, the central figure and his quiet passing away, surrounded by his disciples. Contrast this with the crucifixion of Christ, with blood oozing from the head and the side. He is stretched upright against the cross, with an expression of the utmost pain and suffering, whereas the Buddha looks as if contentedly asleep on the couch, with no signs of distress. The vertical Christ represents an intense spirit of fight, but the horizontal Buddha is peaceful. When we look at the latter, everything that goes against the spirit of contentment is excluded from our

consciousness. The Buddha lies contented, not only with himself but with all the world and with all its beings animate and inanimate. Look at those animals, those gods, and those trees that are weeping over his parting. To my mind this is a scene pregnant with meaning of the utmost significance.

And so, too, is the scene with which it is contrasted: 'pregnant with meaning of the utmost significance.' That scene, too, 'has entered deeply into the religious consciousness of the people.'

It could only have led where it did. The Crucifixion happened everywhere and outside of time, it can never be erased from active presence in racial consciousness, even in cultures where it was never known, can never be forgotten, and *was* never forgotten: those for whose sins He atoned must themselves atone forever for that betrayal which was the Atonement. Eternally clear their eternally re-tarnished consciences. It could only have led where it did. To implacable proselytization, defiant worldliness, ecstatic self-righteousness, the idolatry of power. To the making of History. There's an intersection here, a predestined fertility, of the divine and the human, the eternal and the temporal, against the featureless background of impersonal inexorable cyclic unfolding, that defies articulation. Everything of our lives centers on the Christ.

Kalki Avatar, Maitreya Buddha

Then there's this aspect.

According to Hindu tradition, an Avatar will preside over the final stage of the *Kali-Yuga*. The name given to this Avatar is Kalki.

Hinduism has long been awaiting the rider on the white horse, Kalki, the tenth Avatara of Vishnu, who is to close the present 'Dark Age' and inaugurate a new era of perfection. Maitreya, no less eagerly awaited by Buddhists, is clearly none other than the Kalki Avatara, and the same may be said of the Messiah.

⁓MARTIN LINGS, *The Eleventh Hour*

In the Buddhist tradition, the last Buddha of the present cycle is named Maitreya.

His name is derived from *mitra*, 'friend', 'friendliness' being a basic Buddhist virtue, akin to Christian 'love'... At present, many Buddhists look forward to

his coming. In South Asia these eschatological hopes are little stressed, whereas in Central Asia they are a source of great religious fervor. To be reborn in Maitreya's presence is the greatest wish of many Tibetans and Mongols, and the inscription 'Come, Maitreya, come!' on the rocks of numerous mountains testifies to their longing.
⌒ EDWARD CONZE

And so we read, in *The Prophecy Concerning Maitreya*, in 'a typical Sanskrit version of uncertain date':

Sariputra, the great general of the doctrine, most wise and resplendent, from compassion for the world asked the Lord: 'Some time ago you have spoken to us of the future Buddha, who will lead the world at a future period, and who will bear the name of Maitreya. I would now wish to hear more about his powers and miraculous gifts. Tell me, O best of men, about them!
As soon as he is born he will walk seven steps forward, and where he puts down his feet a jewel or a lotus will spring up. He will raise his eyes to the ten directions, and will speak these words: 'This is my last birth. There will be no rebirth after this one. Never will I come back here, but, all pure, I shall win Nirvana!'

(Seven, of course, is the number in *Revelations*. In which we read: 'And I saw a new heaven and a new earth: for the first heaven and the first earth were passed away; and there was no more sea... And he that sat upon the throne said, Behold, I make all things new... And he said unto me, It is done. I am Alpha and Omega, the beginning and the end. I will give unto him that is athirst of the fountain of the water of life freely' (Rev. 21:1,5,6). There are parallels here; but they defy articulation.)

The enthusiasm of the Central Asian Buddhists recalls to mind the words of Eliade, referring to 'the soteriological function of the *Kali-Yuga* and the privileges conferred on us by a crepuscular and catastrophic history.' To become conscious of our position 'in the descending trajectory of the cosmic cycle' is 'invigorating and consoling for man under the terror of history', and it is precisely in this spirit that I write this book.

In Schuon's summation:

'This Gospel of the Kingdom will be taught among all men, as a testimony to all nations; then the end will come'... if these words refer to the whole world and not just to the West, it is because they are not a command but a prophecy, and because they relate to cyclic conditions in which separating barriers between the different traditional worlds will have disappeared; in other words, we can say that 'Christ', who for the Hindus will be the Kalki *Avatara*, and for the Buddhists the *Bodhisattva* Maitreya, will restore the Primordial Tradition.

Now when you read things like this you really don't know quite what to think. As I said earlier, the water's over our heads. In a sense, the predictive or prophetic dimension of Tradition is rather peripheral to its purpose (and, for many of us, to our concern), which is Salvation or Illumination in any of the many interpretations of the words: the 'recovery' of our true state which was never really lost; therefore we are not particularly impressed by that dimension even when, as now, its unanimous prophecy of terminal decline appears to be corroborated by contemporary experience. It is indeed true that the 'barriers between the different traditional worlds' have disappeared; and it does seem, at the very least, arguable that 'the general conditions of our age... mark the end of a great cyclic period of terrestrial humanity—the end of a *maha-yuga* according to Hindu cosmology.' (SCHUON) But an interpretive analysis of that contemporary experience is absolutely demanded, and alone convincing, and that such an analysis 'proves' a prediction scarcely seems important.

But there's something else going on here, something that immediately rivets our attention. And that is the identification of Christ as the predicted Avatar. Here, in truth, is something to think about. Because things do seem to fall into place around that identification.

Christians in the *Kali-Yuga*

If the Incarnation inaugurates the close of the cycle, then active Christians, as we have suggested, are fated to be an agency of its unfolding. They will be the prolongation, as it were, of the original divine Initiative, unwitting manifestations of the divine Will, or of the impersonal cyclic dynamism, operating 'behind the scenes'.

Missionary work comes first to mind. The spread of Christianity is the expansion of its historical vehicle, Western Civilization, sometimes called 'the market economy', sometimes called 'the White Man'—a procedure described by a shrewd and dedicated worshipper of history, whose canonization now appears to have been premature, as *Imperialism, the Highest Stage of Capitalism*—and we all know what that has meant. To so very many people, so very many living things: indeed to all humanity and the entire ecosphere.

In a more general sense, however, Christians hurl their energy into History, with stalwart generosity into the making of History, through 'good works'. 'Onward, Christian soldiers!' does indeed summarize a divine commission embraced with eager relish. For most decent socially-oriented Christians, liberation theology is really what Christianity and the 'purpose' of Christ is all about, its true message and mission. The suffering that Christians perceive and address is historical suffering, political suffering—not the essential suffering, *dukkha*, inherent in the human condition as such, in Ignorance, to which the Buddha referred in the Four Noble Truths and which called forth His Compassionate Dharma, but the accidental suffering of the relative world: oppression and injustice, economic exploitation and inequality: the massive deprivations suffered by those whom Franz Fanon labeled—so long ago, it seems—'The Wretched of the Earth'.

Christians enter History as Christ entered Time. They march with the cyclic unfolding. Accepting the historical mode as decisive, exhaustive and the principal arena of the concern God expressed in His Self-Revelation as Christ, welcoming martyrdom in its many degrees and guises, they feed with their Christian fervor the great march of events. Through the performance of good works, through self-sacrifice, through love and charity, faith and hope, in the Name of the Messiah, Saviour and Redeemer: Avatar of the Age.

But through love above all. And not love as *libido*, *philia*, or *eros*, which all contain an element of desire, but as *agape*—Latin *caritas*, English 'charity'—which alone is independent of contingent circumstances, affirms the other unconditionally, and 'unites the lover and the beloved because of the image of fulfillment which God has of both... accepts the other in spite of resistance...suffers and forgives.' (PAUL TILLICH, the *Systematic Theology*).

The end of the cycle demands of us our greatest heart, our greatest soul: demands of us nothing less than the Love of God and Humanity that appeared among us as Christ. No lesser love is equal to it. Our love of God and God's love of Humanity, as both are focussed in the Love that is Christ our Lord, is the Love indigenous to the *Kali-Yuga*, the Love specific to it, belonging to it. Native to it. Inseparable from it. Required by it. Christian charity—'There abide these three... but the greatest of these is charity.'

The Deepest We Can Go:
Homage to Frithjof Schuon

I have been wrestling for days, weeks, with the problem of presenting—without first backtracking through a maze of definitions of metaphysical terms, assumptions and categories that could only proliferate into something like an infinite regression that would drive us crazy—Frithjof Schuon's (characteristically) blindingly definitive exposition of the relationship between Christ and the end of the cycle, a relationship he clarifies as originating in, and inevitably and providentially deriving from, the 'Particular Nature of the Christian Religion.' I have decided, in a sort of desperate resignation, to employ (very selectively) the *explication du texte* method and seek to translate the thrust of a primarily metaphysical discourse into the more down-to-earth language of direct experience I have aimed at throughout this study. (Just as, of course, the metaphysical Truth unveiled in that discourse was 'translated' into the direct experience of the Christians whose fate it both explicates and determined.) Metaphysics is not 'abstract', as it can appear, but true, even most true, since it refers us to the deepest layers of universal Reality; and although Schuon, or at least the 'voice' in which he chooses to address us (and this applies as well to others in his school), speaks as if the matters he discusses do not concern him directly as 'one of us', as a *semblable* who shares and feels compelled to expound, out of solidarity and compassionate identification, the common ruin, this rigorous aloofness, even absence of sympathy or empathy—which has generated, in a certain measure, his particular audience—simply means, not that he is indifferent, but that these matters do not, given his vocation, concern him in the same way they might concern the majority. Put in yet another way, his persona, for the most part, doesn't feel called upon to explain human experience, individual or social, in its derivation from the underlying metaphysical realities that experience reflects—although there are, with increasing frequency in the production of his final years, departures from this 'rule' which are penetrating and often beautiful. His eyes, for the most part, are riveted on the Truth it has been given him, in an unprecedented scope and depth, to grasp and articulate. When he does speak about 'us', he speaks about humanity *in divinis* or in sin—a sublimity which yet calls for 'translation'.

I might add, furthermore, that the only writer I am aware of who has taken up Schuon's explication of this... what? momentous? grave? there's really no word for it... issue is Marco Pallis in his beautiful essay, to which we will be referring, 'The Veil of the Temple'. Neither Nasr, at least in *Knowledge and the Sacred*, nor Martin Lings in his *The Eleventh Hour*, where you would certainly expect it, address the cyclic unfolding from this particular perspective; both tend to emphasize the modernist deviation from Sacred Tradition, or 'the human unanimity' (HUSTON SMITH), and Nasr, with respect to the role of Christianity, focusses primarily—we'll be going into his analysis in greater detail—on its historical nature; as does Eliade.

Schuon begins:

> What, for want of a better term, we have been obliged to call 'Christian exoterism' is not, in its origin and structure, strictly analogous to the Judaic and Islamic exoterisms; for whereas the exoteric side of the two latter religions was instituted as such from the very beginning, in the sense that it formed part of the Revelation and was clearly distinguishable from its esoteric aspect, what we now know as Christian exoterism hardly figured as such in the Christian Revelation except in a purely incidental manner.

What this means is that the teachings of Christ, His 'instructions' to humankind both by precept and example, seem directed more to aspirants to sainthood, or to monastic renunciates—to truly rare and exceptional souls, in other words—than to average people living their average lives in 'the workaday world', the common daily round of human existence: ordinary people: the very vast majority. (I said 'precept and example'; but actually the direction of His teaching is fundamentally and inescapably determined by what He was, by Incarnation itself, and we shall soon see why.) 'Christianity, accordingly by its very nature situates itself outside the "actions and reactions" of the human order; therefore, *a priori* it is not exoteric.'

Consider the following familiar passages from Matthew:

> You have heard that it was said, Eye for eye, and tooth for tooth. But I tell you, Do not resist an evil person. If someone strikes you on the right cheek, turn to him the other also... And if someone wants to sue you and take your tunic, let him have your cloak as well... But I tell you, Love your enemies, bless those who curse you, do good to those who hate you... Do not store up for yourselves treasures on earth... You cannot serve both God and Money... Therefore I tell you, do not worry about your life, that you will eat or drink, or about your body, what you will wear... Therefore do not worry about tomorrow, for tomorrow will worry about itself... Another disciple said to him, 'Lord, first let me go and bury my father.' But Jesus told him, 'Follow me, and let the dead bury their own dead...' For I have came to turn a man against his father, a daughter against her mother, a daughter-in-law against

her mother-in-law—a man's enemies will be the members of his own house-hold... Whoever finds his life will lose it, and whoever loses his life for my sake will find it... The kingdom of heaven is like a merchant looking for fine pearls. When he found one of great value, he went away and sold everything he had and bought it... If anyone would come after me, he must deny him-self and take up his cross and follow me... Then Peter came to Jesus and asked, 'Lord, how many times shall I forgive my brother when he sins against me? Up to seven times?' Jesus answered, 'I tell you not seven times, but sev-enty-seven times... If you want to be perfect, go, sell your possessions and give to the poor, and you will have treasure in heaven. Then come, follow me...'

⁓NEW INTERNATIONAL VERSION

And so on. This is the tenor of the entire Gospels.

Perhaps the most striking proof to be found in Christ's teachings of the purely spiritual and therefore supra-social and extra-moral character of His Doctrine is contained in the following saying: 'If any man came to me and hate not his father, and mother, and wife and children and brethren and sis-ters, yea, and his own life also, he cannot be my disciple.' (Luke 14:26) It is clearly impossible to oppose such teaching to the Mosaic Law.

Christ's teaching, then, is clearly not translatable into a viable social legis-lation for that humanity with whose astonishing ways and means we are sufficiently familiar: into a viable way of life for a community of the average 'normal' and invariable majority. Nor are rejection, agony and Crucifixion going to appeal to the average person as a life style to be pursued. The Hindu religion, in contrast, takes full account of human nature in its doc-trine of the four 'human goals' (purusartha): kama, (the pursuit of) sensual and aesthetic gratification; artha, (the pursuit of) wealth, power and posses-sion; dharma, the observance of social and religious law, the address to duty and the pursuit of righteousness; and moksa, (the pursuit of) liberation, spiritual realization at the highest level. These four are legitimate in their social spheres, although moksa implies renunciation, and are understood to be in ascending order. Islam reproves Christianity, in the sense the preced-ing contrast implies, 'when it declares that Jesus was the bringer of an esoter-ism (haqiqah) only, whereas the Prophet Mohammed endowed his followers both with the things of this world and with the things of the other world.' (PALLIS) Christ, however, is uncompromising and relentless. Christ of the Gospels, the Incarnate Word, the Absolute Truth.

It is perfectly obvious that the main teachings of Christ transcend the exoteric viewpoint, and that is indeed the reason for their existence. They therefore likewise transcend the Law... In fact the turning of the other cheek is not a thing that any social collectivity could put into practice with a view to maintaining its equilibrium, and it has no meaning except as a spiritual attitude; the spiritual man alone firmly takes his stand outside the logical chain of individual reactions, since for him a participation in the current of these reactions is tantamount to a fall from grace... Christ did not therefore speak from the standpoint of the Law, but from that of inward, supra-social and spiritual realities.

Remember this last point; because this is where, later, we're going to pick up another 'argument', another level of all this, when we examine the 'gnostic gospels' of the Nag Hammadi Library and the twisted paths, implacable maneuvers and 'providential accidents'—or more aptly, more significantly in the present context where historicity and the Fall into Time are a central theme, *historical contingencies*—which culminated in the establishment of the Church of Rome in the early centuries of what came to be called the Christian era. I don't want to interrupt the flow of Schuon's discussion except to introduce those 'translations' into recognizable concrete human experience, or attempts at such, I mentioned earlier. He continues: 'Christianity accordingly possesses none of the normal characteristics of an exoterism instituted as such.' What are those characteristics?

Schuon speaks a great deal about the esoterism/exoterism distinction. It is fundamental to his entire work, and Huston Smith devotes the whole of his Introduction to *The Transcendent Unity of Religions* to its explication. In the present context, the salient characteristic of exoterism is its offering of a way of life and a vehicle of salvation accessible and practicable, in principle, to everyone. In this sense, exoterism is simply everything we customarily mean by *religion*. In Guénon's phrase, cited both by Schuon and Pallis, 'something that is at the same time indispensable and accessible to all.' In Schuon's words, 'The exoteric point of view is fundamentally the point of view of individual interest considered in its highest sense.' It offers a viable morality for this world, to be affirmed and enacted within a community of mutual support—which for the majority is all 'religion' ever means, effectively—and, with regard to 'the next world', participation in the external forms of the faith—ritual, liturgy, instruction, confession, calendrical attendance, donation, formal observances, and so on—which is equivalent, vaguely, either to 'the one thing needful' for Salvation or to Salvation itself, and this is where its 'interest' begins and ends: exoterism is suspicious of, and even hostile to, anything—'mystical experience', sanctified life, the truth of other religions, the Truth beyond all religious forms, impersonal transcendence, gnosis or knowledge of God, union with God, Illumination or Enlightenment, doctrines, such as *maya*, which deny the independent reality of the world or the human soul—that threatens its exclusivist claims: anything that contests what is deemed necessary or peers beyond what is deemed sufficient by its own restricted criteria and therefore suggests 'intellectual pride'. It 'protects' its adherents in this way, and as it should. There's no 'need to know' certain things. The heights of spiritual discourse and experience, which affirm truths totally beyond any given exoteric formulation, are compelling and accessible, and always have been, whether or not democratic institutions or sentiments approve, only to 'the esoteric minority' motivated or driven to explore them, and which has a right to do so. This is simply the way it is. 'Among thousands of men, one perchance strives for perfection: even among those successful strivers, only one perchance knows Me in essence.' (BHAGAVAD GITA) It would be improper, to say the least, to confuse or undermine the faith of the exoteric majority of humanity, 'for whom this way of talking about religion is sterile if not unintelligible' (HUSTON SMITH), with conceptions that are extraneous to and incompatible with the beliefs that sustain their orientation to heaven. Exoterism is 'religion, the goal of which is to save the largest possible number of souls and not to satisfy the need for causal explanations of an intellectual elite.'

> The exoteric aspect of a religion is thus a providential disposition that, far from being blameworthy, is necessary in view of the fact that the esoteric way can only concern a minority, especially under the present conditions of terrestrial humanity. What is blameworthy is not the existence of exoterism, but rather its all-invading autocracy—due primarily perhaps, in the Christian world, to the narrow precision of the Latin mind.

In this sense, then, 'Christianity cannot be exoteric in the usual sense of the word, since it is in reality by no means accessible to everyone, although in fact, by virtue of its outward application, it is binding upon everyone.' The Christian exoterism, to which Schuon refers—due, 'perhaps,' to the 'narrow precision of the Latin mind,' but also, I believe, to factors we will soon be exploring—is a massive and providential historical development, *and not a betrayal* (as champions of Gnosticism and 'primitive Christianity' have argued), of the original Message of the Messiah and of Incarnation itself, which was, as we have seen, primarily, indeed essentially, *esoteric*.

We have, then, a Revelation 'unbalanced', or better *one-sided*—according to a criterion both easily grasped, in its simple statement, and beyond human understanding, since it refers to a 'method' of God and His departure from it—at its inception, and it is the consequences of this one-sidedness, which is the Christian religion's 'particular nature', that must now be traced. What are, or have been, those consequences? Why did it happen? Where did it lead? What does it mean?

Nothing less than the end of the cosmic cycle.

Let it be added that the esoteric nature of the Christian dogmas and sacraments is the underlying cause of the Islamic reaction against Christianity. Because the latter had mixed together the *Haqiqah* (the esoteric Truth) and the *Shari'ah* (the exoteric Law), it carried with it certain dangers of disequilibrium that have in fact manifested themselves during the course of the centuries, indirectly contributing to the terrible subversion represented by the modern world, in conformity with the words of Christ: 'Give not that which is holy unto the dogs, neither cast ye your pearls before swine, lest they trample them under their feet, and turn again and rend you.'

Here we must pause indeed.

The point seems clear. To reveal esoteric truths to 'ordinary people', to preach the esoteric Way and its other-worldly rewards, is tantamount to casting pearls before swine, who 'in return' will corrupt those truths, hate, reject, contemn and revile them, and turn in homicidal hatred upon those, or Him, who revealed them: who dared to propose them. And this is not an assertion of Schuon's, but a warning from Christ our Lord. Therefore it must be true. A simple, sober, impartial, unjaundiced statement of fact regarding a tendency native to the celebrated human race.

True; but with, I believe, certain qualifications. These words are an English translation (rendered in the 17th century and heard now in the 20th) of a Greek translation of an Aramaic original. The English word 'swine' has accumulated present associations we may be fairly certain were absent in the Aramaic and in the agrarian society of Biblical times, where it most likely simply meant that particular domestic animal with whose appearance we are familiar. Nor did He mean, I believe, or necessarily, that the 'pearls' are singled out for trampling, as if in spiteful and vicious defiance, but rather that they are simply trampled indiscriminately along with everything else, not 'appreciated'; and the 'rending' might well be a reference to the unpredictable natural ferocity of the feral boar raised in Biblical times. The 'swine', in other words, and as Schuon himself goes on to suggest, are something like the darkness in which the Light shines, and that 'comprehendeth it not'. It's a question, I believe, of softening the contemptuous and condemnatory tenor of the English rendering.

But not evading the thrust. Which is that a unique relationship of esoterism to exoterism in the Christian Religion—resulting in the suppression of the former, since it was not 'protected' in its proper place within the structure and economy of 'balanced' Revelation, and the massive overdevelopment and institutionalization of the latter as a tyrannical dogmatism—was the cause of the 'disequilibrium' of European Christendom as a developing civilization, resulting in 'the general conditions of our age, which marks the end of a great cyclic period of terrestrial humanity': the 'terrible subversion represented by the modern world.' No evading that. Schuon, as he soon will make clear, is explicating here the ending of the cosmic cycle, the reign of the *Kali-Yuga*.

How, and by whom, was the Christian 'imbalance' experienced? How did it enter into experience? No one was aware, of course, no theologian, no Doctor or Father of the Church, of the metaphysical impropriety that made of Christianity so fateful a pronouncement to humanity. ('It should be added that the first Christians could have had no notion of such a function attaching to the mysteries of Christ, for they had no idea at all of a "West" that was liable to "founder".') And, as a matter of fact, the 'ordinary people', the 'swine', were in all probability more pious, more 'Christian', than the learned, the intellectuals, who, 'not finding anything in exoterism to satisfy their intelligence', were eventually, in a famous journey called 'the history of Western ideas', 'caused to stray into false and artificial doctrines in an attempt to find something that exoterism does not offer them, and even takes it upon itself to prohibit.' (Which explains, in part, the Church's inveterate indictment of 'intellectual pride'.) The great 'subversion', in other words, originated at the top, in the Mind of Europe, not among the unlettered majority. Christianity was ultimately impossible for those whose intelligence it could not satisfy, i.e. for intelligence itself; the fault lay in exoterism's 'all invading autocracy... which causes many of those who would be qualified for the way of pure Knowledge [*jñana yoga*] not only to stop short at the outward aspect of the religion, but even to reject entirely an esoterism that they know only through a veil of prejudice and deformation.' And this was a suicidal deficiency:

The exoteric viewpoint is, in fact, doomed to end by negating itself once it is no longer vivified by the presence within it of the esoterism of which it is both the outward radiation and the veil. So it is that religion, according to the measure in which it denies metaphysical and initiatory realities and becomes crystallized in a literalist dogmatism, inevitably engenders unbelief; the atrophy that overtakes dogmas when they are deprived of their internal dimension recoils upon them from the outside, in the form of heretical and atheistic negations.

It would appear, then, that the esoterism of Christ's Message was not so much deliberately and consciously *suppressed*, which implies human and therefore contingent agency, but rather *lost*: lost in a strange, inescapable and providential *confusion*; lost because, since the pearls were 'cast' and mingled rather than cherished 'behind the Veil', it wasn't preserved apart or at the Center where it belonged. And so, in time, the intellectuals, the Mind, the Intelligence of Europe sought elsewhere than in religion for answers to questions that cannot but be raised, and cannot be answered satisfactorily within the limited goals and scope of religious exoterism: questions that not only *can* be answered by esoterism, in the form of 'metaphysical and initiatory realities', but which, in the form of that 'answer', engage the whole person, every level of the being, and not merely the instrumental and technological rationality to which the minds of men like Descartes and Bacon and Newton were reduced: answers which address every level of our being, and offer Salvation, Illumination, Peace, by their very totality: because Humanity is *imago dei*, a microcosm containing the All.

But other answers were found, other truths. A new kind of truth. Sought and found, eloquent and compelling, irresistibly enticing, in the material world. The drama of Galileo was the drama of an entire civilization—as that supremely self-conscious civilization is well aware. The cause, as Schuon explains,

> lies within the religion itself, namely the fact that the doctrine and the means of Christianity surpass the psychological possibilities of the majority, and give rise to a secular scission between the religious domain which tends to keep men in a kind of sacred ghetto, and the 'world' with its seductive invitations—irresistible for Westerners—to philosophic, scientific, artistic and other adventures progressively detached from religion, and in the end turning against it.

The esoteric dimension is essential. In its absence the Tradition is doomed to wither. This dimension is the preservation, the prolongation of the original Light, the transforming presence of the Eternal in Time, the presence that *abolishes* Time. In a sense, esoterism alone is of God, purely and totally, and alone can provide us with strength to resist the allure of a captivating and imperious transience that can only betray our choice. It's not only that the Tradition withers: it is replaced. Replaced, in this universe, by what the West became.

> The presence of an esoteric nucleus in a civilization that is specifically exoteric in character guarantees to it a normal development and a maximum of stability... Once this dimension or nucleus ceases to exist, which can only happen in quite abnormal, though cosmologically necessary, circumstances, the religious edifice is shaken, or even suffers a partial collapse, and finally becomes reduced to its most external elements, namely literalism and sentimentality... The fact is that the presence of this transcendent dimension at the center of the religious form provides its exoteric side with a life-giving sap, universal and Paracletic in its essence, without which it will be compelled to fall back entirely upon itself and, thus left to its own resources, will end by becoming a sort of massive and opaque body the very density of which will inevitably produce fissures, as is shown by the modern history of Christianity.

Now none of this career of Christianity was a mistake or an accident or something that, given proper assessment by perspicacious founders of the faith, by human beings, could have been averted or gone otherwise. *Nothing 'went wrong'*. The unveiling of the 'mysteries', the esoteric Truth, their casting before 'the swine', and the subsequent repudiation or exile or concealment of esoterism (it was all those), the confusion, mingling, and fluctuation of the esoteric and exoteric domains, resulting in a suspicious minimization of esoterism and the construction of a massive exoterism (for the 'negative effects' of the descent of Christ into the world 'are also apparent enough, in the extreme exteriorization that took place later; for if the Holy of Holies, with the parting of the curtain, overflowed into the outer portion of the temple, the reverse was also true' PALLIS): all this was as it had to be, as it was 'intended'. The Divine Plan: the way—or, perhaps, one way among others—a cosmic cycle can be brought to an end.

> Now if Christianity seems to confuse two domains that should normally remain separate, just as it confuses the two Eucharistic species that respectively represent these domains, it may be asked whether things might have been otherwise and whether this confusion is simply the result of individual errors. Assuredly not and for the following reasons. The inward and esoteric

truth must of necessity sometimes manifest itself in broad daylight, this being by virtue of a definite possibility of spiritual manifestation and without regard to the shortcomings of a particular human environment; in other words, the confusion in question is but the negative consequence of something that in itself is positive, namely, the manifestation of Christ as such... It was necessary that Christ, by metaphysical or cosmological definition, as it were, should break the husk represented by the Mosaic Law, though without denying the latter; being Himself the living kernel of this law, He had every right to do so, for He was 'more true' than it, and this is one of the meanings of His words, 'Before Abraham was, I am.'

Through Christ, in His Incarnation as Christ, God offers to humanity the way of sainthood: enlightened liberation from this world. He offers Deification. And He offers it, not as the gradually approached esoteric core of a Dharma, a Way, not as the fulfilment of an initiatic *sadhana* conceived and experienced and taught as a journey through states and stages, but in something like a blinding cosmic explosion, a supreme and stupendous Event enjoining total reorientation of the life, total repudiation of the customary, the 'normal', *and at once*: a 'taking up of the Cross'. His Cross. God's Cross. Incumbent upon all.

'My Kingdom is not of this world.' And by His revealing the location of His Kingdom—that pithy and unmistakable 'clue' or 'hint' given to residents in the final *Yuga*—two consequences are assured. First, *rejection* of His Kingdom and *affirmation* of 'this world', because no collectivity can live up to, or *live with*, the demand, an affirmation which culminated, in the fullness of time, in the paradigmatic worldliness of the West, its total secularization and its installation, coronation, as the exemplary civilization. And second, in the secret souls of everyone and not only` the atypically sensitive or those with a vocation, the *affirmation* of 'His Kingdom', of the inwardness of Reality, in a galaxy of perverted forms—from Freud to the cult of 'feelings' and emotions and 'self-expression', in life, literature, entertainment, pedagogy and ubiquitous cultural celebration, to 'Self Magazine' and 'human potential' movements and an inexhaustible variety of 'liberating' therapies *ad infinitum* to the nth degree—and the *rejection* of this world, in consequence of universally suspected incarceration in some kind of Nightmare: in a Madness, in the many Great Lies, in the perfidy of civilization, the dehumanizing machinery of materialism, urbanism, industrialism, the labor process, technology and everything else labelled Progress, in the Universal Bullshit; and this suspicion is not a private secret, an unmentionable, but one of the central themes of the culture: *it is sold to us in the form of Entertainment.* Paradox and polar-ization, 'split personality'. The sense of fascinated, revolted, helpless witness to, and inescapable participation in, a precipitating disintegration and incoherence — 'everything is falling apart' — from which disaffiliation is unimaginable (and might be lonely!); oscillation of temptation and with-drawal, enthusiasm and disgust, guilt and cynicism; the 'doctrine' of Success versus the 'ideal' of Happiness. The whole flavor, the 'life style' of cosmic dis-solution. Yoga for stock-brokers, Tai-Chi at Hawaiian resorts, punk-rock Christ at the Cow Palace, Jesus Christ Superstar on Broadway. Drug-assisted Enlightenment, televangelism, silver-screen science-fiction portrayal of mystical transfiguration through a 'close encounter of the third kind'. Expiring Count Dracula, radiant with the bliss of his release from the blood-sucking thing and experiencing peace at last in the arms of his new-found love, repeating Christ's words on the Cross in the climax of Francis Ford Coppola's 'masterpiece of vampire eroticism' — exquisite choral music in the background, of course. A seething eye-popping lava of pearls, filth, and the swine themselves tumbling like a thousand avalanches down the great mountain of dreams to meet the Second Coming. 'Surely the Second Com-ing is at hand... and what rough beast, its hour come round at last, slouches toward Bethlehem to be born?'

And are we not reminded here, incidentally, of Eliade's magnificent work? 'In History, the separateness of the sacred from the profane — so clear-cut in pre-Christian times — is no longer obvious. All the more is this the case, since for two centuries past the fall of man into history has been precipi-tous.' Not only His Teaching, His laying bare of the mysteries, of the spirit in the letter, but also the *structure* of the Christ-Event, the Incarnation of our Lord in *Time*, in *History*, as the abrogation of the archaic techniques of entry into timelessness and the inauguration of inescapable linear temporal-ity: this revolution too precipitates the 'confusion' of esoteric with exoteric life, of the essential with the contingent, the sacred with the profane. The esoteric Message of Christ — 'My Kingdom is not of this world', and 'But lay up for yourselves treasures in heaven... For where your treasure lies there will your heart lie also' — is simultaneously a repudiation of the very History He had sanctified through His manifestation in Time: the very History, 'the world', which, because He had 'accepted existence' in it, was thereby trans-formed into an epiphany of God. Which is it? Affirmation or repudiation? One or the other or both? Where will Christians take their stand? Is evil 'a transpersonal structure of the historical world,' where 'suffering is equivalent to history,' as ahistorical classes and peoples perceive it. (The citation is from Eliade; I am always suspicious when I read about some Great Leader who succeeded in 'unifying' a large area, achieving, for example, the final 'unification' of China: what did it feel like to be 'unified'?), or is history a great drama of problems and progress, as secular ideologies perceive it, or is it the resumption, through Incarnation, of God's dialogue with mankind? 'And when God the Father 'shows' himself in a radical and complete manner by becoming incarnate in Jesus Christ, then all history becomes a theophany. The conceptions of mythical time and of the eternal return are definitely superseded.' In a word, what Schuon describes as the 'confusion' of the esoteric with the exoteric, 'the confusion in question,' is described by Eliade as a confusion of the sacred with the profane (or stated in another 'dialect', of the cosmic with the historical, the eternal with the temporal) consequent upon Incarnation in Time: 'To the Christian certain events were theophanies (above all, the presence of Christ in history) while others mere merely secular events... He has continually to *choose*.' Implosion and explosion, insupportable tension and the shattering of boundaries and limitations: pearls in the slops, trampled and consumed indiscriminately. Some essential principle of coherence and cohesion, of 'everything in its own place', annulled forever.

But to continue. Clarification is always to be sought in the concrete: where we can identify 'the argument' in our own experience. We want to be able to point at 'the confusion in question' as it manifests, and *must* manifest, in our daily lives, in the 'historical disequilibriums that are both disastrous and providential.' Metaphysical Truth is right here and now.

The consequences of the 'confusion' are readily apparent, initially, in the life of the Church. As Pallis puts it:

> If Christ's kingdom, by his own definition, is 'not of this world' and if the penalty of casting the pearl of great price before swine is that they 'will turn and rend you', then one of the consequences of the removal of the veil between the Holy of Holies and the more accessible part of the temple (to return to our original symbolism) has been a certain blurring of the distinction between the two domains even where it really applies—the shadow, as it were, of an overwhelming grace. This confusion has expressed itself in the life of the Christian church under the twofold form of a minimizing of what, in spirituality, is most interior and of an excessive focusing of attention on the more exterior and peripheral manifestations of the tradition, and especially on the collective interest treated almost as an end in itself. Carried to extremes, this tendency amply accounts for the fact that it was within the Christian world, and not elsewhere, that the great profanation known as 'the

modern mentality' first took shape and became, as time went on, the vehicle of 'scandal' among all the rest of mankind. If this happening, like everything else of a disastrous kind moreover, comprises its providential aspect, as bringing nearer the dark ending of one cycle and the bright dawning of another, it nevertheless does not escape—by force of Karma, as Buddhists would say—the curse laid by Christ Himself on all 'those by whom scandal cometh.' The pain of the cross, in which all must be involved, is there, in anticipation of its triumph.

The veil of the temple, of course—separating the chamber of the Holy of Holies hidden behind the altar, which only the officiating Rabbi could enter and 'containing God in His suchness, the divine Selfhood, transcending even being' (PALLIS again, one of the great 20th-century Buddhist writers), from the main area of the Temple, open to all, the place of formal 'exoteric' worship—which was 'rent in twain from the top to the bottom' when Jesus 'yielded up the ghost,' symbolized the traditional separation, in Jewish spirituality, of esoteric from exoteric: from that stupendous moment, however, when 'the earth did quake, and the rocks rent, and the graves were opened, and many bodies of the saints which slept arose,' the separation is annulled, and annulled forever. 'Henceforth no definable boundary would exist between the "religious" side of the tradition and the mysterious or, if one so prefers, between the exoteric and esoteric domains. As far as the human eye was able to discern they were to be merged... This gives the key to Christian spirituality as such; it starts from there.'

And the consequences of an initiative of the Absolute, of this momentous initiative of Heaven, must also be absolute, irrescindable, eternal, must necessarily reverberate everywhere throughout the civilization or humanity chosen or 'volunteering', 'stepping forward' to carry out the Plan, on all levels of human existence, not only in the career of the Church, whose role as a determinant of human experience is now quite minimal, but in the secular society it spawned, in the great desacralization that emerged from the collapse of the Christian tradition in the West. In other words, the 'confusion' engendered by 'the particularity of the Christian tradition, namely its *eso-exoteric* structure', will still be central right here and now in our modern modem state-of-the-art lives, but in forms that must be identified. I have already indicated, in the passage referring to the two consequences of Christ's location of His Kingdom, split vision and obscene juxtapositions— the pearls and the garbage. But there is, there has to be a 'general idea' among all these forms, a principle, a common factor, and that is, I think, as the inheritance of the mingling of the two domains, something like a radical inability to distinguish between what matters and what doesn't. Between the absolute and the relative, of course, but also between the important and the trivial, the significant and the meaningless. The genuine and the bogus, the beautiful and the ugly, the sublime and the ridiculous, the seed and the fruit—ultimately, between the real and the unreal: Baudrillard's hyper-reality, the 'post-modern carnival', is indeed the terminal form of 'the confusion in question'. The modern world, the spectacular nanosecond screenscape TV techno-havoc we gape at and live in with increasing stupefaction, is permeated, as if by a pungent narcotic all-pervading smell, with something like a radical tastelessness, an absence of intuitive discrimination or moral discernment, with imbecile idealisms and *causes célèbres* as ardent and pious as they are misplaced, idolatries and chauvinisms, passions and obsessions, disproportionate or skewed responses to things: 'disequilibrium', to recall Schuon's word, on all levels. (Those blow jobs in the White House! Those nine million pages of testimony! *Why, O Why, O Why O? Why did I ever leave Ohio?*) Here is, perhaps, an explanation for a central aspect of the Reign of Quantity: all questions of judgment are expressed and addressed *in quantitative form*, in terms of and appeal to statistics and expenses, 'cost-effectiveness', and 'settled' in those terms, because this is now the only 'language' in which the society can speak to itself, and of itself: quantitative facts. Somehow, despite the undeniable and heroic presence among us of truly moral people and truly moral engagements, in a world where there exists 'no definable boundary between the exoteric and esoteric domains', in which the hierarchical structure and proper 'direction' of society has been deranged, or in historical terms, in a society which inherits the consequences, the scar, of the abrogated boundary, whose very *existence* is that inheritance, everything falls apart, and people *feel* that 'everything is falling apart', the basis of judgment or prioritization or balanced placement or appropriate respect and assessment is undermined, and no declaration of intent, no matter how noble-sounding, no effort, no matter how herculean, is able to address or reach the invisible unidentifiable roots of 'the crisis'. Therefore, after the charade, the parody, poignant or shameful, called 'discussing the issues', '*Well, let's look at the numbers.*' Because numbers are all we've got, and all we are. 'Things fall apart, the center cannot hold,' as Yeats wrote. 'Anything Goes,' as Cole Porter warbled. And really *goes*, literally, like the great Saturn Rockets blasting off into the blue, for if there is no basis for discrimination there is none for restraint either. It could be called madness. ('Is this the world or a 3-ring circus?' Title of a column in yesterday's *Press*

Democrat; but any day, any newspaper in the world, would have provided something equivalent.) And of course it is. Everyone knows the human race, in its collective life, has 'lost it'. 'The world has gone mad today, and good's bad today, and black's white today, and day's night today… Anything Goes!' To that irresistibly catchy syncopated rhythm!

I cannot fail to mention here another sector where 'the confusion in question' confirms its subtle ubiquity. In Auerbach's Epilogue to *Mimesis* he seeks the source of the abrogation of 'the doctrine of the ancients regarding the several levels of literary representation.'

> When Stendhal and Balzac took random individuals from daily life in their
> dependence upon current historical circumstances and made them the sub-
> jects of serious, problematic, and even tragic representation, they broke with
> the classical rule of distinct levels of style, for according to this rule, everyday
> practical reality could find a place in literature only within the frame of a low
> or intermediate kind of style, that is to say, as either grotesquely comic or
> pleasant, light, colorful, and elegant entertainment… I came to realize that
> the revolution early in the nineteenth century against the classical doctrine
> could not possibly have been the first of its kind… Before that time, both
> during the Middle Ages and on through the Renaissance, a serious realism
> had existed. It had been possible in literature as well as in the visual arts to
> represent the most everyday phenomena of reality in a serious and significant
> context… And it had long been clear to me how this medieval conception of
> art had evolved, and when and how the first break with the classical theory
> had come about. It was the story of Christ, with its ruthless mixture of every-
> day reality and the highest and most sublime tragedy, which had conquered
> the classical rules of styles.

The Incarnation, a supernova, or an endless succession of them, silent, invisible and irresistible.

> These considerations must not lead us to overlook a complementary though
> more contingent aspect of the question. There must also exist on the human
> side, that is to say, in the environment in which such a Divine manifestation
> takes place, a sufficient reason for its occurrence; so, for the world to which
> Christ's mission was addressed, this open manifestation of truths that
> should normally remain hidden—under certain conditions of time and place
> at least—was the only possible means of bringing about the reorientation of
> which that world had need. This is sufficient to justify that element in the
> spiritual radiation of Christ that would be abnormal and illegitimate under
> ordinary circumstances. This laying bare of the 'spirit' hidden in the 'letter'

could not, however, entirely do away with certain laws that are inherent in all esoterism, under pain of changing the nature of the latter entirely: thus Christ spoke only in parables, 'that it might be fulfilled which was spoken by the Prophet, saying, I will open my mouth in parables; I will utter things which have been kept secret from the foundation of the world' (Matt. 13:34–35). Nonetheless, a radiation of this kind, though inevitable in the particular case in question, constitutes as it were a 'two-edged sword'.
⁓SCHUON

A radiation of this kind. A two-edged sword.

The whole of the West was, and remains, 'a two-edged sword'. No matter what we talk about in the legendary career of historical humanity, there's always the 'up side' and the 'down side', as the latest colloquialism goes. The Price of Progress, of course. Every initiative carries, like a shadow, its 'scandal'. When something is given with one hand, something else is taken by the other—and far more taken than given; every measure instituted is bad news for someone. Or some*thing*. Some river, or some people who live by the river, some obscure amphibian or flower, some habitat, industry, pastime or profession, one of the great creatures, the air or the oceans, an age group or a gender, or a race of people... or a simple joy. The Church of Rome, of course, is the prototype here, the two-edged sword *par excellence*: its excellence, as a matter of fact, its sublime perfection, clearly demonstrated in that those who see both edges are tormented, and those who can see but one—because both are so dazzling that each, seen from the 'right' angle can, as it were, eclipse the other with its brilliance—are blind: specifically, driven either to a fanatical anti-clericalism or an equally fanatical 'fundamentalist' 'right-wing' zealotry, because honest acknowledgement of the grey area would induce paralysis, and 'something must be done!' And the great 19th- and 20th-century revolutions, in the magnificent and agonizing clarity of *their* two edges, were clearly serious and dedicated rivals of the Church. And the miracles, the great technologies: always something gained, we are assured by the 'people in responsible positions', the people through whom the Great Mutations address us; rewards in comparison with which the price paid seems small indeed: the decision was right—although we know, after Ellul, that no one really makes any decisions here. Tracing this seemingly invariable doubleness of things in the West, the two-edged sword feature, to the gesture of Christ in which 'the confusion in question' originated seems, I know, like pushing it too far. But I don't think it is. There has to be something like a cultural-historical geo-political mental structure, a personality, of the civilization in question here, and that structure must be an evolution from its beginnings; this assumption is hardly far-fetched, and indeed is the assumption of an entire archive. And central to that personality must be the unquestioned and unquestionable two-edged enterprise of 'making history', entering purposively, 'creatively', into temporality: perpetually and programatically 'messing with things' as they are, creating what it calls 'problems', and trying to 'solve' them with more interventions. I said 'entering creatively into temporality'; it could just as well be said the other way around: entering temporally into Creation: 'dragging Creation out of Eternity,' as it were, is *the structure of 'falling into Time'*: making of Creation the raw material of History: capitulating to the seduction, the temptation, of Drama: a new mode of existence in which the scenes must continually change, the story continually unfold.

> The West's creative mentality—its 'creative genius' if you will—is moreover accompanied by a singular tendency to be ungrateful, unfaithful, forgetful; if the price of this genius is a propensity to 'burn what one has adored', it becomes compromised by that very token, for the gift of creation is a good only on condition of being accompanied by a sense of values, and thus by stability.
> ⁓PALLIS or SCHUON, most likely the latter. I misplaced the reference. My apologies

We have identified that loss of 'a sense of values', and suggested its source.

Progress. the central 'myth' and mission of historical humanity, is clearly what we are talking about here. The 'two-edged sword' is nothing other than Progress. And the 'weapon', as it were, of Progress is Power. Power is a two-edged sword, as Lewis Mumford argued so eloquently throughout his great work: in this context it is the specific form, the implementation, the *work* in all senses of the word, of the two-edged sword. Was the West always trying somehow to realize the millennium it felt it had betrayed? Realize in the future what it had lost in the past? To realize in outwardness—the letter— what it had repudiated in inwardness—the Spirit? Trying to redeem its tormented forgiven betrayal of the Messiah, the Redeemer?

There are no demonstrable answers to these questions, of course, and they have been asked before, in varying degrees of anguish or animus, by Christians and non-Christians alike, many many times. No; nothing demonstrable. But I believe the drama of Christ is the world's drama, in ways too deep, for this is of God, for us to fully understand or articulate.

There are frustrating lacunae in Schuon's exposition—after 'two-edged sword' in the previous citation, after 'present cycle of humanity' in the one to follow. The question took him, like all of us born of man and woman, to his limit. Let it lie. These are suggestions. He concludes:

> Now apart from the fact that a synthetic mode of radiation such as that just described—with its laying bare of things that a normal exoterism will leave veiled—was the only possible way to give effect to the spiritual reorientation of which the Western world stood in need, it must be added that this mode also possesses a providential aspect in relation to cyclic evolution, in the sense of being a part of the Divine Plan concerning the final development of the present cycle of humanity. From another point of view one may also recognize, in the disproportion between the purely spiritual quality of the Gift of Christ and the heterogeneous nature of the environment into which it was received, the mark of an exceptional mode of Divine Mercy, which constantly renews itself for the sake of creatures: in order to save one of the 'sick' parts of humanity, or rather 'a humanity', God consents to be profaned; but on the other hand—and this is a manifestation of His Impersonality, which by definition lies beyond the exoteric point of view—He makes use of this profanation, since 'it must needs be that offenses came,' in order to bring about the final decadence of the present cycle of humanity, this decadence being necessary for the exhausting of all the possibilities included in this cycle, necessary therefore for the equilibrium of the cycle as a whole and the fulfilment of the glorious and universal radiation of God.

Here it is finished. We sense a mystery, an unknowable, something visible but incomprehensible, like a landscape on another planet. Legacy of Jesus, Shadow of the Cross. Kalki Avatar and Maitreya Buddha, Lord of the End and Life Eternal. True Man and Second Adam, and True God. Blessed be His Name.

> Some say that ever 'gainst that season comes
> Wherein our Saviour's birth is celebrated,
> The bird of dawning singeth all night long;
> And then, they say, no spirit can walk abroad;
> The nights are wholesome; then no planets strike,
> No fairy tales, nor witch hath power to charm,
> So hallow'd and so gracious is the time.
> ⁓HAMLET, I, I

The Gnostic Testimony

I said—after the quotation about Christ speaking from the standpoint of 'inward, suprasocial and spiritual realities'—that we would later pick up, starting from that same point, another strand in the tapestry, although not really an 'argument' here but rather a zone of human experience, where the providential consequences of the original Christian esoterism are clearly illustrated: where the Being of Christ unfolded and, in ever-evolving guises, continues to unfold.

In his Introduction to *The Nag Hammadi Library* (a collection of translations into Coptic of 'gnostic gospels'—Elaine Pagels' term—written originally in Greek in the first two centuries of the Christian Era and discovered in Egypt in December 1945) James Robinson writes:

> The focus that brought the collection together is an estrangement from the mass of humanity, an affinity to an ideal order that completely transcends life as we know it, and a life-style radically other than common practice. This life-style involved giving up all the goods that people usually desire and longing for an ultimate liberation. It is not an aggressive revolution that is intended, but rather a withdrawal from involvement in the contamination that destroys clarity of vision.
>
> As such, the focus of this library has much in common with primitive Christianity, with eastern religions, and with holy men of all times, as well as with the more secular equivalents of today, such as the counter-culture movements coming from the 1960s. Disinterest in the goods of a consumer society, withdrawal into communes of the like-minded away from the bustle and clutter of big-city distraction, non-involvement in the compromises of the political process, sharing an in-group's knowledge both of the disaster-course of the culture and of an ideal, radical alternative not commonly known—all this in modern garb is the real challenge rooted in such materials as the Nag Hammadi library.

It would appear that the esoteric nature of Christ's Message was recognized, by some, immediately. And that these people really tried to live it. This entailed, however, and necessarily, 'an estrangement from the mass of humanity', a withdrawal from the world, and was therefore simultaneously a fidelity to Christ's Message and a forfeiture, or at least a misreading, of His Destiny, which, as He is God and Saviour, Supreme Beatitude and Incarnate Word, could not have been other than—in the 'world' which had need of the Redemption He offered—universal radiation, universal Benediction. As Paul knew.

A responsive esoterism and a nascent exoterism, as it were, confronted each other very early in the post-Crucifixion turbulence, if not in the Gospel generation itself, the former destined for extinction, as an historically continuous movement, and the latter to become the Church, in which the esoterism would still survive, but as the indestructible systematically suppressed divine core or heart of a world religion, always rediscovered and, in a sense, alone real, rather than as the initiatic teaching of a world-renouncing cult. The mystics, repudiated as 'heretics', were forced to retreat into monastic refuges or spiritual communities in the hinterlands, where their witness ultimately faded out, while those who were 'a bit more practical', in Robinson's words, carried the day, and founded a civilization—the civilization with whose awesome destiny we are fully acquainted.

Jesus called for a full reversal of values, announcing the end of the world as we have known it and its replacement by a quite new, utopian kind of life in which the ideal would be the real. He took a stand quite independent of the authorities of his day... and did not last very long before they eliminated him. Through a remarkable experience of his vindication, his followers reaffirmed his stand—for them he came to personify the ultimate goal. Yet some of his circle, being a bit more practical, followed a more conventional way of life. The circle gradually became an established organization with a quite natural concern to maintain order, continuity, lines of authority, and stability. But this concern could encourage a commitment to the status quo, rivalling, and at times outweighing, the commitment to the ultimate goal far beyond any and every attained achievement. Those who cherished the radical dream, the ultimate hope, would tend to throw it up as an invidious comparison to what was achieved, and thus seem to be disloyal, and to pose a serious threat to the organization.

~ ROBINSON

The accuracy of Schuon's analysis, in other words, which points out that Christianity 'possesses none of the normal characteristics of an exoterism, instituted as such, but presents itself as an exoterism in fact rather than one existing in principle'—a blurring or confusion of the esoteric and exoteric domains expressed symbolically in the rending of the veil of the temple—was confirmed at the outset, and assumed its role as a source of uninterrupted tension in the historical career of the Christian religion, always subterranean and sporadically surfacing in innumerable forms, within the souls of the faithful as well as in the politics of the organization, in this immediate confrontation between the esoteric stance we now call 'gnosticism' and the 'established organization' in the first centuries of the Christian Era.

Christian Gnosticism emerged as a reaffirmation, though in somewhat different terms, of the original stance of transcendence central to the very beginnings of Christianity. Such Gnostic Christians surely considered themselves the faithful continuation, under changing circumstances, of that original stance which made Christians Christians. But the 'somewhat different terms' and 'under changing circumstances' also involved real divergences, and other Christians surely considered Gnosticism a betrayal of the original Christian position. This was the conviction not just of those who had accommodated themselves to the status quo, but no doubt also of some who retained the full force of the original protest and ultimate hope. But as Christianity became organized and normalized, this divergence between the new radicals and those who retained the more traditional Christian language became intolerable. Gnostics came to be excluded from the Church as heretics.

⁓ROBINSON

The rejection, of course, was mutual. And in the final analysis, the stupendous cosmic final analysis, the Church was 'right'. God, or Providence, the unsurpassably momentous and decisive Providence we have been investigating, was, as it were, 'on its side'.

Many years ago, before I knew anything of durable significance, a friend of mine, one of those numerous people with a very intense secret inner life, gnostic Christian at heart as I now understand and profoundly impressed, really stricken, by certain speculations in the controversy aroused by the discovery of the Dead Sea scrolls, once lamented to me, indifferent to my nervous incomprehension, Christ's decision to 'leave the Essenes' and come back to preach. 'He should never have left,' I was solemnly assured, eye to eye. This putative decision of Jesus was pivotal, both to him personally and in his 'hit' on Christianity. And if there ever was such a decision it certainly was, to say the very least, pivotal. But I know John himself had no doubt about it; he had 'withdrawn' into a commune, an 'ideal community', in rural Oregon, and I'm quite certain he made that choice in the light of the alternatives which, in his belief, were presented to him by Christ. That is to say, I believe he saw the career of Christ as the tragic consequence of an error: as a lesson. Anyway, John hung himself some years later, on the day his daughter was born. Make what you want of it. Each of our stories can only be a particular rendition of the Music we all hear in our souls, sing with our lives: the 'Unstruck Music' of Kabir.

Formation of the Church

Then there's the Church. The Church and its birth-pangs, the Church and the Empire, the Church and its intrinsic 'problems' and problematic. Billions of gallons of ink spilled here, of course. An issue more fascinating and more vital to more people for more reasons can scarcely be imagined·

It was only by gaining the support of the Roman state after 312 that the triumph of Christianity was assured. Diocletian and Constantine staved off the collapse of the Roman empire only long enough for Christianity to become the universal religion of the Mediterranean world. Thus the history of the disintegration of the Roman world is intertwined with the rise and triumph of the Christian church.

⁓Norman Cantor

I would like to briefly trace here the journey from John 1:14 — And the Word was made flesh, and dwelt among us, (and we beheld his glory, the glory as of the only begotten of the Father,) full of grace and truth — to the pontificate of St. Leo the Great, 440–461. And a few reverberations beyond.

AD 312 : Constantine's famous 'conversion' to Christianity following upon his victory, heralded by the dream of the Labarum and/or the flaming Cross in the sky, at the Battle of the Milvian Bridge. 'Very early in his imperial career Constantine sensed that the church could act as a backbone for the empire. Hence he made desperate attempts to preserve the unity of the church... He laid the foundation and prepared the way for the Christian church of the middle ages.'

The ruler of the Latin-speaking World, Constantine, who had come to his throne in 312... proclaimed his active support of the Christian God and His church. Henceforth the Roman empire was to become more and more associated with the church.

Rome. The Empire became the Church, the Church became the Empire. I doubt that even the most fervent polemicists, on either side — if the fever of their passion ever cooled at all — can have contemplated this spectacle without at least a fleeting moment of (assuredly private) humble stupefaction. That wonderful word, 'caesaropapism', comes to mind. It casts a light on 'Render unto Caesar' which truly beggars irony. Caesaropapist doctrine: the re-emergence, in the fourth century, of the third-century political monotheism of the Roman Emperors (one Deity in heaven, variously and occasionally defined, and one Emperor on earth, frequently an assassin of his predecessor and usually plotting against the lives of rival claimants to his distinction, who was His Representative and a participant in His divinity) in a Christian form. Let's trace it in the text of *Medieval History*, by Norman Cantor, from which the above summation was also extracted; and keeping in mind, with the charity, humility and blithe generosity incumbent upon us, that it is quite impossible, even with the purest of intentions and genuine impartiality, to talk about these matters in a language invulnerable to charges of partisan bias.

From the time of Constantine the Christian Roman emperor played a commanding part in the life of the church... There can be little doubt that the emergence of Christian emperors intimidated many of the enemies of Christianity and encouraged the conversion of pagans to the new religion... the church received a large number of judicial and fiscal privileges which raised it above the common law of the empire and made it a state within a state. From the time of Constantine the clergy had been exempted from the taxes imposed on all the citizens... The church was allowed to have its own tribunals and to develop its own law—the canon law...

By the beginning of the fifth century the Christian Roman emperors in the west had freed the church front doctrinal disunity, crushed its pagan enemies, and granted it exclusive privileges... if the Christian emperors of the fourth century had not unified, protected, and favored the Christian church to the extent that it became a state within a state, the church might not have been strong enough to withstand the barbarian invasions of the fifth century. And thanks to the Christian Roman emperors, the church in the fifth century was still a strong-enough institution to begin the conversion of the barbarian peoples and their education in the Christian Latin culture... The Christian Roman empire in the fourth century had built up the power of the Christian church, and now the church was to supplant the Roman state...

As the Roman state disintegrated in the fifth century, the attention of men in the west came more and more to be directed to the only institution which could provide some unity and leadership to religion and education—the bishopric of Rome, the acknowledged leader of the Christian church in the west. The first pope who seems to have perceived the great role in Western civilization which the bishopric of Rome could possibly attain to as a result of the disintegration of the Roman empire was Pope Leo I, usually called St. Leo the Great (440–461)... The way for this transformation of leadership in the west from the Roman state to the see of Rome was prepared not only by Leo's activities, but even more by the success with which he vindicated the claim of the Roman see to theoretical supremacy in the church...

The claim made by St. Leo to the primacy of the bishop of Rome in the church was based on the so-called Petrine doctrine... Leo's Petrine doctrine claims that Jesus intended Peter and each of his successors in the chair of

Peter to be the primate of the whole church, and should have absolute power over faith and morals as Christ's vicar on earth. Thus the bishop of Rome alone possesses the keys to the kingdom of Heaven. He alone is the vicar of Christ on earth... In the Petrine theory the Roman church found an ideal which gave it the calling of supplanting the collapsing Roman state in the west as the central institution of Western civilization...

In conclusion, we can look back over the whole period between the death of Constantine and the end of the pontificate of Leo the Great and see that, quite unintentionally, the Christian Roman emperors had laid the foundation for the power of the medieval papacy... the emperors did the popes' work for them. They crushed paganism and made Rome into a Christian city... destroyed heresy and assured the doctrinal unity of the Western church. They endowed the church with enormous material benefits and corporate privileges. Then in the middle of the fifth century the Roman state in the west collapsed. All that was necessary was the appearance of a great personality on the throne of Peter, a man of bold ideas and enormous energy, for the bishop of Rome to take over the leadership of the Western church from the empire. St. Leo was the right man. Thanks to the work of the Christian emperors, the foundations of papal power had been laid.

From then on, 'The pope, as the bishop of Rome, regarded himself as the successor of the Roman emperor.'

Now this history is usually recounted, with relish, to illustrate the worldliness, opportunism, hypocrisy, corruption, irreligion, despotism, spiritual illegitimacy, cynicism, treachery, etc., of the Church of Rome. Its betrayal of Christ, of 'primitive Christianity', its commitment, as shameless as it was implacable, to its political entrenchment and supreme hegemony, its scandalous and transparently arbitrary claim to the fabricated privilege of 'apostolic succession', its ruthlessly pursued temporal ambitions, its manifest contamination by the traits and vices of unregenerate humanity, and so on: in Marco Pallis' more diplomatic language, its concentration 'on the collective interest treated almost as an end in itself.' But that would be a misreading. A massive melange of worldliness and spirituality, the latter 'justifying' the former's excesses, the former 'enforcing' the latter's labor of redemption, the latter indeed paracletic, 'even the Spirit of Truth', the former haunted by doubt, guilt, and remorse—all this, this seething cauldron of the sacred and the profane, is yet another spin-off, clearly inevitable, of the esoteric/exoteric 'confusion' which, in Schuon's words, 'was the only possible way to give effect to the spiritual reorientation of which the Western world stood in need.' Yes; there is something almost comic about it: comic, laced with

macabre. A strange 'need' indeed, and a strange 'reorientation'. We must recognize: it was not error, failure, miscarriage or tragedy. It is traceable to
Christ, therefore providential.

Prior to the Christian Roman Emperor scenarios, however, the esoter-
ism/exoterism drama had already appeared, first in the provocation of
'schismatic' and 'orthodox' churches by the gnostic movements, and second
in the Donatist 'heresy' of the fourth century. As the origin of a conflict with
and within Catholicism lasting from the fourth to the sixteenth century,
with a long hiatus from 700 to 1050, it is 'the fundamental doctrinal dispute
in Western Christianity.' The Donatists

> demanded that the sacramental rites be administered by priests of pure
> spirit, and held that sacraments administered by unworthy priests were
> invalid. The Catholic majority maintained their belief that it was the office of
> the priest and not his personal character or quality that gave sacramental
> rites their validity. This was the pivotal point of dispute—a church of saints
> as against the Catholic (universal) church… neither the arguments of the
> Catholics nor even the persecutions waged by the orthodox emperor entirely
> prevailed against the Donatists. They became an underground church and
> disappeared only after the Moslem conquest in the seventh century.
> Donatism reappeared again in the west in the second half of the eleventh
> century. Its absence from the Christian religious scene for several centuries
> enabled the Catholic church to assert its leadership in early medieval Europe,
> a task that could not have been successful had the church followed the
> Donatist ideals of exclusiveness and not attempted to bring all men into the
> fold and tried to civilize them.
> ⌒CANTOR

Here again, the inheritance of esoterism versus exoterism, esoterism 'confused' with exoterism, the familiar, unique, and intrinsic Christian 'dilemma'
guaranteeing instability, drama, and 'church history'. The purity of Christ or
the Redemption of Adam's Seed. For He was True God and true Man.
There could be no compromise, and the issue was only finally 'resolved' with
the most massive convulsion in the history of Western Christendom, the
Reformation.

> In the high middle ages literate and self-consciously moral laymen
> demanded, in Donatist fashion, higher standards of morality from members
> of the clergy. When they were not satisfied in this regard, certain zealots
> among them denied the distinction between laity and priesthood. In various
> parts of Western Europe heretical theories, all traceable to the Donatist out-
> look, made their appearance. The church fought the heresies with all the

means at its disposal because they struck at the foundations of Catholicism, but it was never able to root out Donatism completely. By the sixteenth century many people felt that the Donatist position was right. The Reformation, in the instance of Protestant sectarianism, showed its Donatist heritage: to be a full member of the church, you had to have a conversional experience and you had to have a conviction of reception of grace. The problem the Catholic church faced was that in absorbing society there was the chance that, just as society would be civilized and changed by its association with the church, so too could the church be barbarized by society. Had Christianity remained a religion of the elite, this danger from society would have been reduced, and the Donatist ideal of a church of the saints could have been realized. But a church of the saints could not at the same time be a catholic church bringing the means of grace to all mankind. There never could be a compromise between Donatism and Catholicism.

⟿ CANTOR

We may recall here the words of Marco Pallis: 'If the Holy of Holies, with the parting of the curtain, overflowed into the outer portion of the temple, the reverse was also true.'

Christ changed everything forever. The drama of the final *Yuga*, approaching consummation now in our own times, is inaugurated by 'that "bursting of all bounds" by the mysteries, which the descent of Christ into the world marked from the outset' (PALLIS). Kalki Avatar. Maitreya Buddha.

Consequences and More Consequences: Absence of Maya, Presence of Sin

There is no *maya* in the Christian comprehension of things, in the Christian universe. ('We must draw attention to the Semitic penchant for seeing things in black and white and opting for the sublime, as well as to the absence of the crucial notion of *Maya*' SCHUON.) *Maya*: the 'movement in Consciousness' which is the world, the *appearance* of Brahman to our senses, the 'world-appearance' that both *is* (in the state of Ignorance) and *is not* (in the state of Illumination), known variously as *chit-shakti*, the primal energy, *mahashakti*, the great power, *mahadrishti*, the great vision, *maha-kriya*, the great doing, *mahaspanda*, the great vibration.

The world is and is not. It is neither real nor non-existent. And yet this apparent paradox is simply a statement of fact—a fact which Shankara calls *Maya*. This *Maya*, this world-appearance, has its basis in Brahman, the eternal. The concept of *Maya* applies only to the phenomenal world, which, according to Shankara, consists of names and forms. It is not non-existent, yet it differs from the Reality, the Brahman, upon which it depends for its existence. It is not real, since it disappears in the light of knowledge of its eternal basis. World-appearance is *Maya*; the Self, the Atman, alone is real… The universe, he says, is a superimposition upon Brahman. Brahman remains eternally infinite and unchanged. It is not transformed into this universe. It simply *appears* as this universe to us, in our ignorance. We superimpose the apparent world upon Brahman, just as we sometimes superimpose a snake upon a coil of rope.

⁓Swami Prabhavananda

There is no such 'thing' as *maya* in the Christian revelation; nor, for that matter, in the two other Abrahamic monotheisms either. For the Christian, *this world is real*: meaning, preeminently, *History* is real. Christ made them real by accepting existence in space and time. Jehovah made them real, to a great degree, not only by regarding events here as significant, *unique episodes* in a one-way sequence—as the Prophets testified—but by actually intervening in those events. Incarnation, however, went all the way, beyond interventionism, beyond a divine 'interest' in earthly affairs to actual *presence among us*: a divine presence in our concrete lives, the Second Person of the eternal Holy Trinity. We are henceforth, in our earthly identities, graven in stone, as it were, solid as stone in a solid-as-stone world. Really *here*: permanent, eternal in our individuation, in our material forms, our historical identities (Shankara's illusory 'names and forms'), as Dante's post-mortem cosmos abundantly demonstrates.

Not only that. Not only are we permanent and real in our individual personalities, our biographies, our earthly 'selves', but we are 'sinners', infected by our very birth by an invisible and infinitely consequential contamination.

Christianity… addresses itself to sinners, to those who 'have need of the physician'; its starting point is sin, just as that of Buddhism is suffering. In Islam as in Hinduism—the oldest religion and the most recent religion paradoxically come together in certain features—the starting point is man himself; by comparison, the Christian perspective… will appear as limited to a single aspect of man and the human state, an aspect which, for all its undoubted reality, is not the only one and not exhaustive… Christianity, insofar as it is

founded on the consciousness of sin and the sinful nature of man, has need
of sin and even creates it, in a certain measure, by an appropriate moral theology, sin being, in this perspective, sexuality. In other traditional perspectives, sexuality, in itself neutral, becomes intrinsically positive by a certain
spiritual conditioning.
　～FRITHJOF SCHUON, 'The Human Margin'

　The material world, for the Christian, becomes a place of expiation, trial
and vindication, a place from which there is, furthermore, no exit, in the
Eastern sense of Liberation-in-this-Life, *jivan-mukta*, Illumination or
Awakening; no transcendent goal, fulfillment or Realization, no escape from
'the current of forms' called, in the East, *karma*. (I am tempted to say, *no
peace*, because the peace of Christ—'Peace I leave with you, my peace I give
unto you: not as the world giveth, give I unto you.' John 14:27—although
real of necessity, has always had to contend with a hostile setting, and with
alternative vocations.) On the contrary, it is only by accumulating merit, by
taking action in this relentless omniscient jurisdiction, hurling ourselves forever and again into the current through the performance of good works, that
we can hope to make ourselves worthy of salvation—knowing all along that
'all our righteousness is as filthy rags'—can 'measure up' to His redemptive
Sacrifice, 'carry on' His Work: purge ourselves of Sin and Guilt. No exit
from the world of sin and expiation. It is not a question here, obviously, of a
'fair assessment' of the Revelation of God in Christ, nor exactly an exaggerated accounting, but rather a description of human experience in 'the inter-
mediary plane which we call the human margin,' as Schuon put it, the
'fading' of Revelation into the world.

> Christ, in rejecting certain rabbinical prescriptions as 'human' and not
> 'Divine', shows that according to God's scale of measurement there is a sector
> which, while being orthodox and traditional, is nonetheless human in a cer-
> tain sense; this means that the divine influence is total only for the Scriptures
> and for the essential consequences of the Revelation, and that it always leaves
> a 'human margin' where it exerts no more than an indirect action, letting eth-
> nic or cultural factors have the first word.

Countless millions of people experienced their lives as Christians in the
cauldron of this uncompromising indictment and demand, and still do. It is
the formative, archetypal experience of an entire world culture, the civilization of the West. And the ensuing psychopathology, in its inexhaustible
variety, is sufficiently recognized and acknowledged to have become a basic
theme in our folklore and the governing assumption behind much of the
humor with which Christians console and even relieve their unease.

So, two basics: this world is *real*, and our residence in it is something like a treadmill of perpetually pursued expiation through good works. No wonder energy poured outward! Where else could it go? What other consequence of those 'two basics'? Outward, for outward alone was real, outward alone was escape, liberation, into geography, into natural science, secular learning, secular arts, the construction, elaboration and celebration of individuated personalities; into adventure: exploration in countless forms. 'An excessive focussing of attention on the more exterior and peripheral manifestations of the tradition', as Pallis put it, referring to Christianity, must inevitably lead even further outward, I am suggesting, to what is exterior to tradition itself, to the shining beckoning irresistibly fascinating world beyond that periphery.

Put it another way: the 'laying bare of things that a normal exoterism will leave veiled' entails its consequences. When the esoteric core makes itself public it commits suicide by that very act. Why? Because the world doesn't want to hear these things, never has and never will. We all know that. It turns upon—mocks, invalidates, patronizes, silences, displays the instruments before, questions the sanity of, demands recantation by, ostracizes, burns at the stake, feeds to the lions, crucifies—those who pronounce them: tramples underfoot the message cast before it and turns upon and rends the messengers: whatever's necessary and whatever works. It urges reconsideration with a deadly seriousness fatal to misread. And the world has no other choice, being what it is. The world wants itself. The world has its own agenda. Its own agenda? Well not exactly: an agenda to be sure, which it believes to be its own. What it really has is a fate. Which it blindly and ferociously pursues. Thus the cycle unfolded, and unfolds.

Incarnation and History, Eternity and Time

Seyyed Hossein Nasr, in his magisterial *Knowledge and the Sacred*, traces the Fall into Time to its fulfilment in the history-making and -worshipping of the Christian civilization. It begins slowly, each cosmic cycle being 'comprised of four *yugas*, beginning with what the Greeks called the Golden Age (the *Krita-Yuga* of Hindu sources) and ending with the Iron Age (*Kali-Yuga*) whose termination also marks the end of the present terrestrial cycle of history.'

In one single cycle in which time is divided according to the *Tetraktys*, that is 4, 3, 2, 1, the Golden Age being the longest and the Iron Age the shortest, the process of change or what we interpret as the flow of time is very slow at the beginning, increasing its tempo as the cycle advances so that time, far from being linear and uniform, is itself qualitatively modified during different *yugas*. For men of the Golden Age, time as an element of 'secular' change was not of any significance. Time was identified with cosmic rhythms like that of the seasons. Although the cycle never returns to the same point but follows a helical rather than circular motion, the changes in nonrepeated patterns were too imperceptible to be of any consequence. It was only during later phases of the cycle that gradually the experience of time in its non-cyclic aspect became consequential and that history began to gain significance.

Nasr then proposes a very illuminating symbol to clarify the relationship of time to cyclic unfolding; it explains both the genesis of the historical mode of being, of historical humanity and the historical religions, and the speed-up of time as the cycle approaches its end. It is, fittingly enough, the hourglass.

One unit of time during which the sand flows from the upper compartment into the lower could be considered as symbolizing one cosmic cycle. Now, as the cycle begins, although the sand is pouring through, there seems to be no perceptible change in the condition of the upper compartment which appears as being immutable. The reality of such a condition appears as one of permanence in which the particles of sand are 'seen' as being in space and not in a time which would alter their condition in an ultimately significant way— in the same way that in the Golden Age, although individuals did grow old and die, the world in which they lived seemed to be located in a paradisal permanence in which the cosmos was rejuvenated by temporal cycles but not affected in a nonrenewable manner by time. For so-called primitive man, the cosmos and history were the same, in fact identical, as were time and transcendence and reality and the symbol. But as the sand continues to flow, the very situation of the upper compartment begins to change. It is not only the individual particles of sand that fall through the channel but the whole configuration of sand in the upper compartment begins to change and time gains a new significance.

I might comment here that the 'paradisal permanence' of the Golden Age, in which 'time and transcendence and reality and the symbol' were 'identical', is not lost to us even today, at the end of the cycle: it is the Eternal Now which is the Truth, the Timeless Present which is God, Krishna the

Changeless, the noumenal Reality accessible to us, *deo favente*, in meditation—the World of the Archetypes, in Sufic language—which assumes illusory temporality in the Manifestation as *maya*, as phenomenon; all things, all moments, are eternal *in divinis*; all things, all moments, only actually exist *sub specie aeternitatis*. But this 'true state of affairs' which was visible to any 'ordinary person' in the Golden Age (when we enjoyed, in Schuon's memorable phrase, unimpeded perception of 'the metaphysical transparency of things'), at least in principle, is now only visible in one of the variously defined superconscious states of Tradition, of spiritual realization, or in one of those spontaneous 'mystical moments' with which unconscious lovers of God are occasionally blessed; it is the absolute Unity of *turiya*, 'the Fourth State' which is OM, or, in Buddhist language, 'the world' as it appears to No-Mind or Big Mind, depending on which Suzuki's term we use, or the 'birth in the world of peace and ease' of the Sermon of Master Bassui. All of which is another way of saying, as I have said many times before in this vagrant excursion, that nothing whatsoever has happened, that there is no world, no historical humanity, that all this is indeed 'a head trip to Reality': that the *Kali-Yuga*, the whole content of this book, 'you' and your reading of it, 'me' and my writing of it, are all *maya*, all the Dream from which we awaken into the Bliss of the Void, Nirvana, Brahman Supreme, the Reality. Do you dig? But I digress.

Nasr identifies the speed-up of time as a basic indication that we are approaching the end of the cycle; we perceive and experience an increasing 'insistence', as it were, of linear one-way time, of history. We have only to consider the dazzling pace of life, pace of change and sheer *speed* of everything around us now to get some idea of where we are situated in the trajectory of the cycle. (There are few things in modern 'life' we are more painfully aware of than its pace; but we are reassured, by our mutations, the mutants in the driver's seats, that 'efficiency' in the collective social endeavor—our 'business' in all definitions of the word—is the price well worth paying for the reward of increased 'leisure time'. Everyone knows something is wrong with this argument, but no one knows what!) The pursuit of greater speed is an implicit goal in virtually every aspect and domain of contemporary Research and Development, contemporary 'creativity'.

'Preparing for the Twenty-First Century' is a tour de force on the sweeping impact transnational forces are having on the planet and their likely effects on key countries and all regions over the next 30 years. ('Paul Kennedy, a professor of history at Yale University and author of the highly-praised *The*

Rise and Fall of the Great Powers, 1987, demonstrates that familiar types of change are acquiring an entirely new speed, dimension, and momentum.'
⏤CHRISTIAN SCIENCE MONITOR, April 1993

Why the word processor, the fax machine, the computer in every one of its countless applications, calculators, overnight mail, email, automatic tellers, super-highways, those high-speed trains in Europe and Japan, supermarket check-out machinery, the instant replay, touch-tone telephones, cell phones, credit cards and instantaneous banking transactions, fuel injection? And so on forever, far beyond what a man who lives in the woods like me could ever hope to keep pace with; I'm sure you can add to the list. (The best study I'm aware of on this topic is *Time Wars*, by Jeremy Rifkin, Simon & Schuster, 1987.) The equation of speed with skill in the tasks and occupations where human hands are still necessary is unquestioned. And speed, of course, as an aspect of the temporal dimension, is not only a purely *quantitative* affair, quintessentially quantitative, but also, in its immateriality and intangibility, its 'invisibility', something like a fiendish assault on our sensory limitations — as opposed to the assault in the spatial dimension, where quantification, as it were, congeals and becomes 'gross': statistics, *things* and their *prices*, scientific data, weights and measures. 'Speed', and the speed-up of all things, continuous acceleration, the celebration of velocities, is a central feature of the Reign of Quantity which defines the end of the cycle.

Nasr continues:

> The religions in which time is seen in a cyclic manner and where history is of little consequence as far as man's 'salvation' is concerned are essentially those archaic religions based on the reality of human experience in earlier phases of the cosmic cycle and corresponding to the beginning of the flow of sand in the hourglass. It is the later religions, corresponding to the last phase of the unit of time measured by the hourglass, which had to take into account the temporal experience in a religious manner. Judaism, although in one respect a 'primordial' religion, was destined to play a major role in itself and also to serve as a background for Christianity in the religious life of the humanity of the last phase of the human cycle, hence its concern with history and the metahistorical and metacosmic significance of the historical experience of the chosen people of Israel.

Hinduism and Buddhism, the 'religions of eternity', retain their secure anchorage in cyclic time, the primordial perspective, while Islam 'being the last of the Abrahamic religions and yet a return to the primordial religion confirms the significance of man's actions in history while refusing to identify the truth itself with history in any way.' Time is linear in the Abrahamic monotheisms and cyclical in the Eastern revelations. But neither Judaism, where the Deity is still something of a remorselessly partisan overseer of historical events, issuing dire warnings and intervening at critical junctures but still awesomely, even gratefully transcendent, not actually *here among us*, nor Islam, for the reason just cited—'Many episodes of sacred history are found in both the Bible and the Koran although not always in the same versions. But the Koran seems to be much more interested in the transhistorical significance of these events for the soul of man and his entelechy rather than the understanding of God's will in history or historical events themselves'—ever regarded, or came to regard, history as *spiritually real* in the specific Christian sense, where alone historical events and institutions were regarded as possessing absolute, universal and divine significance and authority in a temporal sequence which was itself providential. (Eastern scriptures, enraptured with what *is*, Western scriptures, obsessed with what *happened*. Peace versus History!) There are no parallels, anywhere, to the Incarnation, to that historical institution which calls itself the eternal 'Mystical Body of Christ', to a man speaking 'ex cathedra'. 'If all of the ways in which Christianity has emphasized the significance of history be considered, even Judaism would have to be excluded leaving Christianity as the only religion with such a particular attitude toward history.'

⌒Nasr

It is most of all in Christianity that one can say that only one part of a complete cycle or one small cycle was taken and treated in a linear manner. As a result, Christianity in its exoteric formulations—not of course in its sapiential teachings which saw Christ as the Logos who said, 'before Abraham was I am'—came to perceive history as marked by three fundamental points: the fall of Adam on earth, the incarnation of the Son of God as the second Adam in history, and the end of the world with the second coming of Christ. This view of the march of time, combined with the idea of the birth of Christ as a unique historical event and the incarnation of the Son in the matrix of time and of history, created a special religious situation which, once Christianity was weakened, gave way easily to that idolatry of the worship of history that characterizes much of the modern world… The worship of mammon as history or historical process came only in the wake of the desacralization of the Christian world, but it was precisely the secularization of the linear concept of time and historical process that gave rise to that historicism and denial of the truth as transcendent that characterizes much of modern thought.

We ought to remind ourselves here that for the enormous majority of humanity history has been something like an autonomously and relentlessly unfolding nightmare, a sequence of guaranteed unpredictable assaults: 'one damn thing after another', as some exhausted historian once concluded. And this History either 'makes itself' (recall Ellul) as the consequence of 'seeds' sown by no one identifiable in some century or another—consider the discovery of metallurgy, agriculture or petroleum, the invention of money, the Industrial Revolution, celestial navigation, chemistry and its antecedents, the Information Age, in the technological order, or the Crusades, the Napoleonic Wars, the Great War, any of the 'great wars' we study in 'world history', the forced migrations, the genocides, the liberations, revolutions, insurrections and suppressions, the dynasties and empires, the inexplicable economic transformations and their stupendous human consequences, the expansion of Western European imperialism over the whole globe, the cultural cross-fertilizations, and so on: how many millions of human beings encountered their distress, their suffering, humiliation and agonized despair, or were simply annihilated altogether, 'for the simple reason that their geographical situation set them in the pathway of history?'—or, if History doesn't 'make itself',

> it tends to be made by an increasingly smaller number of men who not only prohibit the mass of their contemporaries from directly or indirectly intervening in the history they are making (or which the small group is making), but in addition have at their disposal means sufficient to force each individual to endure, for his own part, the consequences of this history, that is, to live immediately and continuously in dread of history. Modern man's boasted freedom to make history is illusory for nearly the whole of the human race.
> ⌐ELIADE

On a more subtle plane, it's clear that all our gnawing inner apprehension, worrying, uneasiness, uncertainty, 'free-floating anxiety' (which simply means nameless dread), *stress*, derives also from our residence in History, and did not exist when our lives were founded in the changeless extra-human Life called—*by us now*, now that we are *separated* from it and hence *aware* of it—'Nature'.

How can we explain the passion for historiography, the 'worship' of all this, this stirring 'Story of Mankind', as it is usually expressed (or *was* expressed in the pre-feminist darkness), as anything other than a face-saving capitulation, a recognition of helplessness, of servitude to an indifferent and overwhelming power that has possessed us?

In many religions, and even in the folk-lore of European peoples, we have found a belief that, at the moment of death, man remembers all his past life down to the minutest details, and that he cannot die before having remembered and re-lived the whole of his personal history. Upon the screen of memory, the dying man once more reviews his past. Considered from this point of view, the passion for historiography in modern culture would be a sign portending his imminent death. Our Western civilization, before it foundered, would be for the last time remembering all its past, from proto-history until the total wars. The historiographical consciousness of Europe—which some have regarded as its highest title to lasting fame—would in fact be the supreme moment which precedes and announces death.

⁀ELIADE

You could also see it this way: we try to get it all down, in hundreds of versions, in hundreds of adroitly argued and mutually exclusive interpretations in almanacs, encyclopedias and CD-ROMs, in thousands of books, in every medium and for every level of response from kindergarten to postgraduate work, down to the most microscopic of minutiae, letting not a detail escape its registration and analysis, because we need to feel 'on top' of what is—'in the event', as it were—quite clearly on top of us, and the only way we can affirm our 'freedom', that defining conquest of modern times, the only way to can ever feel on top of it, is in the after-the-fact recording of it. We say, 'Those who do not learn from the mistakes of history are doomed to repeat them', and we dutifully chart our paths, at least on the planning boards, and demonstrate our humility by appealing to 'the lessons of history'. This is empty crap. By its very intrinsic dynamic, continuous innovation and transformation, history (we ourselves) mocks our claim.

But it begins with the Incarnation, this scenario. 'The entrance of truth into history', in Nasr's succinct phrase: definitely the leading contender for the Most Riveting Observation Award.

Christ, Incarnation, made the world real: does that sound right? Not quite. The word 'real' raises the esoteric/exoteric paradox. On the one hand, the significance of our lives in this world, the reality of our lives here, is confirmed, forever and absolutely, because He took on flesh, appeared here and walked among us as one of us, 'wholly man', 'full of grace and truth'. But, on the other hand, 'My Kingdom is not of this world' and 'Where your treasure lies, there will your heart lie also.' *Maya* can never become independently 'real', never become *the Reality*, anymore than a shadow can become independent of what casts it: the relative cannot become the Absolute, the Manifestation cannot became the Principle or exist independently of It, for the precise reverse is what is perpetually happening: 'The atoms of the universe may be counted, but not so My manifestations; for eternally I create innumerable worlds' (*Srimad Bhagavatam*). *Brahman satyam, jagan mithya*: Brahman is real, the world is unreal. No; He did not make the world real. Incarnation is Sacrificial Love, and the new element it introduces into the world is not 'reality' but *finality: infinite intensity: inescapability: and suffering*: 'the sadness unto death'. All these, but especially finality, for, in Eliade's words, 'The Advent of Christ marks the last and highest manifestation of the sacred in the world.' Christ can be seen as something like a Herald, sent from God, announcing that the Dream is going to end. He brings on that end Himself, by His very appearance here, and His Teaching of the Kingdom, of Eternal Life, is the incentive to awaken, to escape death. As we realized earlier, paradox is everywhere here; the Divine Mercies offered *consequent* upon the Fall are also *stages* of the Fall: we are 'saved' as we are carried onward.

Well, then. Another formulation: *Christ, Incarnation, made the world divine.* No; not that either. His Redemption is eternal. 'Before Abraham was I am.' 'The Redemption is an eternal act that cannot be situated in either time or space, and the sacrifice of Christ is a particular manifestation or realization of it on the human plane; men were able to benefit from the Redemption as well before the coming of Jesus Christ as after it, and outside the visible Church as well as within it.' (Schuon) The world, Creation, has always been divine: *Sarvam khalvidam Brahma*, All this is Brahman.

Christ, Incarnation, casts us into the world, as He was? There you have it. Cast into Time, into History. Incarnation was the Fall into Time. If God consents to be contaminated by Time, then the reverse will be true as well: Time will be sanctified by God: *made real*. It is Time that becomes real, not the world. On that point, between real Time and the unreal World, we burn: explode like fireworks. The *Kali-Yuga*: One-way Time in a Dream, carrying us onward in the great river of Redemptive Love that is the Incarnate Word, toward the Awakening.

Back to Nasr.

The deification of the historical process in secular terms has taken place in the modern world not only because the metaphysical teachings concerning time and eternity have been forgotten as a result of the desacralization of both knowledge and the world but also, as already mentioned, as a result of the particular emphasis of Christianity upon history which is not to be found in other traditions. Christian thought, at least in its main line of development in the West, took history seriously, in the sense of believing in the irreversible directionality of History, the power which history possesses to introduce novelty of even a radical order, awareness of the uniqueness of each historic event... the possibility of certain historical events to be decisive in a final way, the religious significance of human involvement in historical movements and institutions, and the importance of human freedom in not only determining the individual man's future but also the whole of history. From these premises to those of Promethean man, who secularized all of them and decided to mold his own destiny and history, was but a single step. And from this secularization of the Christian conception of history combined with messianism, those materialistic and secular philosophies have been born which are based on the view that the historical process is the ultimately real itself, and that through material progress man is able to attain that perfection which was traditionally identified with the paradisal state... Through historism, secular utopianism, and the idea of progress and evolution, in a sense time has, for modern man, tried to devour eternity and usurp its place, replacing the eternal now, in which the eternal and the temporal meet, with the present moment as the fleeting instant of transient pleasures and sensations.

'The deification of historical process,' of course, is the deification of ourselves—or, put another way, Incarnation, the Fall into Time, initiated the transformation of celestial anthropos, *imago dei*, humanity *in divinis* and *sub specie aeternitatis*, into historical humanity, creator of itself, enactment of its own perceived potentials, the Protagonist of the present study, a transformation required by and inherent in the final unfolding of the cycle. Tradition had set bounds, limits, 'restricted' us within a Law or sacrality or equilibrium, preventing the 'fulfillment' of humanity's potentials. The end of the cycle, the day of secular historical humanity, where the limitations have been eliminated—hence Freedom! Power! Creativity! Progress! Our great themes—is the time of this volcanic 'fulfilment'. As was just suggested, the new element introduced into the world by Incarnation was finality.

Put yet another way:

But the passage from primordial innocence to the 'knowledge of good and evil' and to the experience of centrifugal possibilities is not always presented as a first sin and a fall; according to various mythologies in fact, man was destined *a priori* to this full development of his personality that is represented by the entry into the world of oppositional and moving contingency; it was necessary that he be the witness, in the name of God, of the vicissitudes of cosmic outwardness.

From this point of view the *felix culpa* of St. Augustine can be explained and justified, not only by the saving advent of Christ, but by the necessity of the full development of the human being; Christ and the Virgin—new Adam, and new Eve—then appear less as an unforeseen compensation than as a proof of this paradoxical necessity of human possibility: the necessity to fall in order to be able to carry the consciousness of God into the limits of what is humanly possible.

⌒·Frithjof Schuon

Are we *there* yet? you are thinking!

A Catholic View: Christopher Dawson

It's instructive to glance, briefly, at how a fine Catholic historian and a man of genuine integrity such as Christopher Damson views all this. His book is titled *Progress and Religion* (1960). The title tells it.

He is aware, of course, of the novel Judaic emphasis on the religious significance of History.

> Thus the crisis which destroyed the existence of Israel as an independent nation was also the time of travail in which Judaism was reborn as a world religion. The series of national calamities which culminated in the destruction of Jerusalem and the period of the captivity only strengthened and enlarged the prophetic belief in the sovereignty of the divine purpose in history… The sufferings of Israel and of the Chosen Servant of Jahveh were the necessary means by which God's power and righteousness were to be manifested to humanity. From the beginning the will of Jahveh had set apart this little Palestinian people as his chosen vehicle… Thus all history was moving to a great consummation, the revelation of the power and glory of Jahveh in his servant Israel, and the eternal reign of justice in the Messianic kingdom of God.
>
> Consequently, to the Jews, history possessed a unique and absolute value such as no other people of antiquity had conceived. The eternal law which the Greeks saw embodied in the ordered movement of the heavens was manifested to the Jews in the vicissitudes of human history. While the philosophers of India and Greece were meditating on the illusoriness or eternity of the cosmic process, the prophets of Israel were affirming the moral purpose in history and were interpreting the passing events of their age as the revelation of the divine will. For them there could be no question of the return of all things in an eternal cycle of cosmic change, since the essence of their doctrine of the divine purpose in the world was its uniqueness. There was one God and one Israel, and in the relations between these two was comprised the whole purpose of creation.

But what was this 'divine purpose in the world'—this 'transcendent purpose, this 'moral purpose in history', this 'whole purpose of creation' —manifesting itself now, for the first time, or *visible* or *understood* for the first time, in and as History? It was Progress. For Time is linear—History is the human Reality—and along that temporal line humanity *ascends*, and was now not only to be 'raised to a higher order', but to be fulfilled completely. The divine purpose is Progress, and its fulfilment was the Incarnation.

> The Kingdom of God appears in the Gospels as at once a fulfilment of the ancient prophecies of the restoration of Israel, and as a new world order which would renew heaven and earth, but it was also a new life, a transforming leaven, a seed in the heart of man. And the source of the new order was found, not in a mythological figure, like the Saviour Gods of the Mystery Religions, nor in an abstract cosmic principle, but in the historical personality of Jesus, the crucified Nazarene. For Christianity taught that in Jesus a new principle of divine life had entered the human race and the natural world by which mankind is raised to a higher order. Christ is the head of this restored humanity, the first-born of the new creation, and the life of the Church consists in the progressive extension of the Incarnation by the gradual incorporation of mankind into this higher unity... Thus the Jewish affirmation of the significance and value of history found a yet wider development in Christianity. The world process was conceived not as an unchanging order governed by the fatal law of necessity, but as a divine drama whose successive acts were the Creation and Fall of Man, his Redemption, and his glorious restoration.

I might interject here that Dawson's entrapment within dogmatic theology and Western chauvinisms, and therefore his narrowness of vision and blindness in critical areas, is as obvious as his sincerity; neither require explicit recognition, and both determine his relevance.

A great divine purpose, then, was being played out in the course of earthly events, in History, and any notion that suggested their relativity or illusoriness, any imputation of prejudicial ephemerality, was unacceptable to the framers of Christian dogma, as it is to contemporary apologists. 'There could be no tampering with the reality and uniqueness of the historical process.'

> The irreconcilability of Christianity with the dominant theory of cosmic cycles is obvious, and was stated uncompromisingly by the early Fathers. 'If we accept that theory,' says Origen, 'then Adam and Eve will do in a second world exactly as they have done in this: the same deluge will be repeated; the same Moses will bring the same people out of Egypt, Judas will a second

time betray his Lord, and again Paul will keep the garments of those who
will stone Stephen.'

And it was on this very ground that the Church had to fight its earliest battles, for Gnosticism was essentially an attempt to combine the belief in spiritual redemption with the theory of world-aeons and of the illusory nature of
earthly change, and consequently the whole anti-Gnostic apologia of St. Ire-
naeus is directed to the defense of the value and reality of the historical
development. 'Since men are real, theirs must be a real establishment. They
do not vanish into non-existence, but progress among existent things.' There
is one Son who performs the Father's will, and one human race in which the
mysteries of God are realized.' It was to this consciousness of its unique character and mission that Christianity owes its extraordinary powers of expansion and conquest which revolutionized the whole development of Western
civilization.

St. Gregory of Nyssa, synthesizing the Christian world-view with the
Platonic tradition, had seen in man 'the channel through which the whole
material creation acquires consciousness and becomes spiritualized and
united to God.' The 'intelligible world' and 'sensible creation' were mingled,
'and the bond of this mixture and communion is to be found in human
nature.' 'This created nature, however,' Dawson continues,

> is essentially changeable. It continually passes through a process of evolution,
> which so long as it acts in accordance with nature will always be progressive,
> but which, on the other hand, may become a movement of degeneration and
> decline, if once the will should become perverted. This is what has happened
> in the actual history of humanity, and therefore it has been necessary for the
> Divine Nature to unite itself with mankind in a second creation which will
> restore and still further develop the original function of humanity. Thus the
> Incarnation is the source of a new movement of regeneration and progress
> which leads ultimately to the deification of human nature by its participation
> in the Divine Life. The life of the Divine Trinity externalizes itself in the
> Church as the restored humanity, and the purpose of creation finds its com-
> plete fulfilment in the Incarnate Word.

The notion of Progress, then, is of Christian origin (!) and its secularization in European civilization is the Great Problem: for on the one hand, the
subtraction of spiritual values from Progress, and their replacement by
purely materialist goals, is a calamity if not unintelligible, even perhaps a
heretical view; but on the other hand, the continued and stupendously 'fulfilled' dynamic of Progress is proof that the original Christian impetus is

very vigorously alive. Thus, although 18th-century Deism 'retained certain fundamental Christian conceptions—the belief in a beneficent Creator, the idea of an over ruling Providence which ordered all things for the best, and the chief precepts of the Christian moral law,'

all these were desupernaturalized and fitted into the utilitarian rational scheme of contemporary philosophy. Thus the moral law was divested of all ascetic and otherworldly elements and assimilated to practical philanthropy, and the order of Providence was transformed into a mechanistic natural law. Above all this was the case with the idea of Progress, for while the new philosophy had no place for the supernaturalism of the Christian eschatology, it could not divest itself of the Christian teleological conception of life. Thus the belief in the moral perfectibility and the indefinite progress of the human race took the place of the Christian faith in the life of the world to come, as the final goal of human effort.

Hence the whole tormented ambiguity, the desperate 'optimistic' interpretations, of what is known as 'salvation history', 'the unifying theme that dominates biblical studies today.'

Sacred scripture, in fact, is itself sacred history, or salvation history... God has a plan for man's salvation, a plan that He works for man in man's way— through human mediators—in man's time—through human history— respecting man's dignity, leaving human free choice intact.
⌒SALVATION HISTORY, 1965 (from the Intro. by C. Luke Salm, F.S.C.)

Two of the titles in this anthology are 'Christian Revelation as Historical Process' and 'The Gospels as Theologically Interpreted History'. And it is in this arena of contemporary Christian thought that we come upon the imbecile notion of 'the evolving God'. The ways in which Christians struggle to perceive—I am tempted to say salvage—the 'divine purpose' in contemporary history need not waste our time or gentle irony. It's something like a parody, and not a very funny one, of 'Seek and ye shall find.' (What could be more obvious than the roots of materialism in historicism?) They are right, however, in one sense: the impetus of the Incarnation, as we have seen, does define our lives today—but in a manner so utterly different from the 'salvation history' progressivist interpretation as to reveal the latter as both ridiculous and pathetic, so utterly opposite as to make the comparison seem a derision. For in defining the cyclic trajectory consequent upon 'the entrance of the truth into history' (NASR) as Progress, they have clearly shut their eyes to a rather massive testimony to the contrary.

This is very far out. Very Christian. Very pregnant with great confusion. High drama! To return to Dawson:

In the first half of the 19th century the Idea of Progress had attained its full development. It dominated the three main currents of European thought, Rationalist Liberalism, Revolutionary Socialism and Transcendental Idealism. It evoked all the enthusiasm and faith of a genuine religion. Indeed it seemed to many that the dream of St. Simon was on the eve of its fulfilment, and that 'the New Christianity', the Religion of Progress, was to restore to Europe the spiritual unity which she had lost since the Middle Ages. Actually, however, the course of European development in the following period failed to realize these ideals. The 19th century was 'the Century of Hope' but it was also the Century of Disillusion.

Progress, as we should recall, is the two-edged sword.

A remark by Eliade is apposite here. 'Progress' is an interpretation of history, a particular kind of historicism, and historicism, as all parties agree, originates in the Judeo-Christian innovation. In the Christian view, this particular kind of historicism known as Progress is called 'Salvation history', and, *through Faith*, persists as salvation history simultaneously with the total secularization of life and of the goals of Progress. Here, in this paradox, as we have seen, is what might be called the 'great problem' for those who would be Christians active in the world. Contrast this noble tormented *parti pris* with the following simple clarity:

Yet we must add that historicism arises as a decomposition product of Christianity; it accords decisive importance to the historical event (which is an idea whose origin is Christian) but to the *historical event as such*, that is, by denying it any possibility of revealing a transhistorical, soteriological intent.

For Christians, however, a transhistorical intent, even if it were 'revealed' in history, as it is indeed to certain eyes, is unacceptable: that's not what they're looking for: the 'intent' must be *historical*, part of a divinely intended historical *process*: it must be *concrete*, it must be 'the historical event as such.' This intent, this purpose, never conclusively demonstrable, must be read into the event, in an agony of doubt. For in its absence some kind of paralysis would seem fairly certain. If Christ is not 'working' here, in the sense demanded by historicist theology (and, I might add, with no prejudice intended, for these are generally sincere men, by fundamentalist preachers flourishing their Bibles), how can 'salvation history' be anything but a desperate fiction? A question many Christians have doubtless asked themselves.

Progress, however, in Dawson's view, is still the root idea, the basic 'purpose' of God and of the History initiated by His Incarnation. As he stubbornly insists, in his Conclusion.

> Hence it is in historic Christianity, far more than in any purely rational creed, that the Religion of Progress finds its satisfaction. For here we have not an abstract intellectualized progress, but the emergence of new spiritual values in a concrete historical sense. A new *kind* of life has inserted itself into the cosmic process at a particular point in time under definite historical circumstances and has become the principle of a new order of spiritual progress.

This 'new order' is to be grasped 'not by Reason, which lives on the systemization of the past, but by Faith, which is the promise of the future.' (We have examined the role of Faith in the Christian participation in History, and conceded its central importance, although not quite in Dawson's sense.) The new order, furthermore, a 'return to the Christian tradition', would be supervised by the Church, 'an authoritative organization which secures to the most *spiritual* men the highest rank', and which is 'under all circumstances a *nobler* institution than the State.' Such is his belief.

However, Dawson concedes: 'At the present moment such a solution appears inconceivable.'

Not inconceivable so much as misconceived, as is the entire interpretation Dawson, and theology, proposes. Misconceived, utterly, both with regard to that 'transcendent purpose' of God and the meaning of the historical drama called Progress. Nor is it true that Christians have no choice here. The divinity, the Glory of Christ is not diminished in His identification with the Kalki Avatar, the Maitreya Buddha. Nor is His salvific role. On the contrary.

The Desert Fathers and the End of the World

I found some interesting material, relevant to our pursuit here, in a book I came across several years ago in the monastery library: *The God Possessed*, by Jacques Lacarrière—a survey into the appearance of ascetics, monks and hermits in the desert wastes of Egypt, Syria and Palestine in the 4th century.

Jesus spoke as He speaks, speaks as He spoke: to an anticipation of 'the end of the world'. Hence the esoterism, the esoteric doctrine of the Kalki Avatar. Exoterism addresses the collective, historical continuity, the sequence of generations; esoterism addresses the individual, urges disengagement from the collective, the world, the ever-flowing seductive current of forms: urges the end of an earthly life and rebirth into Truth. Hence the Cross. 'Die before thou diest, so as not to die when thou diest, or indeed thou must perish.' (ANGELUS SILESIUS) 'Callimachus, die that thou mayest live' (ACTS OF JOHN, 76, *Apochryphal New Testament*).

> The purpose of the new religion, as preached by Jesus and propagated by the apostles, was not to conquer the temporal world and establish a place for itself in History but rather to announce that the Kingdom of heaven was at hand, bringing with it the end of the world. Like all great religions, Christianity first made an impact upon its devotees by effecting a fundamental change in the relationship between man and time. For the Gentiles—or Pagans—living in a Time cycle in which religious ceremonies, festivals and sacrifices unflaggingly perpetuated the same original events, within a repetitive (and therefore endless) universe, Christianity brought the sudden, distressing revelation of progressive Time, which evolves and passes, of a growing universe and therefore one capable of *coming to an end*. Is not one of the themes frequently to be found in the words of Jesus the fact and the imminence of the end of the world? The universe is soon to cease to exist, for Jesus, having come once on earth 'to fulfill the prophecies,' will return a second time to bring the history of the world to a close.

No other Avatar, no other Teacher addresses us from this direction. For what is perceived and indicated here as the motive for renunciation is not the intrinsic unreality or corruption or meaninglessness or treachery of 'this world', a 'world of fleeting and therefore 'vain' contingencies' (SCHUON), not recognition of *maya* with its *inherent* perfidy or insubstantiality or seduction, as in the Eastern doctrines, not *dukkha*, the 'pain that seeps at some level into all finite existence' (HUSTON SMITH), but rather a terrible coming event, a catastrophe in the stream of historical unfolding, something that is going to *happen in time*. (Just as in the Christian universe, *suffering* is historically rooted rather than inherent in Ignorance, in the *samsara*, as it is in the Eastern doctrines; or, at least, the distinction is blurred—consequent upon the 'mingling' after the Veil of the Temple was rent in twain—whereas in the Eastern doctrines it is clear.) The teaching of early Christian *kerygma* was that the world was coming to an end, and soon. All around him, the ascetic of the 4th century 'sees nothing but a doomed reality, and to this hopeless

304 ✳ YUGA: AN ANATOMY OF OUR FATE

death agony of the world he reacts by suppressing in its turn, within himself, everything which links him to that world, whether in mind or body.'

The analogy in our own period is, I think, escapism. Where the 4th-century Christian ascetic disengaged himself from the 'doomed reality', the disaster coming down the pike of One-way Time, by 'suppressing within himself' everything that linked him to that reality, the modern prisoners of a One-way Time, experienced as a gradual calamity or falling apart rather than an imminent apocalypse (although some fear both), defend themselves through resort to the great Shopping Mall of escapist strategies we have provided, out of mingled compassion and calculating self-contempt, for ourselves and our children. We're talking about Entertainment. The escapism 'which, we may well suspect, gratifies a secret desire to withdraw from the implacable becoming that leads toward death.' Eliade continues, integrating other themes:

> The defense against Time which is revealed to us in every kind of mythological attitude, but which is, in fact, inseparable from the human condition, reappears variously disguised in the modern world, but above all in its *distractions*, its amusements. It is here that one sees what a radical difference there is between modern cultures and other civilizations. In all traditional societies, every responsible action reproduced its mythical, transhuman model, and consequently took place in sacred time. Labour, handicrafts, war and love were all sacraments. The re-living of that which the Gods and Heroes had lived *in illo tempore* imparted a sacramental aspect to human existence, which was complemented by the sacramental nature ascribed to life and to the Cosmos. By thus opening out into the Great Time, this sacramental existence, poor as it night often be, was nevertheless rich in significance; at all events it was not under the tyranny of Time. The true 'fall into Time' begins with the secularization of work. It is only in modern societies that man feels himself to be the prisoner of his daily work, in which he can never escape from Time. And since he can no longer 'kill' time during his working hours — that is, while he is expressing his real social identity — he strives to get away from Time in his hours of leisure: hence the bewildering number of distractions invented by modern civilization... The 'fall into Time' becomes confused with the secularization of work and the consequent mechanization of existence, and the only escape that remains possible upon the collective plane is distraction.

Which is, of course, quite the opposite of the 'escape' suggested in the present study. 'Walk towards it,' as James Baldwin once put it, look hard at it, think very deeply and seriously about the times you live in, how you might respond… but that has been the theme here throughout. Last Judgment, Second Coming, Apocatastasis, the End of the Cycle—these are all metaphors for an inner event, an inner encounter, which can only be Enlightenment. The following citation from Lacarriere could almost be the epigraph to this book.

> In other terms, the end of the world, in St. Cyprian's text and in the perspective of his day, is no longer an object of terror or wild hope, a source of anarchy or irrational conduct as in the time of St. Paul and Montanus, but on the contrary an object of meditation, a source of reasoned consideration of man's end on the earth.

Benediction

And all this having been said, let us recall the Promise of the Angel:

> And the angel said unto them, Fear not: for, behold, I bring you good tidings of great joy, which shall be to all people. For unto you is born this day in the city of David a Saviour, which is Christ the Lord.

And the Promise of our Lord:

> Verily, verily, I say unto you, he that heareth my word, and believeth on Him that sent me, hath everlasting life, and shall not come into condemnation; but is passed from death unto life… Verily, verily, I say unto you, he that believeth on me hath everlasting life.

XXV

Last Chapter, End of the Book

AUTUMN's in the air on the north coast. High motionless ribbed clouds, the pregnant stillness; cooling air. Soon the flow into the spring box will strengthen, and the rains will set in. Winter. Fire and ice.

May we all be forgiven.

I still have some notes which I'd like to set down here, just for the sake of thoroughness.

Always remembering: *Wa-'Llahu a'lam*: And God is more wise.

The Fall into Time, the Reign of Quantity, the Mutation into Machinery, the End of Nature, the Prison of Unreality. The five hallmarks of the *Kali-Yuga*.

What we call 'ecological consciousness' appears in the *Kali-Yuga* and its exponents perceive a purely physical world: a planet, an ecosphere, an environment. Even 'spaceship Earth'. No other perception can enter into collective discourse. The issue is defined the only way it can be defined in the absence of heaven (just as, for that matter, it was the absence of heaven — of immanent sacrality, the perception of Creation as sacred — that created the 'problem' in the first place, in the West); that is, as a matter of preservation: preservation of physical nature for the utility and 'enjoyment' of future generations, preservation of a world made of matter extended in time and space in order that the drama of historical humanity may continue to unfold. The drama, the Dream: Shakti of Shiva Mahadeva, *Maya*, Samsara. It's the only reality they know, it's all they have. They love it very much, as they should, as we all do. It's Life, it's Beauty, it's Love and Laughter. There's nothing like it. Creation is the supreme manifestation, the supreme Grace, life's home. They fear death, a final death with no rebirth.

But 'the world' was doomed precisely from the moment this mode of perception appeared. Indeed, from the moment when Christ's material humanity, denied by the Docetist 'heresy', was affirmed in the Nicene Creed. As it had to be. There the ecologists' impasse was prefigured, predestined. Spirit and Matter, Spirit *versus* Matter, no quarter asked or given: in the West, warfare and agony until one was finally… what? silenced? neutralized? beaten into submission? annihilated? 'side-lined'? eviscerated? Something like that. In the East: 'no problem'.

The environmentalists' discourse, therefore, is necessarily diagnostic, prescriptive, admonitory, corrective, and always both desperate and hopeful. Like the 'last chapter message' in all historical humanity's urgent warnings to itself. They're trapped.

Who really can believe that 'we', meaning the entire human race, historical humanity, is going to 'take action' *now*, 'before it's too late'?

'Before it's too late.' a brick wall in the protagonist's mind.

In the *Kali-Yuga* good guys and bad guys perceive the same issues with perfect comprehension of each other's position and its origins, and understand perfectly well each other's strategies, devices, constraints and hidden agendas, as they are the same each would employ and dissemble if they were on the other side. Perfect accord with regard to issues and methods. They perceive the same world, the same arena of contesting values and vested interests, and engage each other on common ground. They know perfectly well that victories and defeats are both relative and provisional.

But Enlightenment and Ignorance agree about nothing. Different universes, different realities. Different languages.

> The recollected mind is awake
> In the knowledge of the Atman
> Which is dark night to the ignorant:
> The ignorant are awake in their sense-life
> Which they think is daylight
> To the seer it is darkness.
> ⁓BHAGAVAD GITA II.69

The 'Forests Forever' people, 'eco-warriors', perceive the same 'reality' as the lumber companies. They are in perfect accord about what a 'tree' is, and differ only in their plans for it. The 'sacred', to which the environmentalists occasionally lamely appeal, is enlisted only as a device or argument in defense of the profane, the material world, which is primary and alone real for them. But how could it be otherwise? Where else is Nature vulnerable but on Earth, where it is but the shadow of its eternity in Heaven?

The Reign of Quantity, the Internet, Capital, the media 'shoppertainment' ('a phrase used without irony by the Mills chain of discount malls'), and the identities, the inhabitants, the shining swinging players: the products who themselves produce and become the products they consume, the world they are. *Christian Science Monitor*, January 31, 2000:

PROSPERITY CREATES ERA OF $2,300 DOWN PILLOWS
Greed isn't just good. It's now hip.
GETTING AND SPENDING IN AN ERA OF DOTCOMS

In the 22nd century, historians of the United States may write this about our era: 'It was a time of such ostentation that New York's Russian Tea Room featured a 15-foot see-through revolving bear filled with live fish.' They may note that the mass-market Company Store catalog offered $2,300 pillows full of down hand-gathered in the wild. 'Many popular TV shows had "millionaire" in their title,' they'll say. 'Ringo Starr, a youth icon of the 1960s, became a pitchman for the brokerage house Schwab.' The chapter title? 'The Day Trader Age'.

Dotcom billionaires have replaced investment bankers as the masters of our collective universe... The nature of today's wealth creation, which always seems to involve software or cell phones or something best viewed in Netscape 4.5, lends it a benign image not found in previous booms, say some historians. In a recent *USA Today* poll some 70 percent of college students said they plan on becoming rich. Greed's not just good—it's hip.

Between 1995 and 1998 median family net worth rose 17.6 percent, to $71,600, according to Federal Reserve Figures released this month. Ten years ago the comparable figure was $59,700. And a lot of that money is rolling out the door for new gas grills and pickups. Total consumption has been going up 3 or 4 percent a year since the mid-90s. Spending on luxury goods is rising some four times faster than that. Just look at the sales curve for Porsches, the muscular sports cars beloved by golf pros and successful real estate agents. Porsche sold 3,700 autos in the US in 1993. Last year? Almost 21,000.

'We've never seen consumerism and the shop-'til-you-drop mentality as great as it is now…' This doesn't mean that indulgence is something new in America, unseen before the advent of cell phones that ring with the opening notes of Beethoven's Ninth. One hundred years ago, only a thin veneer of society could afford to conspicuously consume. Today a much deeper strata of Americans look to goods for emotional or cultural reassurance… Bottled water is just, well, water in a bottle. But it can still be a symbol of status… 'The '90s have seen the rise of what I call "opuluxe", luxury on the cheap,' says James Twitchell, a University of Florida English professor and author of books on US materialism. 'A huge number of us can have it, even if only for a short time.' Mr Twitchell argues that possessions are increasingly important because the old markers of middle-class place—religious affiliation, political leanings, school ties—have all become less important. In this vacuum, the purchase of a triple latté becomes an act of self-definition. 'Consumption is what we have,' he says.

But who's trying to kid who around here? I know what elicits the familiar painful disdain, the deep regret, but merits a difficult compassion. I know the demise when I see it.

'The Big Bang' is never invoked with seriousness, not to mention solemnity or awe, or adoration: the very suggestion is absurd. It's always a joke, a sly sidestep in the brain, a leer and a chuckle: because the vestigial traces of Intellect recognize its shameful imbecility. The phrase mocks itself. We know in our hearts that it's a nitwit gambit. But the nitwits are the sages in the *Kali-Yuga*.

'In a certain sense, every single human soul has more meaning and value than the whole of history with its empires, its wars and revolutions, its blossoming and fading civilizations.'
—Nicholas Berdyaev

'I believe that in the history of the world one could easily find a very great number of examples of persons who, suddenly perceiving the truth, seize it… The life of an honest man must be an apostasy and a perpetual desertion. The honest man must be a perpetual renegade, the life of an honest man must be a perpetual infidelity. For the man who wishes to remain faithful to truth must make himself continually unfaithful to all the continual, successive, indefatigable renascent errors.'
—Charles Peguy

'Life is the traversing of a cosmic and collective dream by an individual dream, a consciousness, an ego. Death extracts the particular dream from the general dream and plucks out the roots which the former has sunk into the latter. The universe is a dream woven of dreams: the Self alone is awake. The objective homogeneity of the world proves, not its absolute reality, but the collective character of the illusion, or of such an illusion, or such a world.'
～SCHUON

So we are not to become impassioned about the fate of historical humanity. Historical humanity is *maya*, the Dream of God. Your dream, and mine. As in the spirit of the mantra, the *dhirani*: 'Dreamer, Dreamer, Eternal Dreamer, Eternal Dreamer, Eternal Dream.' *Pax Profunda*. 'The whole of existence is imagination within imagination, while true Being is God alone.' (IBN ARABI) 'The is no spirituality which is not founded, in one of its constituent elements, on the negation of this dream...' (SCHUON)

However: 'This beloved Dream, this beloved Dream: O beloved Dream.'

Ignorant of Heaven, the protagonist is bound to the fate of the world. The Fate of the Earth, in Jonathan Schell's memorable book title. Ignorance, cause of Ignorance, consequence of Ignorance: the *Kali-Yuga* is all of these.

The fact that the people of the *Kali-Yuga* have no knowledge of transcendence, no experience of the sacred, is precisely what binds them so painfully and urgently to the fate of the world, to *samsara*. It's all they have. That's why the crisis is so hypnotic, so supreme a distraction. To the 'intellectuals' above all.

Schuon remarks more than once that we, humanity in the *Kali-Yuga*, have 'lost the intuition of the Absolute.' (Or, lost the intuition of *unconditioned existence*.) This is true; and doubtless the gravest of statements. But it should be pointed out that the loss of that intuition carries with it, following like a shadow, the intuition of loss. For we remain human, *imago dei*.

We know something's missing, but we can't say what it is. Two levels within us. *Duo sunt in homine.*

The forests, the rivers and mountains, all of Nature, already gone forever. There are no more forests and there never will be. Nature in its Truth—as Manifestation, Creation, the quintessential revelation of the Self which we are, the supreme expression of God as infinite Beauty and eternal Peace—is vanished forever. And this because of what has vanished within us. The humanity that can experience forests, disclose them in awareness of their eternity in the Heart, is all but gone.

This departure of the Divine, our departure from our own humanity, is the *Kali-Yuga*. What remains is simply matter, the 'reality' of the *Kali-Yuga*, Guénon's 'Solidification of the World'. The ecological consciousness is at once too late and right on schedule. The eclipse of humanity and nature is a simultaneous episode in the fade-out. Bill McKibben, in *The End of Nature*, sees and states it clearly:

> Our comforting sense… of the permanence of our natural world, and our confidence that it will change gradually and imperceptibly, if at all, is the result of a subtly warped perspective. Changes in our world can happen in our lifetime—not just changes like wars, but bigger and more total events. I believe that without recognizing it we have already stepped over the threshold of such a change: that we are at the end of nature. Not that it could happen, but that it has… We have changed the atmosphere and that is changing the weather. The temperature, the rainfall, are no longer entirely the work of some separate, uncivilizable force, but are in part a product of our habits, our economies, our ways of life… An idea, a relationship, can go extinct just like an animal or a plant. The idea in this case is 'nature', the separate and wild province, the world apart from man to which he adapted, under whose rules he was born and died… Such visions of the world as it existed outside human history became scarcer with each year that passed, of course… Marshall was very nearly the last to see surroundings unpolluted even by the knowledge that someone had been there before…
> The idea of nature will not survive the new global pollution—the carbon dioxide and the CFCs and the like. This new rupture with nature is not only different in scope but also in kind from salmon tins in an English stream. We have changed the atmosphere, and thus we are changing the weather. By changing the weather, we make every spot on earth man-made and artificial.

We have deprived nature of its independence, and that is fatal to its meaning. Nature's independence *is* its meaning; without it there is nothing but us… A child born now will never know a natural summer, a natural autumn, winter, or spring. Summer is becoming extinct, replaced by something else which will be called 'summer'… We have ended nature.

But so what? 'The Sages have been taught of God that this natural world is only an image and material copy of a heavenly and spiritual pattern; that the very existence of this world is based upon the reality of its celestial archetype.' (MICHAEL SENDIVOGIUS) 'You must understand then that the soul makes in the physical world nothing else than copies of the things which Mind makes in the soul itself; and that Mind makes in the soul nothing else than copies of the things which the First Cause of all makes in the Mind.' (HERMES) 'Every form you see has its archetype in the placeless world: If the form perished, no matter, since its original is everlasting.' (DIVANI SHAMSI TABRIZ of Rumi)

We don't abandon the terminally ill. We minister with solicitude, without compromise, even with added concern, to their needs. An added dimension of concern elicited precisely by their terminal condition. We secure their comfort and hope for their Enlightenment, their transcendence of mortality, and not for their sake alone but for ours as well. So with 'the world'. No ill will, no bitterness. No hard feelings. All love.

Cool, Rad, Ragers, High as a noun, Party as a verb. (Supply your own colloquialisms here; they arrive and depart with breathtaking speed— like everything else.) The fate of a generation. A frenzy of terminal Fun.

Every child born into this world is betrayed. As we were. Their lives are, and should be understood as, a response, an accommodation. As are ours.

Practical activity in Traditional (human) Society: addressed to survival, experienced as repetition or mimesis of divine archetypes and paradigms—as was, for that matter, all activity; the modern distinction between 'practical' and 'leisure' activity did not exist—meaningful because ordained by heaven and determined by necessity: all played out in the natural world, the cosmic Reality, Creation: 'Beauty behind me, Beauty before me...'

Practical Activity in Modern (post-human) Society: now become 'work' (a leading contender for the final fatal word), addressed not to genuine needs or potentials but to the production and realization of surplus value — The Accumulation of Capital — and experienced as a daily customary hell, 'the grind,'the rat-race' ('The trouble with the rat-race is that even when you win you're still a rat'), 'my job'; played out in a poisoned, 'stressful', treacherous synthetic environment, the urban-industrial-bureaucratic-vehicular world, 'the Megamachine', the whole nightmare made 'liveable' only by its intrinsic reverse side, the inexhaustible sewage-fountain of compensatory stupefactions called Entertainment.

And what could the presence among us, and *as* us, and *for* us, of something called 'the entertainment industry' possibly mean but that we are lost to ourselves?

The 'environment' we destroy is our own humanity: we are it. Our love and joy in Nature are self-recognition. It is humanity that is lost — not a 'material' creature defined by historical circumstance and 'situation' or by transformist evolution but an eternal and infinite Consciousness, the Self, within which the glorious drama of these delusions, temptations and errors, among many others, unfolds... a Dream and nothing more: humanity as it *is*, an essence, a being, an archetype, an eternal Idea in God, a descent of God, theomorphic and therefore comporting a mutually inherent relation to the world –- humanity, then, that is lost, or polluted, degraded, desecrated, insulted, destroyed, mechanized, laid waste, deforested, strip-mined, clear-cut, raped, not the Earth; or rather both, for their fates are interwoven, identical: we are not 'accidentally' here, 'here' in time and space, on the surface of a 'planet', but rather we, humanity and the Earth, *Jiva* and *Jagat*, are One Eternal Being, mutually present in each other in that One Eternal Being woven of Love and Beauty, Peace and Bliss: One Truth: *Atma*. And *Ayam Atma Brahma*: This Self is Brahman. With the disappearance of Earth-as-Self, of the experience of Earth-as-Creation, 'we' disappear as human. Everything goes.

In other wards, just as we *are* Capital (MARX), or the Reign of Quantity (RENÉ GUÉNON), and as we *are* Technique (ELLUL) or Power (MUMFORD), or the Mutation into Machinery, and as we *are* Hyper-Reality (BAUDRILLARD) or the Prison of Unreality, and as we *are* the Fall into Time (ELIADE), that is, historical humanity, so we *are* the End of Nature. We are the *Kali-Yuga*. '*Please allow me to introduce myself,*' as Mick Jagger sang.

Our mutations in the *Kali-Yuga*: our Spiricide, our Suicide. 'We have met the enemy, and they is us.' (Pogo, again)

Wa-'Llahu a' lam.

We've seen it happen so, so many times, the Moon, the seasons, the diurnal round, the blessed Morning Star, Life, its manifestation, its withdrawal from manifestation, its return. (*This* is Manifestation: *That* is Principle.)

It's never really gone, nothing is ever really gone, it's always there, within, eternal, withdrawing from and returning to manifestation, Life Everlasting. 'Before birth, beings are not manifest to our human senses. In the interim between birth and death, they are manifest. At death they return to the unmanifest again. What is there in all this to grieve over?' (*Gita*, chap. 2, The Yoga of Knowledge) Appearing, withdrawing from appearance to its eternity in God, appearing again. Eternity to Time, Time to Eternity. So with Humanity. Eternal in God, in His Eternal Now, appearing in Time, in the Great Wheel of Birth and Death. Eternal in your Heart, in your Silence. ('The silence within alone is real.') Eternity and Time, Noumenon and Phenomenon, Atman and *Maya*, Nirvana and Samsara, ever *Tad Ekam*, That One. And That One is known directly in meditation. These truths are known and seen directly in meditation. Never doubt it. As clearly, as the saying goes, as a fruit held in the palm of the hand.

Listen to music. Sing and play instruments, maybe start carrying a blues harp around with you, keep it in the glove compartment. 'All songs are a part of Him, who wears a form of sound' (*Vishnu Purana*). 'How splendid it is to drink to the sound of music!' (IBN AL-FARID). 'Allah has not sent a Prophet except with a beautiful voice' (MUHAMMAD). 'Our songs are the same as His songs' (*Chandogya Upanishad*). 'In every strain which the tavern-haunters hear from the minstrel comes to them rapture from the unseen world' (SHABISTARI). Anita O'Day singing 'Sweet Georgia Brown', Fats Domino singing 'Blueberry Hill', Ella Fitzgerald singing 'Starlit Hour', 'That Old Black Magic', Monk playing 'Straight, No Chaser', McCoy Tyner playing 'Satin Doll', Tony Bennett singing 'Fly Me to the Moon', Miles Davis playing 'All Blues', anything by Johnny Mercer and Harold Arlen, the Gershwins, John, Paul, George, and Ringo, Edith Piaf, Jacques Brel, and Old

Blue-Eyes. Or Mozart and Beethoven. Whatever your taste, whatever does it for you.

As the Heart-Intellect, Cardiac Intelligence, the intuition of the Absolute, withers away, it is — with rigorous reciprocity, as one sinks the other rises — replaced by a satanic 'intelligence', the 'mind' of the *Kali-Yuga*, *which is 'smarter' than 'we' are*: we cannot, as the collective, see through its devices, and as individuals only sporadically, and with cynical despair. It is ourselves as self-deception, 'fiendish' as it is the Archfiend, the Adversary. It causes everything to appear to make sense, to appear natural, normal, plausible, from television commercials and freeways to the logic of principal and interest and the 'stock market'. It's terminal form, the terminal 'mind' of the *Kali-Yuga*, is the Computer, in which the whole of reality is transformed into the human absence called 'information', the incontestable 'data'. This is the Great Dead Brain in whose lightless lifeless plastic chambers the world we loved will die. Reality is not Information. The transformation into data is the murder of the real, whatever becomes Information is now dead. The Computer, the Internet, the Web, the Thing we have collectively become, is not human, and our relentless transformation into It is our dying. An 'intelligence' that is not alive is dead, and what is dead knows nothing.

The Garden is the Earth, the Expulsion from Eden is what is presently being completed. We remember our sublime grief, the infinite humility of our contrition. It knew, as we know now, that this was irreversible until or unless a Mercy was offered.

We are conscious of our Fall. And our stupendous efforts to deny the Fall, through the affirmation of Progress, or to drown its memory in the Entertainment narcotic, are proof of that consciousness: that 'memory', Platonic 'recollection', of the present as our fate.

But we were not abandoned. We are never abandoned.

Al-an kama kan: And it is now as it was then.

Acquiring wisdom, learning (or being taught) the truth, 'understanding life'. In the absence of a tradition which affirms these values, and of a way of life that recognizes and rewards those who pursue them, they are no longer goals for any but 'eccentrics'. This tragedy is due, in part, to the massive self-imposed semi-conscious assumption that 'science' and 'scientists', and now at last The Computer, 'know everything', and that we, ordinary human beings, cannot have this 'information' (there's just too much of it, and it's too hard to understand anyway) and need not because it's all there somewhere inside the machines, or 'out there' in cyberspace, and growing greater all the time. Taking care of things.

Knowledge is in the Machine. In the Data Base. Our role is to go to work where we earn the right and the means to have fun.

Even books were a step down from the pre-literate stage in which the wholeness of truth and wisdom were a living wholeness within us, within the whole person, as Coomaraswamy pointed out in his notorious essay, 'The Bugbear of Literacy'. But the words in the books still manage to point back to ourselves, and to the Word. What's in the machine only points ahead, to what we have already become.

Money also, by-the-way, 'knows' things. As we learn from such 'ads' as: 'Which mutual fund knows the difference between acid rain and the greenhouse effect?'

Consider the gulf between inner thoughts and outer behavior and discourse in groups of people at job-site meetings, 'taking care of business'. Within swirls a lazy syrup of weary or amused cynicism, giddy unmentionable crazy thoughts, boredom bordering on delirium, resigned awareness of the necessity to 'go through the motions', 'pay your dues', everyone all the while making sure to do the minimum required to 'look right', being careful to say the 'right things'. And so on. All adults are familiar with this charade. The excruciatingly familiar Great Pretence. The 'leaders', or 'facilitators' or 'presenters', in these sessions are grim, diplomatically relentless, always 'appropriate', shrewdly affable, determined to 'go through with it' at all costs, to 'get the ball rolling here', protecting their hard-won and chronically precarious status, 'covering their ass' and 'playing the game'. All participants are aware, on various levels and from differing perspectives, when their minds haven't 'zoned out' altogether, of Bullshit.

Prison of Unreality, the *Kali-Yuga*.

In the human reality now so far behind us, inner and outer were one. Why? Because the outer was human. The world was a human place, a reflection and creation of the indestructible humanness within. No need for pretence.

The outer now is a creation of the mutations we have collectively become. Capital, Technique, Mechanism.

We are not destroyed, or tormented, by what we call our 'problems' nearly so much as by what we regard as 'normal'. Clock-time, for example. Money. 'Work'. The 'media'. Counselling, vacations, living in cities, driving our cars. Shopping, surfing the net, phoning 800 numbers, reading the newspapers, magazines, and catalogs. The way we live in its totality. Destroyed, in other words, by that in which what we call our 'problems' are rooted.

This truth is generally suspected, widely suspected—which is why it has become possible to sell it to ourselves as Entertainment. We apprehend it in that mode of mindlessness, that relationship—specific to the *Kali-Yuga*—between knower and known in which both are drained of their reality, called Entertainment.

The motif of *violence* in the *Kali-Yuga*, both in reality and as Entertainment (which definitely includes the dazzling electronic amphitheater of TV sports), the lashing out in anger or with impassive technical proficiency, can only be the deformed expression or release of something stifled or constricted whose normal form of expression has been suppressed. This 'something', given the massive all-pervasiveness of dehumanization in the *Kali-Yuga*, could well be our humanity itself, human expressiveness: the exhibition and appreciative reception of the human proposal in all its variety.

Look at it this way:

Presences: cities; the implacable inorganic linear temporality of clocktime: we are always in danger of 'running late', and 'hurrying' to make sure we're 'on time', and therefore tense, harried, fighting and arguing with each other as we glance hurriedly, or impatiently or uneasily or surreptitiously or in alarm, at the clock, flaring up, snapping at each other, speaking rapidly as we lurch to our feet; the unpredictable and equally implacable linearity of history, 'the news', events and their 'pace', 'never a dull moment'; work: the office and the factory; car travel, the daily episodes of screaming hell in 'the rush hour', in 'gridlock', the impatient fury at toll plazas, the grinding corrosive exhaustion daily renewed; perpetual inflammation and frustration of appetite: 'The main activity of our present civilization consists in the creation of new desires and the finding of fresh means to satisfy them' (HARI PRASAD SAS-TRI). And what is Ignorance but desire? We are incarcerated in rationalized structures of inexhaustible variety, tangible and intangible, loyal and answerable only to their inflexible mechanical function and purpose, generated by and comprehensible only to the algorithm and the dollar, trapped in the relentless metamorphoses of Technique.

Absences: Heaven and Earth. Meaning and Silence. Archetype and Ritual. Continuity and stability. Wisdom and Its witnesses. Peace. Beauty. Truth, and Its gift of that Certitude which dissolves the ego, unveils the Joy.

Sufficient reason to be pissed off. To crack. To 'blow up'. To 'go ballistic'.

Archaic humanity did not know it was 'one with Nature', 'living in harmony with Nature', and could never have come up with such figures of speech. The concepts appear only when the oneness is lost, and afterwards any 'recovery' can only be artificial in the collective and momentary in individuals. We didn't even know we were human, only that we were 'the people'; there was no conceptualization of ourselves, no isolation of an abstract quality. When 'we' become conscious of 'humanity', when it becomes a concept 'out there', we are already and from that moment separated from it—as the Tao so clearly teaches. We didn't know we were innocent until we bit the apple. We were simply being what we are, and what we are was invisible to us because we were identical with it.

The analogy, of course, is to childhood. Children cannot know they are 'childlike'; they are simply being what they are. When they 'know' it, when they can recognize 'childlike', they are no longer children. And no turning back.

The linear time to which historical humanity, by definition, is fated is a road of steady loss: loss of what is decisive for our humanity, gain of what is not. Transformation of our humanity, piece by piece, into concepts and memories: into words, intimations, nostalgia: nostalgia for Paradise.

So it went, so it goes. *Wa-'Llahu a' lam.* And God is more wise.

Five and two. Five days of 'going to work', two days of recuperation on the 'week-end'. This image of time is too deeply embedded in our minds ever to be rooted out. We always know whether any given day is a work-day or not. And explain ourselves accordingly.

He rested on the seventh day. We, apparently more exhausted, take two days of rest. But, outside the orbit of the Abrahamic monotheist dispensation no one knew about the seven days. Over all the Earth, all life, since the dawn, no one knew. Only the West. The West: fate of the Earth.

Five and two, and also nine to five. Checkpoints.

There is, however, according to St. Maximus the Confessor, an 'eighth day', the 'Sunday of eternity', which 'announces the passing beyond the created horizon symbolized by the biblical account of the seven days or creation.' (ANDRE SCRIMA, 'The Hesychastic Tradition: An Orthodox-Christian Way of Contemplation'.) 'The death of what is created, on the seventh day—the mystical Sabbath on which death dies—introduces to the Resurrection on the eighth day.' (MAXIMUS) This day is the state of those who have died to this world. Who love this world as it is *in divinis*, in God. Who themselves live in God.

'The economy' is ourselves as numbers. Quantities. The central 'issue' in the 1992 presidential election was 'the economy'. When we talk about 'the economy', about the 'budget', we are talking about ourselves as numbers, quantities, and this is the only way we know to talk about ourselves because it is what we *are* to ourselves. 'Income tax form' and 'checkbook': ultimate reduction of identity to quantity, biography to numbers. Therefore we are, as human, invisible to ourselves. The mind of the *Kali-Yuga* sees no people. Is there any element of our suffering which is not ultimately traceable to this infamy? *Kali-Yuga*: the Reign of Quantity; Sea of acid.

Traditional societies guided and carried upward, toward the Real, out of this illusion, toward fulfillment of the human. Eternity and Immortal Life. Oneness and Joy. No guarantee, but the door was there.

Historical societies point and drag downward, toward the unreal, into this illusion, toward destruction of the human. Time, and Death. Separation and Misery. Brick wall.

In the former the world is revealed in its divinity, its sacredness, its Truth which is Spirit, the Self. In the latter the world is degraded into the unintelligible, the opaque: 'matter'.

And 'tradition, let it be repeated, cannot 'become bankrupt'; rather is it of the bankruptcy of man that one should speak.'

⌁ FRITHJOF SCHUON, from his message to the Colloquium held at Rothko Chapel in 1973)

Al-an kama kan: It is now as it was then.

'Depression' and 'Anxiety' are the two classic 'symptoms' of modern societies. These terms define the states they point to as 'medical', 'chemical', conditions calling for 'therapies' such as 'mood-altering' pharmaceuticals or 'counselling', and the trusting victims perceive *and experience* them as such.

This is all a lie.

The two fundamental experiences of the *Kali-Yuga* are Sorrow and Fear. People are sad and frightened. Sometimes, in waves interrupted only by television, alcohol and sleep, miserable and terrified. They have been deprived of everything they need to fulfill their humanity, everything that makes people feel right in a good world. Separated from Spirit: from Heaven and Earth and themselves. The gaudy surrogates they serve up to themselves with increasingly frantic ingenuity not only rapidly prove empty of their promise but are actually regularly 'withdrawn from circulation' anyway, by 'the system' itself, one of whose iron laws is 'planned obsolescence'; perpetual innovation, the fetish of novelty, is inherent in historical societies under the sign of Progress, and of the very essence of the capitalist 'mode of production'.

Under the circumstances, redefinition was the only answer. Sorrow and Terror, the two dimensions of Suffering in the *Kali-Yuga*, are dissimulated from states into symptoms, from conditions of the soul to conditions of the body. There was no other avenue of approach. Nothing to do but numb the pain.

To lament the ubiquity of violence here is pointless, since it is inevitable and essential in *Kali-Yuga* society. Urbanization, the labor process, capitalism, separation from all that blesses life with meaningfulness and peace, travel in cars, bureaucratization, and of course clock-time—the modern world produces violence, and 'anxiety' and 'depression', as factories produce their products, or a mixture of ingredients its flavor and aroma, or fire smoke. People are driven wild. 'Limits' are pursued with single-minded frenzy, methodical determination. Nothing you can think of that someone somewhere isn't doing: or planning. The absence of Tradition is an abyss that must be filled. 'At all costs'.

The function of a great deal of modern culture, Schuon remarks, is 'to lure man down blind alleys of poisoned dreaming and mental passion, to draw him insidiously further and further away from 'the one thing necessary', to make him lose the taste of heaven.'

Moving through a landscape, through Creation, on foot or animal-back may be compared with moving through Creation inside a machine-driven vehicle—a comparison that has surely been the theme of repeated reverie to millions of people living in the *Kali-Yuga*, composed in varying degrees of bitterness or glum resignation or helpless anger. You can see it through the windshield, feel it in your bones, the imprisonment, the collective suicide. Once there was a natural world here. Nature, and I was there, it was my home, my life.

The former mode, of course, was human. Why? Because the pace of the world was then the same as the traveler's pace, a human pace, a human world; the two, the world and the traveler, lived along with and within each other and were one, and the traveler could feel—prior to words, prior to thought, in the primordial actuality of unity, in ecstasy—*Ahamidam*: I am this. *Idamaham*: this am I.

On the empirical level, we could simply say that everything was *noticed*, because there was *time* to notice it, and therefore became, or was, a human experience: existed as human experience, not as something separate, 'out there'. The world spoke, not *to* us but *within* us. We were one with the world. We paused, looked around, stopped to listen or examine, were part of, *centers* of, what was 'going on'. Whatever was happening was unique. Unique, miraculous: a gateway. Our very own.

> Whenever, in the course of the daily hunt, the red hunter comes upon a scene that is strikingly beautiful or sublime—a black thundercloud with the rainbow's glowing arch above the mountain; a white waterfall in the heart of a green gorge; a vast prairie tinged with the blood-red of sunset—he pauses for an instant in the attitude of worship.
>
> ⌒OHIYESA

Someone asks, in the *Kali-Yuga*, thinking of history, guidebooks and travelogues, about a river, 'Tell me about that river.' Thinking of facts, data: 'information' in the Information Age. This isn't the way it used to be. Guidebooks, 'history' of the river, appear with the changing nature of the river in human experience—specifically, with its *absence* as a river-in-human-experience: fatal absence, fatal for both.

In the *Kali-Yuga* Nature disappears by a subtle magic. Far more decisive, more telling than physical destruction, physical absence, this magic. Anyone can see the urban and suburban 'sprawl' covering the land, spreading like a rash, the network of freeways, the billion-square-mile slab of cement, growing ever larger, the shopping malls and reeking wastelands, the 'managed forests' and the outdoor factories of global agribusiness. But the subtle magic of

Nature's disappearance while it's still 'there'!

Nature disappears when it becomes 'matter' and 'data'. As does the whole world. Because 'matter' and 'data' are external, 'out there'. Nothing can be real 'out there'. Nothing *is* 'out there'. Reality is where inner and outer are one.

What is within us is also without. What is without is also within. He who sees difference between what is within and what is without goes evermore from death to death.

⌇Katha Upanishad, II.1.10

By the 'fall'... Creation, which at the outset was conceived by man as 'interior', has been 'exteriorized' and has become the material world.

⌇Frithjof Schuon

The fatalities and finalities in which we are immersed are too stupendous to be visible. Too utterly incomprehensible. They are everything. We try to escape our own lives.

People can be perceived as imprisoned in this culture, figuratively but intimately incarcerated—in 'cars', in 'entertainment', 'at work', in daily discourse about money matters or things or events in the hyper-reality fantasy world, in pharmaceutical world, merchandise world, 'political issues' world, in their own invaded minds, etc. 'Like it or not, YOU'RE MARRIED TO THE MARKET.' Baudrillard's 'code', the cultural DNA within us and in which we are immersed. Cells in the great invisible penitentiary.

Young people, mid to late teens, tend to view the future with apathy: listless indifference shading off into a tentative deferential cynicism destined to become increasingly hard-edged, 'mature', 'realistic'. The emptiness of historical existence, the emptiness within its furious 'creativity', is, of course, a state of consciousness, and an intolerable one.

The quest for a 'high' is one response. A 'high' is at least *something*, a state of consciousness other than the daily 'normal' *nothing* state generated and sustained by our residence in the empty 'real world'. In The Great Advertizement. The need to escape is urgent, acute. It builds up.

Admonitory writers in our time—their name is legion, it's a seething market—speak to citizens, characters in the historical drama. (As have all social critics, reformers and revolutionaries, from *les lumières* to the latest gay or black or feminist or environmentalist crusaders, good men and women and true all of them.) They speak from and address themselves to the historical identity, which is alone real to them, the conditioned identity, the current moral person. I have hoped, attempted, to speak from the eternal to the eternal, depending solely upon what guidance I have been granted, or believe I have been granted. Ghosts behind me, within me, within us all.

      I have a thick pile of clippings I was going to draw upon to make into a collage titled 'The Future Present'. An Appendix to the book, illustrating the hyper-real hyper-finance supercomputer bio-engineered Information Age Planet Hollywood techno-hell generated by *Kapital* and *Technique*, our terminal mutations. What the utterly innocent jubilant techno-idiots are cooking up. The 'data highways luring billions in investment', Information Superhighways and 'Ultimate Supercomputing'.

> 'The coming merger of home entertainment, computers and communications… movies on demand.'
> 'We think multimedia as education and entertainment belongs in the living room with your television set.'
> 'David and I are trying to anticipate the information and computational environment of the late 90s.'
> 'I suppose you could access all human knowledge through a television set. That would be one way of looking at it.'
> '"The only literature children have that guides them to the future is science fiction," says Martin Harwit, director of Washington's most visited museum.'
> 'More than 12 million Americans are living 'on line' —looking for love, stock tips and therapy on computer networks.'
> 'The technique of gene identification or "mapping" cannot be stopped any more than the technology of the automobile, the machine gun, or the atomic bomb was stopped.'

And so on *ad infinitum ad nauseam* ad see-the-light. As Baudrillard *et. al.*, almost unnecessarily, have pointed out. We become terminals. We ourselves the 'Artificial Life' we foolishly thought we would create in 'test tubes'. *Imago dei*, remodelled into techno-drivel. Call it by its name.

      But there's the evidence and the situation to which it attests; the evidence and the import and interpretation, the perspective on it all. You're reading this because you've already been examining the evidence, suspecting the import—which is something like an 'open secret' anyway. This text has been a perspective, drawn from the illumination of many masters, many champions of our humanity. To adduce further evidence would be redundant here. *Everything is evidence.* You get the idea.

Kali-Yuga: The Age of the wrong Diagnosis.

    I think I want to end this book now. I still have all this material, this carton of stuff, but there's nothing, really, that would add anything significant to what has been said. I think it's been covered. (I know I would have benefited immensely from your assistance—instances, new angles, implications, examples, stories… they're in your mind.) Although God only knows what will have happened by the time you're reading these words.

    Remember that you are Shiva, the I-Consciousness of the Universe. The Self: the Immortal Atman. Time and Space are within the Eternal and Infinite that you are. *Tat tvam asi:* Thou art That. This is the supreme Knowledge, the Truth to be realized.
    Remember that nothing has happened at all, that nothing ever happens, that there is nothing to hope for here and nothing to fear. 'From the beginning not a thing is': Hui Neng. the Sixth Patriarch.

Hearing or reading *Ramayana* you will get from Rama what you wish for, so be aware! Don't ask too little. Good fortune to you all! This is the world's first best poem.
In the first age of the world men crossed the ocean of existence by their spirit alone. In the second age sacrifice and ritual began, and then Rama lived, and by giving their every act to him men lived well their ways. Now in our age what is there to do but worship Rama's feet? But my friend, the last age of this world shall be the best. For then no act has any worth, all is useless… except to say *Rama.* The future will read this. Therefore I tell them, when all is in ruin around you, just say *Rama.*
We have gone from the spiritual to the passionate. Next will come ignorance. Universal war. Say *Rama* and win! Your time cannot touch you! And guard yourself, against the real things. Everything counts, and so be kind.
~RAMAYANA

Long journey home, always a long journey. Through the mind to the Mind, the ego to the Buddha-Nature, circling back to the Center, the Origin, the Heart—from which you never really departed because there was never any 'you' to depart. Whatever you have loved has been God. Find God, love God. Seek to live so that your only joy is in God. And love the neighbor too, of course; that was the second Great Commandment of Our Lord, implicit in the First. Love people. Love them all. Disappear, drown, in the Love that is God.

Your choices are two: to die *with* this world, or to die *to* this world. In either case you're a winner. The former death is an illusion, and the latter your birth into Eternal Life.

Wa-'Llahu a' lam. And God is more wise.

It would appear, it could be argued or suggested, that what marks the end of this particular journey is that you know the cards are on the table. You feel you might have to make some kind of decision, your own decision, from which there's no turning back. You want the will, the wisdom, the strength, above all the strength, to make the decision. And maybe, for you, it's that 'decision' of the Immortal Tao of Heaven and Earth that's really no decision at all—just to flow with things, flow with the great river of life: choiceless awareness. Just *be*. 'Observers of the Tao do not seek fulfilment.' (Or anything else, for that matter) You know? A wink and a smile!

Love people. Love them all. Love existence. 'I was a hidden treasure, and I wanted to be known, so I created the world.' Remember: 'Eternity is in love with the creations of time.' Disappear, drown, in the Love that is God.

Or think of the Buddha. (Never forget the Buddha.) Be a 'mindless wayfarer'. 'Jesus said: become passers-by.' Take Daikaku's advice: 'See all compounded things as like dreams, illusions, bubbles, shadows: don't get hung up in thought about them.' Padma-Karpo, the White Lotus: 'The yogin then looketh on, mentally unperturbed at the interminable flow of thoughts as though he were tranquilly resting on the shore of a river watching the water flow past.' That'll work. And *in* the river, *watching* the river, what's the difference really? 'Detachment abideth in itself.'

Valmiki the Poet looked down into water held cupped in his hand and saw into the past. Before he looked he thought the world was sweet poison. Men seemed to be living in lies, not knowing where their ways went. The days seemed made of ignorance and doubt, and cast from deception and illusion. But in the water he saw—a dream, a chance, and a great adventure. Valmiki trusted the True and forgot the rest; he found the whole universe like a bright jewel set firm in forgiving and held fast by love. Widen your heart. Abandon anger. Believe me, your few days are numbered; make one fast choice now and no second! Come, clear your heart and quickly walk with me into Brahma, while there is time.

⌒RAMAYANA

The End is the Beginning. Gospel of Thomas:

The disciples said to Jesus, 'tell us how our end will be.' Jesus said, 'Have you discovered the beginning, that you look for the end? For where the beginning is will the end be. Blessed is he who will take his place in the beginning; he will know the end and will not experience death.'

Get it? The end is the beginning? It doesn't mean a circle. It means time-lessness. The entire Manifestation, from 'beginning' to 'end', is the wink of an eye, an instant: *nothing. Alpha* and *Omega, Arche* and *Eschaton,* Oneness in the Eternal Now. Your very Self.

Vida es sueno. A Midsummer Night's Dream!

> Welcome them, Theseus! They've arrived!
> Joy, gentle friends! Joy and fresh days of love
> Accompany your hearts!

Remember 'Song for the Little Children'? Such a beautiful tune. Sometimes you can't get the refrain out of your head.

> Chanson pour les petites enfants,
> *Chanson poor tout le monde!*

Oh that smile, it breaks your heart!
Mucha suerte! Bonne chance! Good luck, my friends! God bless!

> Ciao bello! Bella ciao!

Clwyd, Wales—The North Coast, California
1990–2000

Appendix:
Media Technology
and the Computer

Electronic cities, virtual communities, information superhighways, cyberfac-tories, and *cyberias* are among terms already making their way into an evolving cultural technolanguage. As language adjusts to technology, the limits of rep-resentation become clearer. The specificity of the languages of programming are without metaphor, without ambiguity: an instruction set describing logi-cal possibilities is not the same thing as a language whose effectiveness and development is premised on evolving significations. If there is a denominator for the language of technology it is the binary system, the groundwork of the electronic communication. Rooted in the communications technology of the electronic, one can say without doubt that the so-called New World Order will be digital.
Modernity matured in the economies of both capitalism and science... If the shift from modernism was, in some ways, precipitated by the triumph of technology over speculative science, then the assessment of technology within postmodern culture is premised on the triumph of technology over experience.

The goal of cultural critique in the *Kali-Yuga* is to reinforce and substanti-ate the suspicion of suspicious individuals and to encourage their discreet disengagement from the irreversible death trip, the great Death March, whose increasing visibility is beginning to transform their insistent surmise into somber, casual or bemused certitude. And because what we face is not a constellation of vexing 'problems' but an inevitable, providential and ulti-mately illusory cosmic situation, which means, stated bluntly, that there is no possibility of successful ameliorative intervention, no 'solutions' will be proposed. The cycle is unfolding, furthermore, with incredible acceleration; my dear friend, Louie, calls it the *Kali-Yuga* express. (*Utne Reader* just arrived today. The front cover, drawing our attention to its five-part cover story, reads, in enormous letters: 'SLOW DOWN: Finding your natural rhythm in a speed-crazed world.') 'The cosmic substance flows ever faster', as tradition assures us.

Media technology and the computer universe have made enormous inroads into our lives and minds since I began this book seven years ago. Their presence is overwhelming, ubiquitous, aggressive and corrosive beyond anything we might have imagined. Internet, World Wide Web, AOL and all the rest of it. The electronic network, the information infotainment superhighway—the Giant Mindfuck, and this includes TV and videos as well—has become nothing less than our world, our experience, our reality. We are it.

So, fully conscious of the convergence of inherent futility and solemn responsibility involved in this enterprise—a real knee-slapper—I would like to add a few notes and lot of quotes in an Appendix. Media technology and computers, an update. I write these words on February 18, 1997. (By the time you're reading this, if anyone ever does read this, much will have happened: but only in the direction here indicated: away from the eternal invulnerable divine Center within all of us.) Bearing witness as always, nothing more; driven by a resentful implacable compulsion to thoroughness. Finish the job. Then turn your back and forget it forever.

I said there would be a few notes and a lot of quotes here. The quotes, including the two epigraphs above, are all taken from Culture on the Brink: Ideologies of Technology, a collection of essays edited by Gretchen Bender and Timothy Druckrey, Number 9 in the Discussions in Contemporary Culture series originating in the Dia Center for the Arts, Bay Press, Seattle, 1994. The book is praised on the back cover by Neil Postman and Douglas Kellner, two writers you will have encountered in the main text of YUGA. I have not acknowledged the contributors individually, but I wish to express my gratitude for their work. We read in the Introduction:

Culture on the Brink: Ideologies of Technology is not an account of the frenzy of invention but a critical forum for an approach to the question of technology as it pertains to the culture of experience. As technology is assimilated into the structures of the everyday, its ubiquity becomes invisible and necessary. A generation of smart technologies—everything from smart refrigerators to smart cars—will learn to anticipate and to act autonomously based on discernible patterns. Invisible technologies will surveil the intricacies of everything we do. We now assume that technology is comfortably omnipresent. The goal of this project is to frame a critique of technological reason, to deconstruct the mythology that technology is a panacea... directly impacting technology within the forms of everyday life... and demonstrating that disaster will be the likely consequence if the public remains uninformed...

Everything that follows could be categorized under 'The Mutation into Machinery' and 'The Prison of Unreality', two of the five hallmarks of the *Kali-Yuga*.

✳

'Information', on the one hand, and on the other:

Understanding (Remember understanding? Once highly regarded), insight, comprehension, intuition; truth, knowledge, wisdom, depth, ideas, meaning living ideas in a living mind, ideation; realization and intentionality, intellectual curiosity; inwardness, introspection, reflection, rumination, pondering; intelligence, and that supreme faculty, the Intellect, or Cardiac Intelligence.

Information Technology replaces all these, assumes uncontested prestige, and thereby at a stroke replaces the core of our humanity. And this is the outcome for the blindingly simple reason that *'information' is all a machine can contain*; although, in the very deepest sense, the machine contains nothing because it is nothing, is not an entity, is not alive: it is merely the potential, the occasion, for *our* degradation when we sit before it and push the buttons, and it is becoming all that we are. Mumford's 'Megamachine' now fully realized.

For couch potatoes, video game addicts, and surrogate travelers of cyberspace alike, an organic body just gets in the way. The culinary discourses of a culture undergoing transformation into an information society will have to confront not only the problems of a much depleted earth but also a growing desire to disengage from the human condition. Travelers on the virtual highways of an information society have, in fact, at least one body too many — the one now largely sedentary carbon-based body at the control console that suffers hunger, corpulency, illness, old age, and ultimately death. The other body, a silicon-based surrogate jacked into immaterial realms of data, has superpowers, albeit virtually, and is immortal — or, rather, the chosen body, an electronic avatar 'decoupled' from the physical body, is a program capable of enduring endless deaths.

✳

Promises of dizzying access to information, communication, and electronic communities suggest the kind of conjecture that fills science fiction. Virtual futures propose rather than substantiate; instead of necessities they offer only possibilities, a kind of imaginary future in which we will participate as agents of techno-progress and consumption... Technology, in guises touted as 'user-friendly' or as 'radically sophisticated', has become the amorphous foundation of a new social order... Already, the future is being mapped in terms of the dynamics of possible technologies rather than in terms of appropriate or responsible ones.

And that future we, our children, will inhabit, our minds, the collective social mind of that future, degraded into a silly skitzy ditzy Punch-and-Judy series of momentary trivia unrecognizable as such because we no longer possess the confidence or criteria to distinguish what is inherently significant from what is manifestly exploitative and degrading. What we will have lost, have largely lost already, was the integration of mind and personality, faculties and potentials, on a Path, a Dharma, a Way, a proposal to and for humans of their human fulfillment: this was the function of Tradition, and its origins, no matter how incomprehensible this assertion will appear to the modern mind, were celestial. The Technotopia, Postman's Technopoly, Technophilialand, has made the choice for us, and without our even knowing it. We don't know what we're missing.

Perception, memory, history, politics, identity, and experience are now mediated through technology in ways that outdistance simple economic or historical analysis. Indeed, technology pervades the present not simply as a mode of participation but as an operative principle. Beneath the facades of ownership through consumption and conceptualization through use, technology subsumes experience... Immersed within electronic environments, the experience of the individual conforms to the logic of the technological or is characterized as reactionary or sentimental... Deconstructing technology, demonstrating that its effects can rely on superficial notions of progress, is a daunting task.

When we talk about a computer we're talking about a box filled with various kinds of electronic switches and motors, which perform particular tasks according to encoded sets of instructions. This isn't an entirely accurate view of what a computer is or does, though, because it ignores a very important aspect of the computer: it is also a social artifact that mediates a series of social interactions conceptualized as a model *through* these encoded instruction sets. To clarify: human beings conceptualize this model, others encode it in a formal language, still others actually use computers, and still others, even further down the line, are subject to what the computer does... Thus, when we talk about what goes on in a computer, we're talking about an entire complex of relations, assumptions, actions, intentions, design, error, too, as well as the results, and so on.

There is, then, out there in cyberspace, something called the Computer, the Web. Not an illusion. It knows everything it has been encoded to 'decide' we need to know. Which is, since it can contain nothing else, 'information.' It is extolled, in the media environment we inhabit, as miraculous and benevolent, as a great triumph of science, probably the greatest. Through its magical powers our future, maybe even our salvation, is secured. *Noël sur la Terre.* This is the Grand Assumption, impossible to contest, underlying the culture of the *Kali-Yuga*: the enthronement of benevolent technology.

But look at us. Just look at us. Look at our lives. Our faces. Pick an age group and examine its experience. Enter the troubled misgivings within all our souls.

⁂

It is no less obvious that technology is interlaced within the structures of existence. Surrounding us in what Peter Weibel has called an 'intelligent ambience', we assume that technologies will monitor and provide an active presence in life... Adaptability is measured no longer in terms of survivability but in compliance with the conditions of information: biotechnic standards... Accomplishment, experience, and authenticity play little role in the inexorable development of the mechanisms of technology. And what more cogent metaphor for the blurring of the boundary between technology and biology than genetic programming, the reduction of biological change to computed algorithms, artificial life programs, a bank of genetic codes?... Encoding rather than identity could become the signifier of the self, an informatics of domination made possible only by the power of the computer.

The world, and human identities, are being replaced by 'information' about them. This, to a great extent, would appear to be the case. Information, however, is only apparently 'about' anything. It's actually another world altogether, an autonomous world, an artificial universe. Capital reduces all beings and things to exchange value, the Computer now contains and administers exchange value—you and me, our lives—in the form of 'information'. 'Information' is presented to us as images on a plastic screen: the worker, the producer, the consumer, is now a terminal viewing life as information. We lose the world, lose Creation, lose ourselves, lose our own direct human experience, in exchange for words and numbers on a screen, and call it a victory, a breakthrough: success.

> In a slumping, perhaps declining US economy, one sphere, the media-informational, retains uncontested global supremacy. It has another unusual characteristic: it has been nearly totally appropriated for a sole objective—marketing. This relationship, namely, a powerful media apparatus linked tightly to salesmanship, creates a general condition that in time threatens the viability and sustainability of human existence itself... What the record reveals is an almost total takeover of the domestic informational system for the purpose of selling goods and services.

The feel of a 'takeover' is what pervades our lives. A 'takeover' by whom? by what? By ourselves, of course: as technology. Specifically, in the present context, the marriage of information/media technology with Capital, the social relationship of the commodity form, where the principal function of that technology becomes marketing. Information, itself merchandise, administers the production, dissemination and consumption of merchandise. Commodity culture, salesmanship, the market economy, Capital as the social relationship we are, is fueled by the incessant inflammation of insatiable desire, the transformation of the human person into a 'consumer'. ('I'd like some more *things*, please!' as the caption reads on the 'Funny Times' T-shirt, showing a woman with a radiant smile stretching out her arms, surrounded by a mountain of commodities, a huge refrigerator in the background.) The whole picture is tied together in and by the Computer we celebrate. The labyrinth is truly mind-boggling. A pinnacle of fiendishness.

> Entertainment, communication, work—the web of technologized experiences, in Martin Heidegger's terminology, 'enframes' the way things are done... Games, news, film, music, photography, and so on, often serve as the testing ground for technology... The exploitation of culture seems no longer to be linked directly with labor but with a more problematic connection - desire. To be 'disconnected' stands as a form of impotence, of lack, of alienation... The shift from industrial culture to media culture to technoculture represents a phase shift of daunting proportions.

✳

The heart of gnosis, essence of Enlightenment, object of the quest, implicit mission of the Intellect, fulfillment of Love, formula for our consummation as *imago dei*, is articulated: 'What is that one thing knowing which I know everything?' The Answer is given, and it's always a form of recognition of and identification with Oneness, the Oneness which pervades and is the universe, called variously Nirvana, God, Brahman, Tao, the Self, Buddha-Nature, and so on. The Unity of Life. Our Truth. Peace.

This real Answer must now be contrasted with 'access to Information'. Access to a specious 'everything', an inexhaustible multiplicity of jabs to the eager mind, leaving the victim actually 'knowing' or 'having' nothing but an immediately forgotten grab-bag jumble of... what? Trivia? Details? Spurts of excitement? Facts? A shattered skullfull of words on a screen? We are reminded here of Guénon's 'The Great Parody', the 'counter-tradition', 'Spirituality Inverted'. (*Reign of Quantity*, chap. 39)

> The Antichrist must evidently be as near as it is possible to be to 'disintegration'... realizing confusion in 'chaos' as against fusion in principial Unity... The false is also necessarily the 'artificial', and in this respect the 'counter-tradition' cannot fail, despite its other characteristics, to retain the 'mechanical' character appertaining to all the productions of the modern world, of which it will itself be the last.

Contemporary intelligence is not comfortable with Guénon's language, but Neil Postman, in *The Nation*, October 9, 1995, concluded his fine essay, 'Virtual Students, Digital Classroom', with a sentence we all ought to remember. You may interpret it in Guénon's context, or in the gentler, more tentative sense which doubtless inspired it. 'Now computers. I know a false god when I see one.'

> At a recent lecture, one member of MIT's media lab blithely said that we are going to make a transition from computers you're in front of to computers you're inside of where the computer becomes so present that you almost wear it. This would seem to be almost nonsensical if the issue of 'virtual reality' were not already implementing the idea.

Imaging systems have come to echo the forms of representation that so dominate this culture. Digital-imaging technologies now routinely use computed sequences to dramatize their content. Virtual commercials, animation, and 'morphing' have become indispensable components in making imaging

relevant to a generation of users comfortable with the electronic illusory...
The configuration of data used to construct an electronic image is
epistemological—based on a knowledge of how the structure of perception
can be rendered—while the photographic recording is phenomenological.
This is a fundamental reconfiguration of the model of what constitutes an
image, one that raises the issue of whether an image can serve as objective
information.

Viewing photographs or movies we knew we were seeing an image of
something that actually happened or actually exists or existed, whether it
was real life or a performance. This is no longer true, thanks to the Computer. But the assumption is indestructible, built into the very nature of perception. We can't help perceiving the unreal as real. Prison of Unreality. We
are the jailers, we are the jailed. But so what? What does it matter? The fact
is, to some people it may matter very much, and to others it may not matter
at all. The Invocation to *Brihadaranyaka Upanishad* begins, *Asatoma sadgamaya*, 'Lead me from the unreal to the real.' This simple sentence reflects a plea
fundamental to our humanity, the recognition of a confusion and a potential
inherent in our state. For everyone, I would imagine, at some time in their
lives and in one context or another, the plea for this unveiling was felt in the
very depths of the heart. Because maya *is* and we *are* Atma, we demand
Reality, we demand Truth. We were made to know the Truth. It's a question
of remembering what we are. And this is very hard these days.

✳

The corruption of science, fueled by the economics of technology, could herald a culture ornamented with gadgets but devoid of public accountability.
Rarely in the debate about technology does the voice of the citizen emerge.
Specialized discourse, reduced to elemental soundbites, determines policy to
an unprecedented degree. A technologically illiterate culture, inebriated with
the spin-offs of high technology, hardly pauses to address the issue of the
impact this environment will have.

Look at it this way:
We are *imago dei* (I know I'm saying it again, but it can never be said
enough), the central Consciousness of a Manifestation, an Intelligence that
reflects the Divine Mind, the theomorphic being, deiform miracle, 'infinite
in faculties,' 'a little lower than the angels' (although the Tradition, differing
here with Hamlet, asserts we are even higher), made in His Image: we can

know, love, and realize our identity, our oneness, with God. Our stature is supreme.

With the eclipse of traditional societies and the triumph of science and technology we were no longer taught this truth about ourselves, it has been forgotten and become unintelligible, and now, in the 'Computer Age', we have created the Entity that confirms definitely our drastically diminished stature: we are inferior to machinery—even sort of amusing and pathetic by comparison.

It's really quite far out. Technology has expropriated human experience, replaced it, and technology, specifically the Computer, has actually taken our place in the scheme of things, is now the actual *being* in this world, the highest 'life-form' on the planet, the new 'measure of all things', Lord of the Manor, Master of the House. No longer humanity. (Guénon would almost certainly identify the Computer as the Antichrist, Satan; he'd see the final triumph of the Archfiend, the Adversary. But we don't need to think that way literally to *get the idea* of it.) We feel usurped because we are usurped. Usurped, incompetent, subservient, dependent, childlike, vaguely ashamed, sheepish, sometimes resentful, rattling our chains, resigned to a subordinate role… in the latest classroom teacher-talk, lacking in 'self-esteem'.

Information has become the lubricant for a swiftly emerging social structure, that is wholly dependent on the potential, malleability, and exchangeability of data. Evident in the recent merger-mania between broadcast, telephone, and computing companies, the near future of basic communication, broad-casting, and the consumer have taken a frenzied urgency. 'Have you ever tucked in your kid from a phone booth? Have you ever read a book from two thousand miles away? Have you ever faxed someone from the beach?' asks a recent campaign from AT&T. Their reply: 'You will.' Selling the future after 'we're all connected' is becoming a trend in current advertising. Marketed as intimate and essential, communication would seem to eradicate the need for anything other than telepresence…

Who has the information? What has the information? Where is the information? What does information look like? What do you do with infor-mation? Who does it? What is information?

You could say this:

'Information' is our absence—and the absence of the world. Our present collective being, the Internet, the World Wide Web, the Information Age, is the drain into which we, as individuals, flow off into nothingness. Into words and numbers and images without originals—on screens. There we sit.

Human experience, our lives, must now be reinterpreted in the 'language' of machinery and *becomes*, certainly operationally and gradually experientially, the language of machinery, of the Computer. The depth and richness of human experience, of selfhood and encounter, is reduced, mangled and deformed into what can appear on a screen, be 'understood' by an algorithm, conform to a model, be expressed quantitatively, bureaucratically, as on a form. In capitalist society we are our 'assets' and our tax returns, we are numbers. In computer society we are what the mindless binary-algorithm mouth can say, what plastic lips and chips can utter, what can be booted up, downloaded or transferred to a data base.

Computers are unique in that their function is *entirely* determined by the model programmed into them... a model that 'works' in a computer—it is operational and plausible, in other words, algorithmically correct—can certainly be wrong in many other ways: it might be offensive; it might, over time, affect our behavior and assumptions in ways detrimental to our fundamental human interest... These models are typically viewed as exempt from examination and challenge. Yet computers, particularly—I think because of their curiously all-purpose instrumental character—deform the human character to such an extent that the very ability to recognize the artificial nonsense of these systems and models is extinguished.

To such an extent. Oh well. Hopelessness only overwhelms those who are burdened with hope.

❈

Is there really any need to expose 'who' meets 'who' on the Internet 'on-line chats'? Pushing buttons before a screen in imaginary 'communication' with a 'someone' who is nowhere in time or space, both concealed behind pseudonyms, or... I'm sure you can think of the human alternatives here. Cyborgs, of course, don't know what they have become. But we're not cyborgs.

However, there may be a 'sad fact' here. It may be that surrogates for authentic humanity, for human encounter specifically, is all that many people are capable of performing, and all that technoculture is programming them to perform. Uncertain of their own identities and the identities of others, feeling unequal to the challenge of a living human presence, literally and deeply uncertain about who they are or who they should be, and who others are and should be, for many people it's safer to communicate within the ethereal and clearly delimited framework of the electronic model where 'nothing serious' can happen. If nearly all of daily life is small talk or emotional outburst, stereotypical interchanges mimicking TV 'personalities', formulaic discourse, a series of riskless clichés, 'screen talk' and 'telepresence' must be seen as an analogous strategy, a further and now foolproof progress in the 'shallowization' of our lives.

> While information-processing machines are becoming more 'intelligent' by leaps and bounds, much of the world's population appears to be moving in the opposite direction... There are growing indications that large segments of the population are deficient in mastering even the most basic intellectual skills... As the Information Age matures, growing numbers in our population will approach the world in a state of increasing incompetence and bewilderment. Many institutions simply assume this and exploit the situation as an opportunity: in many fast-food restaurants you will not find numbered keypads on the cash register, but pictures of hamburgers, french fries, and milk shakes. A central theme in the time-honored ideology of progress, the belief that technological development and the enhancement of human abilities move forward together, is now effectively undermined by innumerable systems that successfully decouple these two ends through design programs that assume most working people are incompetent. A recurring pattern in modern technological and cultural transformation is that as *new technologies are invented, the kinds of people who will be using them are also invented* (emphasis added).

And isn't that a marvelously thought-provoking insight!

'The Computer' really does 'talk down' to us as if simplifying for morons who can't be expected to grasp something far beyond their capacity to comprehend. 'User-friendly' really means 'talking a simple language even you, a mere human being, can understand.'

> Back-office workers in large commercial banks interact with their video display terminals (VDTs) more than with other human beings. VDT operators sit in individual carrels typing nothing but disembodied numbers all day. Naturally, this numbing boring work causes enormous turnover among VDT operators... Now the old organic self is subsumed under the cyborg self: we are wired, simulacra.

❋

Lobotomized by Capital, 'at one' with commodity culture, we can't see (could never even grasp the idea anymore, because the 'normal' is invisible) that virtually everything in the media Universe we inhabit, and everything on the Internet as well, is trying to sell us something, sell us on something, that the language we hear everywhere in the public sphere is dishonest to the core, the language of advertising, commercials, showmanship, marketing, 'infotainment-speak'—can't see that the whole scene is phony, bogus, a con-man ballyhoo, a massive exploitation. Sales: the supreme commandment. Merchandise: the universal status.

> For advertising to fulfill its systemically crucial role—getting the national output of goods and services into the hands and homes of buyers, and reaffirming daily, if not hourly, that consumption is the definition of democracy—it must have full access to the nation's message making and message-transmitting apparatus. Over time this means the transformation of the press, radio, television, cable, and every such subsequent technology into instrumentations of marketing. This is done with single-minded devotion… In recent years, TV commercials, movies, TV programs, and recordings have called increasingly upon special effects to rivet an audience's attention. Special-effects sound and imagery short-circuit the brain and hit the gut. Content recedes as technique flourishes and reflection disappears… Another writer sees the ultimate effect of special-effect techniques in pop-cultural forms as the triumph of commercialism… Pop music is no longer a world unto itself but an adjunct of television, whose stream of commercial messages projects a culture in which everything is for sale.

The Computer monitor, 'on-line', is now a surrogate for life, *is* life for many PC owners. (Get a life!) People babble about hard drives and disks, megabytes and gigabytes, 'surfing'. Return from 'work' before a screen and go directly to their own home screen, the TV or the PC. ('On line' claims time from our lives, lots of time, time that could have been employed in our own genuine interest: but we no longer have a clue as to what that genuine interest might be, and have no retort, nor see any need for one, to the deafening claims of the machine.) Looking for what? Information, an encounter in cyberspace, the memo-weight thrill of a piece of email, or simply distraction, escape from the emptiness of this incomprehensible play of shadows called life. Anything that can catch the eye: maybe a 'spot' on the Net you never 'visited' before and will be forgetting even as you look at it.

Seated before the computer screen is now the image of success, arrival, glamour, fulfillment, happiness, au courant, 'cool', hip, casual triumph over the whole world, smart, up-to-date: having access to all the joy and magic that technology offers, 'up there'. But where are these people actually in that moment before the screen? (Sitting on their asses is one answer that's been given.) What is the stature of the human spirit in that moment? 'Surfing', imagery of waves, the bracing wind and salt spray splashing rainbows against the crystal blue sky, sun sparkling on the foam: vitality, freedom, giddy excitement endlessly renewed, forever offering you more. ('Surfing': where did that phrase come from? To what end was it introduced as the metaphor here, and by whom? Why, by the celebrated human race, of course! By us!) But where are they actually? What are they, in their innocent obeisance, their hopeful enthusiasm, before the screen, in that moment? What do they have of what they need?

You know, it's really impossible to describe hollowed-out life accurately and meaningfully except in terms of what is absent, and if what is absent has virtually disappeared from human experience and societal recognition, if the vocabulary referring to and identifying these absences has become unintelligible in the technoculture's universe of discourse, in the Age of Universal Bullshit, there's no way to describe it at all. No way to talk about it. 'If I could turn you on, if I could drive you out of your wretched mind, if I could tell you, I would let you know.' Some disaffiliate, probably drug-deranged counter-culture hero cried out those words in the 60s, no doubt talking about 'dropping out.' Teenage-rebel drivel—but the words have a ring and punch still, and with good reason.

'Downloading consciousness' into a computer—which according to Moravek, will be available by the mid-twenty-first century—would simulate brain functions but at an incomparably faster speed. Gerald Jay Sussman, a professor at MIT, once reportedly expressed a similar desire for machine fusion as the wish for immortality: 'If you can make a machine that contains the contents of your mind, the machine is you. The hell with the rest of your physical body, it's not very interesting. Now, the machine can last forever. Even if it doesn't last forever, you can always dump onto tape and make back-ups, then load it up on some other machine if the first one breaks... Everyone would like to be immortal... I'm afraid, unfortunately, that I am the last generation to die.' Far more recently, Larry Yeager's confession of why he 'fell for artificial life' expressed a similar desire to 'live on inside the chips.'

It's hard to regard imbeciles like Sussman as human. Pitiful trash; creeps. Perhaps embittered beyond endurance. They play a major role in the building of the world our children will inherit. Architects of the future.

✳

What is real? How do we know the truth? Today, these basic philosophical questions are harder than ever to deal with. Even if we trust the lessons of daily life, it's difficult enough to come up with convincing answers. For students in rural Pennsylvania, nature may still seem very real; for the kids in the big cities hooked on Nintendo, 'nature' is the name of a computer game. And the video and cable TV addicts around the globe—from the farmers in India to the unemployed former Party officials in Moscow to the graphic designers in New York—leave the misery of a so-called reality behind them and embrace true life in the movies and soaps... Let's have a closer look at the other end of the social ladder: Executives and administrators are dependent on statistics generated by information technology. For them there are no goods or customers or students, the bottom line is numbers, the sole judge of their performance. How real is politics these days? The media is the race-track, polling tells us what we are betting, and success is measured in sound-bites and news outputs. Most people over sixteen pride themselves on being able to easily distinguish between natural and artificial reality, but their own actions will often betray them. It's ten o'clock—do you know which program you are in?... How can we know what is real?

And here is a really profound insight: *Humans don't compute, they understand intentionally.*

✳

Because email and 'on-line' are the latest forms of communication presented to us by technology they immediately assume top prestige and take precedence over all other forms. They seem *most real* because *technology is most real.* They have about them an air of stunning joyous victory, thrilling break-through, arrogant casual power, the liberation of limitless new possibilities from whose constricting deprivation we no longer suffer. We can do so much more now, and so effortlessly. (A central 'ingredient of the pro-technology paradigm,' as Jerry Mander put it.)

It has become increasingly rare to communicate without the help of media-generated forms, role models and channels. Seeing and hearing, which inform our thinking, are overwhelmed by communication technology. Thinking and writing are done within a framework provided by media and follow the possibilities and limits of the chosen technology... Without doubt, our social landscape is being transformed by fax machines, beepers, cellular phones, laptop computers, modems, e-mail, and numerous other devices and systems—all of which facilitate productivity. Any benefits are purchased at a definite cost. Corners of our lives formerly sheltered from direct technological intervention are now bombarded by the insistent call of incoming and outgoing messages. We will have to get used to public spaces— shops, restaurants, taverns, theatres, galleries—filled with people chattering on portable communications systems... Our society has begun to look like a vast electronic beehive in which information processing in search of eco- nomic gain overshadows other personal and social goods. Places and spaces in our lives formerly devoted to sociability, intimacy, solitude, friendship, love, and family are now being redefined as susceptible to productivity, trans- forming social norms and boundaries. Subjected to the pace of productivism, we come to think that if a message can move, it must move quickly. This places strong demands on individuals; communications technologies not only make it possible to reach them but obligates them to remain accessi- ble... Our available time expands into a space of congestion—increasingly frenetic interactions encouraged by our machines... As we fill life's every niche with high-tech gadgetry, we gradually whittle away those quiet, restful places where genuine creativity and satisfaction are nurtured.

Well said! And a lot more than creativity and satisfaction can be nurtured in those quiet, restful places gradually disappearing from the lives of people caught up in all this. Sliced into ever smaller fragments by the pace of elec- tronic communications, attention spans steadily diminish. Bits of informa- tion and snippets of urgent 'communications' become the content and substance of consciousness itself, the very flow of the mind—although it's more like the clatter of a room full of machines than a 'flow'. More and more we are always 'very busy', and we feel, somewhat defensively and with vague suppressed misgivings, that being 'very busy' is the right way to be. We keep up to speed, but are often running late. We become the content of the machinery.

And what are we really? What *were* we really? Four hints:

'Silence is the garden of meditation.'
◠ 'Ali

'Each soul must meet the morning sun, the new, sweet earth, and the Great Silence alone!'
◠ Ohiyesa

'The well-resolved mind is single and one-pointed.'
⌒BHAGAVAD GITA

'At Kugami, in front of the Otono,
There stands a solitary pine tree.
Surely of many a generation.
How divinely dignified it stands there!
In the morning I pass by it:
In the evening I stand underneath it.
And standing I gaze.
Never tired of this solitary pine!'
⌒RYOKWAN, 1758–1831

Our truth is concentration, integration, protracted focus on what matters and ultimately what alone matters. The truth is depth within coherence, Light within the Unity. Simplicity: One.

Americans watch an average of seven hours of television a day, roughly 665 billion waking hours a year in what seems a permanent pattern, an expanding cultural addiction. People do not seem to remember much of what they watch, but they need a certain daily dose of the TV drug in order to feel satisfied. These video habits seem subject to a fascinating developmental logic wherein images and message are broken down into ever-smaller pieces. On MTV, for example, where the vivid images on the screen change from eighty to one hundred times a minute or more, viewers have become acclimated to a frantic pulse and become impatient with ideas or arguments delivered in any less hurried way. Public discourse now assumes a profound fragmentation in the way people process information. American political leaders and their professional 'handlers' are convinced any idea longer than a sentence is too difficult for the television viewing public to endure.

✳

Media technology and Information, that net, that web, that culture, is finally and decisively the snare of worldliness. A relentlessly captivating avalanche of worldly trivia and substanceless minutiae binding us to the seductive ephemera of the world-appearance, of maya, samsara, Illusion, Delusion. Thus it is truly lethal: it is the Adversary. A perpetual and irresistible command to 'disregard the summons of the Infinite.' Our intuition of Something beyond the material world, our intuition of the Absolute, our intuition that we need to and can be saved or illumined by Something beyond and within us at once which we perceive as Truth or God, Peace and Joy and Immortality, Eternal Beauty, the One Reality, is clobbered to the ground by the inexhaustible fatal fascination of *more stuff here*.

The Net, the Web, the Computer, the whole media technology scene, can only be forms of fulfillment and intensification of the potentials for degeneration already existing in a disoriented world. Much more than a simple manifestation of those potentials: a consummation. Immersion in trivia, trivialization of life itself, because the alternatives to trivia no longer have any serious cultural presence or validation; commerce, the circulation of commodities, sales, advertisements which are actually pure deceit, the whole universe of exchange value that is Capital and its climactic electronic flowering; endlessly proliferating dispersion, dissipation, attenuation and dislocation of consciousness until there is really very little left of the integrity of the human person; loss of any sense of priority or of a hierarchy of values and significance; universal leveling; everything is 'information.'

We who are now alive witness the transition from a Path—a Dharma, and 'All is Dharma, there is Dharma alone in the world!' as we read in Ramayana—to... what? The ever-expanding 'Internet Yellow Pages', 908 pages at this writing? A cosmic shopping mall? A cosmic Machine? The Tower of Babel?

> One becomes identified with the object of one's knowledge. For those who believe the world emanates from God, there is a way back to God; for those who believe the world emanates from chaos, there is likewise a way that corresponds with this possibility.
> ∾ WHITALL PERRY

Or maybe we should give the last word to Plato:

> Is not the whole of human life turned upside down; and are we not doing, as would appear, in everything the opposite of what we ought to be doing?'

INDEX

Printed in the United States
2690